1929

1929

America Before the Crash

by Warren Sloat

Cooper Square Press

Published by Cooper Square Press
An imprint of The Rowman & Littlefield Publishing Group, Inc.
200 Park Avenue South, Suite 1109
New York, New York 10003-1503
www.coopersquarepress.com

Excerpt from **That Summer in Paris** © 1963 by Morley Callaghan.
Reprinted by the permission of Harold Matson Company, Inc.

Distributed by National Book Network

Library of Congress Cataloging-in-Publication Data

Sloat, Warren.
  1929, America Before the Crash.
  Bibliography: p. 350
  Includes index.
    1. United States—Civilization—1918–1945. I. Title. II. Title: America
Before the Crash.
E169.1.S5943   97.3.91   79-17149
ISBN 0-8154-1280-0

Manufactured in the United States of America.
  ∞™ The paper used in this publication meets the minimum requirements of American
National Standard for Information Sciences—Permanence of Paper for Printed Library
Materials, ANSI/NISO Z39.48-1992.

To June Walker-Sloat

CONTENTS

ACKNOWLEDGMENTS

Over the course of three years the author read and researched at the Public Library of Plainfield, New Jersey, the Alexander Library of Rutgers University, the Theatre Collection at the Firestone Library, Princeton University, the Edison National Historic Site at West Orange, New Jersey, and the Henry Ford Museum at Dearborn, Michigan. At each institution, staff members provided helpful assistance. The author is also grateful for encouragement from his agent, Knox Burger, and from Charles Corn, senior editor at Macmillan. He also wishes to thank his brother-in-law, Robert Thomas Walker, for tangible aid, and the New Jersey Historical Commission for a grant. He is above all indebted eternally to the remarkable woman to whom the book is dedicated.

Plainfield, New Jersey
March, 1979

1929

The new president, just seven months in office, was making his first extended trip outside the capital. On Sunday evening the light was fading as he and his wife, with a presidential party and twenty-six reporters, climbed aboard the Baltimore & Ohio train to begin a five-day itinerary in the heartland.

At Cumberland, Maryland, the train stopped to change engines, and President Herbert C. Hoover came out on the rear platform of his private railroad car to greet a small crowd of well-wishers. He spotted a small boy in a gray cap and a brown and white sweater. "Son," he called out, "do you want to shake hands?" The boy's father lifted him up to his shoulders, and other parents pressed forward with their children. Soon the president with considerable gravity had shaken hands with two dozen children.

It was October 20, 1929, and the president was on his way to Dearborn, Michigan, for the most extraordinary event of the year—a program and dinner in honor of Thomas Edison.

The entire world was pausing for a unique testimonial to the old inventor. In Detroit, a holiday had been declared, the schools would be closed, and special golden globes would cover the street lights on October 21. In New York, a huge sign in Times Square spelled out LIGHT'S GOLDEN JUBILEE, 1879–1929, in electric letters. In Milan, Ohio, Edison's birthplace, his picture was in almost every window. Forty loudspeakers were mounted in Grant Park, Chicago, so the Dearborn program could be heard over the radio. Philadelphia had scheduled a night parade under golden-tinted searchlights. And the observance was also being marked throughout the rest of the world—in Holland, Italy, Japan, Java. In Shanghai, the Chinese were setting off fireworks for Edison. A street in Buenos Aires had been named for him. A huge reception was to be held at the Mazda lamp factory in Rio de Janeiro, and for three days all the fountains of Rio had been specially decorated with lighting effects.

Light's Golden Jubilee had been celebrated in various ways since June, but October 21 was the fiftieth anniversary of Edison's invention of the incandescent lamp, and to mark the occasion Henry Ford had arranged a gala in Dearborn, a city near Detroit. Five hundred people had been invited to see Hoover dedicate the Edison Institute, a technical school that

I

Ford had founded and financed. The guests would be shown Greenfield Village, an adjunct of the institute that was also to be opened formally. The village consisted of historic and representative buildings and furnishings that Ford had been collecting over the years, including the little red schoolhouse in which he had been a pupil. They had been arranged into a village square to recreate the American past. The highlight of the observance, to be broadcast nationally, would be Edison's re-enactment of his great moment of invention.

Edison, furthermore, would re-enact the past in the same buildings in which he had produced his epochal invention a half-century earlier. In one corner of Greenfield Village, Ford had placed the restored Menlo Park laboratories of 1879, and on the Sunday afternoon before the observance Ford's private auto pulled up at the site and a party alighted to see how the New Jersey laboratories looked in their transplanted state.

In the interest of historical accuracy, even the old outdoor privy was in its proper place. "I wouldn't have believed it," Edison said to Harvey Firestone, the tire magnate. "It's amazing." Edison spoke with some difficulty, for he was storing a chew of tobacco in his cheek, on the side opposite his wife's observant eyes. "Why, Henry's even got the goddamned New Jersey clay here."

When Ford had the laboratories shipped out, he had his operatives move out tons of New Jersey dirt to add further authenticity to the scene. The eighty-two-year-old inventor spat a shot of tobacco juice at the clay and chewed off another bite from his plug. Mrs. Edison approached to button her husband's overcoat. "It's all right," he protested. "I'm just as young as I was when I worked there in the old laboratory." His wife looked unconvinced.

Edison led the way into the laboratory, where the chemicals and apparatus were arranged on the shelves just as they had stood a half-century earlier. As they toured the building, Edison found an organ just like the one they had played so often, and it was on the second floor at the end of the building, where the original had always stood.

In the old days his crew often would halt its work to dine at midnight and then relax while someone would strike up a tune on the organ. Sometimes visitors would drop in and join the meal and the singing. Then, with "Good Night, Ladies," they would slip out and the workers would begin to labor again into the early morning.

Edison sat in a straight-backed chair and took in the scene. He was a tired old man and the flesh drooped from his neck, but his blue eyes were still clear and quick and he was smiling slightly as if in reminiscence.

His companions waited as he sat with his arms folded. Then the spell broke. "Well," he said, looking around, "you've got this just about ninety-nine and a half percent perfect." Edison stood up and walked back to the group.

"What is the matter with the other one-half percent?" Ford asked.

"Well," Edison laughed, "we never kept it as clean as this."

"Tom took me into his plant at Menlo Park in 1881," one of Edison's old cronies at Dearborn for the Jubilee finale told a reporter. "He told me, 'We're here to turn night into day with electric light. But we've also established a policy in the plant of all day and no night. In other words, we're working all the time.' "

"Time didn't mean a thing to Tom," another silver-haired associate said. "He could outwork any ten men in the place. He was always congenial and no matter how long he worked he was always smiling and regretting that there were only 24 hours in the day. I'll bet there were weeks at a time when he never saw a bed. He'd stand over a bench until three or four every morning. Suddenly he'd yawn and then he'd climb up on the bench and with a couple of books for a pillow would fall into a sound sleep."

Another guest had been a chemist who supplied Edison when he was working in his downtown New York office. "It was my job to be at the office every morning when Mr. Edison came down to buy his chemicals for the day's work," he told a reporter. "He never bought more than a day's supply. He would come into the store and we'd go over the stock together and he'd pick what he wanted. His clothes used to be all wrinkled and he told me they got that way from sleeping on benches in the laboratory."

The trip to Dearborn was a homecoming of sorts for Edison. He had spent much of his youth in the Detroit area. That night as he slept in the Ford home he was not far from where he had plied the trade of candy vendor on the train to Detroit, which had been a town of 25,000 when he rode the Grand Trunk Railroad to the end of the line every day. Carrying a basket almost as big as himself, the young Tom would catch the train at Port Huron every morning and make his way through the carriages, calling: "Candy! Newspapers! Apples, sandwiches, molasses, peanuts!" After the three-hour trip he would wait over in Detroit and ride the return train home at night. Edison was a nervy boy and did well at his business. When he grew older he started his own newspaper, which he hawked with the other goods, and bought produce to sell at stops along the way. Eventually he began to move equipment into the baggage and mail car to use in experiments during the long layover in Detroit. He had shelves fitted to the back wall of the car and laid out his bottles, test tubes, and other equipment on them. This project ended when some chemicals, probably jolted from the shelf when the train bucked, started a fire. According to some accounts, a railroad official then hurled his laboratory equipment from the train at the Smith's Creek Junction. Life had held frustrations for the boy, and he returned home very late, but he was equipped to make his way in the world and was fascinated by his introduction to adult life. "The happiest time of my life," he said many years later, "was when I was twelve years old. I was old enough to have a good time in the world, but not old enough to understand any of its troubles."

One of the key people in putting together Light's Golden Jubilee was Edward L. Bernays, a Manhattan public relations consultant. He had worked closely with Ford on developing the Dearborn extravaganza, and on the morning of October 21 he waited with a crowd of guests for the arrival of the president.

The Hoover entourage had arrived at nine o'clock, and Ford and Edison had greeted them a half-mile up the road. A fancy Civil War engine and old-time railroad cars waited to carry them into the depot at the reconstructed Smith's Creek Junction, where Bernays waited in the crowd. The rain beat down upon them.

Huddled nearby in the country store, the court house, the post office and the rest of Greenfield Village waited a group that Ford had dressed in nineteenth-century clothing to people his village and act as guides. Soaked to the skin, a young Greenfield Village man in a derby pedaled up to the depot on a high-wheeled bicycle and leaned against the wall for momentary shelter.

An imposing array of guests surrounded Bernays—virtually a pantheon of American success. They included John D. Rockefeller, Jr., the heir to an oil empire; Charles Schwab, the steel magnate; Otto Kahn, financier and patron of the arts; Julius Rosenwald, the head of Sears, Roebuck; and Gerard Swope, the president of General Electric. A lot of money and power had been attracted to Dearborn and Bernays hoped to make a good impression on possible future clients. He already had made a name for himself as a pioneer in transforming ballyhoo into a science. This, however, was his biggest moment yet. He had brought national and even world attention to the Jubilee. Photographers, newsreel cameramen and reporters from around the nation had poured in to cover the Dearborn affair. Even the preparations for the event were front-page news all over the country.

The train drew near, and a cheer went up as it slid into the depot with a hissing and screeching of brakes. A man in a gold-braided cap stepped in front of the welcomers and placed a platform at the door of the first car for the passengers to alight. The first two down the steps, arm in arm, were Edison and Hoover. The president was laughing and Edison, playing to the crowd, pointed at Hoover and winked. Cameramen encircled them immediately, and the party moved in front of the engine—a gleaming brassbound locomotive with a mushroom-shaped stack—for photographs. As the cameras flashed, Edison turned up his coat collar against the rain. His wife, standing behind him, put up an umbrella and held it over him. "No, no," he said, gesticulating. "I don't need that. It might spoil the picture."

As the cameramen finished their work, it occurred to Bernays that nothing was planned to follow. It would be appropriate, he thought, for the president to meet this crowd in some orderly fashion. He did not want to seem pushy, but if he did not act, nobody else would. He asked several people to organize themselves, and an impromptu reception line was formed, with Bernays undertaking the introductions himself. A good number of the people already knew the president, but Bernays did not know them, so he had to ask their names to present them to Hoover.

Soon horse-drawn carriages—a touch Bernays had recommended to Ford—were lined up to take the guests on a tour of Greenfield Village, to look at authentic nineteenth-century goods in the general store, old telegraphic equipment in the depot, and old fire engines at the fire house. They had lunch at a reconstructed tavern. Many of the reporters left with the Hoovers for Detroit, where crowds were waiting in the rain to cheer the First Family.

Some of the reporters who had come in with Hoover were working up a story about the short train trip over to the depot. When Hoover and the rest had gotten aboard the railroad cars, they found that Ford had filled them with reminders of Edison's youth: the printing press on which he had printed his own newspaper and a little laboratory like the one Edison had set up in a baggage car. Ford had even provided a small boy shouting his wares as a candy vendor.

Edison seemed fascinated by the boy, and when he put down his basket, Edison picked it up. He walked up and down the aisles, shouting: "Candy! Bananas! Apples! Chewing gum! Peaches!" Mrs. Edison, who had been trying to get him to sit and rest, looked shocked at her husband's antics.

But Hoover went along with it. "I'll take a peach, there," he said, and gave Edison a quarter. Then everybody else began to buy as Edison shouted in a high-pitched, singsong voice, and the great inventor passed out candy, gum, and fruit to a cabinet officer, White House aides, and reporters.

Bernays thought the story was silly and embarrassing. But, he reconsidered, if handled properly it might make the international wires.

The reception line that met the president on the morning of October 21 had come from a guest list carefully built up and studied by Ford and Bernays over the summer of 1929. The guest list itself was meant to have a dazzling effect, to convey the importance of the occasion. The guests differed in a number of ways in their views of American society, but they shared a vision of America as torchbearer of an advancing civilization and believed that progress was hereafter to be measured on an American scale. Mockers and scoffers were not invited to bask in the golden globes of the Jubilee.

Nevertheless, skeptics were abroad in the land. Some lived in Greenwich Village where they despised American materialism and wrote obscure verse and surrealist manifestoes. Others belonged to political organizations with little objection to the course of American industrial development, except that it was in the wrong hands. Some, in the tradition of the departed Henry Adams, deplored the ascendance of the Machine Age as a Frankenstein's monster that would turn people into robots and condemn them to a constricted life under the smokestacks. But all of these outlooks were diminuendo in 1929.

There were, however, other reigning rebels impossible to dismiss, for their following among college students and the culturally aware was considerable. They attacked the final product of America—its human types. The United States was chiefly peopled, the rebels claimed, by *Boobus americanus*. Their readers laughed along with them at America's banal pretenses to civilization. Two men were the most important rebels. In his fiction Sinclair Lewis, the first of the pair, had created a gallery of recognizable American caricatures. The most famous among them were the go-getter businessman, George Babbitt, a vapid but vehement slogan-monger; and the rogue revivalist, Elmer Gantry, an operator in clerical garb. The second important figure in the 1920s' rebellion was Henry Louis Mencken, editor of *The American Mercury*. Through his work the magazine spread doubt, disillusion, and debunking across the nation every month. By 1929 Mencken had become, in the words of Walter Lippmann, "the most powerful personal influence on this whole generation of educated people."

The years had not mellowed Mencken. In the March 1929 issue of the *Mercury* he reviewed what he called a depressing but instructive work—

Middletown, a sociological study of a typical small Midwestern town. The authors, Robert and Helen Lynd, had outdone Sinclair Lewis, he wrote, in getting to the truth of the American type. "What it reveals is a man of almost unbelievable stupidities," Mencken wrote. "Well-fed, well-dressed, complacent and cocksure, he yet remains almost destitute of ideas. The things he admires are mainly mean things, and the things he thinks he knows are nearly all untrue. The government he lives under is ignorant and corrupt, the industrial system he is a part of is inefficient and cruel, and the ideals that inspire him are puerile and ignominious."

Even in places like Middletown, Mencken noted, faith was waning, and was being replaced by Rotarianism, slightly less ridiculous. Some thinkers said a new religion based on science would have to be developed to replace such concepts as God, the soul, immortality, sin, and the authority of the Bible. By midyear two social commentators, Lippmann and Joseph Wood Krutch, had addressed themselves to these problems.

"There exists today on a scale never before experienced by mankind and of an urgency without a parallel, the need for that philosophy of life of which the insight of high religion is a prophecy," Lippmann wrote in *A Preface To Morals.*

Mencken was himself working on a book about religion, and in reviewing Krutch and Lippmann he failed to see any more moral chaos in 1929 than in any preceding age, and no need for any religion at all. He was put off by Krutch's book, *The Modern Temper,* because of its traces of the old Christian notion "that human life is animated by some transcendental and grandiose purpose, that a mysterious divine plan runs through it." Krutch said that the light of science alone could not replace religion; but Mencken responded that if science "enabled us to see nothing save the flatulent imbecility of theology it would have served us better than any light that ever dazzled the past. To be sure, we still have wars and politicians, but is it nothing to have got rid of gods and ghosts?"

In July, Lewis stopped at Baltimore to see Mencken. Lewis was drinking steadily, and it showed. His thinning red hair was slicked down, his face was scabby with eczema.

He had just returned from North Carolina, where violent textile mill strikes had plunged areas of the state into anarchy and riot. Lewis was shaken by what he had seen. He regarded it as a harbinger of the future. The nation had hit the peak of prosperity, he said, and the slide was about to begin. "The car's right at the summit of the roller-coaster," Lewis said. "The hair-raising plunge is just ahead. I can see it, feel it, smell it in the air."

Mencken and Lewis delved into such signs and portents while the nation, freed of the bother of gods and ghosts, saw greater prophecy in the celebration of perpetual prosperity at Dearborn.

With the approach of evening on October 21, in the banquet hall of Henry Ford the waiters and waitresses were setting plates and silver for five hundred. The cooks were preparing a meal of boneless squab chicken in butter and Virginia ham with mushrooms. NBC and CBS were setting up broadcasting equipment. Telegrams arrived from Commander Richard Byrd in the Antarctic, Guglielmo Marconi, President von Hindenburg of Germany, and the Prince of Wales. Aides placed printed programs at the settings.

"Never before perhaps has a group met under similar circumstances, to give homage to a simple citizen whose right to homage is based on inventive skill and mechanical ingenuity," the program read. "Here at last is a democracy that rates greatness of achievement principally in terms of social service. For at no age in the past has the scientist been regarded by the people of any nation as anything more than an intellectual novelty."

In Detroit the buses pulled up at the hotels to take the guests to Dearborn and the already-famous testimonial dinner for Edison. But to a considerable extent, the event that Henry Ford had staged was not just about Edison, but about his five hundred guests as well. The businessmen who attended radiated an extraordinary amount of human talent, ambition and folly. They included the well-born gentlemen who continuously feed American finance at its Wall Street concentration; gamblers who played with fortunes at the call of their instincts; go-getters who had climbed upward with energy and salesmanship as their motor; organizers who knew how to put giant industrial combines together; lawyers who had taken command in corporations through their knowledge of anti-trust law, patent law, and labor law.

There were leaders of the trade associations, who worked at the intersection of business and government, and lobbyists for business. There were philanthropists engaged in the business of giving money away. But the guest list also showed how totally American business had become interwoven with applied science. Some of the business leaders had made their mark because they understood Bessemer hearths, or engines, or radio systems, or the mechanics of setting up mass production, or were business architects who designed buildings as machines. Leaders from America's great research laboratories, in the pay of the giant corporations, were there, as well as great innovators like Marie Curie and Orville Wright.

The guests also included individual success stories—like Will Rogers, who had started as a Wild West show performer and then had been successful in every endeavor he had tried, including as a rodeo cowboy, vaudeville circuiter, headliner with the Ziegfeld shows, movie star, author, radio commentator, and columnist.

Some of those who came were promoters above all—selling concepts, social systems, or themselves. Electric light utility executives formed a large contingent representing an enterprise that was at once a business, a technology, and a highly organized promotion. All of them used the rapidly growing press, magazines, and radio and were used by the same communications media. Never before had such opportunities existed for promotion and ballyhoo, and they were being used to the fullest. The Jubilee was for that matter a performance before the photographers, the radio microphones, and the reporters. Ford's dinner was a self-portrait of the American free enterprise system by its own commanders. It had collected the talent that had gone into its making and now was celebrating a business society that claimed to put service above mere acquisition. The clues to understanding 1929 could be seen and heard that evening in the hall.

They gathered to honor a single person—a man already passed into myth as a go-getter, a rugged individualist, a practical scientist—but their meeting implied a national celebration. They converged at Dearborn at the zenith of a remarkable historical development—the cometlike ascent of the United States from a struggling nation riddled by civil war to the leading world power. This transformation had taken place in a single lifetime—the lifetime, as it happened, of Thomas Edison. And the electrical network that he had created had made that world primacy possible. On that Monday evening of October 21, there was no reason to believe that the future would be anything other than a continuation of the golden present. Together these men held the direction of the economy in their grasp—or so it seemed.

The Businessmen

I T WAS 1929 in the United States of America. The people, as could be seen in the advertisements, were all white, and although they occasionally worried about halitosis, falling hair, and common mistakes in English, they were an optimistic lot and spent much of their time showing their new cars, their toasters, and their refrigerators to envious visitors.

That was the year that milk was first delivered in waxed paper cartons. That was the year that Edwin Hubble discovered that the galaxies are receding from one another. The Boston Braves received permission that year to play home games on Sundays, and the New York Yankees began to wear numbers on their uniforms, just like football players. The movie theaters were all installing sound equipment. Prohibition was in effect.

In New York the West Side Highway was being constructed, as was the Chrysler Building. When finished it would be the world's tallest, although plans were announced in 1929 to build an even taller one, to be called the Empire State Building. Congress was debating whether to build a new canal through Nicaragua, and, across the Atlantic, there was talk of a tunnel from Dover to Normandy. In Detroit, police had equipped eight of their patrol cars with radio receiving sets. Criminals were being caught red-handed with the benefit of such communications, and hope was rising that crime had finally been defeated by technology.

It was very hot in Miami Beach on the night of St. Valentine's Day when about one hundred people turned out for a big party at 93 Palm Avenue. The host was installing a lot of improvements in his new home, including the biggest and best pool in the area. It was so warm that the waiters serving champagne were permitted to remove their jackets and shoulder pistol holsters.

The host and hostess, Mr. and Mrs. Al Capone, made an excellent impression on their guests, although some of their neighbors in that exclusive area of Miami Beach had attempted to block their purchase of the property, believing the Capones to be socially inferior. Capone had offered to join the Rotary Club and said he would reconsider the purchase if convinced that he was unwanted. The people who looked down on him in Chicago, he said, were his customers when they needed some Canadian liquor.

13

The guests marveled at his rock pool filled with rare tropical fish and admired his two-story bathhouse. His fortifications were also impressive. He had a wall of concrete blocks built around the estate and put in a phone so callers could announce themselves at the entrance. An armed guard stood watch continuously at the gate. Capone mingled with his guests, discussing his dog track in Illinois, the races at Hialeah, the upcoming Jack Sharkey–Young Stribling fight, and his cabin cruiser. Business was not discussed, though he was known to be concerned that a rival businessman, Bugs Moran, had been intercepting the deliveries of his Canadian goods and appropriating them for his own use.

It can only be conjectured—for Capone and his guests never mentioned the subject that night—whether he had heard of the shocking business in Chicago on that St. Valentine's Day. Seven members of the Moran organization had been machine-gunned to death in a garage on North Clark Street, and the newspapers were calling it a massacre.

But Capone was an exception to the general high esteem in which businessmen were held. At business lunches around the country it was declared that Jesus Christ was the first Rotarian and that there was something divine in the origin of the Kiwanis Club. Bruce Barton had written a book casting Jesus as the supreme businessman of all time, and it was commonly assumed that business and religion were a partnership devoted to similar ends. A few clergymen, like Rev. C. Everett Wagner, complained about it. "When businessmen call on the clergy," he said in a sermon that October, "to say a prayer for success at the opening of a railroad and airplane route from coast to coast and they also ask the blessing of religion upon a profitable enterprise like the opening of a new dam, the Church pays its homage to a new king. They want a businessman's religion, which means that religion must help them to larger profits."

Most clergymen, however, tended to agree with the dominant view that business was basically a selfless profession engaged in helping everybody. Benjamin Javits and Charles W. Wood were the authors that year of a book called *Make Everybody Rich—Industry's New Goal*. In commenting on the book, *The Review of Reviews* noted that the authors "dwell on the new conception of business as a matter of service, of filling human needs."

In January of 1929 Owen D. Young, the board chairman of General Electric, took over the pulpit at one of the most select congregations in New York to speak on the subject of Big Business. He attempted to dispel lingering fears that might have remained from the days when "the trusts" were bogeymen that would raise prices and enter combinations to squeeze the consumer. Not so, said Young—the bigger the business was, the wider its benefits, the stronger its efficiencies, and the more thoroughgoing its sense of responsibility. At some point it even became too large to endure dishonesty. "A storekeeper might short-measure or short-change his customer," Young said. "He might even induce his clerk to short-weigh or short-measure. But he could not organize a vast department store on that basis. Either his employees are honest people who would refuse or he would soon have as employees a vast organization of crooks who would beat each other and soon ruin the proprietor himself. Big business does not lend itself readily to dishonesty and crookedness."

Big Business scarcely needed defenders in 1929. It was generally believed that the inexorable trend of business toward massive structures would solve society's problems. Many of the men who had instilled that belief and had filtered it down to the local Kiwanian oratory about Service were at Dearborn on October 21 for Ford's dinner. Behind their temperamental and even philosophical differences, a common thread ran through their efforts. They had been born into an undisciplined, disorganized and unmonitored capitalism, and they were devoted to socializing and rationalizing the economy to create a new integrated capitalism.

Julius Rosenwald, the head of the nation's leading retailing operation, was intent on developing a free enterprise system in which his private harvest was used to fertilize the society. His theories of philanthropy went far beyond the simplistic money-giving of Carnegie. It was administered systematically as a business, with built-in safeguards so that even Rosenwald's own will would not be imposed perpetually, but his money would be shifted with the changing needs of a time he would never see.

Another guest at Ford's dinner, Charles Schwab, had helped create the image of the business leader as head of a huge Chamber of Commerce. In his view the business leader should be a public spokesman relentlessly presenting the pro-business point of view. He represented not only his own Bethlehem Steel, but the entire steel industry. He sensed that the steel industry underlay all American industry as its basic raw material and thus played a special role in the economy. He spoke for an industry that carried on sustained and crucial business with government.

Henry Ford was the age's great captain of industry. His was an entrepreneurial spirit, but he too worked toward consolidation. His plants were huge integrated machines, and his enterprises were aimed toward the goal of total self-sufficiency. His influence ranged far beyond automotives. No other man so flavored the century; his business philosophy of mass production and mass sales formed the basis of modern industry.

John D. Rockefeller, Jr., was also attempting to integrate the system, but basically by creating cultural loyalties to the capitalist system that would run through the spectrum of social classes, holding in fealty all people from princes to beggars. He intended to create these loyalties by various means, including the overcoming of the system's chronic tendency toward corruption. Capitalism, he believed, could not triumph by force of arms; it would have to win the hearts and minds of the people.

Perhaps no other figure represented economic integration with the force of J.P. Morgan. Like his father, he loathed the wastefulness of competition. The House of Morgan always stood for the right of gentlemen to meet and settle their differences in some huge monopoly. His triumphs were numerous. The twentieth century, under the tutelage of the two Morgans, had been a parade of consolidations, and no other figure had been as important in the alignment of world alliances. Morgan had put the United States on Great Britain's side in the world war, and the pro-German terrorist who tried to kill him may have been mad, but not deluded. He chose the right man.

Owen Young devoted all his efforts at General Electric to remaking capitalism into a fully rationalized system. He believed in monopoly with all the fervor that Cotton Mather had believed in Jehovah. It was Young's nature to consolidate through the resolution of differences. His vision of a consolidated economy was, in effect, a nation administered by regulatory boards watching over a free enterprise system reorganized as public utilities.

The views of these six representative men of 1929 ranged from the populist greenbacker Ford to the liberal Young to the conservative Morgan, but they all influenced President Hoover, who for the preceding eight years had held the pivotal post of Commerce Secretary, and from that post had helped develop such new businesses as radio and aviation. The man who had been rumored to succeed him in the Commerce Department, but whose health was too precarious to permit such a move, was the chairman of the board of Sears, Roebuck, Julius Rosenwald.

Sears, Roebuck still received letters addressed to Mr. Sears, although he had left the company twenty years earlier and had been dead for fifteen. "Honesty is the best policy," he used to tell his partner, Rosenwald. "I know because I've tried it both ways." His honesty had limits. Sears sold a lot of patent remedies that, although they did not hurt anyone, did not cure anything either. He sold, no questions asked, revolvers by mail. One of the gadgets that Rosenwald most disliked—and insisted on paying refunds for—was an electric belt that was supposed to cure rheumatism and other ailments, but had little effect on most people, except for those it burned about the midriff.

Rosenwald studied at the feet of the great Rabbi Hirsch, and he knew there were Biblical and Talmudic injunctions against some of Sears' practices. He effectively kept his partner in check for many years, and when he succeeded Sears as president, he set out to make the mail-order house a model of rectitude in business. The rather discolored prose of the catalogues was converted into forthright descriptions of the products. Out went the patent remedies and in went complete information on all the ingredients in food products. Out went the misleading descriptions of skunk or rabbit fur as "electric seal." Rosenwald set up the world's first testing laboratory. Every article was tested for claims and durability, and the materials that the manufacturers used were analyzed. New designs and materials were developed.

Honesty did appear to be the best policy, for under Rosenwald the firm became an American institution. Bankers, jobbers, manufacturers, and customers relied upon it for its uprightness. Much of its business was rural, and farmers sometimes sent in their savings for safekeeping or to be used for later purchases. Alaskan miners sent in gold dust. A man sent a check, asking that a female employee select presents for his niece and bill him for more if the check was not enough. Lone ranchers sent in for wives, and men asked to be introduced to women whose pictures were in the catalogues. Children wrote for baby brothers or sisters.

The Sears, Roebuck catalogue became, like the Model T Ford, a national family joke, but an affectionate joke. It was used in schools to teach arithmetic. For many rural families it was a chief source of information, along with the Bible, and taught everything from geography, using the postal zone maps, to the female anatomy, learned from corset advertisements. Immigrant families used it to learn English. Rosenwald made his company a national institution, and one of the most trusted.

Some people thought that Rosenwald did too much for colored people. To counter the South's neglect of education for blacks, the Julius Rosenwald Foundation built one-room rural schools and turned them over to the southern states. He had always taken a special interest in helping blacks, and one project of his foundation in 1929 was developing a grant for a health program to help abate syphilis among southern blacks.

It was a typically Rosenwaldian cause. Even public bodies were reluctant to appropriate money to fight venereal disease, and philanthropists who unhesitatingly gave money for tuberculosis or hospitals would never consider such a contribution. Rosenwald welcomed any chance to move into a field that was being neglected.

Generosity came naturally to him. He kept a closet at home full of toys, and no child visiting his home ever left without a gift. Every charity in America called him or dropped by his office, hoping to catch his fancy. His wife encouraged him. Early in their marriage, before they had become wealthy, he came home to make a confession to her. In the emotion of the moment he had pledged considerably more to a Jewish charity than they could afford. Augusta's answer was that he need never worry about such matters. When he said that it would mean sacrifices and economies, she shrugged. The problem had been disposed of, and Rosenwald, always keeping in close touch with his wife's advice, went on to give away millions.

Augusta took an interest in the welfare of those around her. When they were first married she noticed that the mail carrier wore no overcoat in winter, and made a warm vest for him out of materials around the house. Every Thanksgiving the furnace man, the garbage man, the street sweepers were invited to the Rosenwald home for baskets of food. Every Christmas a large party was held for the servants, and the home was kept busy for days preparing thousands of pounds of candy to distribute to children through the institutions of Chicago.

Despite his rotund look, Rosenwald lived intensely. He was always bringing interesting people home to dine with his family. He was impatient about poverty and injustice and wanted everything remedied just as quickly as possible. He dashed about from one appointment to the next, his car always supplied with the freshest editions of Chicago's newspapers. He stuffed his pockets with news articles that he later read to his children at the dinner table.

In spite of his generosities he was not indulgent with himself. His cars were driven to the last mile. He was tightfisted with his children, afraid that wealth might make them wasteful and extravagant. When a new chauffeur came back from Sears with a large supply of razor blades, Rosenwald made it clear that he always ordered in small quantities. "What do you think I would do with all of these blades?" he asked. "First, I would use them up too fast and waste them or probably lose track of them. And another thing, suppose the price should go down."

His own rabbi had denounced him from the pulpit as too ignorant to appreciate the virtues of a cause the rabbi was furthering, but nobody could be more sales resistant than Rosenwald. And to nothing was he more sales resistant than Zionism.

The Zionists had hoped to convert his wife first and through her reach him, but in August of 1929—when murder and pillage broke out again in Palestine—she had been dead for three months. Arab leaders were calling for extermination of the Jews, and when the British finally moved to take hold of the situation, it was out of control.

Rosenwald was donating literally millions to help resettle Russian Jews in Crimea and the Ukraine. He gave millions for medical research, thousands to black people. He was even a major contributor to a forthcoming museum of technology. He told friends that he was ashamed to have so much money and wanted to give it away. And yet he could not be persuaded to support a Jewish homeland. Instead he dealt with a communist government that the United States did not even recognize. The Zionists shook their heads sadly at his errant ways.

The stories out of Jerusalem grew worse. At Hebron forty-eight Jews had been massacred. The Arabs had mutilated all of them. Some were hung upside down and slashed. Some had been set afire. A rabbi's brain had been extracted. A baker's head had been tied to a lighted stove and he was baked to death in his own oven.

The British were scolded at rallies for breaking promises about support of a homeland for the Jews. Unions and capitalists closed ranks to support the Palestine Emergency Fund, and banks were placed at its service. Theaters offered their stages for benefit performances. President Hoover telegrammed his support of a national homeland to a Madison Square Garden rally. Perhaps the best news of all, Rosenwald made a large contribution and took the post of honorary chairman of the fund.

But at sixty-seven years of age, he was not about to change on the subject of Zionism. He welcomed a chance to alleviate suffering in Palestine, but his commitment was still to the colonies in the Ukraine and Crimea. And so, while the Zionists grumbled that Russia had made pogroms before and would make them again, the capitalist Rosenwald worked with the communists. Rosenwald believed that the Soviet government would last and it would in time take over his project as a governmental effort. But he was neither a communist sympathizer nor a Zionist. He was a Chicagoan, an American, and, unlike the synagogues of the East, his temple had no turrets and no cupolas.

He was always outspoken. In January of 1929 he appeared in a Movietone newsreel in which he said that making money did not take much brains and some of the biggest fools he knew were rich. The newsreel fomented considerable editorial comment, most of it chiding Rosenwald. It was better, he had also told the audiences in movie houses around the nation, to be a beggar and spend money like a king than to be a king and spend money like a beggar. Money was no good to him unless it was in use; it had the energy that had once been his, when he used to shout directions to his chauffeur as he bounded into the back seat, change clothes on his way to an appointment, and jump out before the limousine came to a stop.

In March 1929 he and Augusta were in such poor health that they almost missed the inauguration of Hoover, whom he regarded as the greatest of Americans and with whom he had worked closely on postwar relief projects. Attending the inauguration sapped his wife's diminishing strength, and she died in May. Once again he asked himself, as he so often had, what life was about. To look at sales charts? To be lost in business worries always? To hire a lawyer and finagle ways of paying as few taxes as possible? He chose instead to give not grudgingly but gladly and, in his own words, "generously, eagerly, lovingly, joyfully, indeed with the supremest pleasure that life can furnish." Despite his business and civic interests he always had time for his family. Large family dinners were held every week. He visited his mother every day until her death. He walked his younger children to school every day and when they had grown he visited them regularly. His pudgy and undistinguished body had held extra bursts of energy. But by October of 1929 his mother and his wife were dead and he was a bent and shriveled old man, half-crippled with a bone ailment, as he wandered about to see the sights of Greenfield Village.

The general store in Greenfield Village contained a great-bellied stove, and to it on that morning of October 21 some of the guests gathered for warmth. As they rubbed their hands before the stove, they were surrounded by bustles, bedsteads, kegs of nails, barrels of peanuts and apples. Alone by the window, portly and gray-haired, watching rivulets of water run down the panes, stood Charles Schwab. It was a rare moment of repose for the supersalesman of American business.

By title he was chairman of the board of the Bethlehem Steel Company, but by inclination he was cheerleader for the economy. A man of narrow but intense vision, he loved to see the press encircle him, and unlike many press-shy industrialists, he loved to see what he had said the next day in the newspapers. "Idealism rather than dollar-chasing is the motivating force behind big business in the United States," he told a clump of reporters early in 1929, and found it quoted in *The American Mercury* in the monthly parade of what the magazine considered most inane in America. Schwab sounded like the Grand Exalted Head Babbitt in print, but the words failed to capture the dynamic personality that said them. "The late Judge Gary may have been the mouthpiece of Big Business," an *American Mercury* article of 1927 stated, "and young Mr. Morgan may be its mailed fist, but Charlie Schwab is its great, wide-open, throbbing heart."

He might have become a successful entertainer. As a boy Schwab would bombard visiting relatives with jokes, songs, somersaults and magic tricks. When they rose to leave, the boy used to shout: "I can do something else yet!" He went into the steel business as a factory worker and attracted attention in every way he knew how. He came to know almost everything about steel, yet his fabulous rise was not just based on knowledge but on his uncommon ability to make himself trusted and believed. Early in his career his employers discovered his ability to spellbind. He could step out before an angry group of rebellious workers, calm them, and eventually lead them to a table where they would be praised and flattered until they were convinced that Charles Schwab was consumed by an interest in their welfare. It was only when they were back on the job that they would realize that they had won nothing from him.

He could make his plants hum. "How is it that a man as able as you," he asked one of his managers early in his career, "cannot make the mill turn out what it should?"

"I don't know," the manager said. "I have coaxed the men; I have pushed them; I have sworn at them. I have done everything in my power. Yet they will not produce."

It was the end of the day shift. Schwab turned to a workman standing near a furnace and asked him for a piece of chalk. "How many heats has your shift made today?" he asked.

"Six," was the reply.

Schwab chalked a big "6" on the floor, and passed along without another word. When the night shift came in, they asked about it. "The big boss was in here today," a day man explained. "He asked how many heats we had made and we told him six. He chalked it down."

The next morning Schwab passed through the same mill. The "6" had been rubbed out and "7" written in its place. That night he went back. The "7" had been obliterated and a "10" was in its place.

When the United States entered the war, President Wilson realized that he needed Schwab's talents in government. The steel magnate was asked to leave Bethlehem Steel and become a dollar-a-year man to help win the war as head of the Emergency Fleet Corporation. Schwab then made the best use ever of his jokes, songs, somersaults, and magic tricks. The results were spectacular. At one plant in San Francisco a 12,000-ton freighter slid down the ways less than twenty-four days after the laying of the keel. On the 4th of July, 1918, he launched one hundred ships of the Fleet Corporation. At a luncheon in New York, he sold fifty-two million dollars worth of Liberty Bonds in fifty-two minutes. His shipyard speeches to workers, exhorting them on to greater efforts, became legendary. Over his desk he hung a cartoon showing long lines of American-built ships steaming across the ocean. On the European shores stood the Kaiser, looking pained. "Ach," he said, "and Schwab is such a good German name."

On his way back from Europe on the *Olympic* in 1919, his fellow passengers included a group of black American soldiers coming home. Schwab observed some of them standing about the ship's canteen. It was clear that they lacked money for candy and cigarettes. Schwab decided to test them. He lent each of the soldiers a dollar, gave them his address, and then told them that they might return the dollar if they wanted to, but did not have to. Within little more than a month, 138 of the 154 soldiers had returned the small loan. Schwab called in the press to relay the story.

"Those boys were sound to the core!" he said. "That's one of the main reasons I'm not worrying about the United States going Bolshevik at the next election."

Nineteen twenty-nine was a busy year for the chairman of the board of General Electric, and the dinner at Dearborn, at which he was toastmaster, was just another stop on the crowded schedule of Owen Young. At fifty-four years he was a tall, rangy, tired-looking man with dark circles under his eyes and face muscles that had begun to sag into a double chin. As he worked on his address he looked at ease, most of his weight borne by two points—the base of his spine and the upper vertebrae near his neck—and his eyes half-closed. He sometimes claimed when discovered in that attitude that he was just resting—but his legs, braided about one another, gave him away.

All through the spring of the year he had been in Paris for important business; in effect, the final settlement of the war. He sat at a big table at the Hotel George V, listening to Dr. Hjalmar Schacht go on at length about the state of Germany. Dr. Schacht was president of the Reichsbank, the central bank of Germany.

Young listened in what appeared to be a state of advanced relaxation. He occasionally appeared ready to doze off and slide from his chair—but the look was deceptive. Young followed Schacht closely, listening not only to the words but to the note of suppressed hysteria in the voice. The banker had one of those necks that swelled in back and when he became excited it would redden. Young watched for the flush, ready to break up the meeting if the banker showed any sign of losing control of himself. Young relit his pipe and watched Schacht's hands for any trace of shaking.

His gaze wandered around the table. The Japanese delegation looked dignified. The Belgians, to whom the German occupation was still an intense memory, looked more militant. The Italians listened carefully to why Germany could not pay its war reparations. They did not want the reparations reduced by a single lira, for they used them to pay their debts to the United States—as indeed did the other nations whose representatives were arrayed around the table. The French had been twice invaded by Germany within living memory and for them this conference was sweet revenge. And then there were the British, who had witnessed Germany recover more rapidly from the war than had their own nation.

The Treaty of Versailles had fixed the question of war guilt on Germany. Since she had started the war, Germany would have to pay damages for it. And although payments had begun, it was not until February of 1929 that the bankers of various nations met in Paris, with Young as chairman of the Committee of Experts, to affix a final figure for German war reparations and to set terms for repayment. The eyes of the world were on the meeting, which the *New York Times* regarded as the most important news event of the year. It was going badly. Schacht had been playing for time for a month, and that afternoon, even when called to a showdown, he was still stalling.

Germany, he said, was in horrendous shape. Its fields were full of crops stunted for lack of fertilizer. Its people had lost their savings to inflation. It had an unfavorable balance of trade and high unemployment. It was not even paying its reparations bills, really, but just borrowing from one source, chiefly the Americans, to pay another. Germany was aggrieved, he said, by the loss of colonies and territories, and by the continued Allied occupation that now had lasted more than a decade.

What Schacht said, however, was not apparent to the world. Berlin was the most glittering den of decadence on earth. The streets were crowded, and women dressed in expensive gowns and jewels filled the cabarets and smoked from long cigarette holders. On the French Riviera, in Switzerland and in Italy, the hotel proprietors loved to see the Germans arrive; they spent even more lavishly than did the Americans. Rather than give their money away in reparations, the Germans intended to have a carnival with it.

For week after week, the harsh words continued. Young broke up meetings early and broke the committee into smaller working groups to help keep antagonists apart. By June, what appeared to be a hopeless cause had been reversed. The conference that the press had called the biggest poker game in history had ended in sweet success, and most of the credit was showered on Chairman Young. Editorials in newspapers around the world clamored for a Nobel Peace Prize for him. A decade after the shooting had stopped, the war was finally over, and it was hoped that the uncertainty that had haunted Europe for so long would be dispelled. "Say, what do you know about Owen Young getting those hyenas to agree?" Will Rogers commented in his syndicated column. "Remember, boys, he is a Democrat; don't try to claim him, you Republicans." That summer, two hundred businessmen from all over the country attending a session at Harvard Business School voted him the greatest businessman in America, winning out over Henry Ford and President Hoover.

Young did not fit the business stereotypes. There was nothing of the high-powered Schwab brand of Rotarian in him, nor was he a tough-minded expounder of the survival of the fittest. When a reporter of the time overheard Young's friends talking about him in a New York club, they told anecdotes that demonstrated his modesty and his ability to estab-lish contact with all varieties of people. A classmate at St. Lawrence University recalled their undergraduate days together, when Young had been chosen to present the case for a new gymnasium before the board of trustees. They depicted a mellow and soft-spoken man.

"I admire Young just as much as any of you," one of them said after these adulatory comments had gone on for some time. "I went to school with him, too. But I won't admit that he is 100 percent perfect. Everyone has faults."

When the others demanded that he name some of Young's shortcom-ings, he thought silently for a moment. Then he gave up. "I can't think of any right now," he said.

Some believed that his flaw was excessive insouciance—that he lacked sufficient ambition. He did not discourage that image of himself, for he was above all a listener, and his air of languor loosened people up. He was always listening. He was president of his university's board of trustees and would often park himself in a hotel near the campus and listen to under-graduates and faculty who stopped by to talk. He would saunter up the main street of his hometown of Van Hornesville in upstate New York, dropping in to chat with the editor of the weekly paper or the hardware store owner. He faced one of the world's most formidable schedules, but Young knew how to conserve his strength, work efficiently, attend to the problem directly before him, and give the false impression that he had nothing to do.

After his Paris triumph, he immediately became a likely candidate for the Democratic presidential nomination in 1932. An editorial cartoon in The Chicago Tribune showed "Miss Democracy" admiring his photograph and thinking, " '32—Young and nice looking." There was an unwished quality to his success, as if it had fallen into his hands, and he called the presidential boom a lot of bosh. Yet he was not wholly unmindful of his image. Every day while he was in Paris an assistant in New York prepared a digest of editorial comment and other gauges of public reaction to the

reparations conference. They were radioed to Young every night at great
expense, and he read them carefully.

Although he had never run for office, Young was no stranger to the
public spotlight. Five years before the reparations conference of 1929, he
and General Charles Dawes had put together the Dawes Plan, which had
started the machinery of reparations payments, though only as an interim
measure. As GE board chairman, Young had fashioned the Radio Corporation of America, and out of RCA he had spun off yet another cultural
shock—a coast-to-coast program service for radio stations called the National Broadcasting Company. The final settlement of reparations was
soon tagged with his name and called the Young Plan.

After he returned from Paris in June, Young told a story that showed
the new amity in European affairs that had grown out of the reparations
conference. When the major terms were agreed upon by the end of May,
he said, Young began to realize that the details could take weeks to wind
up, and he was hoping to attend his son's wedding in Cleveland and
receive an honorary degree at the Hamilton College commencement. He
quietly mentioned to his fellow committee members that the last ship he
could take to be back in the United States in time for these two events
sailed on June 8.

"From that time on there was no need of my urging that committee,"
he said at a banquet following the Hamilton commencement. "When small
differences of opinion came up someone would say, 'We must get Mr.
Young home for his son's wedding, we must get him back to Hamilton
College to get his degree.' They ended the proceedings at seven o'clock on
the seventh of June and at ten o'clock on the eighth of June I left for the
United States. What finer evidence of the warmth of human feeling and
cooperation could you have than that? How much more helpful to the
committee and to me than any arbitrary statement that I must sail for
home on a certain day?" The story of how the delegates laid aside their
differences to get Young home on time was in all the newspapers that
summer—but how the settlement had really come about was not in the
papers at all.

The American delegates had taken an entourage of assistants from
their firms with them to the conference. The assistants, who performed all
sorts of backup work from research to running errands, were called the
Bellhops Club. At one point the American delegation had become so
gloomy about the obstructionism of Hjalmar Schacht, the leading German
delegate, that they were beginning to set in motion a plan to leave the
conference and return home. One of the bellhops, a prize protégé of

Young's, counseled strongly against such a move. The blame, he warned, would be placed on the Americans if the conference failed. Young, ailing in bed and unable to do much except advise at that point, suggested that his protégé, David Sarnoff, should meet with Schacht and try to start the machinery in motion again.

Sarnoff, an RCA executive, first met with Schacht for dinner on May 1 in the German's suite. What was intended as a brief session to get acquainted continued for eighteen hours and did not break up until the following afternoon.

From that session on through most of May the international conference condensed into a two-man operation. The German financier opened up to Sarnoff as he had to no one else. Sarnoff's desk was moved into the inner sanctum with the major representatives. Realizing that the pattern of negotiations had shifted, allied statesmen began to make their presentations to Sarnoff rather than to Young.

One night they met in a private dining room of a Paris restaurant. Schacht was so angry that Sarnoff was alarmed that he might be taken with apoplexy. Schacht explained bitterly that he was acquainted with a family that had once represented French interests in Germany and had invited him to their French home. But sentiments against Schacht's role in deadlocking the conference were running extremely high in Paris, and the family received a call from the governor of the Bank of France objecting to the welcome extended to an enemy of the French people. Under that sort of official pressure, the family had withdrawn the invitation.

"Mr. Sarnoff," Schacht said, "how prejudiced can people be? Here I am ten years after the war, representing the German government, which is expected to shoulder billions in reparations, to be paid by unborn generations of my people, and yet I am not permitted to dine privately with old friends in a French home!"

Sarnoff's sympathy, with the aid of good wine and the first course, calmed the financier down. Sarnoff suggested that he could well understand how Schacht felt. "After all, you're an amateur in the area of prejudice," Sarnoff said, "but I have two thousand years' experience with it. Besides, your people are not free from such feeling either."

Sarnoff expressed his concern about anti-Jewish diatribes that various political groups in Germany were preaching. Schacht dismissed Sarnoff's fears. He said these extremist views did not represent the sentiments of the German people.

"Do you speak Hebrew?" Schacht asked.

"No," Sarnoff replied, "but I understand it, because I studied the sacred books in my boyhood."

"Well, I'm not a Jew, but I do speak it," Schacht said. He began to recite the first chapter of Genesis in Hebrew. His doctorate, Sarnoff learned, was not in economics but in Hebrew.

The Sarnoff-Schacht meetings led to a basis for an agreement. When Schacht reduced his acceptance of the terms to writing, the letter was addressed to Sarnoff and referred to the agreement as the Sarnoff plan. Sarnoff returned it, insisting that the letter be readdressed to his bedridden supervisor and that all references be changed to the Young Plan. That was how the Young Plan got its name, how Sarnoff cemented his future at RCA, and how Young became a candidate for the Nobel Prize and possibly a presidential candidate.

October 21 was a bad day for the stock market. The ticker tapes were so late that many traders knew nothing of the real standing of most stocks. The tapes had often fallen behind on days of large gains, but it was an upsetting feeling when they lagged on a downward trend. The tickers lost ground after ten minutes of trading and by noon were an hour late. They never caught up until one hundred minutes after the market closed. The market rallied at the close of the day and everyone hoped that October 22 would show an improvement.

The previous month and a half had been disturbing for investors and speculators. Since the great bull market began in 1926, good news had continued for so long that many people seriously believed that the market would continue to rise forever. Over the months of boom there had been a few sudden downturns, but all had been mercifully brief. Since early September, however, the market had been behaving neurotically.

America's intense interest in stocks was in part a response to changes in the personality of banking. The day of the highly respected, kindly banker who advised widows and young people on their investments was passé. The day of jazzy salesmanship had arrived, and bankers were selling stocks and patterning themselves after men like Charles Schwab. They did not wait for people to stop by their offices. Their salesmen knocked on the doors of farmhouses selling Peruvian bonds as though they were selling Fuller brushes or vacuum cleaners. Their bosses sent them telegrams to get out there and sell more—get the lead out, show some spunk. The air rang with Rotarian slogans. The pressure was on, feet were being held to the fire, and the salesmen's jobs were at stake if they failed to meet quotas, so when they fell behind they would sometimes fake orders and buy the securities themselves out of their own salaries.

One leading banker conducted a twenty-five-thousand-dollar contest among his salespeople in 1929. The scoring was an elaborate point system;

the harder the stock to sell, the more points. These salesmen for the most part did not examine the securities with a view as to whether their customers were making a prudent investment. There were no points for that.

Whenever he issued new stock, the great Chicago utilities magnate, Samuel Insull, urged it upon his employees, who believed themselves under pressure to buy. The employees were expected to sell stock to their friends and acquaintances. The man who came to inspect wiring or take a look at the stove was expected to try to interest the householder in a few shares of Insull stock before leaving.

By 1929 the interest in investing had changed into a fever for speculating. In one of New York's brokerage houses a man entered every day wearing the same tattered, crumbling orange tie. He had worn that tie on the day his luck in the stock market changed and, though its ends were frayed and the inner lining showed through, he continued to tie it around his neck every morning.

In New York, stock offices moved uptown to mid-Manhattan, with one on 42nd Street and another on Broadway in the seventies. Strays wandered in. "I want to buy," a woman said, plopping down a huge purse in one of the midtown offices, "a stock that's going up today." The amused clerk suggested that she wanted a fortune teller rather than a broker, and the woman, a bit miffed, replied that she wondered what was his function if not to help customers with such questions.

Brokerage offices were also opening all over the country, especially in Detroit, the home of motor fortunes; the booming resorts of Miami and Palm Beach, where the speculators went to gamble in the sun; Chicago; Boston; Atlanta; and the two up-and-coming West Coast cities, Los Angeles and San Francisco. But about 20 percent of the traffic was in New York. There the houses were increasing their staffs weekly to take care of increased business. New skyscrapers going up along the downtown skyline were rented completely before construction had begun. Cramped brokerage houses were bidding for more office space on Wall Street and throughout Lower Manhattan.

Every day over the financial district the tips went sailing like an armada of balloons. For the amateur—and the great bull market of 1929 was an amateur market, its ranks filled with butlers, bootblacks, and clerks gambling their surplus earnings—tips were infallible signs that came from true insiders. Some were circulated on printed sheets, others were recommended explicitly by brokerage houses, some were planted by manipulators.

Getting close to the inside made the difference, the amateurs said. They told of two waiters who worked at the Bankers Club. Both retired early with heavy winnings—one to a farm on Long Island, the other to operate a Staten Island restaurant. A telegraph operator in a brokerage house made a million dollars in eight years and retired to take his family on a three-year cruise around the world.

Women had caught the fever too. Some traderooms were for women only, with women in smocks keeping the board quotations current and women in charge of the operation. Some offices looked like a missionary society meeting, peopled with elderly ladies in Victorian hats. Others were flashy, with male clerks collecting order slips and lighting the ladies' cigarettes. Still others looked like employment agencies, with cooks and housekeepers playing the market on their day off.

Critics warned that the maw of Wall Street was swallowing all the money, raising loan rates and throwing the economy off balance. They feared that sooner or later prices would topple and in the fall would break things. Out of every outlet, however, poured sunny antidotes to such predictions. "Generally speaking, business is excellent and will be better in most lines," said Walter Chrysler, president and board chairman of the Chrysler Corporation. "I can see nothing but good signs along the road of business for the present year." A sloganeer put it: "Business will be fine in 1929."

Many of these pronouncements of unending prosperity came from the decks of ocean liners, for the ship news reporter, usually young and inexperienced, checked passenger lists of vessels crossing the Atlantic to and from New York and then sought out the famous for a brief interview. In March, Charles Schwab returned from his one hundred sixty-second ocean crossing with his optimism as confectionary as ever.

"Only the old-timers like myself have failed to profit in the present-day market," he said, superseding the caution he had expressed to a ship news reporter a few weeks earlier when outward bound. "Those whom we have considered the reckless speculators have made money." He suggested that everybody ought to buy some stocks.

"Today I do not feel that there is any danger to the public in the present situation," he said. "I no longer see the danger I saw formerly. Money is now being lent in Wall Street by people who never lent it before. As long as the people remain enthusiastic and interested the market will hold up. We must remember that today the United States is doing half the world's business and will continue to do so. Who can compete with us?" It was not a time for playing by note, but by ear.

The question that nagged the old-timers and the hangers-back had to do with whether a share of stock had a certain intrinsic value—that is to

say, a "soul" or an "essential nature." How could the same share be worth
four times what it had been worth two years earlier?

Some of the speculation was mindless, picked up with no more thought
than one picks up a radio jingle. There were reasons, however, to believe
that American capitalism had indeed jelled into an entirely new kind of
economic history. The economy had been transformed by the sudden
growth of credit and installment buying. The nation had emerged from the
war intact—whereas Europe had been torn up—and was richly endowed
with natural resources. The conflicts of the past—the bloody strife of
capital and labor, the vehement jousting of the trusts and the government
reformers—had subsided. Heading the nation was Hoover, a brilliant engineer, a great-hearted humanitarian, an emphatically pro-business thinker
who, as Secretary of Commerce, had graced and guided the business policy
of his two undistinguished predecessors. Behind him were great philanthropists like Rosenwald; Schwab, the advocate of treating labor as a
partner in business; Young, whose enlightened policies at GE promised
decades of business peace; and Rockefeller, the ethical conscience of the
business system.

American business was being rationalized by a terrific concentration.
Banks were combining, railroads were merging, corporations were uniting.
The chain store had arrived, placing retailing on a sounder economic base;
mail order houses like Sears had entered the retail store field. This concentration was weeding out the less able. Those who remained were in an
enviable economic position. They could afford the most extensive research
and the latest technology. Their credit was sound. Their factories covered
the nation, distributing goods more cheaply and efficiently than could the
small manufacturer. Their sales outlets could take advantage of the immense new phenomenon of national advertising.

In 1926, RCA stock had been selling for thirty-two dollars a share; by
1929 it had reached four hundred dollars. Was there something disconcerting about that? Were speculators driving up its price with an inevitable
collapse to come? Or was RCA stock a glittering example of American
foresight? RCA was the leader of an utterly new field of activity, and its
potential had barely emerged. It was developing transoceanic telegraph
services; it was broadcasting on the airwaves into millions of homes; it was
producing the hardware to receive and send the broadcasts; its radio apparatus, constantly being improved, was thus continuously becoming obsolete and requiring replacement; it owned exclusive patents to startling
innovations yet to come. RCA was the epitome of the new business conditions for a new age.

The rocketing stock figures were thus not an overvaluation, it was believed, but an anticipation of the very palpable future. How could one operate on the basis that American prosperity had become saturated when New York City did not even have its own airport yet, and had to use the one in Newark? The possibilities for expansion, especially in power companies, radio, autos, and aviation, were unlimited. This unprecedented moment in history, this prosperity without parallel, could not be measured by the dead rules of what had occurred in the past. All the rules had been thrown in the scrap heap.

The next logical step beyond speculation was eliminating its speculative aspect, doing away with chance. That had also been highly developed in what was called the pool operation, and the most famous pool operation of 1929 was in RCA stock. In this instance the pool was highly formalized, with attorneys for each member, a signed partnership agreement, and the formal hiring of a pool manager.

The pool members had chosen a lively stock for their operation as well as one for which they had access to privileged information. The first job of the pool manager was to get RCA stock moving by frequent purchases and sales. He did this by selling back and forth among pool members. Although transactions with oneself to create the specious appearance of great stock activity—a form of chicanery called "wash sales"—were prohibited both by state law and stock exchange rules, it was easy to get around that prohibition by equally specious transactions among members of the same pool. These transactions were calibrated to make the price rise, not spectacularly but perceptibly. The many transactions kept active trading of the stock reported often on the ticker tape. That attracted attention and drew in speculators. The pool manager's transactions then became more razzle-dazzle. He would sell stock and push the price downward, then buy furiously and bring about a steep rise. In time, it would become unnecessary for him to do anything; frenzied speculators would begin hurtling RCA stock upward by their own purchases. As the speculators took over the momentum, the moment of truth arrived—the point in the operation known as pulling the plug.

Drawing as little attention as possible, the pool manager began to throw stocks back into the market—first in small batches and then by the truckload—just in time to escape the precipitous decline that his selling would create. The operation took only a week. The pool manager and his aides earned a management fee of half a million dollars. The pool members divided a profit of almost five million dollars for doing nothing.

Except for the identities of the pool members, there was little secret about it. It seems peculiar to relate that almost everyone knew precisely what was going on. The RCA pool was reported in the financial papers as it occurred, and when it was over even the amount of the profit was accurately reported. Speculation had become manipulation; it had become intolerable to leave so important a matter as the stock market to chance. Over the course of the year more than 100 stocks were thus raided, and many of them were announced in tip sheets that plainly stated that such and such a stock "would be taken in hand" at such and such an hour.

Did the public demand that such practices cease? Did the pillars of Wall Street shake? On the contrary, the bootblacks, chauffeurs, and minor-league hustlers rushed for a slice of the melon. Though hopelessly out-pointed, they tried to bet on the pool's timetable and come out with a profit. A few lucky ones guessed right. Others went down the drain when the pool manager pulled the plug.

Rather than damaging the faith of Americans, the pool operations seemed a rational development of the market. They strengthened American faith in the stock market, which now appeared not at all a matter of luck, but under the control of powerful men who knew exactly what they were up to, and that was reassuring.

Everyone at Dearborn on October 21 was talking about the fits and starts of the market, and Bernays listened carefully. The publicist for the Jubilee had his work cut out for him, but Ford's gala furnished a rare opportunity to overhear the giants of American business. On the advice of a financial advisor, Bernays had already sold all his stocks, but as he rode in a taxi that morning with Otto Kahn and Paul Cravath, the two Wall Street insiders showed that in their view there was nothing to worry about.

True, they said on the ride from Detroit to Dearborn, the market was fizzling. The same had occurred, however, twice in 1928 and once in March of 1929 and each time it had recovered completely. They were concerned that the confidence of investors, which had seemed through the year to be boundless, was in fact rather shallow. They were convinced, though, that the crux of the difficulty was margin sales. Many investors were buying on margin—putting up only a percentage of the purchase price when buying stocks. When such reverses as the October faltering occurred, the investors were immediately pressed to put up 100 percent of the purchase price. This forced them to sell some of their securities to come up with the money, throwing more stocks on a glutted market and aggravating the slide. The men agreed that the rules should be altered to give the investor some time to come up with the cash.

Kahn was the leading partner in Kuhn, Loeb, the most important

Jewish investment bank on Wall Street, and Cravath, senior partner in a prestigious Wall Street law firm, was a legal counsel for many of the notables at Dearborn, including Kahn and Schwab. Bernays stood among the men who had not only inside knowledge of the boom, but had made the boom. The people surrounding Bernays were the ones who framed the replies when senators called for an end to rampant speculation. They were the people who profited from speculation. They had manipulated the market and added to its frenzy when it suited their purposes. Charles Schwab and Walter Chrysler, both Ford's guests at Dearborn, had been in the RCA pool with Sarnoff.

None of them put any credence in the hokey prophecies of Roger Babson. "Sooner or later," the statistician Babson had said in September, "a crash is coming and it may be terrific. Wise are the investors who now get out of debt and reef their sails." But obviously no such cataclysm was at hand; the relaxed expressions of these well-manicured gentlemen were assurances of continued prosperity. The future had to be prosperous because the inflated values that stocks had reached were based upon a prosperous future. America had already borrowed what the coming decade was expected to produce. It did not seem that anything could go seriously wrong, since these confident gentlemen were in control, and stocks rose and fell at their command.

While Ford entertained that day at Dearborn, his men were at work thousands of miles to the south in another hemisphere. Where once only the chatter of parrots and monkeys had been heard, the throb of motors filled the Brazilian jungle with sound. Fordlandia, not quite as large as Connecticut, lay along the east bank of the Tapajos River, a main tributary of the Amazon. It was a temperate area, not the swamp created along much of the Amazon. The land rose gradually from the river and was covered with tall, well-proportioned trees. The Tapajos, seven miles wide at some points, was a pure translucent blue. Ford's men built living quarters and a temporary dock and had begun to plant rubber tree seedlings for the great engineer's latest and most revealing venture—an audacious plan to produce an entirely new source of rubber.

About a year earlier the advance party of some twenty-five men had begun to prepare the site. In the summer of 1928 two of Ford's private fleet of ships sailed out of the Great Lakes to link up with the advance party in the Brazilian jungle. When they reached the mouth of the tributary, they found that they could not get upstream except in the high-water season, so they removed the tractors, stump-pullers, a sawmill, and a portable powerhouse and sailed without them, then returned for them. One of the vessels carried supplies. The other was set up as a traveling headquarters, with a hospital, machine shop, laboratory, and refrigeration plant.

Ford and technology were almost synonymous terms in 1929. In another Ford outpost in the upper peninsula of Michigan, where his men felled trees by the thousands, the lumberjacks were amused to watch modern civilization planted in the wilderness: single beds, steam heat, electric lights, dining rooms and club rooms, showers, and cement sidewalks. Ford intended to improve Brazil in the same manner.

He planned to bring railroads, airports, banks, stores, daily mail delivery, schools, and hospitals. Assembly-line efficiency would come to the jungle, replacing the amateurish rubber gathering then performed by natives who cut their way through the underbrush in search of individual trees. Difficulties were expected: the site was remote, the river uncooperative, and sanitation and disease control measures sorely needed. Nevertheless, Ford had his name on the land and had what he most wanted —complete power. He had permission to dam the river or do whatever else he chose, including the prohibition of alcohol and tobacco. The people who came to work the plantation would be under the rule of a one-man government.

Fordlandia was the remotest outpost in an empire of one-man rule. The Ford Empire ranged far beyond the auto business. The automobile was for Ford only the initial step in a vast conception of social and economic change to be wrought. Wood had been an important ingredient in the Model T, and when the prices of his lumber suppliers rose, he bought timberland by the hundreds of thousands of acres. He also bought sawmills, docks, towing outfits, tugs, scows, and whole towns. He built huge kilns to dry the wood and designed a chemical plant to convert residues into byproducts. He purchased iron mines all over the Michigan peninsula so that he could mine his own ore, take it by barge to his deepwater island port on the river Rouge, and fire it in his own blast furnaces. By the following day it was molten iron being poured into a foundry mold, and later that day it had become a motor heading down a conveyor system toward the final assembly of an automobile.

Through the decade Ford had purchased coal mines in Kentucky and West Virginia. The coal resources were so productive that he sold a quarter of his output to others. He purchased a nearly bankrupt railroad, sank millions into its improvement, and used it to reach his Kentucky and West Virginia coal mines. He put together his own seagoing fleet that could be used for coal, ore, and lumber.

Scarcity, high prices, and the poor quality of glass produced during the war pushed Ford into the glass business, and his four plants made all he needed for car windows. Ford engineers improved the glass manufacturing process so decidedly that the entire industry adopted the Ford system— pouring directly from the furnace to a moving table and thereby eliminating several steps.

His goal was to become completely self-sufficient. He let his forests grow and bought most of his wood from suppliers, but they knew he was ready to supply himself if he disliked the prices. He had a vision of a huge assembly line covering the globe. Life itself was a mammoth delivery system that included water power, foundries, and power plants. The technology he was creating was, he believed, the most profound revolution in all human history. He was not really interested in money. One day he and Upton Sinclair were talking about his early days, and Sinclair asked if he were happier now that he had great riches. "Yes, of course," Ford said, "because I can do things with it that I could not do otherwise. In those days I was struggling to do something. Now I am in a position to do it, and do it exactly as I want to do it."

By 1929 Ford's revolution had begun to take on global proportions. He had twenty-five assembly or manufacturing plants outside the United States, and his son, Edsel, that year broke ground for a large manufacturing plant twelve miles outside London at Dagenham. England and Germany were to be the keys to his world operations.

There were twenty-five million cars on the road in the United States, one for every five people, and although they eventually were scrapped and replaced, dealers complained that their showrooms were full. "With the United States pretty well motorized," the *Hartford Courant* commented, "the rest of the world is to be put on wheels by American ingenuity, inventive genius, and mass production." Ready or not, the world was about to become Americanized, with Ford as the vanguard, bringing the method that had made him famous and had made America the supreme economic force—mass production.

As had already happened in America, cars in Europe and other parts of the globe were no longer to be made solely for the wealthy. By restoring prosperity, Ford said, he would bring the peace that had eluded the continent for a decade since the end of the war. That prosperity depended upon industry; his expansion, he explained, would provide work for thousands of men, and each new car and truck would start other economic forces in motion. Some Europeans sputtered about economic imperialism, but Ford expected that. Revolutionary upheaval always met with resistance.

The early history of Ford had been revolutionary. He had risen to unparalleled wealth and power while fighting reaction every step of the way. Early in the century he had advocated government ownership of the telephone and telegraph systems and had urged permanent federal public works programs. In 1919 he sided with strikers against the steel industry, assailing Morgan for dictating the labor policies of U.S. Steel and blaming him for the violent turn the strike took. He called private ownership the curse of the railroad system and said major trunk lines should be socialized. The utilities, he said, were being operated not for social good but for the benefit of parasites holding stocks and bonds. He saved his worst epithets for speculators, blaming them even for the carefree morals of the time. One memoir, published in the *Dearborn Independent*, Ford's newspaper, told of a maiden who lost her bloom in an atmosphere of tobacco fumes, nickel cuspidors, and Turkish rugs. It was called "What I Found in Wall Street, by a Girl Who Spent Five Years in a Broker's Office."

During the war he had accused Wall Street of arming both sides for profit. He ridiculed flags and said he intended someday to haul down the American colors over his factory and hoist in their stead a "Flag of All Nations." He denounced Morgan for lending the Allies half a billion dollars while the United States had still been neutral. The cause of war, he said, is "capitalism, greed, the dirty hunger for dollars. Take away the capitalist, and you will sweep war from the earth."

Ford saw himself as the benefactor of working people, helping provide them with an honest livelihood. He hired ex-convicts without a qualm and found that work reformed them. He believed, almost alone, in equal work opportunities for blacks. "I don't want any more than my share of money," Ford said. "I'm going to get rid of it—to use it all to build more and more factories, to give as many people as I can a chance to be prosperous."

Nothing had shaken the foundations as much as his Five-Dollar Day. When he announced in 1914 that he would pay five dollars to all his workers, tremors went through all industry. With a single stroke he had doubled the wages of labor. The *Wall Street Journal* denounced the move as an economic crime. It was assailed as immoral and socialistic; it was said that the working class would be undermined and discontented by so much money. Ford's name was cursed wherever the wealthy congregated. The only consolation for them was that Ford had gone too far this time and would soon be shown for the fool he was.

Against this opposition, however, Ford had reshaped the American economy and had created the twentieth-century consumer. He was selling a mass product and could not succeed by selling his autos only to the wealthy, so he cut prices and raised wages and produced his own customers. The move affected not only his cars but an entire economic system.

His next step was to take over complete control of his company. He told the world he wanted to share profits with his workers and not with a group of parasitic stockholders. He informed the Dodge Brothers, who owned 10 percent of the Ford Motor Company, that they could look forward to no substantial future earnings on their investment. He was placing a ceiling of 1.2 million dollars on profits to stockholders annually. For the Dodges, that meant one hundred twenty thousand dollars. He slashed the prices of his cars—the touring car came down from four hundred forty dollars to three hundred sixty dollars and the runabout from three hundred ninety dollars to three hundred forty-five dollars. This decision alone cut profits by forty million dollars annually.

Ford intended to invest another fifty-eight million dollars in a daring new project—a plant on the river Rouge that would produce a new form of total integration of auto manufacture. It would have its own lumber yards for Model T bodies and make its own cardboard for shipping, produce its own coke for furnaces, make its own iron ore in blast furnaces, make castings from this iron in its own foundries—an entirely self-contained operation on an unprecedented scale. It would require a tremendous increase in factory space, a larger working force, and would produce cheaper cars. Work on the blast furnaces was ready to begin when the Dodges went to court.

They filed a stockholders' suit, claiming that their rights were being violated, demanding that the court force Ford to make a suitable dividend for stockholders and asking the court to enjoin his construction plans on the grounds that it would create a monopoly in the low-priced field. (The Dodges used their dividends to finance their rival auto company.)

Ford took his case to the public. He said he wanted a small profit on more cars rather than a large profit on fewer. Every time the price of a car went down, he said, the number of buyers went up. There were "less profits on each car, but more cars, more employment of labor, and in the end we get all the total profit we ought to make." He would be able to carry out such plans if he could rid himself of the interference of parasites.

The case went to trial in 1917. During one exchange, the attorney for the Dodges questioned the plan to make castings direct from molten metal at the proposed Rouge site, eliminating the need to make pig iron.

"Who," he asked, "is doing that sort of thing now?"

"Nobody," Ford replied.

"You are going to experiment with the Ford Motor Company's money, to do it, are you?"

"We are not going to experiment," Ford said, "we are going to do it."

"Nobody has ever done it?"

"That is all the more reason why it should be done."

"Therefore, you are going to undertake to do something that nobody else has done, that nobody else has even tried to do?"

"Oh, certainly. There wouldn't be any fun in it if we didn't."

Later in the trial, the Dodges' lawyer picked up on Ford's pre-trial comment that he wanted reasonable profits, but not "awful profits," and so was reducing automobile prices.

"Now, I ask you again," the lawyer said, "do you still think that those profits were awful profits?"

"Well, I guess I do, yes," Ford replied.

"And for that reason you were not satisfied to continue to make such awful profits?"

"We don't seem to be able to keep the profits down."

"Are you trying to keep them down? What is the Ford Motor Company organized for except profits, will you tell me, Mr. Ford?"

"Organized to do as much good as we can, everywhere, for everybody concerned."

Ford agreed that in his view profits were "incidental." The lawyer then asked:

"But your controlling feature . . . is to employ a great army of men at high wages, to reduce the selling price of your car, so that a lot of people can buy it at a cheap price, and give everybody a car that wants one?"

"If you give all that," Ford said, "the money will fall into your hands; you can't get out of it."

Although Ford lost the case and was ordered to pay nineteen million dollars in stockholder dividends, he eventually bought out the Dodge Brothers through the subterfuge of a Boston trust company that purchased all the stocks for Ford. Now he was able to build his River Rouge project and fulfill his personal vision unimpeded by others. His very conception of his enterprise was linked to mass production. Up to a certain point there was no profit; the profit came only with great volume. The facilities at his Highland Park plant were unable to produce the number of automobiles that Ford now aimed at—one million a year. Despite the disparaging questions of lawyers, the Rouge plan, as he went on to show, was sound— if the volume were sufficient to make it pay.

Ford now had complete control of his company, only to discover that the consumer economy he had created had a drift of its own. It began to hunger for goods and services—including credit—that Ford was unwilling to give it.

Styles began, with the ascent of the consumer, to change rapidly. Industries began to nurture that whirl of change in fashion. Such preoccupations kept the goods moving, and a billion dollars worth of advertising, by the late twenties, was aimed annually at the American hankering for something different. Styles changed in wallpaper and toothpaste, in skirt length and hair length. One year radio sets were Florentine, the next, Louis Quinze, and Jacobean the next. One year it was chromium radiator caps that had the boys talking at the filling stations. The next year it was rumble seats, or new windshield wipers, or new horns, or heaters. The automobile had produced a standardized America, and now, because of those contradictions that keep the earth moving, people wanted to break out of the standards. There was a new emphasis on color in autos, a preoccupation with styles and comfort. But the Model T Ford never changed: it had the lines of a kitchen pump, a primitive transmission system, no more individuality than a carpet tack, and, as Ford said, you could get it any color you like, as long as it was black.

For years he had been petitioned, from within the company and from the sales agencies, to modernize the Model T. It was argued that women were becoming an important factor in auto sales and, while the hard-riding Model T delivered its passengers exhausted, women bought for design and comfort. The two-gear transmission system, which required the driver to keep a foot constantly pressing on a pedal to stay in low gear, had been long outmoded, he was warned. The Model T went twenty to thirty miles an hour, fine for the days of dirt roads, but America had been paved with modern highways.

A delegation of Ford salesmen who journeyed to Detroit unanimously agreed that change was imperative. They asked to see Ford himself. He came in and took a seat by the door, folding his long arms and crossing his long legs, as if waiting for a certain word or idea to which he intended to respond. When the presentation ended, Ford was asked for his response. "I think," he said, rising, "that the only thing we need worry about is the best way to make good cars." He then swept out, leaving the assemblage breathless.

Bending slightly to the pressure, Ford began to offer the Model T in colors other than black. But something more drastic was required. Every year Ford had set new records for production—until 1926. Suddenly General Motors, operated out of the House of Morgan, had made the Chevrolet into a rival to Ford in the low-priced field. A slow summer was followed by an even slower fall, and by Christmas of 1926 the company was shut down, with more than 100,000 men thrown out of work.

Even during the shutdown Ford denied that he would change the Model T. It was an absolute policy that no change could be made which could not be incorporated into any existing car. The big problem of American business, he said in an interview during the shutdown, was installment sales, and he did not intend to sell on credit to impulse buyers. "I sometimes wonder if we have not lost our buying sense and fallen entirely under the spell of salesmanship," he lamented.

Nevertheless rumors abounded of big changes coming at Ford. Just as they died out, the Ford company announced that it intended to retool its plants and produce an entirely new car. Henry Ford and his son, Edsel, celebrated the old man's birthday by driving over upper Michigan roads testing a model of the car on July 30, 1927.

"Sixty-four today and the biggest job of my life ahead," he told the press. "I am in better health than I was four years ago, more fit in every way. You see, I have got a job to do."

Once he accepted the death of his beloved Model T he hurled all his reserves into the retooling. Through the fall the nation waited to see the results. "The new Ford is completed," the *New York Times* commented on the rumors. "It is on the verge of being completed. It is still in the trial stage. Mr. Ford is through with the new model and has gone back to Colonial furniture . . . It will hang low and sell very cheap. It will hang not so low and sell not quite so cheap." The new car eventually turned up in Brighton, Michigan, about fifty miles from Detroit, when two Ford officials stopped for lunch at the town hotel. "The new Ford is here!" a townsman shouted to the local editor. "She's parked just north of the First National Bank! Come along and get a look at her." The editor rushed off and saw the car, ran back for his camera, and had the picture the nation was waiting for.

The unveiling of what was called the Model A came in December of 1927. At a preview at the Waldorf in New York, an old racing car driver now with Ford waved his arms and gurgled with enthusiasm for the select guests. "Good looking as that car is," he said, "its performance is better than its appearance. We don't brag about it, but it has done 71 miles an hour. It will ride along a railroad track without bouncing, and you can drive across the rails, if you can find a place to do it, without pitching. It's the smoothest thing you ever rode in. And it is a whole new car, from engine to rear axle and from tires to top, and it was designed in all its unity of function by one man."

The nation, just recovering from Lindbergh's solo Atlantic flight, underwent new transports of excitement. On the first day of its showing, a million people—according to a *New York Herald-Tribune* estimate— stormed the Ford showrooms around New York. Crowds had begun to gather on Broadway at 3:00 A.M. to see it. Before noon street traffic was jammed and police requested Ford spokesmen to discontinue their sales talks. Barricades had to be thrown up in front of Ford agencies to keep people from pushing through the glass. The *New York Sun* commented: "It was exactly as if Mr. Mellon had thrown open the doors of the Sub-treasury and invited the public in to help him count the gold reserves." By midafternoon the eastern Ford manager had found the showrooms inade-quate and rented Madison Square Garden. It was much the same around the nation. One hundred thousand people flocked into Ford showrooms in Detroit. Mounted police were called out to control crowds in Cleveland. In Kansas City the Convention Hall was so mobbed that a platform was built to lift the new car high enough for everyone to see it.

One hundred and fifty eastern Ford dealers assembled at the Kearny, New Jersey, plant to see the first Model A Ford come off the assembly line and be driven down a runway into the yard. "Marvelous, wonderful!" said Thomas Edison, a passenger in the blue Tudor sedan. "I don't see how Henry can do it at such a price." When the dealers cheered, the Ford's eastern manager had advised them to wave their hats as well so that the nearly deaf inventor could take more pleasure in the ebullience. Will Rogers received his free Model A at his Beverly Hills home. "Mr. Henry Ford told me he would make me a present of the first new Ford car, and sure enough, when I got here today, here she is," he wrote in his syndi-cated column. "It's the first one delivered for actual use, and believe me, I sure am using it. Nobody is looking at those Rolls-Royces here in Beverly."

The crisis had been overcome, and by the time of the Jubilee Ford was making 8,000 Model A's daily, twice as much as he had envisioned for his River Rouge plant. By 1929 he was preparing to bring the age of the consumer to Europe. "When industry starts this system of prosperity," he said, "it flows through every department of life. In the Ford plants abroad we expect to pay a compensation that will buy the comforts familiar to American workers. We hope to raise the standard of living until it equals —or closely approaches—the standard in America."

Ford wrote to the International Labor Office asking for data about comparative wage scales, costs of living, and taxation in European cities where he had or proposed to build factories. He intended to establish the same scale of real wages for all Ford employees whatever the country in which they lived and worked. The vested interests of Europe in 1929 reacted much like the American interests of 1914. More afraid of Fordism than Bolshevism, they cried that he would stir the workers into restlessness.

Ford now had all the components to bring about the social change he had long envisioned, and in the fall of 1929 he was looking forward to the day when he would share with his workers by making his enterprise a cooperative. He and Edsel controlled all the stock and so he was responsible only to himself for the outcome of policies that affected the lives of 128,000 workers. Ford decided when a glass plant should be built. Ford set wages and hours. Ford approved or rejected plans for daring engineering innovations. Ford set the prices of his cars. His personality was stamped on every machine and even reflected from the skylights of his clean, airy shops.

The total control he had wrought was unique. John D. Rockefeller, Sr., had never owned more than two-sevenths of his Standard Oil Trust; Morgan *père*, who had presided over the birth of U.S. Steel, had owned even less than that. Since borrowing money at an interest rate fixed by the money market was intolerable to Ford, he kept four hundred million dollars on hand—enough to rebuild his entire enterprise without the need to borrow a penny.

Interviewers after the Model A changeover found Henry Ford a puzzling man—footloose and yet parceling out his time sparingly; contemptuous of mere wealth and yet unrelenting in his use of power; modest and without airs and yet demanding absolute obedience of his lieutenants and workers; a man of utter candor, yet surrounded by intrigues among his top aides.

"Probably Henry Ford would resent being called a despot—even a benevolent despot," wrote Waldemar Kaempffert in a 1928 profile. "For all that, he is an industrial Fascist—the Mussolini of Highland Park, Fordson and Dearborn, not to mention works in Europe and agencies in every part of the world. No man in contemporary industry wields such dictatorial power."

The birth of the Model A had come at tremendous cost. The long shutdown for retooling had cost Ford one hundred million dollars, and it was said that some of his best sales agents had been lured away by competitors. But Ford denied that he had erred in waiting too long. "I never made a mistake in my life," he told *Forbes* magazine. "Never! And neither did you ever make a mistake—or anybody else. For what purpose do you suppose you are living on earth?" he demanded of his interviewer. "Do you know what you are here for?" He answered his own question. "I'll tell you what every living person is here for, and that is *to get experience.*

That's all we get out of life." If a man becomes a murderer, he said, it is because he needs the experience. If he lives in poverty or in pain, that was the experience he needed. When he gets that experience, he dies, and then is born into another life which will give him other experiences which he needs.

As for the thousands laid off during his changeover, he told the editor of *Survey Graphic*: "I know it's done them a lot of good—everybody gets extravagant—to let them know that things are not going along too even always."

Kaempffert asked him whether the compelling factor for the change was public reaction or the pressure of competition, but Ford asserted that nobody forced him to do anything. "The old car was too slow," he said. "The public was satisfied with it. And that's a sign we ought to change to something better. Since the public does not tell us what it wants, we give it what it ought to have. Once it needed a car that would go through mud and over the worst roads. It didn't know it, but we did, so we gave it the old car. Now the public ought to have speed, since roads are so much better than they were. Therefore we give it speed. That's the whole story of the new car." He added: "There's too much tradition in all human activities, too much respect for mere precedent. If it stands in the way of human progress it must be broken down." In the mind of Ford, 1929 Model, the unions had replaced the stockholders as the chief barrier to progress. Even the British labor unions, the most powerful in the world, broke ranks and fled before the Ford juggernaut. When he opened his factory at Manchester, he paid higher than union scale, shortened the workday, got the output that he demanded, and shut the unions out.

His employees, he told interviewers, were not yet ready to take part in managing enterprises. He was a complete individualist who did not think people should join armies or unions or even political parties. "People are never so likely to be wrong as when they are organized," he said. "And they never have so little freedom . . . People can be manipulated only when they are organized . . . The safety of the people today . . . consists in this fact, that the people are unorganized and therefore cannot be trapped."

He had little to worry about from labor unions in 1929. The auto workers' union, weak and dispirited, had been suspended from the American Federation of Labor, and the AFL was not at all interested in organizing industries. He felt safe enough to invite William Green, the AFL president, to his Dearborn dinner. But the guest list of union officials stopped with one name.

Every poll found him the winner or runnerup as the most important figure in the world. He appeared to himself as the spirit of modernism, and only he fully comprehended his brusque and solitary purpose.

Old Rockefeller was still alive in 1929. His son, John D. Rockefeller, Jr., found rare moments of peace at the age of 55, basking in the serenity of his aged father. In all his life the old man had never spoken to his son in anger. When his organization of a mammoth oil trust was faced with crisis, his calm had never wavered. Sitting on the lawn of his Pocantico Hills estate, even in advanced age he showed no sign of irritation. He gathered his strength from an inner resource and expressed it with Oriental calm.

On his ninetieth birthday he played golf on his private course and took an automobile ride over his forty miles of private road. A fleet of power mowers snipped through broad expanses of lawn. Trucks lumbered in and out on missions, and uniformed mounted guards patrolled sections of newly acquired land not yet walled in. The representatives of the press waited at the gate until a functionary appeared to hand out photographs of the patriarch cutting his birthday cake. The estate was guarded, walled, fenced, and surrounded by barbed wire because of threats made by radicals years earlier.

When the younger Rockefeller first went to work for his father after college, he had been given no orders and no job assignment. He was forced to create his own niche and set of duties for himself, and, particularly at the beginning, he had stumbled. However costly they might have been, he found that all of his decisions were accepted. His father's supreme confidence also covered his son. Eventually the old man turned his fortune over to his son, in the greatest property transfer in history.

He also transmitted to his son some of his traits. Neither used tobacco, alcohol, or profane language; both spoke in low, unhurried tones and never raised their voices. He instilled in his son a sense of duty. "Heaven help the rich man," the father said, "who does not regard his wealth as a trust for mankind. For that man and his children there is no peace." He also imparted his sense of perfectionism, but not his serenity.

Unlike his father, young Rockefeller lacked any interest in games. Had he played golf, chances are he would have been less skillful than his father. For although both had a passion for taking pains, Junior lacked that calm center that graces the master of anxieties. He found little peace in administering the Rockefeller fortune, and was sometimes overwhelmed by a sense of oppression. His riches had not brought him freedom. He did not, like Ford, revel in power. He said on many occasions that giving was the secret of a healthy life, but it did not keep him from feeling driven.

He began his addresses by noting that he was merely an emissary of his venerated father. "It is my father and not I, his son, who has done the things of which Chancellor Kirkland has spoken tonight," he said in 1928 at a Nashville Chamber of Commerce gathering. "It has been my good fortune and my privilege for thirty years to be associated with him in all of these enterprises, and if you had known him as I have known him, you would realize how sincerely I meant this has been a great privilege."

Many years earlier, young Rockefeller had taught adult Bible classes every Sunday in the Fifth Avenue Baptist Church in New York. The young man often spent three nights a week preparing his lessons—a time-consuming task for a man involved in managing millions of dollars. One of his favorite themes was the common principles that guided both business and the Christian life. Both, he counseled, were matters of duty and responsibility, thrift, cleanliness, and strict adherence to temperance and high principles. Success in one often helped achieve success in the other, he said. Business benefited from the sobering and spiritualizing influence of Christian principles while Christianity needed the power, influence, method, and monetary strength of business.

The great trusts being created in those days, he explained, were examples of a natural law, for the American Beauty Rose was husbanded by pruning all but the hardiest buds. Some thought Rockefeller had Standard Oil in mind when he spoke of the five wise virgins who conserved their oil. He told his class that "in earthly as well as in spiritual things, the law of nature makes for the reward of the man who does something and for the punishment of the slothful."

Rockefeller assumed that the gospel of Jesus had reached full flower in the precepts of late nineteenth century divines and in the splendid example of Queen Victoria, and that God was by and large satisfied with the progress of the world. It came as a scandal to him, therefore, to learn that not everyone was grateful to his father's substantial furthering of God's Divine Plan. His father, on the contrary, was called a blood-sucking vampire of the poor. "John D. Rockefeller," one exercised critic wrote, "can be fully described as a man made in the image of an ideal money-maker. An ideal money-maker is a machine the details of which are diagrammed on the asbestos blueprints which paper the walls of hell."

The muckraking of the time was a trial for the younger Rockefeller and eventually he found the attacks on his father impossible to ignore any longer. They had passed beyond name-calling to documentation; scurrilous accounts of political corruption involving the Standard Oil Trust began to appear in print.

Then the attacks reached a dreadful pitch for Rockefeller. The Congregational Board of Foreign Ministers in Boston applied to the Rockefellers for one hundred thousand dollars to aid in Christianizing the world. Although the family had hitherto limited its gifts to the Baptist denomination, the younger Rockefeller was deeply interested in the concept of an approaching unity. He pressed for approval of this grant, and in time talked his reluctant father into it.

Dr. Washington Gladden, a leading Congregationalist minister of the time, bitterly questioned the motives of the Rockefellers. This powerful family, he charged, was shamelessly dangling gifts before the Congregationalists to try to divert protests about the misdeeds of Standard Oil. He demanded the return of the "tainted money." The imbroglio was quieted when Gladden was shown that the board had *asked* for the money, but his censure had let loose a torrent of new abuse. No longer was it a matter of a few journalists or a few midwestern populists excoriating the family. From pulpits all over the country the Rockefellers were denounced.

Rockefeller was profoundly disturbed. Whatever enjoyment he had found in business dissipated. He was repelled by Standard Oil's political contributions. Although it was explained to him that it was just a way to help good policies to succeed and to reward friends, its conspiratorial nature jarred his sense of right and wrong. By that time John Archbold, the target of so many journalistic exposes, had become Standard Oil's president. Archbold used to take breakfast on his speedboat while journeying from Tarrytown to the city in the morning, and occasionally he asked young Rockefeller to ride along with him. The young billionaire expressed misgivings about practices of the company and asked countless questions about its management. After mulling over the answers, he decided to resign from the board of directors.

Archbold expressed dismay, saying that the publicity would hurt the company. Rockefeller was more concerned, however, about his father's feelings. He discussed with his father his alienated affections for these companies, and the elder Rockefeller told him to go ahead and do what he thought was right. Rockefeller resigned not only from Standard Oil but also as a director of U.S. Steel and various other corporations and banks. Practices were going on in all of them that, as a director, he could not countenance, yet was unable to change. The easy answers of his Bible class no longer seemed sufficient to explain his predicament, and untidy ends stuck out here and there between his convictions and company practices. And so, by the age of thirty-five he concluded that his role would be distributor of the family income because he felt himself miscast as a business tycoon. He would devote his time to presenting bounties to the worthy, to answering attacks upon his father, and to making the name of Rockefeller stand for the highest in business ethics. In May of 1929, when he received a gold medal from the National Institute of Social Services, he accepted in his father's name. What Rosenwald, the Sears philanthropist, did with joy Rockefeller performed through clenched teeth. The attacks on his father had permanently shaped his view of his social role, but perhaps even more telling were the tumultuous events that occurred within the fiefdom of a company in which he had kept an active interest—Colorado Fuel & Iron.

Hundreds of striking coal miners were living in tents at Ludlow, Colorado, in the seventh month of the strike against Colorado Fuel & Iron in April of 1914. Four state militiamen appeared where the miners had turned out for a game of ball. With a crude sense of raillery, they began to point their weapons at the players.

"If anybody pointed a real gun at you fellows, you'd run," a woman shouted at the troops.

"Go ahead," one of the soldiers replied, "get your fun today; tomorrow you'll get your roast."

People laughed off the threat, but the next day a strike leader ran among the tents waving a handkerchief and warning everybody to be careful. The militia was approaching in large numbers.

When the soldiers began to fire, the strikers and their families scattered into barns, wells, and ditches. The militiamen carried torches, which in the distance looked like brooms set afire, and others carried cans. They spilled something out of the cans onto the tents and then set the torches to them.

When the tent of the Petrucci family was set afire, Mary ran out with her baby in her arms and her two other young children with her. They ducked into a large tent used as a maternity hospital, which had flooring and a small cellar. The Petruccis went through the cellar door and found three other women and eight children huddled there in fear. After about ten minutes the soldiers set fire to the hospital tent, and the smoke blew in. The smoke and heat became unbearable, but no one ran out because of the wild gunfire in the street. Mary Petrucci and another mother survived, but two other women and eleven children suffocated and roasted in the earth cellar.

In the town of Trinidad, Colorado, the strikers thronged the streets demanding guns from union headquarters to work vengeance upon the militia. The militia charged that the strikers had opened fire first and denied setting the fires. For the next several days mines were burned and homes looted as the area around Trinidad became a battlefield. The dead children were kept out of sight in the fear that fighting would intensify.

Mother Mary Jones, a strike leader, blamed John D. Rockefeller, Jr., for the "Ludlow massacre." "Let Congress tell Rockefeller that we are not going to have a Rockefeller government in this country," she said, "that these miners are going to organize; that he must treat them decently." Others took up the cry against Rockefeller. Mass meetings were held and hostile parades staged. A soapbox speaker called upon workingmen to shoot Rockefeller down like a dog. Four members of the Industrial Workers of the World were killed in the explosion of a time bomb they were assembling, apparently for Rockefeller's home, and the Pocantico Hills estate was fortified.

It was revealed that the company had paid the wages of the state militia used to bring law and order to the mines. It was clear that state and local officials were sympathetic to the operators; after the attacks, three hundred miners were indicted for various crimes, but not a single operator or member of the state militia faced any charges.

Rockefeller needed help with his public image, and his friends and acquaintances advised him of a man who had started a virtually new field that he called public relations. Thus began the long association of Rockefeller and Ivy Lee.

In those days Ivy Lee was plying his trade in Philadelphia. While working as a reporter, Lee had seen a new field opening. Regulation was coming and it would transform American life. He convinced the Pennsylvania Railroad that it needed him to interpret its activities to the public and that the railroad needed someone to report to them about how the public was feeling.

The willingness of railroad barons to listen to Lee was a sign of change. They had been foremost in the display of disdain for public opinion, even regarding rail accidents as none of the public's business and covering them up whenever possible. Lee encouraged them to further change. Speaking before a gathering of railroad men in 1914, Lee suggested that it was really too callous to advocate railroad fare hikes with the term, "All that the traffic will bear." Furthermore, he added, the railroads had been maneuvered into a disadvantage with such phrases as the Full Crew Law. This heinous statute, he said, should have been called the *Extra* Crew Law; then the public would grasp the burdens being placed on railroads under the pretext of safety standards.

Lee provided a new kind of service. He would prepare a statement in advance of a press conference. He would sit at the side of the great business leader to act as a buffer against brash young people determined to make journalistic names for themselves. He would flick away silly questions from the tabloid reporters and parry subtly with the incisive reporters who appeared intent at getting at the truth. He would cough when an embarrassing question was asked, and the client, as if coached, would smile and express regrets that some matters really had to be kept confidential. He would deflect a businessman's foolish remarks with bright asides. When the press conference was played out, the reporters would begin writing their stories only to discover that they had no more information than had been provided in the printed formal statement.

With the savvy that he had picked up in newsrooms, Lee appeared to businessmen as a wonder. Having heard various reports of the man's slick ways, Rockefeller asked the Pennsylvania Railroad to lend Lee to him. Lee met with Rockefeller for the first time in May of 1914. The best way to overcome the Colorado problem, Lee said, was to issue a series of bulletins explaining the facts and mail them to newspapers and influential people. Lee wrote the bulletins in Philadelphia, but they were postmarked from Denver to make them appear to be the products of the mine operators. He put together a pamphlet, *The Struggle in Colorado for Industrial Freedom,* which was mailed to forty thousand people around the nation. Friendly magazine articles were subsidized by buying large amounts of the issue in which it appeared.

These moves did not come off as smoothly as intended. The national clamor led to congressional hearings that established that the coal operators' information as it appeared in the bulletins was unreliable. The Lee bulletins claimed that Mother Jones, one of the strike leaders, was operating a brothel and that she and others were making huge salaries. Many of the strikers were Greek, and the operators' campaign against one clergyman who tried to aid the strikers consisted of charges that he had socialistic tendencies and a Greek wife, although it was not spelled out as to which was the greater offense. Evidence was produced that Rockefeller, although he claimed to have nothing to do with the anti-strike activity, was actually calling the shots.

Lee eventually was called before the congressional committee. "Mr. Rockefeller told you to be sure to get the truth?" he was asked.

"Certainly," Lee said.

"Just detail now what steps you took to ascertain the facts before you wrote any of these articles. Give all of the steps."

"I had no opportunity, Mr. Chairman, to ascertain the facts from my own point of view. It was their story I was to assist in getting before the public."

"And therefore you did not question any fact that was presented to you, any alleged fact, as to its authenticity?"

Not when it was presented by a Colorado Fuel & Iron official, Lee said.

"Did you make any effort," he was asked, "to secure the statements of disinterested persons?"

"I did not."

"From the workers themselves or their representatives?"

"I did not."

"Your mission," it was suggested, "was that of the average publicity agent, was it not, to give the truth as the man you were serving saw fit?"

Lee called that a characterization. But the public relations campaign had been damaged, making Rockefeller's initial venture into public image-making something less than a complete success.

When Rockefeller went before the committee he spoke of his desire to improve upon the past, to remain open to suggestion. He spoke with such sincerity that he helped to repair his image. On one occasion he entered the hearing room to see Mother Jones, waiting to hear him testify. Then he made a historic move, something that owners never did with union officials. He asked her to stop by his office to talk.

"Well, that's nice of you," the elderly woman responded. "I've always said you could never know what those hirelings out there were doing. I liked the way you testified yesterday, and I can see how easy it is to misjudge you."

Mother Jones and Rockefeller met the next day in the Standard Oil building. She told him of the situation in the mines. She did not attempt to play on his sympathy with tales of the poverty and misery of the miners. Instead she spoke matter-of-factly about the right of the workers to bargain collectively and to air their grievances without fear of losing their jobs. She spoke of the spy system, of the closed camps, of the cheap gunmen who enforced discipline and checked every new arrival against a list. She spoke of the fixed municipal elections, of how the company owned the schools and churches, how they screened teachers, and how these opinionmakers were told what to say; of how union officials were pulled out of bed and pistol-whipped by company thugs; of the company stores where the miners, paid in scrip rather than cash, were forced to buy at exorbitant prices; of how housewives were watched to make sure they were not smuggling non-company store goods into camp. That was how she talked. She did not demean the argument with sob stories, for it was assumed that suffering was part of life. Instead she spoke of the barrenness and chill of mining camp life, and Rockefeller listened.

Reporters met her as she left. "Oh," she told them. "We've just been talking over everything for the best interest of the nation and the cause of humanity."

"Did you tell Mr. Rockefeller about Colorado conditions?" a reporter asked.

"Yes," she said, "I just told him a few things, but I've been in jail so long my head's out of gear." After a few more questions she began to hurry off, then returned to add: "I just told Mr. Rockefeller one thing. We have been misrepresenting him terribly, and I as much as anybody else."

Her soft comments about Rockefeller disturbed some of her supporters. "We are sure," Upton Sinclair telegrammed, "you will not let yourself be overcome by the sweet odor of the American Beauty Rose."

With the help of his adversaries Rockefeller had re-established himself in the American consciousness as a humane force. He still had the image, however, of an absentee owner, and in September of 1914, he set out to overcome that by journeying for the first time to see his Colorado holdings. Nothing like his remarkable trip had ever occurred before in American business. For two weeks he toured the mining camps, walking up to clumps of miners and introducing himself, impressing them with his ease of manner and his fellowship. He put on miner's clothing, descended into the mines, and swung a pick. He ate with miners and slept in their homes. One night after a theatrical performance he proposed a dance, and when the warped floor was cleared he began by dancing with the wife of the superintendent and danced thereafter with almost every woman there. The reporters ran for the telephones, and the world was given a new portrait of John D. Rockefeller, Jr.

Wherever he went, memories of bloodshed, dead children, and gunpowder were still rank in the nostrils, and a large number of the miners' families were living in severe poverty. His father had been anxious about the trip and unsuccessfully urged his secretary to carry a pistol. Rockefeller refused to bring protection with him. The trip was an act of some courage, for Rockefeller's name had been cursed throughout these camps as a monster. Yet he was ever cordial and open, never showing a sign of strain.

He announced that better housing was to be provided. The reason for the shacks, he said, was not company policy, but because the mining families refused to leave homes they had built out of scrap. "We are building these forty new homes," he said at a ceremony, "and we are going to send wagons around and then tear down these shacks. They have no business raising children in such wretched surroundings, and we intend to put a stop to it at any cost. Even then, I suppose, some long-haired reformers will come around and yell their heads off that the corporation is 'turning the poor souls out into the streets.' We seem doomed to get it going and coming."

Everywhere he went he left the same message. "We are partners in this business," he would tell the workers. "Anyone from the inside of the camp or from the outside who has been telling you that we are enemies has been trying to deceive you. I cannot get along without you and you cannot get along without me."

He was dining at the home of a miner in Cameron when a miner's band gathered to escort him to the schoolhouse. Hurrying out of the shack, Rockefeller got into an automobile with his secretary.

Hundreds of miners—virtually every man in the camp except for the night shift then at work—were crowded about the shack in a festive mood. The band struck up a lively tune and began to march. The newspapermen fell into line behind the musicians, and the miners were strung out behind them in a long line.

After riding for a time, Rockefeller noticed that the reporters were walking. "Here! That's not fair!" he shouted. "Let me in on that, too!"

He jumped out of his car and took his place at the head of the marchers, directly behind the band. He caught a huge Irish miner, in grimy overalls, by the sleeve and pulled him into line beside him. "Here, keep up with me," he shouted over the music. "Pair up like the rest of them. That's it!"

Down past the Miner's Club and the village store they marched, Rockefeller grinning and swinging his arms vigorously in step. He joined some of the others in whistling the march. He turned and called to the reporters: "If I had a linen duster and a high hat, I'd think I had joined a minstrel show!"

When they reached the schoolhouse, Rockefeller stepped out of line and took a position at the foot of the steps. The men marched into the building. The billionaire, his sunburnt nose gleaming under the moon, shook hands with each man who passed—not a quick, weak handshake, but a firm, powerful grip that bespoke unsuspected strength of arm. He had a friendly and apt word for everyone. Every man who had spoken with him walked into the schoolhouse smiling.

At the end of his two-week investigation, Rockefeller appeared before a joint meeting of the officers and workers to explain his so-called Colorado Plan, designed to give workers a voice in the operation of the company through employee representatives. His remarkable campaign had already persuaded the workers, and his speech began with a tone of confidence. "Had this meeting been held two weeks ago, I should have stood here as a stranger to many of you, recognizing few faces," he said. "Having had the opportunity last week of visiting all of the camps in the southern coal fields and of talking individually with practically all of the representatives, except those who were away; having visited your homes, met many of your wives and children, we meet here not as strangers but as friends, and it is in that spirit of mutual friendship that I am glad to have this opportunity to discuss with you men our common interests."

As Rockefeller spoke, bringing the Colorado Fuel & Iron affair to a triumphant end, he sounded more like a politician visiting his ward than a great prince visiting his demesne. The world had taken another of those sudden turns. Rockefeller had begun a fight to keep the family name pure and to convince the public that capitalism in its more developed stages was democratic, charitable, and honest. In 1929, in an unprecedented stockholders' battle growing out of the Teapot Dome scandal, he attempted to show that it could also regulate itself.

Whiting, Indiana, looked like the site of a political convention on the raw and cold morning of March 7, 1929. Merchants expected a crowd of up to two thousand people and lunch stands had laid in extra supplies of food. The police force, augmented by firemen sworn in for special duty, reported early to handle traffic. People began to arrive by automobile, bus, street car, and train. "All out," one train conductor called, "for the Standard Oil rumpus."

Colonel Robert W. Stewart, chairman of the board of Standard Oil of Indiana, was meeting with people in his office in nearby Chicago, giving out the 1928 annual report to newspapermen and assuring people by his bearing that he was not finished yet. The colonel, a former Rough Rider, could once ride like a Sioux warrior and shoot like Buffalo Bill, but he was sixty-two years old and the pleasures of the table had thickened his girth.

On his desk lay a copy of the seventy-two-page report that his nemesis, John D. Rockefeller, Jr., had sent to stockholders in the massive campaign to knock the colonel out of office. The report documented the colonel's involvement in the huge oil scandal known as Teapot Dome.

The pamphlet, assembled by Ivy Lee, told of how Stewart and other oil men had met in the Vanderbilt Hotel in New York on a November day in

1921 to buy millions of barrels of oil. The seller, when he arrived at the hotel, had learned to his surprise that he was not selling his oil directly to the oil companies represented around the table. Instead he sold the barrels to a Canadian firm that had just been created, the Continental Trading Company, for $1.50 per barrel. Then the Continental immediately sold the oil to the companies represented around the table for $1.75 per barrel. The lucky people who had formed Continental made three million dollars before it was liquidated and its holdings distributed in Liberty Bonds. Three-quarters of a million dollars worth of these Liberty Bonds ended up in the hands of Colonel Stewart. Stewart told a Congressional committee in 1928 that he did not know why the bonds were delivered to him, and had never asked. When the story became public, Stewart produced the bonds, which he had never cashed. He said he had been holding them in trust all these years for Standard of Indiana, and presented them to the board of directors.

All this was presented in the pamphlet as an indictment of Stewart for his participation in a fishy scheme. "I cannot believe," the colonel said on first seeing the heavy document, "that Mr. John D. Rockefeller, Jr., ever gave his approval to the publication of such a slander."

Rockefeller and his wife were traveling in Egypt, but his forces had settled in a Chicago hotel, bearing seventeen steel filing cases containing their proxies. The cases were loaded into taxis and taken over to the Standard Oil office for a committee to count and check.

Winthrop Aldrich, trusted ally and brother-in-law of Rockefeller, led the assault. The Rockefeller forces had studied lists of the stockholders in the twenty-four largest cities around the country and had lists of all those holding more than five hundred shares. They had the foundations, the Eastern connections, and the old Standard Oil families—and the majority of shares. Stewart, however, had the popular vote, if each stockholder had one vote. His Chicago headquarters resembled a political campaign office, with large pictures of the dashing colonel on the wall. Hundreds of signatures covered a sheet that stated: "We're with you, Colonel Stewart, 100 percent."

The stakes had become high and the rhetoric hot. It was the biggest proxy fight ever seen in America, the most open conflict ever to take place in business history, and everybody, not just stockholders, had taken sides. Clergymen talked about it from the pulpit. Senators went on at length about it. "Rockefeller never served his country better than he is serving it now in his fight with Colonel Stewart," stated one widely quoted newspaper editorial.

Because of the anticipated crowd, arrangements were made to adjourn the annual meeting from the administration building at the refinery to the Whiting Community House, which held a thousand people. In case of an overflow, other rooms, connected with the main auditorium by loud-speakers, were in readiness. Telegraph lines were strung into the basement pressroom under the main stage, and special telephones were installed to flash the results to all parts of the country. Newspeople were there from all over the nation; the Standard proxy fight had been a day-by-day front-page story for two months. The orchestra pit had been equipped for their use.

A squad of motorcycle police pulled in front of the building, followed by several limousines. Drawn by curiosity a crowd assembled in front of the community house. The proxy committee of some twenty-five people led by Aldrich strode confidently through the crowd and into the building built with Rockefeller money.

As the meeting was about to begin, they walked down the aisle and took front seats reserved for them on the left side. The crowd watched silently. The president and directors were applauded when they appeared on stage. Then, as Stewart strode in from the back of the stage, the room shook with an ovation that lasted for four minutes.

Stewart plunged into business. In his report he stressed that 1928 had been Standard of Indiana's greatest year, with earnings far above any in its previous history, and at the conclusion there was another prolonged ova-tion from everywhere in the theater except the Rockefeller corner. People cheered, whistled, and stamped their feet.

After a break to authenticate votes, the meeting began again with two different slates placed in nomination. The slate that Aldrich nominated was the same as the Stewart slate, with the omission of the colonel and another who had been adjudged unnecessarily offensive.

The colonel displayed crisp good manners and his voice was firm, pleasant, and controlled, almost nonchalant. He recognized a stockholder who moved that—inasmuch as there were two board vacancies—the present board be re-elected and then two more directors be selected, one by shareholders having five hundred shares or less, the other by share-holders having more than five hundred shares. The motion was seconded and the crowd was about to vote when Aldrich, his shoulders tensed, sprang up to protest that the proposal was clearly out of order, that neither the bylaws nor the laws of Indiana provided for any such procedure, and that he would be forced to vote his proxies against it. A voice from the audience asked if the stockholders could not amend the bylaws. Stewart, enjoying the irony of a situation in which he was cool and his opposition tight and nervous, replied that of course the stockholders were the supreme power. That too brought applause and cheers.

When Stewart announced that he was about to make the motion, Aldrich sprang up again, demanding to know whether the vote was to be by stockholders or by shares. "Now just leave that to me and I think you'll be satisfied, Mr. Aldrich," Stewart said. Smiling broadly as Aldrich sat down, the colonel called for the vote. There was a deafening roar of "ayes." He then called for the negative votes, and a dignified chorus of "noes" came from the Rockefeller corner. Stewart let the tension gather for a few seconds. "The 'noes' seem to have it," he shouted. "The motion is lost." Laughter filled the hall and Aldrich settled back in his seat, his tension playing out.

During the counting of ballots Stewart swung down from the stage to shake hands with the Rockefeller party and talk earnestly with them for several minutes.

As the vote tally was to be announced, Stewart grew grave for the first time. "Well, then," he said, "let's have the news. It may be bad news to some of us, but I'm sure we'll all take it standing up." The secretary read the report of the inspectors and without a tremor in his voice Stewart announced the winners. The Rockefeller slate had won decisively, with about 60 percent of the votes to 32 percent for the Stewart faction.

Aldrich expressed thanks for the fair manner in which Stewart had conducted the meeting and for the help of the employees in checking proxies. "Why," Stewart replied, "that's the kind of people these boys out here are." His smile had returned. He obligingly posed for photographers, and stood talking with friends who came forward to shake hands. Presently he left the stage, walked down to where his wife sat in the front row, embraced her, gave her a kiss, and they walked out of the auditorium into the afternoon with the applause of the crowd still ringing in their ears and a fifty-thousand-dollar-a-year pension in their grasp.

"A battle of such proportions over a moral issue has never before been fought between American captains of industry," wrote the bulletin of the Federal Council of Churches. "Mr. Rockefeller and his associates regard this contest as a moral crusade which will have far-reaching results for American business."

His principal support west of the Hudson came from Sears president Julius Rosenwald. Rosenwald, who did not own a share of Standard of Indiana stock, was convinced, as was Rockefeller, that the private enterprise system had to be credible, even in the face of public apathy or worse, popular support for the colonel. Rosenwald devoted considerable time to campaigning among his business associates for Rockefeller and became publicly identified with the cause.

Chicago saw the struggle more as a contest of East versus West, and contended that behind the high-sounding Rockefeller prose lay the old urge for monopoly and combination. Rockefeller owned only 15 percent of the Standard of Indiana stock and a much greater share of other Standard Oil companies. Stewart's supporters believed he was just too competitive; he had run up against territorial agreements left over from the old Standard Oil Trust. It was hard for worldly people to believe that Rockefeller would spend hundreds of thousands of dollars on a principle. But they did not see the kind of letters that came to him. "If you will look up the record of your father," one stated, "in the early days of the old Standard Oil Co. you will find it pretty well smeared with black spots ten times worse than the charges you lay at the door of Col. Stewart . . . There is not enough soap in the world to wash the hands of the elder Rockefeller from the taint of fifty years ago. Only people with clean hands should undertake to blacken the character of other and better men."

Rockefeller and Rosenwald shared the view that capitalism had reached a stage in which it had to present a humane face to the society. For Rosenwald, this meant working with people that other capitalists might shun as troublemakers or socialists. He had long been active in the Immigrant Protective League, an agency established to help newcomers from being duped and swindled while learning America's new ways. He helped the league financially and also had the political influence to help stop such proposals as a literacy test for voting that had been designed to keep the franchise away from the foreign-born.

One night at a meeting of the League, at about the same time that Rockefeller was wrestling with Colorado Fuel & Iron, Rosenwald watched a woman, a strong-minded activist, put on her coat and prepare to slip out into the bitter Chicago winter. She was heading across town to speak at a rally for strikers in the clothing trades. Rosenwald intercepted her on the way out. "You're going to that strike meeting, aren't you?" he asked, walking downstairs with her. She nodded. Rosenwald said he was sure that there was nothing she would say that evening with which he could agree, but he was concerned that she would catch cold on the way. When they reached the street he escorted her to his limousine and told the chauffeur to take her to the strike rally.

Both Rosenwald and Rockefeller translated their social views into a drive against prostitution. Chicago was a center, with everything from streetwalkers to the most elegant sporting houses. The Chicago Vice

Commission, of which Rosenwald was a leading figure, reported in 1911–
12 that five thousand women were engaged in the trade in the city. Many
of them were shopgirls and factory girls. Jane Addams wrote in her book
on prostitution, that such a woman sometimes "yields in a moment of utter
weariness and discouragement to the temptations she has been able to
withstand up to that moment . . . The long hours, the lack of comforts, the
low pay, the absence of recreation, the sense of 'good times' all about her
which she cannot share, the conviction that she is rapidly losing health and
charm, rouse the molten forces within her . . ."

In 1913 a state committee held hearings on prostitution in Chicago.
The city's politicians, smarting from the questions the Vice Commission
had raised about the toleration of prostitution in the city, applied pressure
to show Rosenwald up. He was called as a witness. Sears had made 8.5
million dollars in profits the previous year, while the average pay of its
women workers was nine dollars a week. Rosenwald was asked why he
could not have applied another two hundred sixty thousand from that large
profit to pay a thousand female workers another five dollars a week.

Rosenwald thought over his answer. He had grown up in the clothing
business—a tough field in which people fought for advantage without
much concern about the wages of their employees. The rule was to pay the
minimum. Anything more was provocative and drove prices upward. "I
would answer that as I said before the vice commission," Rosenwald
replied, "that I think the question of wages and prostitution has no practical connection. I think there is no connection between the two."

One day two Pullman porters were talking of who was on the Chicago–
New York train that day. One of them said, "I've got Julius Rosenwald."
When the train pulled in, the other porter asked how he made out with the
philanthropist. He replied thoughtfully: "I guess Mr. Rosenwald is more
for the race than for the individual."

Likewise the shipping clerks at Sears, Roebuck may have been skeptical of his standing as a philanthropist. Even those people to whom he had
lent money—in most cases to go to college or to start a business—sometimes expressed disillusion. Rosenwald insisted on repayment according to
schedules established with the granting of the loan and pursued the smallest debt with vigor. Anything less dissipated the tension that is part of the
creativity of a loan, he thought. His debtors looked at the matter differ-
ently, and hard feelings sometimes resulted. Rosenwald was not in philanthropy just to be a soft touch. He had a system.

In 1929 he was asked to be an executor of philanthropic funds for
Conrad Hubert, a Russian Jewish immigrant who had died the previous

year, leaving an estate of more than six million dollars. Hubert, who had developed the battery-powered flashlight and formed the American Ever-Ready company, had left three-quarters of his fortune to worthy causes to be selected by an all-star panel of executors. The men selected were Alfred E. Smith, unsuccessful Democratic candidate for president in 1928; former president Calvin Coolidge, and Rosenwald.

At the first meeting, held in July, Rosenwald expressed the tenets of his philanthropic philosophy. Hubert's money could be made to yield fifteen million to twenty million dollars of philanthropic money, he said, if it were given to projects on the condition that additional funds would be raised from others. He said he would gladly include himself among the donors. He urged that no money be given to the operating expenses of any project, since that would only relieve others and would generate nothing.

In articles and interviews over the course of the year he further developed a theory of philanthropy. Perpetual endowments should be avoided, he said, because they are static and a drug. Money should be used up quickly and turned over often. Philanthropic money should be used sparingly and for as short a time as possible, to put it back in circulation. He would start projects, but they had to be viable—eventually able to support themselves or become government-supported.

"It is trite to speak of the burdens of wealth," Rosenwald said in an interview early in 1929, "but there are few possessors of large fortunes in the country to whom the worthy disposal of their wealth has not become a genuine concern. Viewing the matter in retrospect, I can testify that it is nearly always easier to make a million dollars honestly than to dispose of it wisely."

His philanthropy was capitalist, and its most important tenet was that philanthropy was a business. He understood that the rise of finance capital, with bankers in basic control of the economy, had abandoned whole areas to neglect—such as medical research and schooling for blacks—because to financiers anything innovative seemed risky, upsetting to the established order, or unprofitable. Rosenwald's view of philanthropy was dynamic and entrepreneurial.

At the end of the nineteenth century business interests were continuously wrestling with the problem of competition and the volatile economy that it fostered. At times competition within an industry would be intense, and at other times the industry leaders would be able to fix prices and allot territories. Just when the agreements were most needed, however—in a business downturn—they would come unstuck. The best way to eliminate competition was to create a trust, and the biggest trust of all, until 1929, was put together in 1900 by J. Pierpont Morgan.

Old Morgan was attempting in 1900 to erect a giant combination in steel. He was unable to corral one key company. That firm belonged to the wealthiest man in the world, Andrew Carnegie. He had built an impregnable position for Carnegie Steel. It controlled its own mines, had its own source of coke for its furnaces, controlled its own steamships and railroads, and above all dominated in the production of crude steel. The units of Morgan's combination were chiefly engaged in finished products—rails, beams, steel plate, or wire. The little Scotsman Carnegie controlled crude steel, and Morgan knew he could not be dislodged. Relentless in his search for ways of cutting costs, Carnegie could undersell any challenger and, because he avoided the inflated stock schemes of Wall Street and the encumbrances they produced, he was able to eliminate profit altogether if he had to.

By 1900 the stubborn and combative Carnegie had become intolerable to the great Wall Street bankers who had swooped down to take control of much of the American economy. Morgan was about to declare war by producing his own crude steel. Carnegie heard of it while on vacation in Scotland and immediately sent word to his troops to authorize a new tube plant on Lake Erie to go directly against Morgan's tube plant. He told his chief executive at Carnegie Steel to buy more land around the lake for additional factories. "No use going halfway across a stream," he advised, "[one] should aim at finished articles only." Carnegie was preparing for a showdown. It was his nature to glory in competition. He always fought to the last inch and always won.

The Morgan forces could not put together a combination large enough to outflank the crusty Scot, who had all the crude steel he needed. "The cooks who were preparing this meal . . . found that they had prepared and were ready to bake the finest plum pudding ever concocted financially," one steel magnate said, "but that Mr. Carnegie had all the plums."

The chief executive of Carnegie Steel and the Scotsman's right hand was Charles Schwab. He had been working for Carnegie most of his life, and Carnegie had taken an interest in him early. When he was just a stripling he had been sent to the Carnegie home with a message. He had to wait for the millionaire to return and sat down at his piano and began to play. Schwab had a good voice and played well. It happened that Carnegie loved music, and on entering the parlor was charmed by Schwab's voice and bade him continue. He asked the lad if he would sing and play at a party the millionaire was giving in a few days. Schwab agreed, and within the next few days he discovered what were Carnegie's favorite tunes and learned to play and sing them. He was a marvelous success, and from that time on Carnegie shepherded the melodious boy upward in his organization, all the way to the presidency.

While consternation grew at the House of Morgan about how to eliminate the quarrelsome Scot, his fair-haired boy was in New York. In 1900 Schwab, then thirty-eight, was guest of honor at a dinner at the University Club. Although his reputation was secure in steel circles, he was not widely known outside the industry, and so in effect was being introduced to the banking establishment of America as a rising executive figure.

Eighty of the nation's leading financiers gathered to honor him, and at Schwab's right hand was sitting Morgan himself. Schwab intended that evening to speak only briefly; he went on for almost an hour. His voice was as pleasing in speech as in song, and on that night he was at his most eloquent. The theme was bold and intended principally for the ear of the man at his right side.

The Carnegie executive spoke of the unlimited prospects that lay before the steel industry if it were properly organized. It would have to be totally integrated: a single authority would control the entire process from the mining of the ore to the shipping of the finished product. That economy of operation would have to be translated into *lower* prices. The use of monopolies, pools, and trade agreements just to raise prices was exactly the basic fault that hindered American supremacy in steel. The huge concern he foresaw would not stand for such practices. It would enforce not higher prices, but lower, and that would be the key to the expansion of markets in the nation and around the world.

Morgan listened without a word, his piercing eyes fixed on his plate. Although he was able to make men quail with his anger, he sat without expression. Both he and Schwab knew that the steel executive was not just speaking pretty sentiments. Morgan had been a party to such practices on many occasions, and the rebuke was aimed at him. At the conclusion of Schwab's address the table burst into cheers. The glories of consolidation had been sung before, but never in such heroic tones.

Morgan took Schwab by the arm and led him to a corner. For half an hour the two men talked privately, with the banker posing questions and Schwab replying.

For days afterward, Schwab's words rang through the mind of the great banker. He kept bringing them up to his partners. The thought of undertaking a supercorporation in steel, the most ambitious financial project ever by an American banker, was arresting enough. But the address had also stirred his depths. J.P. Morgan was as implacable a foe of competition as Carnegie was its knight. Schwab had awakened Morgan's sense—often forgotten in the pursuit of gain—of harmony, of the transformation of competing systems into coordinated regional patterns. Morgan loved order and smooth-running operations. Schwab had expressed that vision in a new way. It was an idea just emergent: the idea of a single economic unit stretching from the iron mines of Mesabi all the way to girders being placed on a gondola; the idea of assembly lines; the idea of low costs, low prices, profits based on volume rather than scarcity. It was an idea later to be stamped with the imprint of Henry Ford, but when Schwab expressed it in 1900, Ford was still an obscure visionary in Detroit.

Morgan's intuition told him that Schwab had arrived at precisely the right moment, that the great steel corporation that seemed impossible weeks ago was about to be born, and that this was the moment to move. The first step, he reasoned, was to eliminate Schwab's boss.

Advisors told Morgan that the way to Carnegie was through Schwab, the only person with influence over the steel magnate. When contacted, Schwab was elated but apprehensive, since Carnegie focused much of his contempt for the Wall Street money crowd on Morgan. Schwab suggested an accidental meeting with Morgan. Plans were made to meet in a Philadelphia hotel but Morgan, sick in bed with a cold, failed to keep the appointment.

Throwing his caution aside, Schwab went to New York to meet with Morgan and other cohorts in the big deal. In the Morgan library Schwab discussed the companies that should be brought into the combination, why this one was essential and that one superfluous. Morgan, his eyes looking out from behind his huge discolored nose, told Schwab his aim was not to buy Carnegie out but to prevent him from expanding. Unless Carnegie retired, Schwab responded, there would be no checking him. The conference lasted all night. At the close Morgan stood up and said he would buy if Carnegie would sell. Go and find his price, he told Schwab.

The Carnegie executive left the library with the sense that, just as he had hoped, all of his plans were coming together. The next step was slipperiest of all. He knew that Carnegie had been thinking about retirement, but would the stubborn old man step aside for Morgan? He went to consult with Mrs. Carnegie.

She advised him to play golf with her husband and talk to him afterward. They played on the frosty links of Yonkers. Then Schwab said his piece and the white-bearded little millionaire listened with a downcast air.

"The amassing of wealth," he had written in a memorandum he had saved for three decades, "is one of the worst species of idolatry, no idol more debasing. To continue much longer overwhelmed with business cares and with most of my thoughts wholly upon the way to make more money in the shortest time, must degrade me beyond hope of permanent recovery." He had planned all these years to retire and devote all his time to philanthropy, but now that the awaited moment had arrived, Carnegie wanted to keep up the fight. But he did not reject the offer, and when he asked for a little time to think it over, Schwab knew what the answer would be.

The next day Carnegie wrote his price on a slip of paper and gave it to Schwab, who took the slip to Morgan. With hardly a glance, Morgan accepted. The thing was done. The most far-reaching and largest of all American companies was created—the United States Steel Corporation. Hundreds of steel companies were to be brought under a control that would rest in the hands of one man on Wall Street.

There was almost a weird resemblance of outlook and manner between the elder J.P. Morgan and his son, who bore the same name. When the old man, troubled in his last days by mental instability, died in 1913, a new Morgan took over the monumental institution. He seemed more pedestrian than his father, more deliberate, less brilliant, less bold, less prone to make mistakes. He called a meeting of the partners shortly after his father's death. His manner was pleasant but grave and firm, as he told his associates that the House of Morgan had concentrated its capital beyond the limits of wisdom into huge industrial units such as U.S. Steel. The company would gradually withdraw from its directorates in outside companies and concentrate on bonds and securities. The tranquil, rather savorless son spoke with new authority as hereditary head of the house, and the partners exchanged wondering glances, as if the spirit of the father had passed into the son.

The Morgan partners announced on New Year's Day, 1914, a wholesale withdrawal. "The necessity of attending many board meetings has been so serious a burden upon our time that we have long wished to withdraw from the directorates of many corporations," the statement said, and the house also intended to extricate itself from national and international politics. But Morgan soon learned that even great power does not allow complete freedom and that often the opposite is the case. Other banking houses went after Morgan's businesses, and Europe exploded in war. He had to reverse his policies sharply, as France and England came to him for help, in desperate need of money. The loans to the Allies established a new era in international finance, re-established the firm as a political force, and drew the United States closer and closer to taking sides openly in the European war.

On a July day in 1915, a man who called himself Frank Holt came to the front door of the Morgan estate at Glen Cove, Long Island, extended a card and asked to see Mr. Morgan. Holt's real name was Muenter, he was a rabid German nationalist, and he wanted to keep the United States out of the war. He did not bother with intermediaries like the secretary of state or the president.

"What is your business with him?" the butler asked.

"I can't discuss that with you," he replied haughtily. The butler was used to people who could not discuss their business with him and the card, if not impressive, looked legitimate. It stated: Summer Society Directory, Thomas C. Lester, representing. "I am an old friend of Mr. Morgan's," Holt-Muenter-Lester added. "He will see me."

The butler's suspicions were raised. The stranger on the threshold did not have the air of a friend. "You must tell me what business you have with him," he said firmly.

The man put his hands into his coat pockets and brought them out with a revolver in each. He pressed them against the butler's body, pushing back into the doorway and forcing himself past. "Don't dare and try to stop me," he said. With two guns at his back, the butler led him into the hall.

"You will find Mr. Morgan in the library," the butler said. He walked ahead of the gunman toward the library, which was located at the west end of the mansion, as far away from where Morgan actually was as any area of the house could be. As the intruder went through the library door, the butler stood back respectfully and as soon as the revolvers were out of his back he ran down the hall toward where the Morgans and their house guests were breakfasting.

"Upstairs, Mr. Morgan! Upstairs!" the butler shouted. Not wanting to betray Morgan to the gunman, he did not run directly into the breakfast room, but went down the stairs into the basement to throw the gunman off and to find other servants to help him.

When Morgan heard the shouts from the hallway he leaped up and ran upstairs by a rear staircase, followed closely by his wife and their house guests, the British ambassador and his wife. They went searching room to room in an attempt to discover what the butler had been shouting about, and met servants who were equally puzzled.

Suddenly one of the servants shouted that a man was coming up the stairs. Morgan and his wife, Jessie, hurried to the head of the stairs to intercept him. "Now, Mr. Morgan, I have got you!" the intruder shouted. Jessie sprang forward to throw herself against the gunman, but her husband pushed her aside and jumped at the man as he reached the landing.

Morgan flung his 220 pounds at the tall, slender gunman, who fired twice before his weapon jammed. The gunman was knocked down and fell with his feet toward Morgan, who threw himself forward on top of him, catching the wrist that held the revolver and forcing the hand open so that the gunman dropped his weapon. Holt-Muenter-Lester tried to bring up the other revolver, but Morgan pinned his left hand to the floor with his body and kept it there. Jessie and a servant jumped on the arm and wrenched the revolver away. The butler, carrying a heavy lump of coal, smashed the intruder in the right temple with it, stunning him. Morgan got off the gunman and servants bound the prone man hand and foot. Then Morgan walked to the telephone and called a physician who lived three miles away. He asked the physician to come at once to attend to his injuries. When he left the telephone the others realized that he had been shot. One bullet had gone through his groin near the right thigh and emerged at the rear of his thigh. The other was lodged near the base of his spine.

The police arrested the man who, as it transpired, had changed his name to Holt after fatally poisoning his wife. He had remarried and until recently had taught German at Cornell. A stick of dynamite was found on his person, two others in his bag, and another on the Morgan lawn, where he had presumably dropped it. He said that he had not known that the British ambassador and his wife were guests in the house when he had paid his call.

"I have done what I can," he responded when asked what other steps he had taken to further his views. "I have argued with people to keep them neutral. I have written to the press. I wrote several letters in favor of preserving strict neutrality in the *Ithaca Journal* and they were printed. I have a well-trained mind and I studied for a long time as to what would be the proper course for me to pursue before I decided to take the matter up with Mr. Morgan personally." Three days later he committed suicide in jail, slipping from his cell and hurling himself twenty feet downward into a corridor.

In its collection of printed books and manuscripts, Paris was the principal city of the world, and the *Bibliothèque Nationale* was the most impressive library of all. Every year it mounted an exquisite show. In

March of 1929 it produced one of its best, an exhibition depicting the evolution of bookbinding through ten centuries. The exhibition, illustrating the French sense of beauty and genius for assimilation, contained volumes bearing the arms of Catherine de Medici, Diane de Poitiers, and Marie Antoinette. Also on view was a remarkable series of old maps, one of which was supposed to have been annotated by Christopher Columbus.

Among the visitors was a rugged-looking man of sixty-one years, dressed impeccably. When he came upon a volume in green morocco that had originally been given to François I, a look stole over his face that suggested an emotional nature beneath his outward reserve. It was part of the collection of Jean Grolier, who had been Treasurer of France and one of the great Gallic financiers. He lingered for a time to drink it in. The two men—Grolier and the visitor—had much in common. Like Grolier, he also loved fine volumes and perfect bindings, and had some of his own. He was owner of one of the most engrossing private collections of manuscripts and first editions in the world. His library, an annex to his Manhattan home, was open to qualified scholars. Like Grolier, he was also a financier. Although he walked unrecognized in the *Bibliothèque*, he bore the fourteen-year-old scars of two revolver shots and a mighty name. J. Pierpont Morgan was the foremost financier in the world—the war had clinched that title.

His late father had been mighty too. But the elder Morgan had been concerned largely with America. He had juggled railroad lines, shipping lines, and thought in terms of millions. Morgan *fils* and his eighteen partners in the House of Morgan thought in terms of billions and, since the war, in terms of the world. Up to the elder Morgan's death, the largest foreign loans made had been fifty million dollars to Japan during the Russo-Japanese War and two hundred million dollars to Great Britain at the time of the Boer War. The five hundred million dollars loan to the Allied nations in 1915 had begun the modern era of international finance.

Through that loan the House of Morgan became vastly more powerful than it had been in the days of the elder Morgan. His son had planted the dollar where it had never been seen before. He had come to the aid of bankers, businessmen, kings, and the rulers of the earth. Torn apart by the most destructive war in history, the European nations had often been financially embarrassed, and Morgan had provided the money.

The plodding and pedestrian son had became the international banker of all time. The Morgan office was located in America, and in fact financed such companies as United States Steel, General Motors, and General Electric, but its face was turned always to the Atlantic.

The quality that set him apart had been born with him. He was raised with the elegant selfishness that passes for good manners and grew up to be a pleasantly brusque lad who took nothing without asking and always was sure to say "thank you" in a tone that showed how little it meant. He learned to speak in a charmingly precise manner. On joining his father's firm after attending Groton and Harvard, he was assigned to the London office, where he adopted the English mode of living, including the custom of afternoon tea during banking hours. It made him only slightly more distant than before.

He was a large and aristocratic figure and like his father looked out of deep-set, sharply inquisitive eyes. There was a droop in the left lid that suggested cynicism but might have been the result of neuralgia. He used his imposing presence to magnificent effect. More than once senators and congressmen, believing themselves ready to stare down the great Morgan, had summoned him before committees, but none bested him. "I am a proud man," he said one day, fixing an entire committee with a defiant flash, "and I will tolerate no further heckling." When the lawyers and solons made their apologies, he continued to answer questions on New York subway contracts. Yes, he said, he had received a quarter of a million dollars just for talking to certain officials of the transit company. "And," he snapped, "it was well worth it!"

He disdained the public. "I have lost all hope of receiving fair consideration from the people of Massachusetts," he said in Boston during an investigation of New Haven railroad financing. "Don't talk to me about appealing to the public. I am done with the public, for the present anyway. The public reads the headlines and that is all. The story itself is fair and shows the facts. That would be all right if the public read the facts. But it does not. It reads the headlines and listens to the demagogues and that's the stuff public opinion is made of."

He reached the acme of the supercilious at another committee hearing. A cameraman was inches from his nose. Every time his mouth opened, cameras flashed and newsreels turned. As he grew stiffer, a member of the Industrial Relations Committee asked him whether he considered ten dollars a week sufficient wages for a longshoreman. "If that's all he can get and he takes it," Morgan sniffed, "I should say that is enough." The editorial writers thumped for days about that one. His partners in the House of Morgan read it and groaned. In hundreds of rundown flats, weary freight handlers cursed Morgan, who received a fortune for an afternoon's work but thought ten dollars a week plenty for them.

He considered it weak and contemptible for a man to go out of his way to explain his motives, or even to remove a false conception of his motives. The aloofness covered a sentimental heart.

His wife's room in the mansion near Glen Cove was still kept in 1929 just as it had been at the time of her death four years earlier. In her memory he continued to support her tiny philanthropies. He would arise in the early morning, don work clothes, and hoe and rake to keep green the corner that she had planted for her Garden Club. He dug with such care that his tulips won prizes at shows.

With the same wounded heart he worshipped the memory of his father. The frowning portrait of J. Pierpont Morgan *père* looked down upon him every day at his Wall Street office. He took his father's place in the Protestant Episcopal Church. Like his father, he was vestryman at St. George's Church; as his father had done in 1892, he singlehandedly bore the financial burden in 1928 of the revision of the Standard Book of Common Prayer.

Like his father, work was not allowed to interfere with Episcopal affairs. Morgan would quit his office to convene with Episcopal ecclesiastics in discussions of all manner of dusty subjects. He felt about the Church as his father had. It was a great mystery, a blessed assurance that bestowed peace on his soul. There was in him nothing of the questing soul, the seeker of truth. His religion was, like the memories of his wife and father, a gift to be venerated in secret, a talent wrapped in a napkin and laid away in his heart.

He did not work hard. It was often late in the morning when he would board the *Corsair*, his black yacht, at the pier of his Glen Cove home and take it across the Sound to the New York Yacht Club landing. It was often only midafternoon when he could be seen leaving the office for his Manhattan home, there to spend hours in solitary study in the library. At quitting time the stray scholar would leave and the librarians would tiptoe out, leaving Morgan, alone in the cool white marble building, seated under the portrait of Milton as a youth, with his manuscripts of Keats, Byron, Cellini, Milton, and Dickens, arising to pace among the rich carvings, bronzes, and marbles—the treasures of queens and courtesans, popes and kings.

After having fled public involvement all his life, he found it necessary in 1929 to become a member of the Committee of Experts in Paris, serving with Owen Young. It was believed that to discuss reparations without the presence of Morgan was like playing cards without the ace of spades.

He dwelt apart from the rest of the American party, in an out-of-the-way lodging at the Hotel Princess, where he could enjoy both elegance and contemplation. In Paris, pursuing art treasures and dining on Ostend oysters, lobster à l'Americaine Pouilly 1919, drinking splendid Bordeaux, he also pursued a dream of consolidating not just an industry but the entire capitalist system. And Morgan had a way to do it—a world bank.

The Bank for International Settlements, as Morgan proposed to call it, would be created to handle the single largest financial transaction in history—German reparations. The reparations, according to the plan, would be converted into a loan and Germany would float a bond issue. The bank would act as intermediary in marketing the bonds with, of course, the indispensable help of Morgan in America.

But the bank, according to Morgan's view, would do more than that. It would reorganize the entire capitalist system on the principle of cooperation. Another war, he reasoned, would be a disaster. The last one had created a socialist nation in Russia; another one could bring about a socialist world. The world bank represented one aspect of the total integration of the earth that the international bankers fostered.

Paris was lovely, but Morgan was happiest in England—shooting game birds at his Scotland lodge or tramping about his Hertfordshire estate. He also had a home in London, and that spring he longed to be there. Everything at his London home was in readiness for him at all times. Even if he arrived unannounced it was expected that his maids, butlers, cooks, and chauffeurs would be uniformed and able immediately to make plans for dinner. Upstairs the cool covers of his bed were turned down, and a detective novel lay on the bedside table with his ash tray and pipes. He had come to value such harmony and tranquillity highly. Back at his home near Glen Cove, his mail was still checked for bombs, and guards were posted around the estate and at the barrier that had been erected at the entrance.

While the international bankers, led by Morgan and Young, worked to foster financial peace, American business interests pursued similar aims in the domestic economy. Stability, consolidation, and the avoidance of disruption appeared in 1929 to be all but achieved in the arenas of business, labor, and government.

Business needed an instrument to stabilize the effects of competition and selected the trade association. Labor was in a quiescent period but had been disruptive after the war, and the solution appeared to be Rockefeller's concept of the "Colorado Plan." Government's chief task was to stabilize the economy and break the cycle of boom and bust, and to the business leaders the key to the solution appeared to be full employment.

These three elements amounted to a grand scheme for the American economy in 1929. The goal was a frictionless economy in which all elements operated in harmony.

Trade associations dealt with the mutual problems of all the companies in an industry. In 1929 the most famous and most photographed trade association head—and a guest at the Dearborn dinner—was Will H. Hays, president of the Motion Picture Producers and Distributors of America.

The film industry had been created by tough, competitive men, but by 1921 they saw a need to cooperate. A damaging series of Hollywood scandals had brought about censorship boards in various states and clergymen all over the land were decrying Hollywood as Babylon.

They went to ask Hays, then postmaster general, to take over. He later explained that he had sympathized, but did not feel compelled to change jobs until he went home for the Christmas holidays. "I took with me some cowboy suits for my boy, Bill, then aged six, and his two cousins, aged five and eight," he explained. "But did they begin playing Wild West as I anticipated they would?" No, he said, instead they began to act out a western movie they had seen. "A new vision of the motion picture came to me," he continued. "I saw them not only from the viewpoint of men who had millions of dollars invested, but from the viewpoint of the fathers and mothers who have millions of children invested." He did not take the job as a showcase for his presidential ambitions, or because it paid one hundred thousand dollars annually. He took it because Will Hays could never resist an opportunity to do good.

Hays opposed governmental censorship, but at the same time proposed censorship from within. He took a train west and presented his views at a large meeting of the movie colony, where he told them that self-regulation was the answer to censorship. Even more important than the threat of official censorship, he said, was the global role of films. Movie people had a patriotic duty to be sexually virtuous, for trade no longer followed the flag, it followed the film. The United States was winning the world, not by armies of occupation and the pursuit of empire, but by its cultural sway. American films thus had to reflect credit on the nation.

Every film proposal was subjected to review, and if Hays rejected it, the movie was not made. Nothing was to be filmed containing swearing, nudity, deprecation of the clergy, or romantic attachments between people of different races. In addition to the "Don'ts," Hays had a list of "Be Carefuls," including violations of the Prohibition laws, lustful kissing, sympathy for criminals, and any attack on the institution of marriage. The important thing was that wickedness be punished and virtue rewarded in the end—a film could get away with a lot if a moralistic ending were tacked on. Legally it amounted to restraint of trade—often the surreptitious aim of a trade association, but Hays made no attempt to hide it.

By 1929 he had beaten back every effort to impose more stringent censorship in America, and the censorship problems had begun to emerge on the international level. In January the Chinese government banned *Ben Hur*. The film, the Chinese said, was "Christian propaganda decoying the people to superstition, which must not be tolerated in the present age of revolutionary enlightenment."

Mussolini was so annoyed about another American film, *Street Angel*, that he dismissed all the members of the Italian Board of Censorship for allowing such a slander on the city of Naples to be shown. "Perhaps in the remote past conditions approached those shown in the picture," an Italian critic wrote, "but in Mussolini's Italy certainly nothing of that nature exists. Gypsies, underworld characters, prostitution, cheating, misery, vice, overdressed peasants, gamin life, people in rags, filthiness, superstition, thuggery, human landscape immersed in endless fog—even the classic sun of Italy was obliterated."

France and Spain had taken action against American films that they thought misrepresented their nations, Hungary was planning legislation against United States films, and the British complained that the American talking film was corrupting their speech patterns. The American film industry—the biggest, busiest, most productive in the world—was taking as much as 80 percent of the film business in some countries and returning most of the money to the United States. Hays knew that other nations believed they could help the film industry blossom in their own countries by rationing American films, and saw economic rivalry lurking behind protestations of wounded pride. International irritants kept his phone jangling, but the basis for a powerful trade association had been put together.

Hays also helped to promulgate the trade association idea to other developing industries. Aviation sank into a full-scale depression after the war, and when it had failed to recover by mid-decade, its leaders turned to him for advice. In 1924 an aeronautical trade magazine invited Hays to speak at a luncheon for representatives of the aircraft interests in New York. His advice was: play down private interest and accentuate the public interest in a vital aviation industry. Once the public was convinced that the product was essential, support would follow. Second, find out what the government needs and supply it. Third, set your own house in order.

He continued to meet weekly with an aviation group and was indispensable in bringing the industry together. The paramount rule, he advised, was that all differences were to be solved by the aircraft interests themselves. For internal peace, more recognition and profit had to be allotted to the design innovators. Under the cross-licensing system then in effect, many plane companies had enjoyed a free ride in appropriating the ideas of others. "Design rights" were established in the industry. Parts were standardized so as to be of greater service to the government. For twenty-three aircraft companies that had been quarreling since the war, the closing of ranks was a startling development. Early in 1925 the aircraft committee met with the secretaries of war and the Navy, and then with President Coolidge, who said the government did not need that many planes but that a sound industry able to produce large quantities in a crisis was crucial. By July the Army and Navy had agreed to protect design rights, to follow a purchase procedure that the industry favored, and to cease competing with private industry in construction and engineering. The growing influence of a united aircraft industry was a crucial factor in producing the Kelly Act, which took the government out of the airmail business and gave the routes to private companies.

The growing importance of trade associations was related to the increasing complexity of business-government dealings. The trade association also fostered more rationalization and socialization and the abatement of what the aeronautics industry called "destructive competition." In several states, trade associations pressured state legislatures to enact "fair trade prices," or price-fixing by law. Rival businesses agreed, via the trade association, to stay off each other's turf. Such understandings had become so widespread that a committee of the American Bar Association in 1929 urged Congress to face the facts and make them official so that they could be regulated.

The labor policy that business was developing had begun in effect in the coal fields of Colorado with Rockefeller's plan for employee representation. It was variously called the American Plan, the Colorado Plan, or the Rockefeller Plan, and usually only its detractors called it a "company union."

After the Colorado strike, Rockefeller had developed a permanent staff that specialized in reform, led by MacKenzie King, the Canadian liberal. Without the staff, Rockefeller believed, he could only scramble for information in a crisis; with it he could control and channel unrest.

Rockefeller had to fight his own industrial managers to get them to accept employee representation. The managers sabotaged it in every way possible, and the workers tended to react with apathy, so it failed to work well. King told him that it lacked a psychological appeal for workers and that only in labor unions did workers feel power and develop a sense of dignity and self-respect.

Rockefeller regarded employee representation as a weapon against labor organizing. All the concessions made in other industries were based on a similar impulse. Rockefeller, like most businessmen of the time, hated labor unions, which he found discordant. It appeared in 1929, however, that the heyday of the labor union had passed; unions were continuously losing membership and power. It seemed yet stronger evidence that all interests were coming together in a new era. "Trusteeship" was industry's watchword, and many companies offered stock ownership, savings plans, visiting nurses, safety lessons, and recreation.

"There has been a change—an enormous change—and within the last ten years," a director of the U.S. Chamber of Commerce wrote in 1929. "We are acquiring a new industrial philosophy . . . that the fundamentals of decent and right conduct laid down by Jesus of Nazareth constitute the soundest, most sensible and workable economic system possible to devise."

Charles Schwab, a staunch opponent of unions, was also ready to pour syrup on the situation. "I have gone through some rather dark chapters in American industrial history," he said that spring of 1929. "It is a great joy to realize that humanity rules today; that industry has awakened to the fact that the employer, in engaging men's services, is entitled to use them but not to abuse them . . . Let us hope that the new order which we find in industry will hasten the day when we shall cease altogether to talk about a separation between labor and capital and begin to think of ourselves as contributing to a cooperative undertaking in the advancement of which every supervisor and every employee is an important and essential factor." There were exceptions. Bloody textile strikes—like the one to which Sinclair Lewis had journeyed—raged through North Carolina that year, but most businessmen thought the era of the strike was over.

In government, too, a new era seemed about to begin. One of the foremost champions of the trade associations had entered the White House in 1929. As secretary of commerce, Hoover had husbanded their development, contending that they would eliminate waste, promote standardization and provide statistical backup for industry-wide decisions. While he was Secretary, the U.S. Supreme Court in 1924 in effect gave a stamp of approval to trade associations by sanctioning the free flow of information to various industries through them. Hoover recognized that trade associations could promote conspiracies, but he trusted most businessmen to be honest and fought the prevailing opinion at the Justice Department that trade associations should be treated with suspicion.

Hoover had been the principal government force for the development of the Merchant Marine and the radio and aviation industries. He believed that the free enterprise system was condemned to waste unless a way could be found to eliminate the periodic cycles of boom and bust. As early as 1921 he established, using President Harding as a mere showpiece, the President's Conference on Unemployment, with Owen Young as chairman of the committee on business cycles. As president, Hoover intended to use government planning and public works projects as a means to combat business downturns.

Young, the GE board chairman and his possible presidential rival in 1932, was prepared to go much farther, in the areas of trade associations, labor, and government.

In 1926 he and Gerard Swope, the president of GE, met with William Green, the president of the AFL, in an attempt to interest Green in organizing GE workers—an unprecedented and daring overture.

Swope and Young were skeptical about the prevalent belief that the labor union was passing away. They regarded labor unions as a permanent force and if so, they reasoned, the prudent move was to cultivate them and foster a domesticated labor movement. They even expected advantages in the stabilization of the work force that unions encouraged.

With its employee representation system, Swope suggested to Green, GE had already created the AFL's organizing base. Green was interested. He had been president of the Ohio Mine Workers and had been involved in the Colorado Fuel & Iron strike, and was one of the few AFL leaders of the time who looked with favor on industrial organizing. He promised to look into the dimensions of this strange offer. But his colleagues were trade unionists, skilled craft workers who opposed organizing the unskilled plant workers, and the offer came to nothing.

In the development of trade associations as well, Young and Swope were prepared to go much farther. The two GE progressives favored the expansion of powers, via government charters, that would actually give trade associations control over industries. The powers of the trade association, according to their plan, would include the control of prices and production. It would mean that trade associations could limit production —and thus the government would be able for the first time to deal with the problem of overproduction of goods, which they saw as a leading factor in unemployment and business downturns.

Such a plan appeared to run directly into the prohibitions of the Sherman Antitrust Act, but the act was held in such wide disrepute in 1929 that it was commonly assumed to be due for revision or scrapping. Young maintained that various Supreme Court interpretations of this act suggested that an electrical trade association with broad powers could be set up under federal supervision as a model. The court, he held, would sustain such a move. The law was not created to hamper progress, he said, and when it ceased to serve the purpose it was created to serve, it had to be changed. Their plan was a new form of government for an industrial age—official, sponsored trade associations acting on behalf of the government and dealing with official domesticated big labor organizations speaking on behalf of the worker. What the GE leaders had in mind was still nascent in America. To find such a government in practice one had to look across the Atlantic.

On one side of the vast Piazza San Giovanni in Rome on a February day in 1929 stood a huge crowd of Fascists. On the other side, near the window of the Lateran Palace, an equally large crowd of priests and ecclesiastical students were cheering. Applause broke out as automobiles drove to the palace gates of the Vatican and entered. The car carrying Benito Mussolini sped by so quickly that it was gone before they realized who was inside.

When Mussolini reached Cardinal Gasparri, the two exchanged greetings and sat down together to sign each page of the treaty with a solid gold Papal pen. The Cardinal then presented the pen to Mussolini.

Outside, the tension was broken by a hastily written communiqué announcing that after sixty years the Italian government and the Papacy had signed a treaty and concordat. Cheers broke out on both the Fascist and Papal sides of the piazza.

Inside, the Fascists in morning coats and silk hats and the Papal delegation in black, scarlet, and gold chatted as they passed through a succession of great halls. Standing by a curio—a relic of some missionary expedition to heathen lands—Mussolini heard the ecclesiastics outside sing a Te Deum and heard the Fascists shout "Viva Mussolini! Viva Il Duce!"

All over Rome people celebrated, and Italian and Papal flags festooned almost every window. "History will say," one of the headlines stated, "that this is Mussolini's masterpiece." A new era of amity and peace was proclaimed. The conciliation had ended a sixty-year quarrel that had kept the Pope a prisoner within Vatican walls. Once again, as in the Middle Ages, he was a sovereign ruler. He would have his own railway station, landing field, mint, postal service, and radio station.

Around the world it was forecast that the treaty and concordat would dominate the history of the second quarter-century as the war had the first. "This will stamp Mussolini," said an American lay Catholic leader, "as the greatest man of his age."

The following month Mussolini appeared in triumph to proclaim that the conciliation with the Vatican would cause the Fascist regime to live forever in history. The enthusiastic audience at the Royal Opera House in Rome consisted of four thousand Fascist chiefs, military and civilian, from around the nation.

Il Duce (his title as Party Chief) appeared in good humor, smiling at his friends on the stage and nodding his head to acknowledge the waves of applause. The cheering redoubled as he stepped on the elevated platform and raised his arm in the Fascist salute. When the ovation reached its height, he put out his hand in an imperious gesture and listeners immediately fell silent. He spoke forcefully, in quick sentences, as if he were eager to finish. He seldom gave his audience time to applaud.

"Only with conciliation," he said, "has the separation of church and state become complete. Each now has its own rights and duties and each can collaborate with the other as a sovereign independent state."

Giving the Roman Catholic Church special status in Italy and control over matrimonial questions hardly seemed the usual way to promote the separation of church and state. The crowd, however, was more inclined to be spellbound by his presence than critical of his argument. "Mussolini," according to one of the newly promulgated Ten Commandments of Fascism, "is always right." Although only Fascists were allowed to run for office, Il Duce proclaimed Italy to have the freest elections in the world. It had, he said, the freest press in the world, although totally government controlled. He was always right.

He was, in 1929, at the height of his adulation by the world. Journalists described him as one of the world's wonders. He had balanced the budget, made the trains run on time, ended labor disputes, drained the marshes. He was a penetrating thinker, an intellectual, and a fiery lover whose romances included fifteen-minute matinees with starstruck young ladies. He was resolute, bold, and manly. He was compared to Caesar, Napoleon, Bismarck, and Garibaldi.

A former journalist himself, he loved being interviewed, and flattered the foreign press shamelessly. One American journalist told him that in America he was often compared to Theodore Roosevelt. "For that I am very glad and proud," he said. "Roosevelt I greatly admired. Roosevelt had strength. He had the will to do what he thought should be done. He had greatness."

Strength and will were what Mussolini attempted to personify—and, like Roosevelt, he also had a theatrical style, as well as scant interest in principle, and a gigantic ego that could swing him in any direction. Only a few years earlier he had dared God to strike him dead at a public assembly. In 1929 he was photographed praying to a statue of the Virgin in lone splendor. It had more to do with theatrics than religious belief.

He understood how to gain the world's attention. "I told you three years ago when I saw him that he was the biggest man in public life," Will Rogers wrote of him in his syndicated column in the summer of 1929. "I have never seen a thing that he has done that wasn't based on common sense. He has done more constructive things for his country since the war than any hundred men in any other country."

A more constant and committed propagandist for Mussolini was the Wall Street banker Otto Kahn, who, despite liberal convictions on other subjects, had fallen under his spell. "Mussolini," Kahn said, "has substituted efficient and energetic and progressive processes of government for Parliamentary wrangling and wasteful, impotent bureaucracy. He has engendered among the people a spirit of order, discipline, hard work, patriotic devotion and faith."

But the most persistent ally of Mussolini was the House of Morgan, and the man in charge was Morgan's chief aide, Thomas W. Lamont, who engaged a newspaper clipping service to keep Il Duce informed of American reaction to his regime and was treasurer of the Italy-American Society. He served as an unpaid business consultant and was in a splendid position to boost investment in Italy.

On some occasions Mussolini's publicists concentrated on how he had restored Italy to fiscal sanity and prosperity. When debt payments came up, however, the same publicists lamented Italy's impoverished soil, dense population, and limited resources. The Italian government owed the American government for wartime loans. After consideration and debate, the U.S. Debt Commission gave Italy a unique break. Although it did not lower the principal on the debt, the interest rate was reduced to a miniscule four-tenths of one percent. The British were paying 3.3 percent. Thus the United States made an unmistakable show of friendship to the Fascist regime.

That out of the way, Lamont secured a hundred-million-dollar loan from the House of Morgan for the Fascist government. The renegotiation of the war debt made the loan possible. The State Department had informed the Italian Embassy, in language difficult to misunderstand, that "once the debt is funded it will be far easier to get money in America." The American ambassador jokingly warned the Italians not to overdo the poverty story if they intended to borrow money immediately afterward.

The impoverished nation was, it transpired, an excellent risk for a Morgan loan. The loan, said to be budgeted for land reclaiming, water-power development, and electrification of railroads, was easily subscribed. It was Mussolini's greatest prestige victory to date—an official stamp of approval from the money headquarters of the world. The House of Morgan placed confidence in the future of the Fascist regime. The former radical Mussolini, who had railed against the Morgans and Rockefellers and their crimes against humanity, was now their ally. Now that his debts to the American people had been reduced, he could afford to be in debt to Morgan.

After the Morgan loan, and partly as its consequence, the admiration of Mussolini grew. His image also underwent a change; from Mussolini the conqueror, a bit too operatic for American tastes, he evolved into Mussolini the business genius. "He is quite charming, listens attentively, and with every show of keen interest to what his visitors have to say, answers their questions with wit and brilliance and in every way behaves like a polished and cultured man," a *New York Times* writer stated of him in the summer of 1929. "There is no reason, of course, why he should act otherwise, but it comes as a complete surprise to the majority of people, who had been led to expect the exact opposite."

He was called the great advertising man of his time. When the Third International Congress of Scientific Management met in Rome in 1927, those apostles of efficiency named him honorary president. The man of action had been recast in a mode of action more comfortable for Americans—the man who got things done.

American business leadership soon saw what the House of Morgan liked in the Fascist regime. Financiers, industrialists, and chambers of commerce became taken with the evolving philosophy of the Corporate State. Italian corporatism was heading in the same direction as was the U.S. economy—toward a planned economy, toward government husbandry of business, control over business cycles, incentives to help emergent industries like radio and aeronautics, everything that Hoover had been doing in the Commerce Department for eight years. The corporate state seemed made for a dynamic industrial society. Corporatism put the divergent interests of such a society together and dealt with them as blocs: Big Business, Big Labor, Big Government. It radiated efficiency. Em-

ployee organizations would represent workers. Trade associations would
represent business. It seemed a sound and intelligent adaptation of the
principle of checks and balances. The Italian citizen, according to the pro-
Mussolini faction, was better represented via corporatism than by some
parliamentary method based on whether he happened to live in Rome,
Milan, or Naples. There were clear parallels between the ideas of American business leaders and the Italian model.

Mussolini and Fascism were not universally admired in America,
particularly not in unions, in Congress, and in liberal circles. William
Green, the AFL president, was staunchly anti-Fascist, and the AFL regarded the corporate state as a shell game in which the bankers and
industrialists always won. Many Congressmen regarded Il Duce as an
enemy of representative government. Many Americans, however, were as
impatient as was Mussolini of forums and debates. Will Rogers's barbs at
politicians rose from his exasperation with "hot air" when there were jobs
that needed doing. In a society in which action was admired above all,
Congress seemed the antithesis of modern business methods. The liberals
were upset about Mussolini's use of secret police, his terrorism, the loss of
freedoms in a totally controlled state, and they were appalled by his boast-
ing about his jackbooted strides over the decomposed corpse of liberty.
But such swaggering did not much seem to bother the guests at Dearborn
on October 21. They were swaggering a bit themselves at the zenith of
American optimism and energy.

No one person could embody all the angles and shapes of American
business at that moment, but the collection at Dearborn represented a
useful composite portrait. Young captured its smug optimism in his sermon on Big Business. Its autocracy was encapsulated in the trim frame of
Henry Ford. Hays was the sort of hustler destined to head the trade
associations—fixers operating at the bulging intersection of business and
government. Rosenwald showed the tensions and contradictions that grew
out of developing a humane capitalism.

By inviting these people to congregate, Ford for a moment had brought
most of the disparate elements of American Big Business together. He had
even possessed an astute enough sense of the occasion to invite people of
whom he personally disapproved, for the great enemy of the trusts had
invited trustifiers and even Wall Street speculators like Nicholas Brady;
Otto Kahn, who had helped finance Hollywood's Babylonian enterprises;
and Hays, whom Ford dismissed as a fraud who talked Presbyterianism
while the screen continued its salacious ways. Whatever their shortcomings
in Ford's eyes they were admitted because society regarded them as re-

spectable. The one important element of American big business that Ford failed to invite was the underside.

Two detectives were standing under a theater marquee in a twilight in May of 1929 in Philadelphia when a pudgy-faced, thick-lipped man came walking out of the movie house.

"You're Al Capone, aren't you?" one of the detectives asked.

"Yes," Capone answered genially. "Who are you?"

They showed the Great Scarface their police badges. "Oh, bulls, eh?" the Chicago gangster said, still tractable. "All right, then, here's my gun." He handed over a .38-caliber pistol. A bodyguard walking behind his boss also pulled out his pistol and peacefully surrendered it to the two Philadelphia cops.

It was the end of a trying day. Motor trouble, Capone said, on the way from Atlantic City to Philadelphia had caused him to miss a train. By the time the automobile had been repaired, it was a wait of several hours until the next express left for Chicago, and he and the bodyguard had whiled away a few hours in a movie theater.

Capone poured out his heart to the Philadelphia Director of Public Safety. The life he had been living, he said, was not glamorous, but constantly filled with anxiety. Having turned thirty years of age, he had just retired and planned to live on the wealth, reputed to be two million dollars, accumulated in his various rackets. "Once in the racket," he sighed, "you're always in it, it seems. The parasites trail you, begging for money and favors, and you can never get away from them, no matter where you go. I have a wife, and a boy, who is eleven—a boy I idolize, and a beautiful home at Palm Island, Florida. If I could go there and forget it all, I would be the happiest man in the world. I want peace, and I am willing to live and let live. I'm tired of gang murders and gang shootings."

When the Philadelphia police checked with Chicago, they discovered that Capone had a blameless record out there and was well regarded in Chicago police circles. Capone found Pennsylvania to have a sterner brand of justice. He and his bodyguard were indicted the following morning for carrying concealed deadly weapons, and a jury was drawn to begin trial immediately.

When the indictments were read the two Chicagoans stood mute. The judge gave them half an hour to confer with their lawyers and then at noon reconvened court. Before the Commonwealth could begin its case, Capone's lawyers approached the bench and talked with the judge for fifteen minutes. At the conclusion of the conference it was announced that the defendants wanted to plead guilty.

"All right," the judge responded, "each of the prisoners is sentenced to one year's imprisonment." A shadow crossed the scarred face of the great gangster. The arrest had become no joking matter. Only twenty hours after having been taken in custody, America's biggest mobster was about to serve time for the first time in his life.

It had come at what Capone hoped was a turning point in his career, for during his three-day stay in Atlantic City he had met with other gang leaders to begin the initial steps in the most far-sighted project of his life. He was determined to end the long reign of terror in Chicago and to inaugurate an era of harmony. All past grievances, including the St. Valentine's Day Massacre, were to be forgotten in an age of peace.

The press reports, though partly guesswork, contained an inkling of what the Atlantic City meeting had been about. It was reported that the gangs were to unite in one supermob with departments of Booze, Gambling, Vice, and Protection Agencies. "Did you hear about the latest big financial merger?" Will Rogers chuckled in his column. "It's in Chicago. All the various competing gangs of racketeers have united under one board of directors headed by the chairman. It's a $16 million corporation. Each gang gets preferred stock in proportion to the notches on their present machine guns. They figure it will reduce their present overhead which consists mostly now of flowers and caskets. With everybody working in harmony it should increase service to its customers. So don't sell 'American Racketeers Corporation' short."

Capone's plan was actually more like a trade association than a merger. It consisted of an agreement to establish territories, set fair-trade prices, and provide an arbitrator, patterned on the Hays model, to settle disputes, replacing with modern methods the blood vendettas of the old-fashioned gangsters.

"I'm like any other man," Capone told the Public Safety Director while under arrest. "I've been in this racket long enough to realize that a man in my game must take the breaks, the fortunes of war. Three of my friends were killed in the last two weeks in Chicago. That certainly is not conducive to peace of mind. Even when I'm out on a peace errand we must hide from the rest of the racketeers, even to the point of concealing our identity under assumed names, in hotels and elsewhere. Why, when I came to Atlantic City I registered under a false name." Hearing of the death of three friends may have imparted a sense of urgency to Capone's peace efforts—even though, since he had ordered their executions, it could hardly have been much of a shock.

On the day of the Jubilee dinner, Capone was serving a term in the Eastern Penitentiary in Pennsylvania. His imprisonment was interfering somewhat with his administration of his business empire, but he was able to issue instructions to Chicago almost daily. The helpful warden let him use the telephone in the administrative offices whenever he liked, and Capone could be seen there many an afternoon chewing on a cigar and making big decisions. The warden also allowed him an unlimited number of visitors at anytime. Capone had a cozy, well-furnished cell that was nothing like the standard at the penitentiary, with a rug, pictures, a chest of drawers, a desk, a bookshelf, and a five-hundred-dollar floor model radio console.

Capone's arrest had been arranged through one of the Philadelphia detectives who had been waiting outside the theater—an old friend of Capone's who had first met the gangster at the Hialeah racetrack and often renewed acquaintance while in the South. Capone had asked him to arrange the arrest as a hideaway from the Bugs Moran gang, which had been outraged by the St. Valentine's Day Massacre. He had expected a short sentence, but a starchy judge had sent him away for a goodly term.

Making the best of it, he made plans for his Pax Caponi. The plans went far beyond Chicago. The Atlantic City conference had been a more ambitious project than merely a settlement of Chicago's messy gang war. It had been the second in a series of meetings toward the formation of a national crime syndicate. More than thirty big names from Chicago, Philadelphia, Newark, and New York had met to plan a modern, rationalized national syndicate that cut across nationalist and ethnic divisions. Slavs had sat with Jews and Irish, Sicilian Italians with mainland Italians. The age of the ethnic gang was closing and in its stead was arising an organized crime operation.

Capone was as intrepid a foe of competition and as full-blooded an advocate of monopoly, pooling, and cooperation as was J.P. Morgan. The gangs in various cities were eager to work out exclusive local franchises and wanted a national organization for supportive services.

Like Young and Swope, Capone believed in setting prices and limiting production through industry-wide decisions. The protection agencies of Chicago were trade associations in which fair-trade prices were enforced against mavericks who tried to undersell their competitors. When a dry cleaning business, for example, charged less than the agreed price, the place was bombed.

But that was not senseless violence. It was the organization of rational enforcement. Capone was enforcing laws that had not yet become legal. The more he was able to shape events, the less violence would be necessary and the more profit for all. Sometimes, as so many leaders have testified, it is necessary to make war to bring peace. That was what the St. Valentine's Day Massacre was all about—it was a step in stabilizing American crime and moving from untamed gangs to the smoother age of crime as Big Business. The same economic forces were at work in the mobs as in other fields of business. But when Capone warned against the perils of "murderous competition," he meant it literally.

Machinery, the New Messiah

ON THE EVENING of October 21, 1929, the sun set on a resonant moment in the century. Most of the inventions that had shaped the age—the telephone, the motion picture, the automobile, the electric light and power complex, the airplane, and the radio—were a quarter-century to a half-century old. They had developed fitfully, but on the night of the dinner they were at work in the world. More than machines, they conveyed information, exchanged ideas, transported goods, and sang through wires. These systems, intricate and global in scope, had made the United States more sophisticated and more powerful and more envied than any other civilization hitherto known. The United States was at that moment the only nation with both feet in the twentieth century.

The tables in Ford's banquet hall were filling with representatives of each of these concerns. They had mounted and spurred their technologies to remarkable successes. A technological base had been developed in which new gadgetry replaced old. The new screen-grid radio tubes of 1929 made earlier radios obsolete; the new headlights with two intensities of beam were another inducement to trade in the old car. Technological change had become one of the chief propellants of the economy. The systems, furthermore, were becoming more interrelated—innovations were coming in the use of telephone lines for radio broadcasts, of sound in the motion picture, of the transmission of light waves as well as sound waves, —creating a complex, man-made environment.

Not the least remarkable of the successes of technology was its uncritical, almost hypnotic public endorsement. No philosophers or magazine writers could swerve the public from an enthusiasm for applied science almost religious in its faith. The faith was essential, for everyone involved in making technological change is a sorcerer's apprentice, opening a vulnerable society to changes that profoundly affect human life and even human nature.

The opinion-makers and leaders of the nation were pleased with the widespread public approval of technological advance and, to reinforce this attitude, made such advances a matter of national pride. An advancing technology was often taken in America to be the measure of civilization.

87

Edison was being honored at Dearborn as an avatar of "inventive skill and mechanical ingenuity"; in effect, the society was toasting its own technological health. The dinner at Dearborn was, therefore, more than a mere celebration of Big Business. It was an official observance that the United States had become principally a technological society.

It was June 1929, and the manager of the General Electric lamp factory in New Jersey was perspiring gently. About two hundred people, most of them GE workers and officials but also including reporters, photographers, and newsreel cameramen, were facing a group of men seated at a table. The June sun shone on the deeply tanned face of Thomas Edison, who had just returned from his Florida home. The GE manager rose to speak. "Today we are going to part with one of our most treasured possessions," he said, indicating with a gesture the building on a grassy knoll behind him, "the original lamp factory of the Menlo Park days." As he continued to speak, Edison's gaze wandered to the young milkweed growing in the field about them.

Edward L. Bernays, the public relations consultant for Light's Golden Jubilee, looked at the clump of newspeople with a sense of accomplishment. He watched Edison closely, as if seeking a clue to his greatness that might be capsulized in a press release.

Ford was in a jovial mood, joshing with reporters and smiling broadly. He had been putting Edison's old Menlo Park headquarters together for his Greenfield Village project and this, the old glass-blowing building, was a vital addition. GE was making a great to-do of the donation. When Edison left Menlo Park many years earlier for his larger facility in West Orange, he had abandoned his laboratories, and over the years they had been rifled, demolished, and scavenged. Some of the lumber had been loaded on trucks and used in homes constructed in the area; some of their doors had been ripped off and repainted to grace the doorsteps of barber and millinery shops; the rafters of his laboratory had been torn out and installed in a sawmill. The brick of the machine shop had been found, forty years later, still scattered at the site. With the assistance of Edison himself, paid operatives, and the former Edison employees who had incorporated themselves into the Edison Pioneers, Ford gathered as many parts of the buildings as he could locate or reconstructed what he could not find.

He had managed to find a single shutter from the old office building. It was taken apart and mingled into reproductions, so that every shutter on the restored office building in Dearborn contained a piece of the real thing.

One of his luckiest findings was the dump. Behind the Menlo Park office building had been a hole into which Edison and his men dropped the debris that came out of the laboratory. Over the years it had settled and been forgotten, and in the forgetting it had been transformed into historical artifacts. Ford had the discarded equipment, old bulbs, broken porcelain, and the rest of the debris dug up and shipped in one hundred twenty-five boxes to his Dearborn project. Edison's chemical supplier had been able to find early bills of sale to determine what Edison had on hand in those days, and the same chemicals were shipped to Ford's ambitious restoration.

It was as if Ford were creating a movie set. Now he was getting, already restored by GE, what was in effect the world's first lightbulb factory. It had been used as a shelter for a family of squatters, and as a chicken coop, until GE had rescued it and shipped it to Mazdabrook, a recreation area for its New Jersey lamp factory employees.

At the Mazdabrook ceremony the manager was finishing his remarks. He handed the deed and the key to the building to the auto magnate. Ford turned slightly in his chair to see the white placard printed with large letters in front of the chair. "THIS ORIGINAL LAMP FACTORY WILL BE GIVEN A PLACE OF HONOR AT THE EDISON MEMORIAL INSTITUTE AT DEARBORN," it read. "THIS KEY I PRESENT TO YOU." He smiled self-deprecatingly as he read the words aloud to the group and, turning at the proper cue with key in hand, he gave it to Edison, who was seated beside him. The inventor glanced at his placard, which read: "THANK YOU, MISTER FORD. I SHALL BE GLAD TO KEEP THE KEY AS A REMEMBRANCE OF THE OCCASION." He said those words, the audience applauded, and the two old friends smiled again.

Although an experienced and sophisticated man, Bernays felt a rush of excitement at getting his first glimpse of two of the most important figures in modern history. He hoped that being able to converse with them would aid him in the months of public relations work still ahead before the Jubilee's climax in October.

He thought himself fortunate, therefore, to get a chance to stroll briefly with both men through the fields around Mazdabrook before lunch, but there were only shreds of conversation. Edison was fascinated with the milkweed and stooped over continuously to examine it, making humming sounds and squatting on his haunches. He mentioned to Bernays that milkweed might be the answer to his search for a new domestic source of rubber.

As Bernays sat with the two men at lunch, he hoped the change of locale would start their conversational juices flowing and even considered writing some of the talk down. Ford brought him up to date on his digestion, the merits of carrot juice, and the dangers of mixing foods improperly in the stomach. "You're looking fine!" Ford shouted, cupping his hands at Edison's ear.

"Yes, that's my wife's liver pills," he said. "She gives me some every day."

They munched, they talked digestive subjects, or they slurped. The thought crossed Bernays' mind that he could have learned more about them in ten minutes at a library. He slipped his pencil back into his jacket pocket.

Bernays had one objection to the advance of American technology. He feared airplanes. On one occasion because of the urgency with which he was needed, he took his first plane ride—from Newark to Dearborn. He preferred the more leisurely pace of the Detroiter, which left New York in the evening, provided a fine dinner and a comfortable Pullman, and arrived in the morning in time for the business day. Through the summer and fall as he shuttled between Dearborn and New York, working closely with Ford on the development of Light's Golden Jubilee, he took it on several occasions.

Every time he arrived in Dearborn he found more crates and clutter. Acres of goods, everything from spoons to locomotives, were piling up. Ford's galleons returned with such treasures as hoopskirts from the Alleghenies, Sandwich glass from Cape Cod, hooked rugs, wheat flails, army boots, Conestoga wagons, grist mills, cider presses, daguerreotype machines.

Ford had been collecting such objects for a decade. He had begun modestly enough with a whale-oil lamp or a spice mill, a Chippendale cabinet, and a wooden chandelier. But as time went on his purchasing took on a wholesale aspect. He used the former Fordson tractor plant to store his treasures, and they even overflowed the plant. Ford had become the principal collector of Americana in the world, and in that summer of 1929 his finds lay in crates on a one-hundred-twenty-five-acre tract. Ford was assembling a museum—not a marbled hall with niches for naked Greek gods but a homespun, down-to-earth museum of objects that came from the everyday lives of people—the technology of the past.

Nor had he stopped at buying objects. He had taken to purchasing whole settings and was a collector of buildings—dismantled, shipped to Dearborn, and the pegs and nails driven in again in his lot. Ford intended to group these buildings into a village to reflect a vanished way of life. He and Bernays kicked about the grounds, formulating plans to show this village to the invited guests on the day of the Jubilee dinner in October. Bernays suggested that the horsedrawn vehicles be hitched to meet the guests at the railroad depot and carry them about, and Ford liked the idea.

Both the village and the museum were to be adjuncts of the Edison Institute, a technical school named in honor of his friend. On Edison's birthday, Ford announced that he was throwing five million dollars into the institute as a beginning. In 1928, when Edison was poking around in the artifacts, Ford had persuaded him to immortalize his footprints by walking across freshly laid cement, and Edison added his flourishing signature to the display. Upon seeing the squares the following summer Bernays asked: shouldn't Edison's footprints be walking into the building, not out of it? Yes, Ford said, you're right, and forthwith he had the squares dug up and turned around. Bernays found that was the way with Ford. Once Bernays suggested that an area near Ford's office looked too bare. "Liebold," Ford said, immediately picking up the phone, "I want some planting done." When Bernays left a short while later men were planting and landscaping at the spot.

He and Bernays would talk as they strolled through the warehouses, packed to the ceiling with crates. In one room workmen were repairing antique firearms. Those already conditioned, hundreds of them of all kinds and periods, were hanging on pegs. Farther along, men were mending, scraping, and polishing furniture. There were fifty spinning wheels lined up in rows on a mezzanine platform. All about them were stoves, apothecary bottles and jugs, boxes of children's games, toys, puzzles, and dolls, sausage stuffers, coffee roasters, cotton gins, steam engines, autos. Ford and Bernays ended up in a corner of the warehouse where a craftsman was putting together music boxes, reed organs, cornets, zithers, and harmoniums. Behind him a dozen large cases awaited his attention. Ford turned on a music box, and another, and another, and another, and soon twenty of them were spinning out long-forgotten tunes.

Only one of Ford's forays had been unsuccessful. His emissaries returned empty-handed, unable to buy Independence Hall. It was not for sale at any price. According to an architect who told the story to Bernays, Ford's eyes had narrowed, then he had thumped the table and ordered the construction of another Independence Hall, bigger and better than the one in Philadelphia. Within Ford's improved version of the historic building the music boxes ran down.

While Ford collected his antiques in Dearborn another technological museum was in the making in Chicago. Julius Rosenwald had conceived of such a collection years earlier, but it was not until 1929 that he offered three million dollars to the city of Chicago to undertake the Museum of Science and Technology. The grateful city added five million dollars of its own and was hoping to complete it in time for the Chicago Exposition of 1933.

According to the conception, the Chicago museum was to be dynamic and functional. Wheels would move, valves seat and unseat themselves, meshing gears would cause large masses to rise and fall rhythmically, and engines would be cut open so that the workings were visible. The Rosenwald-backed project would show not just how an elevator worked, but how elevators produced modern cities. When elevators made it feasible for twenty thousand people to work in a single skyscraper, this led to the growth of subways, buses, street cars, taxis, elevated railways, and other means of urban transit, and generally to the characteristics of a modern metropolis.

One would be able to walk through five centuries of streets in two minutes. First there would be the filthy cobbles of Elizabethan England, through which any sort of gentleman would have to be borne in a chair. Then the paving would improve. Gas would come, with sewers and water mains, and street lights would appear. Finally, ablaze with light, the pavement below it honeycombed to provide conduits for pipes and electrical cables, would be Broadway. The layout emphasized systems. It was obvious, furthermore, that it consciously expressed a belief in evolution. Technology had transformed human possibilities from the pitiable squalor of London three centuries ago to the glory and promise of the Great White Way, the pinnacle of civilization. Ford and Rosenwald and most of their contemporaries believed in evolution as a basic premise. The Hebrew concept of the Promised Land, the Christian belief in the Kingdom of God, the Darwinian theory of progress in animal species all had been funneled into a belief in a constant technological evolution. It was as true of the Dearborn museum as the one in Chicago. Those who believed that they had discovered a vein of regret in Ford for a bygone age were mistaken. His museum of outmoded technology was, as conceived by his mechanistic consciousness, a hymn to progress.

The celebration of American civilization as a fusion of business and technology recurred as a motif on many occasions in 1929. Owen Young, the reparations committee chairman, explicitly stated the case at midyear when accepting an honorary degree from the State University of New York. The imagination of man, he said, "appears to be stimulated by a demand for new things. Curiously enough, it has a relation to business and to profits.

It matters not whether one speaks of Sir Walter Raleigh or Sir Francis Drake or William Shakespeare or Thomas A. Edison."

Human imagination blossomed in Elizabethan England, Young said, out of the furious commerce of the age. Great companies were organized to reach world markets. The Armada was swept from the seas and England became a world power. Almost at once, the population of London tripled, and as wealth increased, a civilization was created. In the next half-century a language and a literature flowered.

Three hundred years later another burst of human creativity occurred. This time its bent was technological. "Graham Bell comes with the telephone, Edison with the electric lamp and a system to work it," Young said. "Power, whether developed by steam or water, once stationary, is now mobile. The motor car replaces the horse, the flying machine conquers the air, and radio waves, knowing no physical barrier, become carriers of the valuable intangibles of life to all people everywhere." The modern counterparts of Shakespeare, Marlowe, Ben Jonson, and Milton, he concluded, are the physical researchers. "There may be enough poetry in the whirr of our machines," he said, "so that our machine age will become immortal."

Henry Ford was the exemplar of technological society. "He has had more influence on the lives and habits of this nation than any man ever produced in it," Will Rogers wrote in his newspaper column on July 30, 1929, Ford's sixty-sixth birthday. ". . . So good luck, Mr. Ford. It will take a hundred years to tell whether you helped us or hurt us, but you certainly didn't leave us like you found us."

Despite general approval of the ascendancy of the machine, concerns were occasionally expressed about the social effects of Ford in particular and technological advance in general. "Much as I believe in the automobile as a social and business necessity in modern life, I cannot fail to see it also as a force in breaking up the home," Archdeacon Joseph Dodshon of New York reluctantly admitted in February 1929. The auto, he continued, had taken the place of the red-light district in many American cities, and some college presidents, in an effort to preserve moral standards, had banned autos from the campus. In its portrayal of criminal life, he concluded, the motion picture was probably even a more formidable enemy of the home.

In the meshings of Ford's mind there was no gear that represented the bad effects of technology. In spite of evidence to the contrary, he believed that technology would reinforce his own puritanical code of behavior. In May, while collecting doodads and gimcracks for his museum, Ford stopped in Washington to have lunch with the president. "Absolute Prohibition must come," he proclaimed afterward to reporters. "The law must be strictly enforced, and the country made absolutely dry. The present progress in the United States is due greatly to Prohibition, and the development of aviation calls for a dry nation."

"Why aviation?" a reporter asked him.

"No one wants to ride in an airplane with a drunken driver or ship anything by such a plane where there is a possibility of liquor causing an accident," he said. "We do not want airplanes flying over us with intoxicated pilots in command. Also, airplanes are used for smuggling liquors and, therefore, the control of the liquor problem revolves around aviation directly." He denied the rumor that he intended to abandon automobile manufacture and devote his energies solely to aviation.

A new technology always produced initial resistance. In the case of the automobile, class antagonisms had broken out. "When the automobiles were first introduced the farmers were hostile to them," Congressman Robert H. Clancy, whose district included Detroit, remarked at hearings held earlier in the year. "They regarded them as a sort of blowgun sent out by the city people to kill their chickens, and so forth; and I remember that they used to throw tacks on the roads."

But in time the plaything of the rich became the necessity of the farmer. "I think that the members of the House were surprised," he continued, "to get the information a couple of years ago that there are more automobiles per capita in Iowa, an agricultural state, than in any other state in the union, and of course, the automobile had this—I will not say persecution—criticism and analysis and regulation from the ruralites at first, but they have passed that stage. I think the radio is in that stage now. The same was true with regard to the movies; they were opposed to them; and the same was true with regard to aviation. They aimed to kill the United States air mail, and one of those men was from Texas, which would profit most by aviation—a large state without adequate roads or adequate railroads. But now aviation has passed that stage, due to Lindbergh and General Mitchell and the various trans-Atlantic fliers."

After the resistance wore off and full production began, the new technology became an element of the American Way. Big business and technology ran parallel, like the red and white stripes in the flag. Some intellectuals grumbled that the machine would produce a faceless society. Hoover, when still secretary of commerce, addressed himself to that.

"From the savings made by greater efficiency in production—that is, in the time we have saved from other occupations—we have added the automobile and the good road, the movies, the radio and the phonograph directly to the standard of living," he said. "We have increased the diffusion of electric light, power, telephone, plumbing, better housing, and a dozen other things. Some feel that in all this we are deadening the soul of men by machine production and standardization . . . I may observe that the man who has a standard telephone, a standard bathtub, a standard electric light, a standard radio, and one and a half hours' more daily leisure is more of a man and has a fuller life and more individuality than he has without the tools for varying his life."

To the foes of standardization, fifteen million Model T Fords, all black and completely interchangeable, might appear as an American nightmare. Yet fifteen million owners had gladly bought them, pleased that their parts were so easily replaceable. Young spoke of technology in terms of romance; thinkers and philosophers glorified it; but the plain truth was that everybody wanted it. Everybody hoped that technology might continue to prosper and pour out more goods upon them.

On the day of Ford's dinner, a parade of crude-looking men on hasty errands were entering and leaving a two-story frame building in Atlantic Highlands, New Jersey. Autos could be seen driving down from the hilltop on which it stood, over a winding dirt road that was the sole access to it. From the cupola a man kept a lookout over the wide clearing, which no one could approach without being seen. The house was a link in the Capone organized crime empire, but the only unusual outward sign—and one had to possess sharp eyesight to see it—was a fine wire that ran diagonally from a second-story window to the foot of a tree one hundred fifty feet away.

Within, the upstairs was devoted to radio transmission and reception. Next to the transmitting room a man in work clothes, standing at a bench, repaired radio equipment. Behind him was arrayed a storeful of spare parts. The radios maintained communication with six ocean-going vessels and a fleet of small boats; the operation had enough trucks to distribute ten thousand cases of liquor a week up and down the Eastern seaboard. Several of the bay windows were protected by metal sheeting for use as machine-gun emplacements. Not wanting to take a chance on breakdowns, the ring had five different styles of receiving sets, designed for operation under varied meteorological conditions.

If law enforcement had the technology first, the underworld was not far behind and was willing to innovate to pull ahead in the use of hardware. The more crime organized itself into Big Business, the more ready it was to purchase and operate the technology it needed. "Ford and his mass production," Will Rogers noted, "is where the bootleggers got their ideas."

At fifty-seven, Thomas W. Lamont was tall, slim, fair, with a full head of white hair. Inside this distinguished structure was an Anglophile sensibility, a cultured bearing, and a well-spoken manner. He looked every inch a member of the House of Morgan, for they were a pedigreed breed. Lamont was more than a partner. He was the brains of the firm, and, especially in the non-European connections—in such heathen lands as China, Japan, and Egypt—he was chief diplomatic emissary. A former newspaperman, he regularly contributed his thoughts on various subjects to magazines. In 1929 he wrote chiefly about the virtues of an international bank. He handled the press with aplomb. As spokesman for the House of Morgan, he took on a task that Morgan detested. Owen Young was allied with the House of Morgan and he and Lamont often worked together. That spring in Paris they had occasion to confer on an undertaking of great consequence.

Early in the year RCA had created a subsidiary and stacked it with such directors as Young, Sarnoff, and Paul Cravath, the Wall Street lawyer. It was called RCA Communications, Inc., and it held the company's radio–telegraph business. While Lamont and Young were in Paris carving out that big war settlement—Lamont was an alternate delegate to the Committee of Experts and Morgan's chief aide—plans were made to sell RCA Communications to International Telephone and Telegraph. It was an easy matter and disposed of quickly. Young represented RCA, Lamont represented ITT, and the House of Morgan was the banker for both.

Such business affairs, however, had become overlaid with the complication of government, and so by October it was established that Young would be coming up before a congressional committee to explain the proposed merger. Young's philosophy, however, was no secret. In Young's view competition in the field of communications, which was so delicately interrelated, would not work. Air communications should properly be a monopoly, in a single set of hands, under governmental regulation, like a public utility. In this field, competition was ruinous and wasteful, he contended. He would prefer to have the government take over the cable-radio field outright rather than live under competition. Great savings in expenses, overhead, and management could be effected by combination. Useless and expensive duplications could be avoided in circuits and plant investments. Young knew what he would say; he had been saying the same thing about every combination, every monopoly that came up in his bailiwick.

Lamont's view was even more elevated. Like so many of the partners in the House of Morgan, and indeed many in that rarefied social class, he had a certain overt disdain for money and mundane matters. He was, therefore, for all his travel and experience, perversely naive. In such a state of lofty innocence, it appeared to him that everything he did was for the most high-minded and purest of motives. What he and Young were undertaking that spring was, in his eyes, not a mere business deal but a public service of the highest order. The world was being netted into a vast, all-encompassing communications system, and great interests and great nations were engaged in getting their strands connected first. Thus, Young and Lamont solemnly assured the Hoover administration, the merger was not aimed at stifling competition, but at meeting it: namely, the competition of the great British wire–wireless octopus that would entangle the world if RCA–ITT did not merge and close ranks.

Lamont and Young made it sound urgent, as though it should have been done long ago. The only problem was that it was illegal. The agreement Young and Lamont had signed was a violation of the White Act of 1927, which specifically extended the Sherman Antitrust Act to include communications companies. The agreement could not take effect unless the government changed the law. To that purpose RCA officials in October were preparing to appear before a Senate committee to advise that all laws interfering with the company's plans be repealed at once. It was the government's patriotic duty to do so.

Shortly before the World War began, Owen Young had received a call from Guglielmo Marconi asking him to stop by. When Young, then GE's general counsel, met Marconi at the Holland House, the great inventor told him that the British Marconi Company was interested in buying the Alexanderson alternator. Young replied, in that low-pressure style for which he was famous, that he would have to take the question back to GE to kick it around a little.

The first thing Young did when he returned to his office was find out what an Alexanderson alternator was. Young was a lawyer, not an engineer, and knew little of such matters. He soon learned that what Marconi wanted was valuable indeed.

Dr. Ernst F.W. Alexanderson had been developing a new high-frequency radio transmitter. What he had come up with was more effective in relaying signals for long distances than any previous transmitter.

Before Marconi could make a deal the war intervened, and he was called into the Italian service. When the U.S. entered the war the Navy took over all radio patents—those belonging to GE, Westinghouse, AT&T,

Western Electric, and others. Development continued quickly under that pressure. America could not have conducted such a long-range war, a huge land engagement fought on the other side of the Atlantic, without radio to maintain communication between field generals and national leaders. "It was the war which brought radio into its own," Alexanderson recalled later. "Before the war it had been interesting. With the advent of the war it became vital."

After the war Marconi resumed talks with GE about purchase of the Alexanderson alternator. In April 1919, two highly placed American naval officers turned up at GE to talk in private with Young. When he emerged, Young had changed his mind about the sale to Marconi.

The Navy still held all the patents. With such control, the development of radio would be smooth, without lawsuits or competition. The control of radio should belong to the U.S., not to the British, who already had control of cables. President Wilson himself, Young was informed, was concerned about this matter.

Young, in a series of brilliant maneuvers with Marconi, the U.S. government, and other electronics manufacturing companies, created a new company to hold the patents and named it the Radio Corporation of America. With the formation of RCA Young established his reputation. Every leading technician and official of RCA was a reserve officer of the Army or Navy, and the company was geared for instant conversion to war duty as an arm of the government. An Admiral sat as an *ex officio* member of the board of directors and served as a liaison with government. The Commerce Department under Hoover had fostered it and approved its operation. The State Department assumed that RCA acted with an eye ever on America's national interests. The government itself had created this monopoly for reasons that allowed Thomas Lamont, the Morgan partner, to indulge in a bit of self-congratulation. It was difficult for RCA to understand why the Federal Trade Commission had to collect seventeen thousand pages of testimony before abandoning its conjecture that RCA might be in violation of the antitrust laws.

Colonel Manton Davis, RCA's general counsel, found it hard to conceal his disdain for his company's detractors when he appeared before the House Merchant Marine Committee in 1929 to remind them that independent tube manufacturers who called RCA names were questioning "an organization created to protect American interests in time of war and in time of peace, an organization which has carried American prestige worldwide." Its policies, he said, "are dictated by Owen D. Young, honored at home and abroad and whose integrity and patriotism no one save propa-

gandists such as those who have addressed you would likely question."
When the words "radio trust" were used, RCA people stared at the
speaker as if he had spit upon the flag. RCA had rescued radio from the
threat of foreign domination. One did not question RCA. There was thus
nothing at all odd about RCA's lecture to the government about the coincidence of the company's interest and the national interest.

In 1929 the electrical giants, GE and Westinghouse, held the controlling interest in RCA. It was the ultimate symbol of the age of merger, a
merger even of the private and public sector, and it was the ultimate glamor
stock of the decade. Owen Young had outdone himself. The Navy-held
patents created what was called a patent pool, which the participating
companies shared. The radio industry was thus in large measure rescued
from the wearisome and debilitating court battles that had attended the
development of other technologies. With more than one thousand engineers engaged in developing radio, RCA had made the United States the
radio capital of the world and changed the course of the century. The
patent pool, they argued, did not monopolize radio. It created radio.
The patent pool did not restrain trade. It removed trade restraints.

Behind the merits of this argument lurked a ruthless and monolithic
bent of Big Science that had to be understood in terms of power. RCA
hired away all the engineering talent it could find for its huge research
laboratories. Much of this research was devoted to turning out inventions
to be rushed to the patent office and jealously guarded so that whenever an
outsider came up with something new, the radio trust could claim en-
croachments on their patents. The continuing relationship with government was used to exclude the unanointed. Lee De Forest's radio company
was consistently passed up in bidding for Navy contracts in favor of radio-
trust companies that submitted higher bids. "The reason given," one of
De Forest's former employees told a congressional committee, "was that
Government officials considered the apparatus of the other companies to
be superior . . . although in each case I had agreed to supply apparatus
that fully met the specifications of the government."

The Navy held a number of patents with which it could have challenged RCA's claims to primacy, yet it chose not to move. It was Navy
policy to do nothing that might disturb the RCA monopoly. RCA was able
to refuse to sell transmitting tubes to owners of broadcasting stations who
built the rest of their apparatus instead of buying it from RCA. RCA was
able, because of other patents that radio setmakers needed, to compel
them to put RCA tubes in their sets. The RCA trust was able to force
manufacturers to pay royalties not only on the sets they made, but on the

cabinets in which they were placed and the packing cases in which they were shipped. It placed spies in De Forest's laboratories, and when they were discovered it was explained that they were not there to steal secrets but to make sure RCA patents were not being used surreptitiously by De Forest. These activities did not lower the price of tubes. Some, including De Forest, called them outrageously high. The independents fought back; De Forest won a series of court victories in 1928 and 1929 and proclaimed better and cheaper tubes on the way. But the chances for victory for the independents against such a giant were dim. RCA controlled the technology and used its power in ways that did not increase volume and decrease prices. The Young–Swope philosophy (control volume, stabilize prices) was in opposition to the tradition of Schwab and Ford, of higher volume and price-cutting. RCA lusted after the control of all radio, and that control rested on higher prices. It had become omnipresent and omniscient.

Technology had become a national resource. The Navy had decided that monopoly was good for radio technology and had placed it in specific hands, judging that the Siamese twins of Big Business and Big Technology would thus be nourished—but the Navy had no tradition of popular review, popular input, or popular control. The Navy also had no conception of rates, of business cycles, of profits, or of how to regulate a public utility in the public interest. Business and technology were being rationalized in undemocratic ways.

Patents lay at the intersection of business and technology and made inventors weep. Improvements to the telegraph, the phonograph, the motion picture camera, the electric light—patent disputes over all of them through the years had turned Edison's hair white. Alexander Graham Bell and Elisha Gray had fought over the telephone. Isaac Merrit Singer had to pay heavily for his own sewing machine. America was not a land of law, the inventors said, it was a land of lawyers. The most revealing episode in the patent wars was the battle of Henry Ford against the Selden "road engine."

George Baldwin Selden applied for a patent for his invention in 1879, but he was in no hurry. The life of a patent was limited to seventeen years, and the car was still years away from development. For many years, therefore, he avoided being issued a patent by numerous amendments and improvements to the original application. He could afford to wait. His protection dated from the application date, but the seventeen-year right to control it began to run out only after it was granted.

In 1895, when the time for the automobile had ripened, Selden pushed for his patent and upon receiving it, without ever having made a car based on it, he established the Association of Licensed Automobile Manufacturers. His patent covered all internal-combustion engines; anyone who wished to make one had to pay royalties to Selden and his partners. Ten companies signed up, but Ford's was not one of them. To him it looked like just another trust, organized by Wall Street financiers for their usual aim of getting something for nothing.

Soon after the Ford Motor Company began operations, Ford and his partner, James Couzens, met with association representatives at the Russell House in Detroit. A spokesman for the association said Ford was infringing on the patent and proposed that he join and pay the royalties. "Selden can take his patent," Couzens shouted, "and go to hell with it." An association official warned that suit could be brought immediately. "Couzens has answered you," Ford said. The association thereupon threatened to lay waste the Ford Motor Company. Ford leaped from his chair, shook his finger at the official in a fury, and hissed, "Let them try it!"

The court battle began in 1903 and lasted eight years. Eventually the U.S. Circuit Court ruled for the Selden group. Legal costs, damages, and payment of back royalties loomed to push Ford into bankruptcy. The Selden group could put him out of business simply by denying him membership.

Selden and his Wall Street partners took out advertisements threatening Ford's customers with prosecution. Answering with his own campaign, Ford offered to post a bond with every car sold, protecting buyers against any financial damages. Only fifty buyers ever demanded a bond, a development that underscores the public's sense of a political issue. While Wall Street cheered for the Selden group against the Detroit crackpot, the people supported Ford as their champion. In 1911 the Court of Appeals shattered the Selden monopoly with a decision that said his patent only covered two-cycle motors. Ford's was a four-cycle motor.

Firestone was on Ford's side. He was fighting a tire patent at the same time, and common outlook brought the two men together. In 1906 Ford placed an order with him for eight thousand tires—at that time the largest automobile order ever made. Ford decided patents were immoral and ran for the Senate in 1918 on a platform that included the abolition of all patent laws.

Technology is mistakenly regarded as only peripherally involved in American politics; yet it is the issue that strikes the American nerve. Here, on one occasion, the issue was clear. The people were involved. They supported Ford. They wanted cars.

The Hoover inauguration in March 1929 was brought off with something novel in news coverage—broadcasting that was switched from one spot to another. Graham McNamee of NBC took his microphone with him into the sentry box at the north portico of the White House, describing the callers as they arrived to bid goodbye to the departing president. Then NBC switched to an announcer flying over the Washington Monument. They heard a description of President and Mrs. Coolidge leaving the White House, then heard crowds cheering Hoover as he appeared in the street. They heard a corps of announcers describe the parade's formation and procession—some at vantage points along Pennsylvania Avenue, some at the Peace Monument, some from a booth on the Treasury steps. A microphone was poised near Hoover as Chief Justice William Howard Taft administered the affirmation of office (as a Quaker, Hoover would not take an oath). They heard the first broadcast ever of a vice president being sworn to office in the Senate Chamber. They even heard a transcontinental transmission: the program was switched to Palo Alto, California, where the Stanford University orchestra and chorus serenaded two of its graduates, the president and first lady, at lunch a continent away.

Sam Pickard was aloft for CBS, describing how the cowboys, Indians, veterans, and marching bands looked in a drenching rain. H.A. Bellows listened from the ground on earphones. They were both former members of the Federal Radio Commission who left to work as CBS announcers. The new chain, in its rivalry with NBC, was attempting to add strength to its Washington coverage. "We had feared the roar of the motors," Bellows said of Pickard's description, "but this really formed a realistic background. The reception was fine and the voices from the plane clear and distinct." The NBC air broadcast was also acclaimed. The NBC chain used the Army Air Corps' flying laboratory, a tri-motor plane with radio equipment, to fly in from Wright Field in Dayton, and corps officials said it set a new standard of voice quality in broadcasting from airplanes.

By the time the inaugural ball ended, according to NBC, about sixty-three million people around the world heard the day-long program. The audience, which included Byrd's Antarctic party in Little America, was the largest in all human history. Coolidge, four years earlier, had been the first president inaugurated on radio, but radio sets in 1925 had been a novelty owned only by the wealthy.

Some people went to theaters to listen. Patients at Walter Reed Hospital and at many others around the nation heard it in wards. People dropped in for lunch at restaurants that had advertised their radio receiving facilities. In many cities pupils in the public and private schools heard the ceremonies as part of the day's lesson in civics. In some cities the municipal auditoriums were opened for people to listen to broadcasts over loudspeakers.

Despite some blown fuses and losses of transmission there were surprisingly few difficulties. The most disappointing failure was that the short wave to England ran into trouble just as Hoover began his address, and after fifteen minutes of continuous fading the British Broadcasting Company abandoned the attempt.

Both NBC and CBS called the broadcasts the most successful and most intricate ever attempted. The razzle-dazzle was possible because of technical apparatus not available until recently, and advance planning of each segment of the broadcast. The networks were busy for several days in Washington getting ready, and NBC said it set at least thirty microphones around the city. More than a thousand people, including announcers, technicians, aviators, messengers, and people to keep tangles out of the pickup lines, took part in a mission with as many specialized facets as an expeditionary force. The world would never be the same again.

Radio broadcasting had come from nowhere to engulf the nation in less than five years. A decade earlier only a few pioneers like De Forest and Sarnoff had any vision of broadcasting. Radio was regarded then as a medium for ships at sea and for private messages. Suddenly it had become the most pervasive means of mass communications ever known, and by 1929 there were nine to ten million sets in operation. A witness before the House Merchant Marine Committee that year called it "God's greatest gift to the twentieth century."

A new concept was being tried, called "superpower." In November of 1928 the Federal Radio Commission licensed forty radio stations to broadcast at extremely high wattage. The little stations believed that they were being squeezed off the dial and that these superpower stations were an attempt to create national radio stations. The superpower stations protested that no signal was powerful enough to broadcast across the entire nation and that the superpower experiments were concerned with providing a more reliable signal in a limited radius.

The superpower stations were right about that, but more important was the shape that the debate was taking. The Radio Commission was turning for advice to the leading radio engineers of the nation. These engineers by no coincidence worked for Westinghouse, RCA, GE, American Telephone & Telegraph. Only these companies had the money to invest in superpower experiments. The radio giants were inexorably drifting into control of the airwaves. The giants were the very group that the Radio Commission was supposed to be regulating.

"We believe the certain tendency of high power, cleared channels and chain hookups is to centralize and monopolize the industry," said a lawyer for a labor radio station before the House Merchant Marine Committee in 1929, "[and] that the ultimate result will be to eliminate the smaller stations, to force all the rest into chains and central control, and to place in the hands of a few corporations the power to select the kind of message that shall flow daily into the homes of the land. The power to do this insures the power to dominate the thoughts, habits and culture of the nation. Granted that their musical programs are superb, that their talent is the best in the world, that at the present time there is no harmful propaganda, still, is it in the public interest, necessity and convenience for all the people of this nation to be dependent for their radio programs on the city of New York and on a few great corporations?"

One of the "chain hookups" sent its president from New York to Washington to assure the committee that it was no danger to the republic. Merlin Aylesworth, head of the National Broadcasting Company, said NBC was a dinky little operation that owned a single radio station in New York and managed two others. But it was not NBC's physical assets that made it powerful. With its new rival, the Columbia Broadcasting System, the two chains had signed up one hundred eight stations in seventy cities coast-to-coast—all the more impressive because the first coast-to-coast telephone call had been made only fourteen years earlier.

The chains were the real superpower. They could do what no single station, whatever its wattage, could do. They could broadcast all over the nation, not over the air but through telephone trunk transmissions hooked to individual stations. In late 1928 the American Tobacco Company became the first firm to sponsor a national network program, and since then eleven other companies had joined the trend by the time of the hearings in early 1929. Idaho farmers and New York playboys were swaying to the same rhythms and reaching for a Lucky instead of a sweet.

"Radio has helped to create a vast new audience of a magnitude which was never dreamed of, which weighs and judges our political and social speakers, our musicians and our educators," Owen Young wrote in a 1929 report for RCA. "This audience, invisible but attentive, differs not only in size but in kind from any audience the world has ever known. It is in reality a linking-up of millions of homes."

He may have been thinking about his own political possibilities when he added: "Radio is exerting a profound effect upon our national life. No illustration is more strikingly significant than the appearance of radio on the stage of politics. There is a psychological difference which the political speaker must take into account when he addresses not a closely packed and often hysterical mass meeting in an auditorium, but this vast invisible audience coolly sitting in judgment around the family fireside . . . Let us consider the effect upon those sections of the country where, through habit or convention, one or the other of the great parties has had a practical monopoly of the political stage. In some cases the rival party has virtually never had a hearing. It is radio that evens the scales and affords a fair hearing to both sides. Who can say what radio may not accomplish in destroying sectionalism and creating a new national unity?" What some worried about as the standardization of people, others perceived as a new strong national unity.

The chief public argument about radio in that time was not control, however, but advertising. Important figures in education attacked it as vulgar. Some Congressmen suggested that we might re-examine the practice of allowing salesmen to hawk their wares over the air. Others disagreed.

"Radio in America had a birth by advertising," a member of the Federal Radio Commission told the House Merchant Marine Committee in January. "It is well birthmarked and it has grown now to manhood from the stripling, so that it now looks like the thing that gave it birth." Although there were complaints—some about the plugging of fraudulent securities over the air and much fuss about false claims in the Lucky Strike cigarette advertisements—radio advertising, he said, was generally well-behaved. The superpower clear-channel experiment, he said, showed the dominating role of advertising, for he saw it as geared to reach larger audiences so that news of products would billow outward to the farthest reaches of Radioland.

The commissioner contended it would be a mistake to forbid advertising, which pays for entertainment. The only alternative, he said, would be to charge listeners for the programs. To the Merchant Marine Committee, which had maintained congressional oversight of radio since its days as a means of ship-to-shore communication, those seemed the terms of the argument. Then Merlin Aylesworth, NBC president, presented a strikingly different view. Radio and advertising, he told the committee, are two separate phenomena. As far as NBC was concerned, advertising was a byproduct, an appendage, an afterthought tacked on to radio's grander scheme.

Aylesworth had an enviable job. NBC did not have to make a profit.

Its owners showed little interest in whether it came out in the black or the red.

A couple of years earlier Aylesworth, then an executive with the National Electric Light Association, was summoned to the office of GE Chairman Owen Young. He was told that GE, Westinghouse, and RCA were forming a new company called the National Broadcasting Company. Aylesworth was going to be its president. Young said he had no idea how the company was going to support itself and indicated that he did not think it could. But that was of slight importance. Forget about it, he told Aylesworth, sucking on his pipe; the main thing was to keep the public listening to the radio. He was insouciant about it. Up until that point—the interview took place late in 1926—public interest had not emerged as a problem. Radio had been a great novelty, and people would listen to anything. In time, however, the novelty would wear off. New programs had to be designed and broadcast to keep people glued to the set. They would keep buying radios and tubes and equipment, and plunk their money down for improved models when they were marketed. What GE, Westinghouse, and RCA wanted was a company that developed program content.

NBC had begun to show signs of making profits, but the radio giants were not overly interested. They had grander notions. Up to that point they had just been trying out programs to get people to listen. The coming phase would be more ambitious. They intended to produce a magnificent American cultural awakening. People would listen to the radio and receive an education never known to a previous civilization.

"Do you suppose," one of the more skeptical Congressmen on the committee asked, "that your advertisers are going to be willing to sponsor these educational features?"

"If they do not, we will," Aylesworth replied.

"You think that the sponsors of your programs and your owners would be willing to lose money in order gradually to come to that?" the incredulous Congressman asked.

Aylesworth unhesitatingly assured him of it. Great educators and scientific talents, he said, should not be confined behind academic walls but should let their intellects run riot on the airwaves.

"If sponsors like the Lucky Strike people are willing to sponsor these things," the congressman continued, "it does not matter much to you who the sponsors are as long as they give us what we need?"

"If the sponsor is reputable and honest," Aylesworth said.

"And Lucky Strike is as reputable as anything else?"

"Why," Aylesworth said with surprise, "I smoke them."

The Congressman began to wonder whether the president of NBC was having some fun with him, and with narrowed eyes he told Aylesworth that he was not buying such bedtime stories. He demanded to know what was really behind it all.

Aylesworth realized that there was no use trying to outmaneuver such an intrepid questioner. He dropped the veil and let the House Merchant Marine Committee in on NBC's innermost ambition. The network, he said, is planning to use radio to unite the United States, to make a single nation out of this patchwork of states. And it had already begun. Around the country people were chortling at the same comics and swaying to the same foxtrots. The nation was becoming culturally homogenized.

It would be done from New York. That was the way the communications business was being established in America. Even a football game on the West Coast was run over the telephone trunk lines to the NBC Fifth Avenue studios. The Los Angeles station plugged into NBC might be a mile from the football field, but to get the program it had to apply to New York. The signal traveled transcontinentally twice, from California to New York and back again.

"I have always had the feeling and it has been borne out by my experience in the last two years that New York is naturally the center of talent," Aylesworth said. NBC encountered difficulties, he said, in originating programs out of Chicago because the talent was not there, and people wanted to hear programs from New York, not Chicago. He brightened up the session with a story about a woman who had written to NBC asking for no more jazz—she wanted to hear Paul Whiteman and Al Jolson. Everybody chuckled.

Al Jolson was "The Jazz Singer." Whiteman was the King of Jazz. The woman from outside of the big city did not know the proper terms. NBC was talking about cultural control, out of New York, in a form of stewardship exercised by Aylesworth and Young and others for the people. Another form of standardization was being created. Another form of tightly centralized control was being established. Another Big Business was growing out of an irresistible technology. Yet there was no devious plot involved. Everything had been openly revealed. Rather than a cabal of plotters, NBC was rushing to give people what they clamored for. The control was narrow, but in the direct service of democracy.

Yet there were a sizable minority of people in America who thought that Chicago had supremely exciting music, possibly the best in the country. Chicago had a cornet player named Louis Armstrong, who played a jazz quite different from what went by the same name on Broadway.

Armstrong's music was by turns tender and bawdy, sorrowful and joyful. He moved to New York in 1929, but that did not put him on the radio. Neither did Aylesworth mean uptown New York—where Duke Ellington played at the Cotton Club—when he talked about New York talent. He meant New York's official music, from Broadway, brassy, sentimental show-business music, one inch deep. That was what America was going to hear.

More wonders were still to come. In April of 1929 several guests met at the home of Dr. Alfred N. Goldsmith. On a little console cabinet, with a screen about five inches square, appeared the image of a man. He was in a studio three miles away, but he performed for over an hour, doing things that could be seen on the screen.

At times Goldsmith adjusted dials to improve the quality of the image. He called the studio and the guests saw the man at the other end answer the call. Goldsmith asked him to stroke his hair and to give other evidences that he was actually following instructions, and the man could be seen complying. When Goldsmith joked, the guests could see the man on the video screen smile. The definition was so good that at times it was possible to detect, by means of reading lips and facial expression, whether his reply to Goldsmith was yes or no. There was no sound.

The reception was so clear that when the man on television wrote "Hello" on a small blackboard the viewers could see where the chalk had slightly slipped in drawing one of the letters and had made an extraneous white line. He corrected it by thickening the line with another stroke of the chalk.

Television was regarded as the most astounding of the coming miracles. Lee De Forest was predicting that it would be in general use in five years. There was no stopping it. Light waves could be broadcast as easily as sound waves, and all the major problems of transmission, it appeared, had already been resolved. Through the work of Ernst F. W. Alexanderson at GE, Secretary of Commerce Herbert Hoover had in 1928 been the first national figure to appear on television. In February of 1929 D.W. Griffith, the film director, was seen in Los Angeles while broadcasting from the GE studio in Schenectady. Research, led by the big laboratories, was intense in television. De Forest and Alexanderson were only two of the big names interested in its development. RCA was broadcasting experimental television daily from 7:00 to 9:00 P.M. At Bell Laboratories, work was continuing on the development of color television.

No one knew what the program content of television would be, but one thing was certain. Like radio, it would be primarily an advertising medium, and the programs it presented would be interspersed with inducements to buy products.

That fall an experimental television station in Jersey City telecast a cartoon movie. It depicted the rescue of Charlot the Cat from the Bastille, because the tear in its pants was repaired with the thread of the Spool Cotton Company. The French-made film was not only the first television commercial ever broadcast, but the first animated film to be supplied with musical sound effects.

More than a half-century of research had gone into the story of Charlot. Almost fifty years earlier Edison had discovered the "Edison effect" when experimenting with incandescent lamps. Although Edison failed to explore his epochal discovery—that a negative charge of electricity collected on an extra filament or plate introduced into the vacuum of a lamp—Lee De Forest and others used the discovery to develop the radio tube for transmission and reception of radio.

Then George Eastman began to produce a substitute for glass as a medium for prints and put celluloid in easily loaded rolls for the Kodak Company. Edison induced Eastman to produce the flexible film in long strips for his movie camera and projector. All of these discoveries, plus the phonograph, were put together to make the sound film and then the sound television commercial.

Thus the various facets of electronic technology were converging in 1929 and the age of electronics was emerging. Early in the year William Fox announced that his studio was changing over exclusively to the making of sound films. Broadway was being united with the movies. Over two hundred Broadway personalities signed up with Fox and would not appear on Broadway again until their contracts expired. Among the singers, dancers, and comedians the most important name was Will Rogers, who had a two-year contract with Fox and made his first talkie in June.

RCA that year acquired the Victor Talking Machine Company. "It is clear that in the new era of electrical entertainment now expressed in broadcasting, in talking motion pictures, and in theater installations, radio and the phonograph play distinct but complementary parts," David Sarnoff said in announcing the merger. The unification, said Owen Young's protégé at RCA, would make the developing technology interchangeable. The Victor Company at Camden, New Jersey, put the sound into sound pictures and made recordings for the phonograph.

To complete its leap into entertainment, RCA acquired two creaking vaudeville circuits, the Keith and the Orpheum, and organized them into a new subsidiary, Radio-Keith-Orpheum. RKO, as it was called, now owned an army of its own entertainers. More important, it now had an armada of theaters. With movies, radio, television, records, and even theaters in its possession, RCA was the biggest entertainment giant of all time.

Rivals were also emerging. "It is hard to tell just how television will be handled," said William S. Paley, CBS president, in 1929. "Whether it will be confined to the home solely, or whether entertainment houses will also show it on the screen is still problematical . . . Let us imagine for one minute the field of the newsreel. Imagine flashing on the screen instantaneously in sight and sound a news event of major importance as it is taking place. Our imagination can run wild, I know. I only want to point out, that whatever comes, be it television or any form of new entertainment which in any way has to do with screen, stage or radio presentation, that our amalgamation of interests finds us wholly prepared to take advantage of it. And that should be a comfortable feeling of satisfaction." The amalgamation of interests to which he referred, which came at almost the same moment as the RCA-Victor merger, was the purchase of half of CBS by Paramount Pictures.

"The question of monopoly in radio communication must be squarely met," Herbert Hoover had said a few years earlier as commerce secretary. "It is not conceivable that the American people will allow this newborn system of communication to fall squarely into the power of any individual, group or combination." Yet if the president were to inquire of Lee De Forest, a fellow guest at Ford's table at Dearborn, the radio pioneer could have told him that the leaders of the radio trust—from the House of Morgan to the new board chairman of Westinghouse—were present in the room. Radio had fallen to them, entertainment was being consolidated, and nobody appeared disturbed. It gave everybody, as Paley said, a comfortable feeling of satisfaction. Despite Hoover's concern, key figures in his administration looked favorably upon such a monopoly, and the public believed that such centralized control was necessary to its continued amusement.

Whereas radio had only problems of success in 1929—such as how to create mass production and mass sales while keeping prices artificially high—aviation was faced with the need to stimulate demand.

Aviation had always been a problem technology that required injections of aid and disguised subsidies, such as the federal decision to turn airmail over to private enterprise. Nowhere in aviation, nor for that matter in radio, could be detected that spirit of laissez-faire capitalism that was supposed to permeate the 1920s. On the contrary, Hoover's Commerce Department had continuously intervened actively to help struggling industries.

The aviation industry, with the aid of Will Hays, had been organized into a trade association, and its major task in 1929 was to overcome public wariness about the airplane as a means of passenger service. Lindbergh was a godsend. Orville Wright, still alive and half-forgotten, was resurrected as a figure, to the extent that his uninspiring personality permitted. And other heroes were coming to the fore.

While he was in flight on January 27, 1929, Commander Richard Byrd discovered fourteen mountain peaks over King Edward VII Land. He named the Antarctic range for John D. Rockefeller, Jr., calling him "a man who with his great power stands for progress." Rockefeller had been a major factor in financing the expedition, along with Edsel Ford and Adolph Ochs, publisher of the *New York Times*.

A little later an aerial photographer surveying the Rockefeller Range on another flight discovered them to be only part of a majestic range stretching as far as the eye could see. Then three men of the Byrd party at Little America, including a geologist, flew to the Rockefeller Range in March to examine rock formations. The examination, it was hoped, would ascertain not only their origin and structure, but a possible connection with other mountain chains.

The Byrd expedition was the first to rely heavily on the new technology. Airplanes and radios had speeded up the process of exploration a hundredfold. For the first time, photographs of Antarctica were being taken from the air. The airplane covered large areas much more quickly than the dog sleds that had been the chief means of transportation in past polar expeditions.

At supper, Byrd learned that his three-member party had landed safely between two large peaks and were preparing to go to work. They had taken a tent and plenty of supplies and could live comfortably for some time if bad weather delayed their return. Byrd was in continuous radio contact with all his men—on ships, on planes, in encampments, and dog-sledding—and was able to direct their field movements. He was even in daily contact with his representatives in New York. Radio and airplanes had changed the character of polar exploration.

The party at the Rockefeller Range had run into terrific storms and intensely high winds. So as not to be blown away, they sometimes had to lie flat and hold themselves in place with knives and ski sticks. The gale began lifting the plane off the ground, and eventually broke tent guys that had been tied to the airplane skis. For hours and days they fought the wind, sometimes all three of them riding a bucking plane as they piled snow blocks on the skis to keep them down. Driving snow hit their faces with the bite of needles, caught on their eyelids and froze. Lumps of heavy snow swept from the mountain two miles away crashed into them.

Eventually, as they were in their tent, exhausted, a sudden gust of one hundred fifty miles an hour tore the plane from all moorings. It burst clear, its propellers turning, rose in flight, and flew backwards for half a mile then crashed on the ice, a complete wreck. The radio equipment was damaged, and although they could receive messages from Little America they could not transmit.

Anxiety increased as nothing was heard from them for days. Byrd and his men could not understand how both the standard and the emergency radio sets could be out of commission, unless the plane had crashed. But Byrd could not leave to find them because of thick overcast weather that made flying impossible. He moved about quietly, sent out dogsledding teams in a desperate attempt to reach the party, exhorted them to greater effort by radio, asked hourly for weather reports and hoped for a change in the weather, but it was too risky to go aloft.

In the Antarctic, clouds hide the horizon and merge it with the snow so that a pilot flying low to get under the clouds can lose his bearings and fly into the ground. In the air there was no way of telling if the plane were one hundred or one thousand feet up. And under such conditions a safe landing was entirely a matter of luck.

Byrd had given orders to keep a plane warmed up so that he might leave if there was a promise of even four hours of good visibility. The wind was about twenty-two miles an hour and there was little drifting when Byrd saw a chance of flying some distance eastward to the Rockefeller Range. He did not know what conditions were there. He conferred with the meteorologist, who thought the weather was as good as could be anticipated. It was 3:00 P.M. on March 18. Byrd sat down in the library and thought it over. He wore a green knitted wool hood and swung a fur hat in his hand. The flight would be a gamble, but he felt it had a chance of success. He looked up suddenly and rose. "All right, we'll try it," he said, and climbed the steps that led from the subterranean building to the surface above.

Mechanics had the motor in perfect condition. The blow torch hissed under the fireproof funnel that led to a hood covering the motor. Hot oil was poured into the tank. The hood was removed and the engine started with a sputtering and barking that soon steadied to an even, powerful roar. The pilot nursed it carefully and tested the mixture as he opened and closed the throttle, listening intently. When the radio operator had loaded the last of his equipment and the pilot had looked up with satisfaction from his tachometer, which measured the engine speed, Commander Byrd climbed in. With some difficulty the plane was moved from the bed of snow in which it had been for days and the pilot turned it up the hill for takeoff. The sky was clear over the field but olive green to the east, exactly on the plane's course.

The pilot taxied up the slope, then headed into the stiff wind. The surface was uneven and the plane bounced alarmingly, the skis badly pummeled. But the wind lifted the plane and it climbed slowly and in a few minutes had vanished.

Everyone's work was dropped, and the radio room quickly filled with men who talked over the chance of success. A brief message came that all was well, but it did not mention that the horizon was indistinguishable from the sky and the fog hid the ground and the clouds closed in. An hour and a half later word came that they had reached the first mountain. They passed another mountain but there was still no sign of the missing men.

Men around the buzzing radio loudspeaker could hear the sound of the plane's motor. Signals ticked in, dots and dashes, and looking over the radioman's shoulder as he copied the message, his pencil could be seen forming the letters: "See the plane now. Someone below waving."

A cheer went up. It was followed by concern about the other two men—whether they were dead or lying near death in the tent. They looked at each other, sucking at pipes that had gone out. "Waving and working blinker," the radioman wrote on his pad. "Landing," the pencil spelled out. There was a long period of silence.

The radioman looked up and said they had taken in the radio antenna and he could no longer hear the engine after it had been throttled down for the glide. They could only imagine the resourceful pilot, stalling in over a surface he could hardly see in the poor light. The moments dragged as the radioman twiddled his dials, turning them back and forth without results. Suddenly he picked up his pencil. "Landed OK, everyone OK," he wrote.

Men jumped up and down and pounded each other on the back until the radioman glanced up with an annoyed gesture. He was having difficulty listening for any further messages. After a short wait a message came from the plane. It was on its way back with two of the stranded men. Byrd remained behind with the third until a second flight could be made. They tumbled to their feet and ran out into the field. They waved their fur parkas and stared into the darkness. Then they started to set up kerosene lamps in two rows to guide the plane in for a landing.

Little America lay on the edge of the Great Ice Barrier and was two thousand four hundred miles from Dunedin, New Zealand, the nearest point of civilization. Yet in addition to all the contact and communication within the Byrd expedition there was continuous contact with the unfrozen world.

Reporters had worked in strange places—in airplanes, front-line dug-outs, aboard sinking ships, in burning buildings and mines, and in the mountain vastnesses of Tibet, but no reporter had a stranger beat than Russell Owen of the *New York Times*.

Owen covered a continent all by himself. Had he gone to Antarctica a decade earlier, he would have been at least a year late in getting his story to the paper. But long-distance reporting was no longer a matter of writing it when the correspondent got back. His copy was in the hands of editors sooner than that of a police reporter phoning in a story to a rewrite man. Some of his story was already set in type before he finished sending the last paragraph. As his last sentence came in from Antarctica, the first sentence was being set on linotypes in Tokyo, London, and Paris. The isolation of exploration was over. The whole world, day by day, was following the adventures of the Byrd expedition.

"Getting news on an Antarctic expedition," Owen said, "merely demands going somewhere. No matter where one goes, there is news. This country is strange and fantastic. Life is so different from anything conceived at home that everything is new by contrast. And every day something exciting happens, even though one never knows exactly where it will occur." News came to him from his own circulating, reports of dog-team drivers, pilots, and the constant stream of radio messages. The difficulty was not to get news but to keep up with it, and getting it was not half as hard as finding a quiet place to write it. There was a desperate hunt every day for Owen to find a place to be alone with a typewriter. Work was continuously going on around him; a table he was using was needed for another purpose, a phonograph was playing, conversations blossomed around him, and quarters were so close that people were usually in each other's way. Owen wrote on, trusting his copy to the vagaries of short-wave radio.

It was easier to send messages to the Antarctic than to receive them, and every Saturday the Byrd expedition would receive a special broadcast from America. One Saturday in April at 4:00 P.M.—it was 11:00 P.M. in New York—the group assembled in the mess hall. Outside it was twenty-five degrees below zero. Fog, storms, thousands of miles of land and sea, and desolate wastes of ice—the broadcast cut through all of it. General Electric's Radio Station WGY in Schenectady, a superpower clear-channel station, picked up the broadcast from Times Square and sent it over the Byrd antenna to the bottom of the world.

Invented by Ernst F.W. Alexanderson, the inventor of the Alexanderson alternator, the Byrd antenna increased the power of radio tenfold. Over the antenna that Saturday the explorers heard Ochs, the *Times* publisher, tell them that "never before in the history of newspaper enterprise has there been anything to compare with these daily reports from a remote and inaccessible part of the world. It is journalism at its best." They also heard a message from President Hoover and were told of Alexanderson's work on a new flight instrument that might help them in future Antarctic expeditions. "Through the ages," Ochs said later in an interview, "men who went into the polar regions lost touch with civilization completely. Now in a way that is almost matter of fact they listen to entertainment that is being given to them right at the other end of the world. This communication we have effected with the South Pole opens up a new era, perhaps more remarkable than any of which we have hitherto dreamed."

Yet this age of wonders may have been just a replay. "This globe has been inhabited by intelligent people millions of times, and very ancient people, I believe, were highly developed in the arts and sciences," said Henry Ford in an interview published in *McClure's* magazine in 1928. "I believe they had all or most of the things which we think are the creations of modern progress and some things that we haven't heard of. I am sure they had the automobile, the radio, the airplane—everything that we have, or its equivalent, and perhaps many things that we have yet to discover."

If there was nothing new under the sun, it was small wonder that Ford refused to pay royalties to the purported invention of Selden. Perhaps a millennium before, a priest in a Mayan temple looked up and saw a great silver bird in the sky. What happened to all these civilizations, Ford explained, is that they lacked a correspondingly advanced moral development. Perhaps, he ventured, our civilization will last longer, because the moral sense has been evolving through many incarnations and helps increase the stability of each succeeding civilization.

"I believe the time will come when man will even know what is going on in the other planets, perhaps be able to visit them," Ford said. "The mind is traveling faster than it did. Ideas circulate more freely. We make more mental progress in five years than we formerly did in a century. The distribution and reception of new ideas have been greatly increased."

One-half of the team that had created one of the modern wonders was still alive in 1929. Not only were Orville Wright's hair and moustache gray, but there was a similar cast to his flat and inexpressive face. The first man ever to fly an airplane was a surprisingly gray man who dressed in gray clothes and lived in the most ordinary surroundings in Dayton, Ohio.

Of all the ambitions that man had ever displayed, Orville and his brother had chosen the most vulnerable. At the turn of the century, the idea of a flying machine was the subject of continuous ridicule, and people who attempted it were town jokes—especially if they happened to be a couple of obscure bachelors who ran a bicycle shop. "There's no use fussin' with that thing, Wilbur," an old farmer advised. "It's against nature to fly, and even if anybody does, it won't be anybody from Dayton."

The people of Dayton underestimated the Wrights. Nobody had ever attacked the problem with the right combination of scientific genius, engineering skill, patience, and absolute courage. Wilbur Wright also brought to the task vision and a desperate thirst for glory. A brilliant future had once appeared to lie ahead for Wilbur Wright. Then, while still in high school, all of his upper front teeth and some of his lowers were knocked out in a hockey accident. The shock produced medical dysfunctions of the heart and stomach, and he remained at home, a semi-invalid, for eight years. Flying was his last chance to live up to his own adolescent dreams.

Two brothers gambled their lives on their dangerous experiments, but even after they did it, almost nobody believed it—not for almost five years.

On a spring day in 1908, five journalists were trudging across Kitty Hawk, North Carolina. The day was hot, the sand ankle-deep, and the walk tiring, but after about two hours of slogging they galloped across a narrow clearing, afraid of being seen, and dropped into cover on a scrub-timber cape. They were within a mile of the camp of Orville and Wilbur Wright.

In the distance they could see the roof of a shed. On the sand, shimmering in the heat, they could faintly make out the outline of the boxlike plane with its twin sets of wings. Swatting chiggers and speaking quietly if at all, they crawled out as near to the point of the cape as possible. They remained hidden and watched. The blurry rectangle of the plane gleamed and flickered in the sun as it was warmed up, and a throb wavered across the sand flat like a reaper working far away in a field of grain.

The newspapermen had reason to believe that if the secretive Wrights knew they were being watched they would shut down activities immediately. They remained like hunters under cover, stalking a big story.

It was the hot afternoon of May 11, 1908. No one remembers it as a date of any significance in aeronautical history, but in a sense it was. The Wrights had performed their first flight in this same area on December 17, 1903. Since then they had made countless flights in Dayton, Ohio, and had stayed aloft for long periods of time. Yet in all that time there had been virtually nothing about it in the newspapers. Many editors did not believe such spurious tales were worth the telegraph fees or the time of a reporter. The brothers, though eager to have their story told in print, were so circumspect and secretive about details and so protective about their trade secrets that they raised suspicions about the authenticity of their claims.

By 1908 the newspapers had found a new interest in the Wrights' claims, because of a burst of publicity from Europe. Two months before the journalistic expedition to Kitty Hawk, Leon Delarange had won the Aero Club prize at Issy-les-Moulineaux with a six-hundred-meter flight and in April he had flown two and a half miles. Suddenly editors were wild for aviation stories and warning reporters not to come back without them. Find those two bicycle makers from Dayton, they were told, and check their story. When a Norfolk paper reported that they were back at their old Kitty Hawk haunts, several reporters raced for the Carolina coast.

Having reached it, they were peeking from behind trees on the cape. There was little to be seen but a few half-wild razorbacks and cows wandering about. They swatted bugs and waited on that particularly bleak stretch of coast.

The throbbing in the distance increased in speed and intensity, the hazy rectangle began to rock across the sand, and the straining journalists could suddenly see air between the ground and the plane. But before it got very far, and no more than twenty feet up, the pilot saw that he was heading for a dead tree and quickly touched down again. The plane was trundled back and restarted for a second try. This time it went aloft, about sixty feet in the air, and chugged tantalizingly toward the spot where the journalists were hidden. It came closer and closer, then maneuvered a slow right turn and swept past in profile. Several cows looked up quickly and fled in terror. Unable to restrain himself, the photographer for *Collier's* jumped out of hiding, aimed his Graflex at the plane, and took the first photograph for a publication of the Wright machine in flight. Turning sharply to the right, the plane disappeared over some high dunes and came down on the farther side.

What the journalists had seen was enough for a fine, well-fleshed story. The only wire in the area belonged to the Weather Bureau and soon it was ringing with the news that the Wright brothers had a machine that would rise of its own power in sustained and serious flight. The writers cabled their stories with a tone of urgency as if they had been present at a historic event.

After producing their stunning invention they believed that great events would happen to them. But when their mansion was only half-built, Wilbur died in 1912 of typhoid, and the vision and genius went out of the partnership. Orville was left alone. The fearless flyer was timid on the ground. His misery at meeting people was so keen that most backed away as soon as possible. He had spent thirty years dodging cameras and interviews, and early ridicule had taught him to be tight-lipped.

He opened a small private laboratory for aeronautical research but little came of it, and he played no significant role in the further development of aviation. For a while he ran a drowsy little flying school. He was usually in his office in a drab brick two-story building. The interior was uninformative. The front room was a bare box, covered on its uneven floor by a faded scrap of rug. The walls were bare of pictures, the room empty of mementoes. A rolltop desk stood against one wall, a small table against another, and the room held three flimsy chairs.

Orville Wright was a Chevalier of the Legion of Honor, a doctor of technical science of the Royal Technical College of Munich. He held a fistful of degrees and an array of medals. He was a great historical figure, and no one would have considered him vain were he to remind himself of it occasionally. But the roof leaked, and on rainy days, every nine seconds, a drop of water flashed past the pale light of the window into a little pool on the floor. He watched it flash with wincing distaste.

Tired and listless, apparently in pain, he answered some of the truckloads of letters that still came to him: boys asking for advice on models, inventors trying to interest him in their own ideas, reminding him of the Wrights' long battle for acceptance, letters of admiration, and letters from cranks.

He could no longer do much traveling. In 1908, while he was conducting the first flying tests at Fort Myer, Virginia, for the Army, his plane had crashed. The result was a spine injury that sometimes caused excruciating pain, and though pillowed like a rajah in a Pullman, the journey was too rough. The bumpy landings made plane travel impossible. Yet in spite of his disability he had been getting around more during the last year than he had in the previous decade and had left Dayton on several occasions. In December 1928 the nation had observed the Silver Jubilee of Flight, and he went to Kitty Hawk for a monument dedication. On the same journey he attended the International Civil Aeronautics Conference in Washington. When Colonel Lindbergh was called to the platform to receive the

Clifford Harmon Trophy, Wright was asked to accompany him. Lindbergh offered his arm and they walked arm in arm up the aisle—the tall, lanky figure whose face was recognized all over the world and the short gray man so easily lost in a crowd.

In February 1929 the Secretary of War presented Wright with two Distinguished Flying Crosses, one for himself and one for his late brother. In May the men of the Army Air Corps, holding maneuvers at Wright Field in Dayton, leaped to their feet and applauded when he was introduced during a critique of the operation.

The Wright brothers were still not established in all quarters, however, as inventors of the airplane. Stuart Chase's *Men and Machines*, published in 1929, listed Dr. Samuel P. Langley as the inventor. In 1928 a Congressman, seeking to clear up a controversy that had lasted a quarter-century, had introduced a bill to determine what had actually been the first heavier-than-air flying machine. The source of this challenge to the Wrights was the powerful government-sponsored Smithsonian Institution, of which the late Langley had been executive secretary.

Langley had designed and built a flying machine as early as 1896 but had never been able to get it off the ground. A few days before the Wrights' first flight he had been attempting flight without success along the Potomac. The Smithsonian claimed that the Wright brothers' plane was based upon Langley's principles, a claim the brothers had always vehemently denied.

In 1914 Glenn H. Curtiss lost a patent suit to the Wrights. Among the court findings was that the Wright patent claims were entitled to a liberal interpretation because they had been the first to build a plane capable of flight. Curtiss intended to appeal and reasoned that if he could convince the court that a machine preceding the Wrights' was able to fly he would have a stronger case on appeal. Perhaps, he thought, he could get the Langley plane in the air. The Smithsonian was delighted to lend him the plane.

Curtiss, after making extensive changes in the wings, rudder, and vertical surfaces, succeeded in making several short hops of less than five seconds with the altered machine in May and June 1914. The Smithsonian was greatly pleased. "It has been demonstrated that with its original structure and power, it is capable of flying with a pilot and several hundred pounds of useful load," the institution reported. "It is the first airplane in the history of the world of which this can truthfully be said." Another report falsely stated that the Langley airplane had been flown "without modification." Even in 1929 the Smithsonian continued to maintain that the Langley machine on display was "the first man-carrying aeroplane in the history of the world capable of sustained free flight."

After years of indecision, Orville Wright in 1928 sent the Wright plane to the South Kensington Museum in London where, he said, "the plane will have its proper place and credit." That would never happen in the Smithsonian, he charged. There was no reason to believe that it would be "any safer from mutilation than Langley's had been, or that the label put on it would be any more true than the label on his."

Charles G. Abbot, the Smithsonian secretary, smarted under the attack, and arranged a meeting with Orville Wright when the inventor visited Washington. Abbot asked Wright if the plane could be returned to the United States and in the custody of the Smithsonian. Wright agreed, but only if the Smithsonian recanted its campaign of two decades of trying to make the Langley airplane look like a precursor of the brothers' invention.

Orville Wright went back to Dayton without any satisfaction from Abbot, and returned to the shadows that he preferred. He refused to write an autobiography and was annoyed when anything was written about him. He occupied himself in his office putting his brother's papers in order, so that the painstakingly recorded early data of aerodynamics that the brothers had developed would not be lost. He denied access to reporters and researchers.

Those who gave the Wrights credit for the invention of the airplane regarded Orville as co-inventor, but he never claimed to be. In the latest edition of the *Encyclopaedia Brittanica* a long article appeared about Wilbur Wright. It sounded as if he were the sole inventor, developer, and pilot of the airplane, and there was only the slightest suggestion that Wilbur even had a brother. The author of the article was Orville Wright.

Edsel and Henry Ford believed in the Wrights, and in October they sent him an engraved invitation to attend a dinner in honor of Thomas Edison. It had been a busy year for the reclusive Wright, but he decided to attend. Otherwise he lived alone, a bachelor with two servants, and every day made the short trip to his office, where he worked with a secretary, seeing no one if it could be avoided, saying nothing if he could help it, a little frightened and overcome by the world. He had long ago sold his interest in the company that bore his name. He had no talent for acquisition, and none of the millions that had gone into aviation had found their way into his pockets. For years the Wrights had tried without success to attract investment in their experiments. Charles Schwab, the great steel man, had told them flying was a pipe dream and would not back them; in 1929 he was making money speculating in aeronautical stocks. Orville

Wright was watching the puddle spread in his seedy office on a non-descript little street in Dayton. The age had chosen another hero to lead aviation—chosen on a May day in 1927 when he landed outside Paris after a thirty-three-hour trip alone in his plane out of New York.

Colonel Lindbergh, twenty-one months after his historic flight, flashed his signal lights as he headed for the Havana airport in the dark. Below, the airport personnel responded as best they could, trying to illuminate the airfield with floodlights and spotlights. His arrival was six hours late and the crowd had dwindled, but a cheer went up as the two-motored amphibious plane came to rest in a perfect landing. The U.S. ambassador shook hands with the slim, boyish twenty-seven-year-old aviator as he emerged.

Colonel Charles A. Lindbergh and his party had left Belize in Central America earlier in the day on February 12, 1929, and had been expected in Havana in early afternoon. They spent more time than anticipated, they said, making a survey of possible airfield sites for Pan-American Airways along the coast of British Honduras and Yucatán. Lindbergh was delayed further on landing in the harbor at Cozumel Island for refueling; small boats ferried gasoline to his and an accompanying plane in a tedious process that took four hours in heavy seas. When they landed again at La Fe, an isolated Cuban port west of Havana, they phoned to say that all was well and were surprised upon arrival to learn that their tardiness had caused concern around the world.

Pan-Am officials assured American newspapers through the afternoon that, despite reported bad weather over the Caribbean, there was no cause for worry about Lindbergh. When Lindbergh called the Pan-Am traffic manager in Miami to report in, a New York newspaper was talking to the manager on another line.

Pan-Am was a small but ambitious company that two years earlier had taken over a mail-passenger service from Miami to Havana, shuttling Yankees over for a Cuban vacation that included the forbidden pleasures —alcohol, roulette, and readily available women. The firm, which saw itself as the cutting edge of business expansion into Latin America, had taken on Lindbergh a few weeks earlier as a technical advisor for its latest move—the first airmail run ever from the United States into Central America.

Lindbergh was an excellent consultant, but his more obvious asset was his ability to generate publicity. The inaugural airmail flight, with him at the controls, became an event attracting world attention. When he set off on the first leg from Miami earlier in the month, more than a thousand people bid farewell to him at the airport at dawn, some of them still in evening clothes. When his plane was heard over Tegucigalpa people rushed from their homes and gathered in the streets and on the roofs, shouting "Viva Lindbergh!" as his plane circled low over the capital city of Honduras for five minutes, then dipped down over the airdrome and winged away.

When he landed in the Canal Zone a crowd broke around the plane and struggled to get a look at him. Finding it impossible to leave the plane, Lindbergh began to putter with the cargo as officials came aboard. A movie cameraman called out to him to turn, so he could get some good footage. "I haven't time now," he shouted, "I've got to check this mail." And he did. He noted carefully the number on the rotary lock of the sack of registered mail. Then he took the receipts of the postmaster, signed reports of his arrival and registration of his plane's entry, and checked out requirements with the quarantine officer. Instead of dwindling and wandering off through this wait, the crowd grew bolder and pressed closer, shouting his name. At last he had to appeal to them to move so that the plane could be pushed into the hangar.

Since his fabled success in 1927, Lindbergh had been devoting most of his time to promoting the hot aeronautics industry. He had toured the United States talking about the civic improvement made possible by airports, traveling with the financial backing of a fund for the promotion of flight. He had also undertaken, in 1928, a goodwill tour of Latin nations as a spokesman for an air link between the two American continents. That night in Havana, it was obvious that his work was succeeding.

Standing among the floodlights at the Havana airport, Lindbergh knitted his brows in a scowl as the reporters began their questions. Someone showed him an Associated Press dispatch from Mexico City in which the U.S. ambassador to Mexico, Dwight Morrow, had just announced his daughter's engagement to Charles Lindbergh.

Everything he did furthered the image of a young Mercury, but the cries of adulation, the excited crowds, and a life lived in floodlights and searchlights troubled him. His behavior grew quirky, and he would take off unexpectedly, traveling always by air, for nowhere in particular, and land wherever night came upon him.

If he walked into a building, a crowd would form waiting for him to emerge. If he threw away a corncob while picnicking at some flying show in a Midwestern hayfield, a matron would climb a restraining rope to rescue it from the garbage heap. If he sent his underwear to the cleaners it would not return. Women pinned to their walls the hotel pillowcases on which his head had rested, and tourists tore the shingles and flooring from his boyhood home.

What disturbed him most, however, was the press. He glowered at photographers when they asked him to smile and most despised the reporters who asked him his opinion of love, marriage, or girls. In Havana that night they were ready to ask him about his engagement to Anne Morrow, which he considered a private matter. "Well, I see you know all about it," he said, glancing at the Associated Press story. "I will confine my remarks to aviation."

The growing antipathy between the Lone Eagle and the press, however, had done nothing to still the enormous public interest in aviation. Most big newspapers were publishing an aviation section, and it was almost as important a subject at the barber shop as the Model A. The aviation companies were making bigger planes in expectation of the advent of passenger service. Although it seemed inevitable as soon as the technology permitted, there was still no coast-to-coast passenger flight. A new service of Transcontinental Air Transport came along that year, however, that was the closest thing to it. When it worked on schedule, the combined air-rail transport operated like this:

The customer bought a ticket in New York for Los Angeles, checked his baggage on a train, and boarded at 6:00 P.M. on a Monday evening. After a night in a Pullman, he found himself the next morning at 9:00 A.M. on a siding alongside a large airfield outside Columbus. Nearby was a new kind of building: an air-rail station. It hardly looked like the traditional railroad depot but was designed to be, as the expression went in 1929, "futuristic" or "moderne." Through the waiting room was a dining room for breakfast and beyond that a terrace from which he could watch activity all over the airport while dining. The outdoor terrace ran the full length of the station and beyond and was designed to attract people who were not yet prepared for air travel but liked to watch airport bustle while eating. In the waiting room at the center of the station there were none of the iron-armed wooden benches that filled the typical railroad station. Even in decor, this was luxury travel. The room was cushioned and as comfortable as a clubhouse.

When the plane was ready, the passenger trooped aboard to find an interior more posh than any he had ever seen before in a plane. The cabin was carpeted, curtained, had colored wall coverings and deep, comfortable chairs. Attempts, largely unsuccessful, had been made to soundproof the cabin from the roar of the engines. The passenger might also be surprised to find the pilots separated from the passengers in a separate cabin, and that talking to them was discouraged.

From a leather-cushioned seat, adjustable to a reclining position, he could press a button at his elbow for a cabin boy. The boy was there not only to serve, but to entertain. He knew all about the plane, the engine, and the route, and it was his job to satisfy the passenger's curiosity and relieve the tedium of a long flight by volunteering information about the passing scene below. He was ready with an air-sickness remedy for anyone who became ill. The plane had a two-way radio system that supplied the pilots with weather reports and other information that helped them to fly in safety.

The passenger left Columbus after breakfast, traveling with as many as thirteen other passengers at speeds up to one hundred twenty-five miles per hour. There was a fifteen-minute rest stop at Indianapolis where the airport was smaller than the one in Columbus. During the stop a passenger might leave and another join the group.

The next stop was Lambert Field in St. Louis at noon. Here, instead of embarking and debarking passengers and luggage in midfield, sometimes in the rain, and invariably on ground hazardous to the high heels of women passengers, the plane landed on a runway and taxied in under cover. Between two buildings was an arched roof, like a train shed, over a two hundred-foot-wide concrete platform, for passengers to alight. One of the buildings was for passengers, the other for administration. Passengers here ate lunch and could watch preparations for flights to Chicago and Atlanta.

The St. Louis stop lasted a half-hour and was followed by another fifteen-minute rest stop at Kansas City. By evening the passenger arrived at Dodge City. Here he had a choice—to continue by night on a Santa Fe sleeper or to try another novelty: an air sleeper that flew by night over the historic Santa Fe trail. The so-called Air Pullman would carry twelve slumbering passengers in berths convertible into seats for day travel. It traveled by following lights—blinker lights on the ground marking the course every three or four miles and giant revolving beacons every twenty-five miles.

The passenger who flew by night would reach Los Angeles Wednesday morning, coast-to-coast in about forty hours. The passenger taking the railroad would return to the air next morning at Las Vegas, New Mexico, and travel almost all day in sight of the mountains, to arrive at Los Angeles in late afternoon, in forty-six to forty-eight hours.

Lindbergh, a consultant to the company, had approved the night flight after nearly four months' study. In a larger sense, most of what was happening in air travel in 1929 was his work. His advice on building

airports had started a rush of cities to get one quickly. The advent of
passenger travel, it was believed, would cause airports (a phrase just coming into popular usage) to grow rapidly in efficiency and appearance.
Thousands of new jobs were being created; in a period of months, airmail
had quadrupled in volume; and aeronautical stocks soared. Appearing
before a joint committee of Congress that April, Lindbergh advised the
American aeronautics industry not to wait for the helicopter.

"We have at present no prospect of a commercial plane which will go
straight up and down," he said. "There may be a great many years' development before we have one which can be used economically. I believe at
the present it would be good policy to go ahead with large airports. Even if
we do go straight up and down, we will need the big fields for a larger
number of helicopters."

So they built airports. The old airfield, the cow pasture with a hangar,
was being replaced by a new use of space, at least a mile square and
representing at least a million dollars in investment.

Lindbergh was also plugging bigger airships. "I expect to see safe
transportation between here and South America soon," he told the committee. "Within a year or two we should fly direct in multi-motored ships
from Washington or New York to Buenos Aires or Rio." Based on his
recommendations, the air-rail service purchased ten Ford Tri-Motors, a
big break for Ford's new enterprise. Henry Ford celebrated in a characteristic way: he reduced his prices.

The automobile had begun to bore Henry Ford, and in keeping with
the spirit of 1929, he talked about flying all the time. Ford turned up in
December 1928 at the International Civil Aeronautics Conference—the
one at which Lindbergh and Wright walked arm in arm—to speak to the
press on the future of aeronautics, which lay with him and his Tri-Motor,
nicknamed the Tin Goose. The age of the bigger plane had dawned, and
while others hesitated he concentrated on the multi-motor plane. He was
out to dominate aeronautics as he had automobiles.

Safety development, he said with Lindbergh standing by his side in
apparent agreement, had to be the first priority now. "I've heard Mr.
Edison say that flying was five percent mechanical and ninety-five percent
man," Ford said. "We must reduce that balance, and try to reverse it."

Power control was important, he said. "A method must be found so
that an airplane can use its power in landing. That's where many serious
accidents occur. You see, when an airplane starts to land the power is shut
off and it is helpless—in the power of the elements—from that time until it
stops."

His obsession with flying began in 1927, when Lindbergh visited Dearborn and took him for his first ride, but his interest had begun three years earlier when his chief engineer, William B. Mayo, had brought around another engineer, William Stout. Ford asked Stout to choose an airfield site at Dearborn. Stout looked at several and chose a two-hundred-sixty-acre tract near the engineering labs. Ernest Liebold, Ford's secretary, objected that the site had been tagged as a housing subdivision. "Oh, Liebold," Ford responded, "maybe it was a subdivision yesterday, but it is a landing field today." Fordson tractors began grading the land almost immediately.

In April 1929 almost all Detroit turned out to see the All-American Aircraft Show at Ford's airfield. The great manufacturer himself was the leading attraction. He appeared to enjoy himself greatly, rubbing school-children on the head and talking about how the future of aviation lay with them. He seemed especially taken with the exhibits of airport lighting equipment.

About eight thousand people were at the airfield for an air circus when two planes collided in midair. The planes fell to the ground fifty feet apart, endangering the lives of hundreds of spectators who had run onto the field. The two pilots were killed and a rider in one plane was found alive but gravely injured.

About forty planes were waiting to land, but had to remain in the air as the crowd swarmed over the field. Officials in charge became alarmed and a lane was quickly cleared for the large Keystone plane *Patrician*, which landed safely. Mayo, who was at Ford's side, turned to a woman and said, "Do you wish to go up now?"

"Sure I do," replied Evangeline Lindbergh, mother of the famous flier. While the piles of wreckage were being cleared of the dead and injured, Mayo and Mrs. Lindbergh stepped into the *Patrician*. Ford waved goodbye as police and Ford employees pushed the crowd back. A frozen smile clung obstinately to his lips.

Nineteen twenty-nine was the big year of aeronautical safety, with the government and private enterprise working in tandem. Army pilots from Wright Field in Dayton had visited Schenectady to lay the problem before GE's leading research scientist, Ernst F.W. Alexanderson. Pilots were still flying with their eyes. In rain, in fog, in the dark, the pilot was helpless. Working to order, by 1929 Alexanderson, who had invented the Alexander-son alternator and the Byrd antenna, had produced a new invention called the altimeter. Using radio beams, bouncing them from the plane and back, it measured an airplane's altitude. A warning light went on when the plane was fifty feet or less above the ground. The altimeter was a novel application of the principle that objects can be located by bouncing waves off them.

"Fog flying will have more effect on future air transportation than anything else," Lindbergh told a congressional committee that spring. "We must develop air transportation to approach accuracy comparable to land travel. For landing we will be able to use, I think, intersecting radio beams, sonic altimeters and other instruments. We will be able to land on a field we cannot see. This will be tried first on the air mails and then be available for passenger travel. Fog flying is hazardous now, but I expect that within the next few years we will be able to fly through any kind of weather."

The altimeter, a major safety advance for plane instruments, was on display at the Dearborn air show of 1929. It was one more piece of hardware in the campaign to make the airplane into a means of passenger transportation. All that was needed now for the onset of the age of passenger travel was the customers. People had to vote for technology to keep it rolling on, and men like Lindbergh and Ford were attempting to lead the way. If only the damned things would stop falling out of the sky.

They had an ally in that campaign in one of the most beloved and trusted men of the time—the cowboy-humorist Will Rogers. He always traveled by air. If a person's time was worth anything to him, Rogers said, he might as well fly, and if it weren't he might as well walk. He and Lindbergh had become close friends; Rogers had spent a lot of time in Mexico with Ambassador Dwight Morrow and had been around while Lindbergh was courting Morrow's daughter. Transcontinental Air Transport hoped to have Rogers as a passenger when Lindbergh piloted the inaugural Los Angeles to New York air-rail hookup, but Rogers had been unable to make it. He had been, however, the first person ever to fly coast-to-coast round trip as a paying passenger. The flight, on regular airmail planes from Los Angeles to New York and back in four days, was no mere stunt. Rogers had to get to New York on business and wanted to return home to Beverly Hills as quickly as possible. The trip saved a full week's time.

Rogers boosted aviation constantly—in his syndicated newspaper column, on the stage, and on the lecture circuit. From 1925 to 1929 he flew nearly twenty-five thousand miles in keeping his schedule. He praised continuously the skill of pilots, the merits of ground crews, and described the rapture of being over a lighted city at night. He campaigned for airports and passenger service, and concentrated on overcoming the fear of flying. He said there was no safer way to travel. "After Lindbergh, Will

Rogers is aviation's best press agent," one aeronautics manufacturer said. "The industry owes him more than he is ever likely to collect."

On one of Rogers' tours the pilot lost his bearings and they landed in a field to find out where they were. The predicament so impressed the humorist that he undertook a campaign for all towns to identify themselves so as to be seen from the air and offered to pay for the paint. The response was startling, and he was soon inundated with paint bills from all over the nation, some of them asking for the money in advance.

"Well," he lamented, "right there is where I stepped into paint plum up to and over my financial neck. Say, Sherwin Williams didn't have enough to have supplied the demand. I started with an awful poor idea of the number of towns in this country. I sure did mean well, but I just gnawed off more than I could chew. For instance, Pontiac, Michigan, sent me a bill for ninety-eight dollars. I thought somebody must be going into the paint business up there. But they told me they had some pretty big buildings up there. If they've got buildings that big, however, I'm going to fly up there and land on 'em someday. The *Saratoga* ain't that big, and all the Navy lands on it."

He was forced to limit his offer to towns with four-letter names, then to three-letter names, and eventually he offered only to supply the paintbrush. But it started something. The Kansas Legislature adopted a law requiring every town in the state to brand itself so as to be seen from the air, and other states had similar bills before them in 1929 for consideration.

When Lindbergh nearly crashed while flying with his new fiancée, Rogers congratulated both of them for going back up again as soon as possible. "I knew he would," Rogers wrote in his column. "Flying is Lindbergh's business. He spent years perfecting himself at it. Because he tips over on his nose once out of a million miles, a lot of editorial writers start howling about it." Rogers had been in two crashes himself, but he said that he intended to keep flying until his beard became caught in the propeller.

He traveled by air on his way to the big dinner for Edison, and when he reached Chicago, he learned that his flight to Dearborn had been cancelled because of the heavy rain. He located a pilot willing to take him in a two-seater, and soon they were aloft.

When they reached the Dearborn airfield they found no lights on and they had no way of signaling to the ground. They circled the field a few times, stuck in the sky. The pilot said the only course open was to return to Chicago.

As the plane circled over Chicago, the pilot passed a note back to

Rogers. The plane, he wrote, was running on empty and he should brace himself for an emergency landing. Rogers was sure that they would hit something, but the pilot, with the help of some flares, located an empty lot, and the little plane headed for it. When the wheels touched down, Rogers sighed with relief.

Roaring across the vacant lot the wheels struck something and the plane flipped over, throwing Rogers against the side of the craft and stunning him. They were in the middle of Chicago. The pilot helped him out of the plane and they hailed a passing taxicab. When the driver asked him where he wanted to go, his head was still confused. "Chicago," he said.

"Well, buddy," the cabbie said, "you're in Chicago now."

A doctor strapped up his side, but he managed to get out his newspaper column. "Got an invitation from Henry Ford to come to Dearborn tomorrow," he wrote. "Was headed over there and ran into a thick fog and had to come back here . . . Old Chicago might be wicked, but that lighted field looked mighty good at night, and I sure want to thank Mr. Edison for inventing those little things." The Ambassador of Flight did not mention his accident—one did not joke with the future of aviation at stake.

On a Sunday afternoon in March 1929, a Newark motorcycle policeman watched a plane struggling in the sky. It was a Ford Tri-Motor and two of its engines were out. He jumped on his motorcycle and sped along the South Street ramp into the state highway across the meadows, in the direction of the crippled plane.

The plane was in service at Newark Airport as a sightseeing craft over the lower bay and downtown section of Manhattan and then, with a wide half-circle, over Fort Lee and back to the airfield. The thirteen passengers had paid five dollars each for a twenty-minute excursion ride.

The plane climbed painfully and appeared overloaded at seventy-five feet up. The pilot turned it slightly to the south, barely clearing the roof of a factory. It was unable to get more than two hundred feet up and then ran into an erratic wind.

The pilot decided to land wherever he could. He looked at the ground, looming up quickly as the plane lost altitude, but he could see no safe ground—only the treacherous marshes, the criss-crossings of railroad tracks, embankments, and telephone wires.

The plane was traveling about seventy miles an hour when it hit an iron flatcar on the tracks. The impact tore off the cockpit, and the pilot and a friend riding in it were pitched to the other side of the flatcar in the cockpit.

Officials of the transport company said the plane had not been over-loaded, but the Department of Commerce insisted that the Tin Goose was licensed to carry only fourteen persons. The plane had fifteen. The management, measuring load limits in pounds, claimed that it was flying with a safe load margin.

It was the worst airplane crash ever on American soil and tied the world record set in Rio de Janeiro in 1928. Fourteen were dead and the pilot seriously wounded.

Six months after the Newark crash, another Tin Goose—one of the ten purchased by Transcontinental Air Transport for its air-rail service—was in trouble in the Southwest.

Borrowing a plane, Lindbergh and his new wife left from New York, arriving in St. Louis in less than three hours. When they landed there were reports that survivors may have been sighted, but no further confirmation came, and it was believed that they may have been excited Navajos who had never seen an airplane before.

On the following day, as the Lindberghs flew to New Mexico, there were forty planes in the air looking for the wreckage of the *City of San Francisco*, the missing tri-motor. Hope was still being held out that the giant liner may have reached earth safely in the inaccessible regions of northern Arizona or western New Mexico, where they would be stranded and unable to reach civilization. The Navajo and Hopi Indians, it was said, shunned localities in which there were dead and sealed their lips against the finding of any bodies. It was feared that the superstition might mean that the crash had gone unreported if it occurred in Indian country.

By the time the Lindberghs reached the airfield at Winslow, New Mexico, the wreckage had been found. There seemed little hope that any of the eight aboard, passengers and crew, had survived.

Before the Lindberghs landed a pilot found the burned wreckage on the south side of Mount Taylor. He spotted the left wing of the plane lying upside down; the rest of the plane lay about one hundred yards beyond.

Ambulances and searchers left from Grants, a little town of three hundred people. Pack teams were organized in the mountains. The following day, the bodies of the passengers and crew were reached. They were all burned beyond recognition. They were placed on the backs of horses for the trek down the mountain. Ambulances met the pack team at the Canyon Lobo station.

While a Mexican orchestra, with an accordion carrying the melody, played a few doors up the dirt street of Grants, an inquest was held in the

Red Ball Garage. A woman was identified by her jewelry; a man by a Masonic ring; the crew by their blackened gold buttons; the last by elimination. The left wing had apparently been torn off when it struck a tree. There had been speculation, but no evidence, that the pilot had tried to turn back for Albuquerque in a severe local electric storm. It looked as if the plane had failed to gain enough altitude. As had happened in the Newark crash, the aeronautics bureau of the Department of Commerce undertook an investigation. The federal government was taking a great interest in airplane crashes that year.

Transcontinental, which had discontinued all operations while searching for the wreck, undertook plans to restore service, but passenger air travel took a dip. That was only due, it was said, to the decline in travel now that Labor Day had marked the end of summer vacations. The crash came just as Roger Babson predicted another catastrophe, this one on Wall Street. The nation's leaders assured all once again that there was nothing wrong with the stock market. It was, however, having some trouble gaining altitude.

Nor were plane crashes the only new way that technology had provided in which to perish. Mrs. Quinta McDonald, a thirty-four-year-old mother, had worked for several years at the United States Radium Corporation plant in Orange, New Jersey, and on the day of the dinner at Dearborn she was dying at New York's Memorial Hospital. Like many of the women who worked at the plant, applying luminous paint to watch dials, she often used to point the paint brush end with her lips. That was probably why the first pain most of the women experienced was toothache. The sore limbs and chronic fatigue followed later. One fellow-worker was growing lame; another had maddening toothaches; a third had undergone a series of jaw operations. They were radioactive and eventually they would all die of it, their skeletons slowly burning away.

Technology produced breakdown as well as development, and to systems as well as to individual people. It created congestion and ate up natural resources; it produced fearsome weapons for the next war and created an increasingly vulnerable society that could be crippled by power failure, natural disaster, or strike. But most people were no more disheartened by technology's death tolls than by its effect on moral standards. The dominant answer, in many of the leading magazines of the time, was that when scientific minds like Edison's and Ford's ruled the world, the cure for technology's harmful effects would be solved—by more technology. Applied science would in time solve all problems.

It would end work. "Human slavery will not have been fully abolished until every task now accomplished by human hands is turned out by some machine," Edison said. He suggested late in the year that a machine should be invented to take a piece of cloth at one end and produce a suit of clothing at the other. "We have the Naval Academy and the Military Academy to develop sailors and soldiers," he said. "Why should we not have a government school of automatic-machine designers? Our delay in adopting full automatic-machinery is due to a lack of men who can design it."

The depletion of natural resources would be at least partially solved, and farming abolished, with the development of synthetic foods. Man would soon be able to control the climate and change the geography of the world. All energy problems would be solved because enough heat could be produced by fifty thousand tons of ocean water to maintain the polar regions at the temperature of the Sahara for a thousand years.

Mankind would soon be emancipated from all forms of limitation. The cure for cancer, Dr. Charles Mayo announced in August 1929, would be along soon. Test-tube babies would be produced and pregnancy could take place without the attendant discomforts. Even aging would be abolished; biologists would learn all the secrets of the human body and eventually rejuvenation would be perfected.

One of the chapters of Ford's latest book, published in early 1929, was entitled "Machinery, the New Messiah," and it summed up the wisdom of the age. Engineering and technology would cure alcoholism, dirt, ugliness, confusion, and noise. Technology would not produce a terrifying war; it would make war obsolete. "The prejudices and enmities are due to the fact, in no small degree, that the people of the Continent are not well enough acquainted," he told an interviewer. "When motor cars cross boundaries freely and bring the people into contact with one another, the strongest assurances of peace will be created." He was speaking to a *New York Times* reporter in the summer of 1929 about his full-scale expansion into Europe.

In the book he expanded that vision: "Machinery is accomplishing in the world what man has failed to do by preaching, propaganda or the written word. The airplane and the radio know no boundary. They pass over the dotted lines on the map without heed or hindrance. They are binding the world together in a way no other systems can. The motion picture with its universal language [he had apparently not yet acknowledged the talking film], the airplane with its speed, the radio with its coming international program—these will soon bring the world to a complete understanding. Thus may be visioned a United States of the World. Ultimately, it will surely come!"

Led by the United States, the mechanized world hailed every new manifestation of its spirit. In September, the same month that the tri-motor crashed in the Southwest, Fritz von Opel flew in a rocket for seventy-five seconds at a minimum height of fifty feet over a little more than a mile at Frankfort, Germany, in the first manned rocket flight in history.

Cordons of police guarded the site from the curious, newspaper reporters from all over the world watched, and the credulous world received word within minutes, in a notable contrast to the lonely experiments of the Wrights at Kitty Hawk.

Of far greater significance than this showy flight, however, was the rocketry of Professor Robert Goddard in the United States. He was more interested in developing liquid fuel and studying the earth's atmosphere than he was in taking his rocket for a ride.

The rocket needed no atmosphere to lift it, but kicked itself forward solely by fuel energy. In July 1929, Goddard's latest rocket shot through an isolated part of Worcester, Massachusetts. Its roar was heard for two miles. Scores of residents called police headquarters, reporting that an airplane was aflame in the sky. Two police ambulances searched the area for crash victims and an airplane was dispatched on an aid mission from Grafton Airport.

Goddard explained that he was not trying to reach the moon with his rocket, as rumors had it. At present, he explained, that was not possible. To carry one pound to the moon would require five hundred to one thousand pounds of any known fuel or explosive. It might be possible to send a rocket to the moon, but there was no way to get the craft and passengers back—the first people to land on the moon would have to stay there. It would take a while, but the majority of people accepted the notion that it would happen eventually. Men like Edison and Ford had shifted the burden of proof to the scoffers.

Technology accomplished such marvels not merely through scientific genius, but through scientific organization, and Germany believed it understood this process of scientific codification better than did the United States. When Edison established his research center in Menlo Park, the chemical industries of Germany had already begun organized research. The Germans tied their efforts not primarily to individual profit or to entrepreneurial instincts but to national resurgence, and were ready to enter into any alliances for the Fatherland.

Henry Ford's expansion into Germany was being financed with the help of the huge German chemical firm of I.G. Farben. In return, Ford was contracted to help I.G., the largest industrial corporation in Europe, with an American project—a plant it was opening in Louisiana.

Over the years I.G. Farben had shown itself adept at chemical sorcery, not the least examples of which were several varieties of deadly gas, and the company had been decisive in making Germany the chemical capital of the world. By 1929 I.G. had just developed a new process that was expected to revolutionize the oil industry—a new method for cracking petroleum out of crude oil that produced a much higher yield. I.G. was also involved in experiments to convert coal into gasoline and to produce synthetic rubber from coal.

The ownership of American I.G. Chemical Corporation would be partly German, but stocks were being sold in the United States, and there were a number of American directors, including one representing the investment banking house of Otto Kahn. Edsel Ford represented the interests of Fordlandia. The president of Standard Oil of New Jersey was also a director, signifying the enlarging involvement of the Rockefeller company with I.G.

Under a new agreement the Rockefeller company would take over I.G.'s market in oil all over the world, while I.G. would take control of chemical matters. The two fields of oil and chemistry were closely related and used many of the same raw materials. Standard Oil was willing to cede the field to I.G., which would have charge of all research in Germany and in the United States—including dyes, pharmaceuticals, fungicides, solvents, lacquers, light metals, photographic supplies, artificial silk, and nitrogen fertilizers. I.G. retained all rights to basic chemical techniques, products, and markets.

"The threat in this newest maneuver of the I.G.," said one of the few people who appeared to be disturbed, "lies in the danger that research in this important field (which is the source of explosives, as well as most of our medicinal specifics and our dyes), is once more in danger of gradually being left exclusively to the Germans. The leaders of German industry and finance know industrial progress is dependent upon unremitting research and if they can lull this and other countries to sleep by graciously taking over all the research work of these international combines and alliances they are forming, they will once more place the center of world scientific knowledge in Berlin."

General Electric had also just entered a significant agreement with a German company. Dr. Zay Jeffries was a rising executive who had been placed in charge of GE's tungsten carbide project. GE had developed the alloy, harder than sapphire and almost as hard as a diamond. It promised to be the best edge for machine tools ever developed. Tungsten carbide cut steel as if it were cheese.

GE was excited about its prospects. But across the Atlantic, tungsten carbide was nothing new for the chemical wizards of Germany. The House of Krupp had developed the alloy several years earlier, and had cut the Big Bertha cannon of the world war with it. Having the alloy had provided Germany with an edge over the Allies in armament production. Krupp and its close associate, the Economic High Command of the German Army, were aware of the alloy's invaluable advantage in drilling, threading, and shaping a mass. They hoped to keep it as a monopoly. Unfortunately that was no longer possible, since GE had come up with its own process, but the next most advantageous step would be to restrict production elsewhere as much as possible.

Luckily for Krupp, the company into whose hands it had fallen was the great proponent of restricted production, stabilized prices, patent pools, and licensing. The House of Krupp and GE had been able to sign an agreement to their apparent mutual advantage. GE would control the American rights to tungsten carbide through its own patents and would pay part of its profits to Krupp, which agreed to stay out of the United States. Krupp had the additional right to rule on which American firms would be allowed to manufacture tungsten carbide. The effect would be that in the United States production would be severely limited, prices exorbitantly high, and profits huge. Claiming that the process of making tungsten carbide was expensive and almost superhuman in its demands, GE would severely limit production—an example of what it actually meant by "stabilizing" production. Meanwhile in Germany, tungsten carbide would be sold at one-tenth the cost, in ten times the volume, and its use throughout German industry would be encouraged.

Modern business, said GE's Swope and Young, regarded the Sherman Antitrust Act as a relic. With Krupp, GE would control commerce, fix prices, and eliminate competition in the sort of illegal arrangement that the Sherman Act was designed to prevent.

Germany had taken the organization of technology one step farther. In the United States the control of technology still lay in a setting of individualism; in Germany it lay in the hands of the nation, to be socialized in what one might call national socialism.

Three years earlier, in 1926, the German Army had formed an Economic High Command studying the deficiencies of the German economy and making plans for its transformation. The chemical industry and the army cooperated closely, and the policies and management of the chemical giants were an instrument of military planning. The military effort to rearm Germany was concentrated on the same aim for which Germany had striven before and during the last war: the creation of scientific monopoly. United States companies jumped at baubles such as profits when the Germans dangled them. With synthetic oil, synthetic rubber, and tungsten carbide in Germany's hands, Britain's command of the seas and control of raw materials would not be so important—next time.

The sticky and interlocking web of technology was a creation of capitalism, but it did not stop there. If anything, the Russians were as enthralled with technology as their class enemies, and before such urgencies, ideology was forgotten. There were approximately one hundred members of the Soviet government in the United States that October of 1929, treading about in stolid search of heavy machinery, tools to make tools, dyes, locomotives, and oil-refining equipment. The United States government did not recognize the Bolshevik government, but American business had lost any hesitancy about dealing with the foes of private enterprise. Although the imminent demise of communism was being preached, and a few implacable anticommunists called it treason, by 1929 trade with the U.S.S.R. had emerged suddenly into the open. American companies were doing more business with the commissars than they had ever done with the czars, and the Soviet Union was getting the most liberal credit terms of any nation in the world.

Many Americans found it hard to believe. On one occasion, a suspicious U.S. Immigration officer detained several Russians at Ellis Island, ignoring their explanation that they were here to buy a number of complete steel mills to ship back to the Soviet Union. They were rescued just in time to make a luncheon in their honor at the Bankers Club.

The icebreaker had been International General Electric, which opened the credit field to the Bolsheviks in 1928 with a twenty-six-million-dollar deal. The Board of Directors was shocked when Owen Young sprang the proposal, but eventually agreed. The credits were for machinery to help construct a large dam to be called the Dneiperostroy. The story making the rounds was that GE had accepted a lien on the Red fleet as security, and Wall Street laughed at the prospect of Swope and Young steaming into New York Harbor with a Russian battleship when the Reds defaulted.

The contract (which contained not a word about the Red fleet) was of global significance. Young had persuaded GE to drop all claims the company held against the Soviets for debts incurred by the prerevolutionary czarist government. These were the very claims that the United States government insisted had to be honored prior to any discussion of diplomatic recognition.

In many Soviet homes the pictures of Lenin, the political genius, and Ford, the technological genius, were hung side by side. The Theater of the Revolution in 1928 had presented a dramatic sketch in Moscow that portrayed Henry Ford as an idealist who wanted to help humanity. He supported good causes and paid his men well so that they could have the good things of life. Worn out by his efforts, Ford went in secret to Paris for a rejuvenation operation. He returned to the United States an unrecognized young man. At home nobody, not even his son Edsel, would admit that the young man was Henry Ford. Cast off and penniless, he took a job in his own factory and became an ardent communist agitator.

When Soviet engineers visited the enormous Ford plant at River Rouge, they found no reason to change their estimate of the genius of Ford. They were thrilled by a conception of total efficiency built into the system from wharf to foundry to assembly lines in which each move of the worker was closely calibrated. The Russians were putting up automobile factories at Nizhni Novgorod near Stalingrad in southern Russia, with cotton mills and other plants. A Cleveland firm had won the contract to build a great industrial city where five hundred thousand cars and trucks would eventually be built annually. The city would be built for a work force of fifteen thousand to twenty-five thousand and would include homes, schools, theaters, clubs, parks, streets, sewers, railroads, terminals, warehouses, and docks. It would be as hygienic as the crystal skylights in the Ford plants and would have the same brisk air of scientific management. The Soviets engaged the architect for Ford's River Rouge project, Albert Kahn of Detroit, to plan and supervise the Nizhni Novgorod manufacturing plants.

"I hear you have a contract to build for the Russian Soviet government," Ford told Albert Kahn over the telephone. "I wish you'd come out here and let's talk it over. My thought is this: we are willing to be of any help in this matter. I wish you would tell the Russian commission that anything we have is theirs—our designs, our work methods, our steel specifications. The more industry we create, no matter where it may be in the world, the more all the people of all the world will benefit. The more industry there is in America or Russia or India, the more comfort and the more profit there will be for everyone, including us."

Ford jumped into the burgeoning trade picture. In May of 1929 he signed an agreement with the Russians. They would buy thirty million dollars' worth of his cars and he would construct a factory and furnish technical advice at the Nizhni Novgorod factory. International General Electric also included extensive technical help in its contract with the Soviets, in construction of apparatus and generation and transmission of power. Soviet engineers would visit America under GE auspices to study American methods used in the manufacture of electrical machinery. Before the end of the five-year plan state farms plowed by Ford's tractors would be waving with wheat and Young's electrical machinery would be whirring and helping factories spring up everywhere with cheap power.

The Soviets were creating a communist counterpart of the process that the financiers had promoted in the United States—organization far beyond the cautious centralized planning of Hoover. In the five-year plan, every detail of what the U.S.S.R. would be doing until 1934 was set down to minute specifications: what factories were to be built and where, what mines would be opened, what railroad lines laid, what kind of cars and locomotives would be run on them, how many bricks and yards of cloth and pairs of shoes would be made, what crops would be grown, how much each worker was to produce, what the production costs would be, what prices would be set for agricultural and industrial goods, what capital would be needed and where it would be used, what the total population would be, how many workers would be employed, what wages they would get, and how many square feet of housing each family would live in.

The admiration of the Soviets for American technology was returned in the privately expressed admiration of American business leaders for the Soviet grand design. The two opposing systems were equally immersed in a business technology in which all was measurements and graphs. The American businessman and the Soviet commissar thought remarkably alike—in terms of statistics and quantities. In the U.S.S.R. the buttoning-up process was total. Nothing would be left to chance or discretion. Mythical creatures like the unicorn and dragon had disappeared from the earth, replaced by such creatures as six-tenths of a child.

"The great tasks set by the five-year plan," said the U.S.S.R., "is that of attaining and surpassing the economic level of the advanced capitalist countries in the approaching historical period, and of thus assuring the triumph of the Soviet economic system." The deepest implication of the 1929 five-year plan was this: if the U.S.S.R. remained a backward, undeveloped agricultural country subject to periodic famines, it would be vulnerable to counterrevolution within and conquest from without. If, however, it developed an adequate industrial sector, the Soviet Union would become a world power. That was the political situation that sent Soviet industrial experts and engineers scurrying to the United States in search of machinery. Young and Ford, whether they knew it or not, were helping to cement the Stalin regime in place.

In early 1929, Charles Lindbergh was flying over the dense, inaccessible Guatemalan jungle when he saw what seemed to be two emerald eyes staring at him from a tangle of vines. As he dropped lower he found the ruins of an ancient Mayan city, some eight miles in diameter, crumbled away and devoured by the centuries, but protected until the coming of the airplane from the scavenging expeditions of white men. The jungle bush had matted the city over, but out of the thick brush rose numerous small pyramids and a stately pile of stone, about two hundred fifty feet high, holding aloft the ruins of a temple. It looked like the center of the civilization. At the foot were two green pools of water that looked like eyes gazing out of the bush. Apparently formed by breaks in the earth above the course of an underground river, they had been caught by the Mayans and held in basins of white stucco. Lindbergh sensed immediately that he had found a lost city.

That same day, February 12, his engagement to Anne Morrow had been announced in Mexico City, and when he arrived in Havana six hours late he found a crowd of excited reporters waiting. He made various excuses for his tardiness, but said nothing of his find.

By October, however, the news had come out, and in that month he and Anne, now Mrs. Lindbergh, made several air expeditions from Belize into the Guatemalan jungle to the Lost City. Other temples were found, some barely visible through the humid growth that had swallowed them. There was no way of landing. On the ground, Indians seeking chicle fled from a huge silver bird, just as terrified as their Mayan ancestors would have been.

Whatever had caused the decline of that civilization, however, was not visible from the air. Whether they had searched the steaming entrails of human sacrifices for portents of that decline, whether they had felt the brush of the advancing jungle, whether they had measured their time in seconds, whether they had discovered such useful tools as the wheel and the census, whether their shamans had told them of Paradise or the end of history, of evolutionary progress or of cycles of death and rebirth, of honors for the valiant in the next world or of the grave's silent void—if they had left clues to any of these questions they were beneath the latticed canopy of vines. Charles and Anne, who was carrying in her womb their first child, flew back to Miami on October 9 in the service of **Pan-Ameri-**can Airways, master of the southern skies.

On October 20 he visited the Fokker installation at Teterboro, New Jersey, to look at a new plane, and when he flew back to Roosevelt Field on Long Island he found three thousand people there to cheer him. A mechanic drove Lindbergh's car out to his surrounded amphibian plane so that he could jump in and slip away. He almost made it, but near the gate the crowd forced him to stop. Full of excitement, they pressed against the car. He shook hands with those close to the auto, feeling crowded by eccentric passions. In response to cries for a speech, he made some brief remarks and then, with police help, he made his escape.

The following day, which was the day of the Dearborn gathering, Lindbergh and his bride were flying over Bergen County, New Jersey, in the biggest airplane anyone had ever seen. They had flown in from Roosevelt Field to Teterboro to take the new plane for a ride. It was a four-engine Fokker Giant, with seating for thirty-two passengers, and it made the Ford Tri-Motor look like a midget. They were almost one-third of the way through a century that brought new wonders every year.

In 1920 the world had almost forgotten Marie Curie. The Nobel Prize winner, dressed always in black and looking older than her fifty-two years, lived in genteel but threadbare circumstances near the Sorbonne in Paris, without the funds to purchase radium for her work or to keep her laboratory in operation.

That was how Marie Meloney found her on the day that she knocked on the Curie door for an interview. The editor of a women's magazine called *The Delineator*, Mrs. Meloney came seeking an interview and stayed to become Madame Curie's public relations advisor, head of the Madame Curie Radium Fund, and friend. She called it a scandal that a woman who had contributed so bountifully to human progress should scrape along in such poverty. America had numerous wealthy women who would willingly contribute to such a worthy campaign. The name Curie still had a market value, if the world were just reminded of it, and preparations were made to bring the once-famous scientist to the United States in 1921.

Mrs. Meloney, whom everyone called Missy, proved adept at fostering publicity. The New York dailies had been supplied with copy every day as buildup to the ship's arrival. The press eagerly jumped at the story. One magazine and newspaper after another played variations on the same theme, summarized in the title of the *Literary Digest* story: "She Discovered Radium, But Hasn't a Gram Of It." The stories described how Madame Curie and her late husband, Pierre, had worked year after year in a dreary, ill-equipped laboratory doing heavy labor to extract radium from pitchblende. Yet she had never patented any of her discoveries. She had never tried to obtain a fee for information rendered. She had never concealed any of her methods. Everything had been done openly so that others could repeat all the work as soon as the papers were published. She and her husband had even sacrificed their small savings in order to buy chemicals, vials, containers, and other equipment with which to pursue their work. She had devoted her life to a selfless pursuit of scientific knowledge. Yet she was living in tatters in Paris, raising her two fatherless daughters. Missy's own story, the central piece of the April 1921 issue of *The Delineator*, was entitled "The Greatest Woman in the World."

The only problem for Missy's campaign was academia, which was even more prickly than she had anticipated. Some scientific departments concluded that with two Nobel Prizes on her mantle, both of them in effect for the same work, Marie Curie had already been amply rewarded. Some universities found the Curie campaign dividing their faculties. Harvard, to Missy's chagrin, withheld an honorary degree. The physics department largely concurred in that decision, and even one of Madame Curie's champions had admitted that "since her husband died in 1906 Madame Curie has done nothing of great importance."

Many other universities, however, were eager to bestow honors, and Missy, a frail, tubercular woman confined at times to her bed, easily raised the funds for a gram of radium. The greatest woman in the world accepted the radium, valued at one hundred thousand dollars, from President Harding, a man with whom Missy enjoyed considerable influence. Marie Curie remained in the United States for a seven-week schedule that included industrial and university tours, fund-raising, and sight-seeing. As she toured factories and laboratories, Madame Curie was also promised high-precision galvanometers, X-ray tubes, electromagnets, voltmeters, and other hardware to equip a physics laboratory.

Even when she had been in good health Marie Curie had found social events a strain. With a continuous buzzing in her ears, with failing eyesight, and with a body that tired easily, she found the pace disabling. She found handshaking painful and took to wearing her right arm in a sling. Her poor health, it was explained, had something to do with her long exposure to radioactivity. She canceled some appearances, begging off on grounds of health. She was also uncomfortable about the Radium Fund venture which, however Missy disguised it with the trappings of a triumphal parade of honors, contained an element of alms-gathering. Curie insisted that all publicity underscore that she had not asked for a fund-raising campaign, but that the radium was an offering at the insistence of her admirers.

What fascinated Americans most about this visitor was the belief of the Curies in pure science. Never even considering the commercial possibilities of their work, they had lived that belief. Americans, who had acquired a reputation for vulgar acquisitiveness, thought that she might be saintly. A Columbia University scientist wrote during the 1921 visit: "It seems strange that America, which has always been credited with the development of materialism to the nth degree, should desire to do honor to one who has cared nothing for the material things of this life."

A writer for the *Scientific American* pursued a similar theme in a rare interview with Madame Curie. "Both from within and without, we Americans have got into the habit of believing that little we do is done for anything else than to make money," he wrote. "But our dollar-chasing habits have been grossly exaggerated, so it seems. For we asked Madame Curie if she found our scientific laboratories interesting, and she replied that she did. Following that we asked, in a somewhat abashed way, if she thought we were contributing anything to science, instead of taking science and molding it into the ways of industry for the pure and sole purpose of making money . . . Madame Curie believes that much of the work done in our leading laboratories and universities is done for the sake of science— pure science—and does not contain the slightest trace of industrial motives."

One of the gatherings for the Madame Curie Radium Fund was held at Missy's Washington Square apartment in New York's Greenwich Village, and among the guests was a twenty-nine-year-old public relations man named Edward L. Bernays. He found the great scientist a bit aloof but pleasant. She seemed anxious to return to solitary labors. Missy, lame from a childhood fall from a horse, limped about the room keeping people entertained with her vivacity. She glowed with the commitment that this campaign had bestowed upon her life.

As a professional, Bernays was impressed by Missy's amateur work. It was as if Madame Curie had never been forgotten. She had become once again a full-sized famous world figure. Bernays himself had a radium public relations account, representing the United States Radium Corporation. The company was coming up with ingenious new ways to put radium to work: painting it on house numbers, gunsights, instrument dials, and illuminated watch dials to make them all give off an eerie glow in the dark. The company made a lot more money out of radium than Madame Curie ever had.

The publicity campaign for Madame Curie was a double triumph for Missy, both for what she got into print and what she kept out. She had created the image of Marie Curie as the embodiment of pure science. That image, however, had replaced an earlier one. There had been a time when elements of the press had called her a love-mad scientist and churned out prose about the radioactive flame burning in her soul.

Marie Curie had been the focus of intense public scandal, most of it packed into the single year of 1911—the year that she applied to become the first woman to be admitted to the *Academie des Sciences*. The application created a debate in the French magazines and press that soon spilled over the bounds of scientific argument. For the progressives, Marie Curie was a symbol of the rise of feminism and her election a cause for womanhood and against obscurantism and clericalism. She was staunchly opposed by the rightist press, which turned its attention from strident nationalism, anti-semitism, and the hunt for monsters like Dreyfus to belittle the Curie contribution. They insisted that Madame Curie had been little more than a technical assistant to her husband. The discovery of radium and the work on radioactivity, they said, was chiefly the contribution of Pierre Curie, who had cut his wife in on the honors. She had seen the accusation coming for years and had guarded against it by the careful wording of her scientific papers to bear her imprint. Nevertheless the Curie application failed and the *Academie des Sciences* remained a male bastion.

Politicking was distasteful to Madame Curie and the effort left her exhausted. But an even more enervating episode followed. Paul Langevin, a brilliant physicist five years her junior, had worked intimately with Madame Curie for a number of years. In time their involvement had spilled over the laboratory into their nonworking hours. In 1911 Langevin took a Paris apartment to save late-night journeys to his suburban home. It was just a ten-minute walk for Madame Curie from the laboratory. She joined him there often and those who saw the pair together had no doubt about their relationship.

The sanctuary was invaded by Madame Langevin. She and her family broke into his study, forced a drawer, and made off with a packet of Marie Curie's letters to him. Within days the story of a scientific tryst between a famous woman scientist and a father of four was being printed in papers all over the Western world. Madame Langevin said she had proof of her husband's infidelity for a year and a half. The letters, which were damaging, were published. The right-wing jingo press, lying in wait for Madame Curie after the heat of the *Academie des Sciences* campaign, fell upon the letters and produced torrid prose. "The fire of radium," reported *Le*

Journal, "had kindled a flame in a scientist's heart, and his wife and children were now weeping." They played upon her Polish nationality and sympathized with the honest Frenchwoman whose home had been wrecked by a scheming foreigner. They saw in the freethinking woman a menace to Catholic France. Noting that she and Langevin had taught together at Sevres in the year preceding Pierre Curie's accidental death, they raised brutal questions. Had her husband been driven to suicide by his wife's infidelity with his former pupil? Had he flung himself in front of the horse and carriage that trampled him?

Marie Curie had been a widow for five years. Langevin's marriage had been disintegrating, and the two scientists had been drawn together gradually during a long professional association. But the cries of the nationalist press created ugly passions. Crowds began to gather in front of the Curie home, hooting and hurling insults. Someone threw a stone at the wall. One day the crowd was at its most hostile when friends arrived in a horse-drawn taxi to take Marie Curie to safety. They pushed their way through gawkers at the gate. Marie was inside, pale and frightened. They walked back out through the crowd and picked up the Curie children at their schools. Marie sat in the taxi, stunned and unable to speak.

In the midst of the scandal, word came from Stockholm that Marie Curie had won a Nobel Prize for the second time. The first had been in physics for the discovery of radioactivity; the second was in chemistry for the discovery of radium. The second prize underscored the incalculable importance of the Curie research; no one, man or woman, had ever won two Nobels. Yet it appeared that Marie Curie might not have been so honored had not the scientific community sympathized with her plight, for many believed that the work she had done since the earlier award in 1903 did not justify a second in 1911.

Marie went to Stockholm weakened by ill health and strain, but bore the ceremony with dignity. She established in the speech her partnership with her late husband, making it clear that they had been coequals in the work and that she was accepting in his memory as well as for herself. At the same time she laid claim to her work. She had been the pioneer in radioactivity and Pierre had joined *her* in collaboration. It was *her* hypothesis that radioactivity was an atomic property of matter. *She* had coined the term radioactivity to describe phenomena *she* had observed.

She left Stockholm a woman who had struggled successfully against professional and political hostility directed against her sex. Although the Langevins parted by legal separation, the love affair was over and never again would she become involved with another man. The story might have created insight about the situation of women who refused to submit to secondary roles in a male society. But Missy saw to it that nothing of the story was printed.

Missy visited editors and asked for cooperation in preventing even a whisper of the scandal from being revived. She did not want a controversial feminist figure in America for a fund-raising tour. She wanted a brilliant, aging scientist in pathetic circumstances. Missy was concerned above all with the Hearst papers, which had played up the scandal in 1911, and she met with Hearst's leading editor, Arthur Brisbane of the *New York Evening Journal*. When her presentation was finished Brisbane had the paper's back files on the 1911 scandal delivered to his office and handed them intact over to her. He said he had no need of them anymore. Missy thanked him, and then asked for a contribution to the Madame Curie Radium Fund. Brisbane gave her one hundred dollars.

In 1929, Marie Curie came back for another triumphal tour, once again to raise money. She was now sixty-one years old and looked much older—bent, tired, pale, and white-haired. America, as she was to discover, had changed in eight years. Most important, she was, owing in large part to Missy's earlier promotion, one of the great world citizens. It was mid-October when she arrived in New York on the *Ile de France*. She sent out a typed statement to the press that she was unwell and unable to stand the strain of an interview.

On the occasion of her first arrival in 1921 she had been exhausted by a long interview, delegations of Girl Scouts, Polish-Americans and French-Americans, marching bands, and the recitation of a maladroit ode to radium. This time she had made the rules to Missy clear, and they came straight from her doctors: no interviews, no autographs, no pictures. "And," she added in that mixture of English, French, and Polish idioms, "no shakehands." She also wanted to avoid large dinners and receptions, although Owen Young, the board chairman of General Electric, had arranged that she and Missy would attend a large gathering for Edison, the American inventor. Since she would neither have to speak nor be interviewed, she had consented.

When Young stopped by with General Charles Dawes, with whom he had served on the Dawes reparations committee, Madame Curie was wearing her gray coat and black straw hat. Her failing eyes looked huge behind her thick glasses. General Dawes, who had also been a passenger on the voyages, left the ship with Young and Curie, avoiding a crowd in front of the pier by walking down a back stairway to the lower level and leaving in three limousines. Madame Curie's luggage was sent over to Missy's apartment.

Missy found her friend Owen Young eager to help with the Curie schedule. He had set up an honorary degree for Madame Curie at St. Lawrence University, where he was chairman of the board of trustees, and he had planned a tour of the General Electric plant at Schenectady. The plant, he told Missy, would be entirely at Madame Curie's disposal; she could shut the whole operation down and conduct experiments if she chose.

Missy knew the movers and shakers of the nation, and even had lined up the president. Hoover had extended an invitation for Madame Curie and Missy to stay at the White House as overnight guests—a rare honor, and one never extended to non-Americans. Although Madame Curie could not recall having met him, Hoover had been a supporter of the Madame Curie Radium Fund in 1921, and a member of its committee. As president, he would oblige again by handing over a bank draft, encased in silver, for Madame Curie, and speaking of how honored America was to have the great scientist for a return visit. There would be so much activity, and Madame Curie would be so much in evidence, that no one would notice that the fund-raising was not actually for her, but for her sister, Bronia.

For several years Madame Curie had been helping to support an Institute of Radium in Warsaw. Bronia had organized it to provide a Polish resource in the fields of radioactivity and radium treatment for cancer and, by promoting her sister's name, had been able to build it and keep it in operation. The directors, however, had never been able to come up with enough money to buy a gram of radium, and so rented one.

Missy, now editor of the *New York Herald Tribune*'s Sunday magazine, was back in Europe in 1928, interviewing Mussolini and other luminaries. When she stopped in Paris to visit her beloved friend, Marie Curie asked her to help the struggling Polish facility, and she agreed.

On returning to the United States, however, Missy found it was not as easy to come up with a gram of radium for an obscure Polish institution as it was to raise funds for the greatest woman in the world. Floundering and ready to abandon the effort, she wrote to Madame Curie that there was only one way to promote such a project: for Madame Curie, ill and tired as she was, to make another visit and make it appear as if the campaign were for her.

According to Missy's clever promotion, Madame Curie would be the ultimate beneficiary. In 1921, she explained, an account had been established to supply her with a small income, the money coming from an oversubscription of the Radium Fund. Instead of spending this endowment on herself, however, Madame Curie sent it to the Warsaw Cancer Hospital to help provide treatment through rental of a gram of radium. Frustrated in their efforts to make Madame Curie's life more comfortable, the women of America had begun the 1929 campaign to raise the money so that she would no longer have to support the rental of the radium. At least that was the way Missy told it.

Madame Curie almost upset Missy's campaign by deciding to bring Bronia with her. Missy, who feared that this would refocus attention on where the money was actually going, fought that intention with an aggressiveness that offended her old friend. "I am almost always ill when I travel in the cold season and the return in November will be dangerous for me," she wrote to Missy. "I easily succumb to crisis of fever and of sore throat and bronchia from the middle of October until spring. It's because of this that my doctor has tried to dissuade me from making the journey, and my daughters insist that I either do not go, or I at least should be accompanied by someone from my family. It would certainly be difficult for me to decide to leave against the formal advice of my doctors. My sister is a doctor and can take care of me."

In the end Bronia withdrew from the opportunity to see America. The two Maries were still sole partners in the venture. Missy had a curious blend of selflessness and egotism, but Madame Curie could understand it. The same blend was found in devotees of pure science.

Thomas Edison was a young man when he was granted his first patent, for a telegraphic vote-tallying machine. As a trained telegrapher he was appalled at the delay involved in polling members of Congress for the votes by voice, and devised a much quicker and more efficient method. He was surprised to learn that legislative bodies were not the least interested in his invention, since the slow and mellow ritual of the voice vote gave the opposing sides leverage and time in attempting to strike bargains and was highly cherished. The chagrined Edison vowed never again to invent something unwanted. The research laboratory that he built at Menlo Park—and many researchers regarded that as his greatest invention—was conceived in the spirit of commercial enterprise. All American research, all the other laboratories built at Standard Oil, GE, RCA, and other centers of American technology could trace their origin to Edison's Menlo Park laboratories. RCA, the ultimate monopoly and the ultimate in government and private enterprise as a joint venture, was a direct consequence of the course Edison had laid out for American research.

When the guests at Dearborn saw the transplanted Menlo Park laboratories, they were visiting the shrine of the birth of American research enterprise. That spirit was even more important in understanding the Jubilee than the birth of the lamp or Edison's other contributions in batteries, phonographs, movies, and the power industry. It was only fitting, then, that a rival scientific spirit attended embodied in Madame Curie.

In 1865, Napoleon III had expressed surprise to Louis Pasteur that the great French scientist had never used any of his discoveries for his own financial profit. A true scientist, Pasteur replied, would regard himself as lowered by resorting to commercial enterprises. "A man of pure science," he said, "would complicate his life and risk paralyzing his inventive faculties" by attempting to make money from his work.

That was the tradition of the amateur, and it pervaded European science. Nobody had needed Newton's or Galileo's discoveries. Many scientists had suffered persecution and opprobium for their work, rather than testimonial dinners. Faraday refused to patent his induction coil, and indeed there was no market for it anyway. Often the scientific laboratory had been in a pavilion in a formal French garden, where aristocrats demonstrated their superior intellectual capacities. They had no regard for or interest in the needs of industry or of human welfare.

When a new breed of nonaristocratic scientists took over they kept such traditions, and in that tradition Madame Curie had worked. In attending the dinner, that tradition crossed paths with the Edisonian spirit of America. The great European and the great American, two of the leading scientific figures of all time, represented two rival traditions.

Missy would see to it when the hour of the banquet had arrived that the two great figures were introduced, though perhaps it would be a pathetic meeting, with Madame Curie unable to see him clearly, and Edison unable to hear her at all. If Missy could get a few minutes with Ford she might pull him aside and ask if he would donate an automobile to Madame Curie, for she always looked out for her friend's interests.

Madame Curie would be surrounded, however, by men who represented the Edisonian conception of science. Through her thick glasses she would see Young and Swope, the leaders of GE and RCA, and their lieutenant, Merlin Aylesworth, the president of NBC, who intended to develop a national chain of radio stations; Lee De Forest, who had done so much to develop radio and television; Ernst Alexanderson, who had fostered television, the Alexanderson alternator, the Byrd antenna, and the altimeter; Will Rogers, the promoter of aviation; George Eastman, the manufacturer of celluloid film; Paul Cravath, working with Young on the proposed merger of RCA and ITT; Orville Wright, whose experiments had always .

been directed toward practicalities; Charles Abbot, secretary of the Smith-sonian and in charge of the artifacts of aviation; Julius Rosenwald, spon-sor of a technological museum for Chicago; William Mayo, who had fostered Ford's venture into aviation; Zay Jeffries, in charge of developing tungsten carbide in cooperation with Krupp; Adolph Ochs of the *New York Times*, who sent Byrd to Antarctica, with the cooperation of Edsel Ford; Congressman Clancy, who testified on how technology sometimes meets with initial hostility and is later embraced; and Albert Kahn, about to bring mysteries of technological organization to an auto plant in the Soviet Union. She was outnumbered. And overlooking it all as the public relations consultant was Edward Bernays, who had met her eight years earlier while he was working for the United States Radium Corporation. Light's Golden Jubilee was, in an unmistakable sense, celebrating the United States' conception of science, although that was not what Bernays had specifically been engaged to do.

The success of Madame Curie's and Missy's campaign was assured. Once again they had raised more money than was needed for a gram of radium. Madame Curie had been to Owen Young's New York apartment while he explained how to negotiate a good price from the Belgian radium manufacturers.

The downpour of the day at Dearborn had soaked through her cloth-ing, and with more than two weeks of appearances ahead of her Madame Curie had a bronchial cold and a fever. She was working on her speech for the forthcoming honorary degree ceremony at St. Lawrence University. She intended, in the face of all that she had seen, to speak out for pure science as the source of true progress and civilization. It did not appear that such advice would change the course of American enterprise. Science was no longer practiced in formal gardens. It created dynamos, automo-biles, and airplanes. Its raw materials were imported from other countries, and so it was intertwined with trade, politics, even with war debts and reparations.

The sheer massiveness of American technology awaited her. At Schenectady, Owen Young would take her through building after building, block after block, connected by covered walkways. She would see thou-sands of identical high-precision instruments gliding down an assembly line. At Columbia University she would stand before a colossal experimen-tal magnet that dwarfed the human figure. American development in research since her last visit in 1921 had been breathtaking. The society's course had been determined by the infusion of more than nineteen million dollars, much of it coming from the Rockefeller fortune, into the scientific departments of selected American universities. In addition, millions of dollars of profits from mass production were being reinvested in vast research laboratories, and all of that research was ultimately aimed at the market, for consumption in America or for trade around the world. The radio, the movies, the airplane, and the automobile had carried American life everywhere, and no society rejected it.

This science belched out of smokestacks and shot through braided cords of copper. It was an expression of the personality of Thomas Edison. Calling it commercialism was a disdainful and glib way of dismissing its power, for there was in such a practical science an expression of a democratic system, a science in the service of, and even influenced by, ordinary Americans who made their own choices as consumers. It faced into the society rather than away from it. It was informed by the entrepreneurial spirit. It was a technology created by those not merely interested in money, but in writing their names in concrete. Edison's passion for glory was fed by ordinary people, and it was there, among the ordinary, that he sought it.

Madame Curie had come to this jazzy country late in life, and there was something in it that ran against her grain, but as she was treated as a celebrity, as she slipped out side doors to avoid reporters and rolled on to the next American appearance with police escorts and sirens, there was a smile on her weathered and punished face that hinted she might be not only amused by but envious of America's adolescent and gritty energy.

The Promoters

VY LEE'S OFFICE was at 111 Broadway, a short walk from the Bankers Club and the Wall Street financial center. Some people called him a press agent. He called himself a public relations counsel. He said that he interpreted his client to the public and the public to his client. He did not wear the flashy checkered suits, the yellow gloves, or the derbies of the press agent. He did not buy reporters drinks, slap them on the back, or tell them off-color stories. He did not even enter newspaper offices. When he had something to tell the press, he had his secretary call the newspapers, inform them that a statement would be released at such and such an hour, and wait. They came, because editors knew that Lee would not take up their time with a worthless bit of fluff. He would not do it and get away with it a second time.

At the appointed hour on a day in January of 1929 the press sidled in—bleary-eyed, unshaven, and in bad humor—a dozen representatives of New York's dailies and wire services. One reporter expected it to be about Bethlehem Steel's patent fight with U.S. Steel. Another had been told by his editor that it probably had something to do with the Standard Oil of Indiana proxy fight. A third guessed that Rockefeller, at that point traveling in the desert, had donated something to the Egyptians.

When the release was handed to them, it was unquestionably a front-page story. Rockefeller had leased a large piece of property in midtown Manhattan from Columbia University. The lease included almost all of the three blocks from 48th Street to 51st Street between 5th and 6th Avenues. The nucleus of the building project was expected to be a new home for the Metropolitan Opera House, and the whole development would include a two-hundred-foot plaza and would be built "in architectural harmony" with the opera house.

The project was in the thick of Fifth Avenue shopping, opposite Saks, and encouraged the hope that New York would at last build a plaza to match those of the great European cities. The project would include hotels, apartments and offices, double-decker shops on a mezzanine or balcony, and auto ramps under the opera house, with elevators to take the patrons up to their seats, a relief for the clogged traffic of midtown. Lee said

Rockefeller intended to give the center a monumental quality, meaning that he did not intend to squeeze every inch of rentable space out of it.

That was it. Lee expressed regret that Mr. Rockefeller was not available for comment, but reminded the reporters that he was on an extended trip. Were there any questions? Lee was cordial and smooth but not greasy.

He occasionally reminded reporters that he was once a New York reporter himself, but he neither looked nor acted like one. He looked much like the men he represented, and their values were his. He was listed in the social register, belonged to the best clubs, and his daughter had been presented at the Court of St. James. The reporters finished their questions and stuffed the sheets of flimsy in their pockets. One grumbled on the way out about how newspapermen were becoming little more than messenger boys, picking up news and delivering it to the city room. Lee relaxed as they left. He had not cajoled anyone, nor begged old drinking buddies for space, nor suggested how to play the story. He was too professional for that. Yet he managed to convey the impression that he imparted important news, and the next day, on their front pages, the newspapers agreed.

Light's Golden Jubilee was a celebration of Big Business, and a celebration of Big Technology, but above all it was a Big Stunt—a red, white, and blue three-decker birthday cake. It came at the end of a decade of unprecedented ballyhoo and attracted the great promoters of the age. They fired the economy. The communications media were created by technology and supported by business and sold the products of business and technology. People wanted the technology because they were bombarded with information about it.

A similar celebration could have been held earlier in the century, but its impact would have been limited to print media. It was not until the end of the Twenties that the radio had penetrated to every corner of American life, and was even imbedded in the dashboards of automobiles; the films, including the newsreels, talked; and the transcontinental and transoceanic telephone had brought in the age of global newsgathering. Appropriately, Edison had made it all possible. He had invented the phonograph and developed the motion picture; created the power industry; improved the telephone transmitter; invented the microphone; discovered the effect that made radio possible; and had even produced important elements of the mimeograph machine that Ivy Lee and Edward Bernays used to churn out their information, and that the *New York Times* used to send to its clients buying the Byrd story.

Dearborn was overrun with promoters. Will Rogers extolled the joys of aviation; RCA waved the Stars and Stripes; Missy had promoted a forgotten scientific genius back into world prominence. Otto Kahn, with his waxed moustache and pearl-handled cane, could not walk in public without attracting attention. Ben Lindsey used the magazines to become an internationally known figure while serving as a juvenile judge in Colorado; Jane Addams was the first media saint though, it was suspected, not the last. Ford and Schwab had been extolled and seared in the public press. President Hoover, although he preferred to let others take the spotlight, was a master of behind-the-scenes promotion. Edison was one of the supreme promoters of the age. The dinner was an extravaganza.

Grace Fisher was in Milan that year, studying voice with her maestra, and as she walked past La Scala, dreaming of the day when she would be a celebrated soprano, she carried in her bag a letter to Otto Kahn.

Will Rogers called Kahn the King of New York, but to Miss Fisher he was one of the great Pharaohs of the earth. She had met him the previous year. In his early sixties, his hair had turned to silver, but his eyebrows were black and his silver moustache was so obsessively waxed that it looked like a surrealist trick. She kept in touch with him by letter and telegram, informing him of the rather predictable developments in her career. Would he be coming to Italy this year, she asked, and thus have a chance to hear her sing? Alas, he responded, he was not including Italy in his 1929 itinerary. She responded that she was coming home for the summer to see her family in Buffalo and could see him in New York before leaving in the fall. "Not with the view of doing anything in the immediate future," she wrote in a letter of April 4, "but to have the benefit of you possibly suggesting to me one or two opera managers over here for the purpose of making my debut in Italy, perhaps in January or February." He nurtured her confidence. If she had the mettle he would eventually aid her, as he had experimental playwrights, ballet troupes, tenors, and even radical writers.

Kahn was an important figure on Wall Street and his financial reorganizations had established him in railroad history. He was famous, however, for being the busiest man about town of his age, and the foremost patron of the arts—laying cornerstones, endowing a theater group, welcoming a visiting virtuoso at the pier, and attending every opening.

His base was the presidency of the Metropolitan Opera Company, and his innovations upset the digestive juices of boxholders. In January of

1929, over the objections of other directors, he produced the American premiere of *Jonny Spielt Auf*, an opera that included a lead male in black-face, a jazz idiom, a chorus line, and an onstage auto crash. "I think this is disgraceful!" an outraged boxholder shouted at him in the foyer. "You ought to be ashamed of yourself!" With frail elegance, standing like a ramrod, Kahn asked a companion, "Who on earth was that?" He had known the man, an unblushing anti-Semite, for years.

Even saxophones in the orchestra pit at the Met were not as disturb-ing, however, as Kahn's plans to move the opera house to a new site west of Carnegie Hall. He had left for his annual European trip in 1927 with his architects already at work on designs. "There is only one style of architecture that would do for a new opera house in New York," a Metro-politan official said, "and that is the modern New York style. It should be representative of New York, a skyscraper with towers and terraces in the revised Babylonian style of New York."

The interior, Kahn said, would express "that genuinely democratic sentiment which ought to be characteristic in all ways of America." It would be designed more favorably for the true opera lovers who had to climb to the second balcony to afford the existing Met, and would break the hold of the rich on opera. The number of boxes would be reduced and instead of outright ownership they would be leased. The so-called "Diamond Horseshoe" of parterre boxes would be arranged to face the stage.

But the owners, who included the Morgans, were appalled. They went not to see but to be seen and their tiaras and stickpins glittered to more conspicuous effect when they faced each other in the diamond-shaped seating. Some were in their seats only during intermissions, anyway; during the performance they retired to play bridge. Above all they objected to the "commercialism" of Kahn's plan to support the opera on rentals of the remainder of the building. Opera, they said, had to be supported by the cream of society. An opera house deserted by the important people would not survive, even with rents. Kahn returned from his tour to find a develop-ing resistance that led to a long impasse.

Eventually he switched ground. Planning to sell his site west of Car-negie to William Randolph Hearst for a big hotel, he managed, through Ivy Lee, to interest Rockefeller in a new scheme—to lease land owned by Columbia University for a monumental midtown center with an opera house. Shortly before the announcement of January 1929, Lee suggested that Kahn undertake a "special campaign of publicity to be carried on unremittingly while the new opera house is being erected with reference to the building itself, opera houses in general, and the development of music in New York and throughout the country." He added: "There is an opportunity here to do a national service and the publicity campaign should be worked out independently of the current publicity for the opera itself."

Kahn's conception of America, like his conception of railroads, favored consolidation. America, he held, had entered the age of which it was to be master. The cultural maturity of America was as imperative to him as ethical integrity was to Rockefeller or monopoly to Morgan. Culture stamped a nation with greatness. America was not just a matter of dollars but of style, and would overcome its detractors. "In the last century this country had the formidable task of conquering a continent, physically, industrially, economically, and it was necessary that the intensest energies and activities of its people should be devoted to that stern and exacting task of material effort," he said during an interview in the fall of 1929. "That task has been accomplished. We can now afford and ought to occupy ourselves increasingly with art, science, culture and other things of the spirit. In my opinion this evolution is, in fact, taking place." He had worked to make it evolve and in so doing he had shaped the nation. But in 1929 one of his collaborators in that vast cultural project lay wounded in the psyche.

In a mental hospital in France a man in a loose dressing gown lay on a low mattress. Month after month he crouched in his cell, playing with his wrists or tearing at his nails until the blood came. In the last week of 1928 he received his first visitors in more than two years—the great impresario, Serge Diaghilev, and one of his celebrated dancers, Serge Lifar. Hoping that he might cut through the madness by evoking the past, Diaghilev talked of ballet. The madman listened. Sometimes a look of suspicion glimmered, as if the identities of his visitors had slipped from his mind.

Thirteen years earlier that madman, Vaslav Nijinsky, had been the most famous dancer in the world. When he walked into a party the sound level decreased. With Diaghilev, Otto Kahn, and a publicist named Edward Bernays, he had delivered America culturally into the twentieth century.

Diaghilev's Ballets Russes had created excitement all over Europe just before the world war. On the night that The Rite of Spring premiered in Paris, the audience had come close to riot. Divided by Igor Stravinsky's angular atonal score and by the assault of color and movement on the senses, the crowd in the theater began to argue and shout about whether the ballet was a work of genius or degeneracy, and then spilled out into the street only to grow louder.

Kahn saw the Ballets Russes while on his annual European trip. What, he wondered, would American innocents make of Nijinsky dressed as a Negro slave in a harem? Or as the ghost of a rose in limp silk petals of pinks, reds, and purples? Or as a faun in a skin-tight costume spotted with animal markings? Nijinsky, the legendary Polish dancer who strode and leaped across the stage with a disconcerting feline grace, would shock the nation, and the themes of blood and bacchanal would be too powerful for naive Americans, he thought. Nevertheless he felt compelled to help America deepen its sensibilities. He had been through the Midwest and was appalled by its aesthetic undernourishment. Scarcely more attractive for Kahn was the flashy and brassy style of New York. In 1915, over the objections of some associates in the Metropolitan Opera Company, Kahn decided to bring the Ballets Russes across the Atlantic for a national tour to open in New York. It was his boldest move ever in cultural innovation.

He hired the twenty-four-year-old Bernays to scurry around promoting the American tour. Bernays glibly informed editors that the dancers had been together since infancy and had been "trained in Ballet of the Czars from earliest childhood." Bernays knew nothing about ballet, but he could recognize trends, and it was obvious that the Ballets Russes was a total assault on the sensibilities. Using what he called "the segmented approach," he broke the total effect into categories. Leon Bakst's costuming for the ballet company was conquering women's fashions in Europe, and so he sent stories to fashion editors. Stravinsky had shaken the foundations of music, and so Bernays sent material to music editors. At times he met puritanical resistance. When he called on *The Ladies Home Journal*, Bernays was told that his photographs of the troupe were unacceptable without retouching, because readers would never allow pictures of so much flesh into their homes.

The publicist concentrated his energies on building up the stars, Tamara Karsavina and Nijinsky. But shortly before the troupe was to set sail for America, Kahn received word that Karsavina was in Russia awaiting the birth of a child and Nijinsky was being held in Austria-Hungary as a prisoner of war.

Diaghilev, who had neither under contract, had apparently assumed that the warring powers would call a truce to accommodate him. His troupe, supposedly together since childhood, had been picked up on the run all over Europe. Diaghilev sent cables assuring Kahn, meanwhile, that his new stars like Léonide Massine were as great as those he had lost.

Theater owners grumbled about the absence of the stars, but the American tour was nevertheless a critical success—and an administrative disaster. Kahn, who underwrote the losses, found the temperamental and histrionic Diaghilev running up expenses with extra rehearsals and bigger orchestras, passing off singers as dancers, and issuing anti-German statements. Bernays found the anti-German feeling among the troupe a good source of copy and made a news story out of the refusal of the conductor to perform the works of living German composers. But John Brown, the Met business manager, was appalled at Diaghilev's behavior. "We have already encountered the antagonism of the German element in Milwaukee, St. Louis, Cincinnati and other cities where the Teutonic element is strong," he told Kahn. "It was only after the most heartrending work that I was able to book the ballet with them."

In February of 1916 while the tour was going on, Kahn, in an astonishing feat of influence, succeeded in getting Nijinsky released. When Nijinsky arrived at the dock in New York, Diaghilev waited to meet him. Recrimination surfaced and old wounds ached slightly as they met. Until he had slipped away and married the daughter of a wealthy Budapest family, Nijinsky had been the star not only of Diaghilev's company, but of his life. The monocled and heavy-lidded Diaghilev, however, presented Romola Nijinsky with a bouquet and kissed her husband on both cheeks. Nijinsky put his baby daughter into Diaghilev's arms and they all walked off together.

Kahn soon discovered that Nijinsky's gratitude had limits; the dancer asked for the unprecedented figure of three thousand dollars per performance. The Metropolitan offered him a maximum of two thousand five hundred dollars per week. Brown, the Met business manager, reminded Nijinsky that he owed his release to Kahn and that a promise had been made to return him when the engagement was concluded. If Nijinsky did not come to a reasonable agreement, he said, Kahn would see that he would not work anywhere else and would be sent back to captivity. Nijinsky relented.

The tall, theatrical Diaghilev and his greatest protégé, Nijinsky, who looked ordinary and nervous in his street clothes, were together again. The truce did not last. They quarreled over who had the right to select ballerinas to dance with Nijinsky. Brown fought continuously with Diaghilev over programing and repertory. Nijinsky would stand motionless on the stage for a full quarter-hour while the other dancers grumbled and the orchestra fretted.

Nevertheless, in performance Nijinsky metamorphosed into the epitome of modernity. The interweaving of brilliant music, ravishing decor, opulent costuming, and spectacular effects, all providing the background for a burst of iconoclastic dancing—these elements embodied the changes that were sweeping over all the arts and over Western sensibilities. America was shocked by its shamelessness and its half-concealed eroticism, but it was fascinated. The tour came to a triumphant conclusion.

Kahn was willing to underwrite the losses that would be run up in a second tour, but Diaghilev was bored with puritanical America. Kahn asked Bernays to approach Diaghilev about another tour. They went to lunch, Diaghilev carrying his gold-topped cane and wearing his long black fur-lined coat with sable collar. The impresario, his monocle screwed into his expressive face, listened while Bernays presented the case for a second season. Perhaps because the war was limiting his opportunities, Diaghilev agreed.

With Bernays' role ended, Kahn sprang the second half of the arrangement—Mrs. Nijinsky did not want her husband's former lover about. Diaghilev agreed to let the company tour without him.

A *New York Sun* reporter was aboard, interviewing Nijinsky in French, when they left for Boston to begin the second tour. In Connecticut, Nijinsky asked when the interview would appear, and Bernays explained that no one could be certain about an interview, even about whether it would be printed at all. "This man has taken my time under false pretenses," Nijinsky shouted. "If I do not have a guarantee that the interview is printed, I refuse to permit him to ride on this train to Boston. Have him put off." Soon Romola Nijinsky joined the din, and the Nijinskys relented only when advised that an unscheduled stop could create a lawsuit.

Reporters were waiting at the hotel's registration desk in Boston to interview Nijinsky, so many that Bernays suggested they move to a reception room. He led the way down the hall with Nijinsky, followed by the press. They had gone only a few feet when Nijinsky asked what was happening.

"So many newspapermen are here to interview you," Bernays explained, "that it would be better to talk in the reception room than to have a standup press conference."

"I will not walk that far for any newspaperman," he said. Then he turned back toward the lobby, walking briskly on the balls of his feet. He had become a reigning prince.

By December of 1928 the spring was gone from his step. The flabby Nijinsky shuffled as Lifar, the dancer who had come to the sanitarium with Diaghilev, helped the demented man to shave and get ready. Diaghilev had decided to take him to see the Ballets Russes. Unwilling to admit to a good deed, Diaghilev said it would make good publicity. Nijinsky sat perfectly still in the car all the way to the theater. At the performance, the word spread that he was present, and people came to pay their respects, but found him unresponsive.

Count Kessler, an old friend, was standing in a corridor behind the stage waiting for Diaghilev. He saw the impresario approach in the company of a short haggard man in a tattered coat. "Don't you know who he is?" Diaghilev asked.

"No," the count said, looking closely, "I can't really call him to mind."

"But it's Nijinsky!" Diaghilev said. The count was astounded. The face was slack, the bearing sloppy. The man who had been a young Dionysus faintly smiled.

Diaghilev held him under one arm and, to get down the three flights of stairs, asked his friend to support Nijinsky under the other arm. The count held him fast, reassuringly pressed his thin fingers, and tried to encourage him with gentle words. The look that Nijinsky gave from his great eyes was mindless but touching, like that of a sick animal.

Serge Lifar, the dancer who had been with Diaghilev at the sanitarium, came to Venice eight months later, in August of 1929, to find Diaghilev bedded in a hotel, feeble and waxen. The young dancer took care of him, massaging his legs, administering his medication, and helping him dress.

The mask of hauteur and contempt with which Diaghilev had once confronted the world had dropped away. His health had failed. The slightest symptoms of illness had once sent him to physicians, but now that he had diabetes he took no care of himself at all, ignoring medical advice and drinking and eating whatever he pleased.

Lifar stayed up all night to minister to his illness, though the love between them had ended in reproaches and temper. With most of his old friends alienated, Diaghilev was alone except for Lifar. A clairvoyant once had told Diaghilev that he would die on the water; Lifar recalled the prediction as he looked out the hotel window into the canals of the city.

"I've still such a number of unfinished schemes," Diaghilev said. "There's so much to be done that I don't want to die, and yet death seems near. Terrible thing, death! All my life, I've been terrified of it—and always shall be, I think—even to the very last moment."

According to Russian superstition, Lifar recalled, it is a sure sign of approaching death when a very ill person asks to be put in another person's bed. The thought emerged in his mind as the impresario grew worse and Lifar began to fear that he would die.

Boris Kochno, an assistant to Diaghilev, had been summoned to Venice because of his master's serious condition. He and Lifar went to lunch. When they returned to the room they found that Diaghilev had crawled across the floor to Lifar's bed and was trying to pull himself up on it.

The sick man's temperature climbed to 106 degrees; the folds of his body were scorching to the touch, yet his sweat was cold; he was delirious and suffered from choking fits. A Greek Orthodox priest was summoned and began to read prayers for the dying. When the last breath left his body, Kochno and Lifar flung themselves upon the corpse. Each tried to push the other away. While a nurse and a doctor watched, they struggled for the body of the founder of an aesthetic movement. It was necessary to remove them forcibly from the room.

He died in debt to pharmacists, far from the pinched faces of the respectable, but within the Church. The artists he had nurtured changed fashion, changed music, changed dance, and with a wild combination of energy and decadence had changed America more than Kahn and Bernays would realize. Nijinsky had appeared in skirts and jeweled chokers, as a slave loosed in a harem, and joggled the American mind. Diaghilev's troupe was seen only by thousands but it may have been as sexually transforming to America as the motorcar and the roadhouse.

"Try as we may," an American reviewer had written during the 1916 tour, "we can never come away from the Russian Ballet to think of it merely as an achievement of art. It is also a gospel, a philosophy." That philosophy, or gospel, whirled in contradiction to the cadence of the machine. Mystery and magic had come cascading and leaping back onto a stage.

When *Afternoon of a Faun*, with Léonide Massine in the role originated by Nijinsky, was presented in its first New York performance, it immediately ran afoul of the decent-minded. At the conclusion of the dance the faun, who had frightened away the Grecian maidens bathing near his cave, picked up a filmy garment one of them had dropped. He placed it on the ground and lay upon it, nuzzling it, and the ballet ended with a convulsive jerk of his hips. Acting on complaints from the Catholic Theatre Movement, the police called the Metropolitan management into headquarters where certain "objectionable features" were discussed. Otto Kahn ruled that the ballet must be denatured. At the following performance, instead of falling upon the veil, Massine placed it on a rock and sat gazing at its silken folds as the curtain fell. Diaghilev had walked from his seat in the orchestra circle down the aisle to where the Met management was standing and said with a smile, "America is saved."

But he was joking. America would never be the same again.

When Egon Erwin Kisch, a German writer, reached California he looked up his friend Upton Sinclair. Kisch, who was touring the United States in 1929, was eager to see the film colony, and Sinclair, a well-known writer, knew some of the big moguls, so together they visited the studios, gawking and meeting the famous. While they sat in front of a gigantic studio surrounded by walls with iron grille gates and guards, Kisch mentioned whom he would most like to see. "Charlie?" Sinclair said. "Yes, we can stop and see him if you want to."

Kisch was overjoyed. Some film magnates had warned that he would never get to see Chaplin. Every braggart in Hollywood boasted of being his friend on the strength of having seen him once in a restaurant.

"Yes, he is terribly pursued," Sinclair said. "Every day more than a hundred people come to see him for all sorts of reasons." Sinclair drew his car up before a group of red-roofed buildings, a homey contrast to the grandiose scale of the studios they had been visiting. A small metal tablet on one building stated: "Chaplin Studios." The two men entered a reception area, then proceeded to a waiting room where two men greeted them. Even meeting Chaplin's aides told Kisch something about the operation. They were intelligent and sensitive men, with no trace of the hustling spirit that typified film people. "Here comes the boss," one of them said.

Chaplin came in and greeted Sinclair. The comic was dressed in expensive, dapper clothing, yet he wore neither tie nor hat and his vest was open. He little resembled the Chaplin seen in films. He had no bamboo cane, no battered little derby, no moustache, no oversized shoes. At forty he was prematurely gray. He looked princely, with a strong brow, jaw, and mouth. Yet the modeling about his temples was girlishly tender, and his eyes looked as if he were constantly retreating into himself.

Sinclair introduced him to Kisch. Chaplin began at once to talk about *City Lights*, his film in production. He told it with animation, but it was not until he began to move that he captured its spirit, for its comic genius was expressed in the gestures, the perfect sense of timing, with which Chaplin explored human behavior. The new film was his most ambitious work yet, and even as he told it, his listeners sensed the growing somber note in his comedy. There was laughter as always, but salted with tears. It was a comedy deeper and darker than the custard-pie throws and furious scrambling that had once typified silent comedy. He had become that rarity, a popular hero who had in time enchanted the critics as well.

"Now we've come to a dead stop and can't seem to get any further," he said. "Won't you help me, Upton?"

The visitors were delighted at the opportunity and they all went to the projection room. Chaplin, so farsighted that he could not even write his name without glasses, put on a pair of horn-rimmed spectacles. Kisch found him charming; while the takes were being prepared for showing,

Chaplin made up imaginary Spanish words to a tune he played on the harmonium.

Only a quarter of the film was ready, but the clips were impressive. During one scene Kisch laughed aloud and Chaplin, with an admonitory hand on his knee, silenced him. The film ended, the projection room lit up, and Kisch and Sinclair immediately proclaimed what they had seen as great.

"Can you tell me what you have seen?" Chaplin asked.

"Certainly. A girl is selling flowers on a street corner. Then Charlie comes."

"Oh, not yet," Chaplin said.

"Before that comes a man with his wife and buys a flower."

"A man?" Chaplin asked. "What kind of a man?" He induced them to describe the man as elegant, and they described the action in which the tramp approaches a running spring on the street. Chaplin was displeased.

"No, that is not clear," he said. "We must shoot that scene again." They had not grasped his intention. He began to pace. He went through the motions in every detail that they had just seen on the screen, then asked them to continue their summary.

"Now Charlie takes the drinking cup from the wall."

"Have you recognized the part I am playing?"

"What do you mean?" one of the guests asked. He had looked just like the same little tramp he always played.

"I am a little different this time from what I have been before."

"Yes, you have a little bat tie and gloves. You want to look like a rather dandy tramp this time, don't you? That is the significance of the incident with the drinking cup."

"Describe it, please." Chaplin addressed his visitors, but his eyes were far off.

"Charlie takes the cup, which is hanging on a chain. The chain falls across his stomach and, noticing that it would make a splendid watch chain, he tries to tear it loose from the wall, while he is drinking. He fails and toddles away with a resigned air in the direction of the flower girl. She is begging."

"Stop, stop!" Chaplin said, ceasing his pacing. "There is something in between."

The guests, who could remember nothing, looked blankly at each other.

Chaplin prompted. "An automobile comes."

"After the automobile arrives," said one of the guests, picking up the cue, "a gentleman gets out of it and passes Charlie, who greets him in his usual fashion."

"What does the auto do?"

Kisch said he didn't know. Sinclair said it went away.

Chaplin swore in his distress. "A complete failure," he announced. His aides stood about in attitudes of dismay.

Kisch hesitated, then continued his description. "The girl naturally offers a flower to Charlie. It falls to the ground; both bend over and Charlie picks up the flower, but the flower girl keeps looking for it, although he is holding the flower out to her. Realizing that the girl is blind, he buys the flower and goes away. Then to discover whether the girl is really blind he returns again."

"No, no!" Chaplin interrupted, unhappy at the paucity of detail. "How does he come on the scene the second time?"

"The second time he enters very hastily, as if he were hurrying past, but actually he stands in one place and lifts his feet up and down so that the noise of his footsteps seems gradually to fade in the distance. Then he turns about quietly, on tiptoes, and comes back to the girl and sits down beside her. She has been sprinkling her flowers and throws the water from the pot into Charlie's face. He sneaks away, comes back a third time, and once again buys a flower. The little girl wants to pin it on him and, as she is feeling for the buttonhole, discovers that the flower he had bought before is already there. In this way she realizes that it was on her account that he returned. Charlie indicates that his other buttonhole is still free, but she replies that people don't wear flowers in both buttonholes. Then he begs her to keep the flower, which she fastens in her bosom. And now she is in love."

"With whom?" Chaplin asked.

"With Charlie."

Chaplin swore again.

"What is it?"

"Didn't anybody go by?" he asked, with a touch of irritation.

"No, not so far as I know."

"Didn't you notice," he inquired, "the auto again and the gentleman?"

"No, I noticed nothing."

Chaplin buried his face in his hands. His assistants appeared ready to do the same. The reason for such despair was not just that the visitors had missed the point of a scene, but the fundamental point of the movie. The scene takes place on an elegant street, signified by the elegant couple who first appear on it. The flower girl mistakenly believes that the man who climbed out of the automobile purchased the flower from her and had returned to see her again—that the little tramp, in other words, is a rich man. Sinclair and Kisch had missed the automobile remaining on the corner throughout the first scene and had not noticed its reappearance when the blind girl gives the tramp a second flower. The little tramp sees the confusion of identity at once and through the rest of the film passes himself off with her as a rich man. He steals money to pay a doctor to cure her blindness. He is arrested. Upon his release from jail he meets the girl, her sight restored. At the sight of him she bursts into laughter, for he *is* funny-looking and she has no idea who he is. If the public failed to grasp his sensitivity to his poverty and his desperate decision to win the girl's affections, the film would be incomprehensible.

"We must film the whole thing again," Chaplin said evenly. His blue eyes were so darkly shadowed that they were almost purple. Pity and bitterness looked out of them. Despite his charm, his eyes held back, as though he truly lived only in solitude.

By 1929 Chaplin had assumed complete control of his films. If he wished to junk a scene that had taken fifty thousand dollars and a long journey to shoot, he answered to no one. He was a slow worker and a perfectionist. The corps of workers had champed and chafed through months in which little seemed to happen. At last certain scenes had been accepted, carpenters and plasterers had begun work, and the sets had gone up. It was a departure from the frantic pace of Hollywood, where precision was limited to financial matters.

He was at a high point of his career. The veneration among critics, after *The Gold Rush*, was universal. They found him articulate, intelligent, and amusing. He was a true film author—a writer, director, and actor—not interested in cheap gags but in irony and poignance, a filmmaker with the heart of a poet.

"He has enriched the commedia dell'arte with an immortal figure," said Max Reinhardt, the great German producer. ". . . It is impossible to speak of the motion picture without beginning and ending with him. For in the beginning of this wordless art was Charles Chaplin."

For eight days Kisch and Sinclair visited the studio. One afternoon they were drinking tea in the little bungalow when the famous actress Edna Purviance arrived. Chaplin left for the reception building while Kisch fled into Chaplin's dressing room to comb his hair. On the dressing table lay a comb with a mass of tangled hair on it. Kisch pulled out the hair, made a face, and dropped it to the floor, then looked in the mirror and combed his hair. On his way out he saw the hair on the floor; realizing that in his haste he had infringed upon Chaplin's preserve, he picked it up rather than leave a telltale mess. He placed it back on the comb.

Just then one of Chaplin's staff walked in to clean himself up. "Look," he said to the German visitor, "that's the moustache." He pointed to the mess on the comb. "He has had the same one for fifteen years. A New York theatrical barber picked it out for him especially. No other moustache can stand all kinds of weather as this one can and we have entirely lost track of the New York barber from whom we got it. Charlie has always said that if this moustache is lost he will play smooth-shaven."

It was not, however, the loss of his moustache that threatened Chaplin, but the passing of the silent film. All the other studios were investing heavily in sound while Chaplin made the only silent film in Hollywood. He mocked sound films. As for a mixture of the two—he slammed the door shut while moving his lips silently, showing how ridiculous the concept was. The producers, he said, did not know what to do with sound. It was artificial; the voices came from somewhere but not, no matter how well-synchronized, from the images on the screen. He put his fingers to his ears, explaining that a friend had done so in a theater where a talking film was being shown. It was frightful, he said, to unplug one's ears and hear the voices after watching for a time with the sound blocked out.

His treatment of the tramp was non-realistic, puppetlike, as if Nijinsky were dancing Petrouchka. He did not even move his lips on the screen. The silent screen had been made for Chaplin and his expressive movement, his supreme choreography. He was in the tradition of the great clowns—energetic, fresh, inventive, silent. He dodged between the legs of clumsy policemen. He had created a language in movement, and was not about to scrap it for some foolish and superfluous verbiage.

He would come up with an idea about the flower girl scene and would step out the part with his small silly movements. Kisch would play the flower girl, Sinclair the man getting out of the car. As it always was for Chaplin, the period of gestation was painful and seemingly interminable. He would lie abed all morning in thought. His sense of film, though infallible, was inarticulate, and he had no words with which to convey the sense of rhythm he wished to impart to a scene. While he lay brooding in bed at his Beverly Hills home, the air was tense at the studio.

When he was ready, at the exact instant, he would jump out of bed, get into his clothes, step into the limousine that had waited all morning at the door, its engine throbbing, and drive to the studio.

He joined the group in the bungalow. Moments of the film were brought up, altered, discarded. Details were studied and acted out: gags,

postures, properties, business. Chaplin paced, accepting or rejecting concepts after submitting them to the rhythm and translating the rhythm to his
movements.

The defect of the flower girl scene was clear. The audience could not
grasp that she mistakes Chaplin for the man getting out of the car because
it had not been established that she is blind. That had to be moved up—but
Chaplin wanted the tramp and the audience to make the discovery simul-
taneously. Could the automobile be so vividly shown that the audience
would remember it? How would it be if the man climbed out of it and said
to the chauffeur, "Wait here."? Suppose the little tramp were to close the
door politely and the girl take a few steps in that direction?

Suppose the man walks behind Charlie, in step with him, remains
standing behind him, so that Charlie thinks that the flower held out to the
other man is meant for him? Should the man in the auto be of indifferent
appearance, or a very handsome man? Of course the flower girl would not
see him, but the audience could feel that he must be making a grand
impression on her. The audience would see the illusion in the mind of the
blind girl.

How would it be, it was suggested, if the girl, whom the audience now
realizes is blind, were to say when the tramp buys his second flower, "Give
this to the chauffeur."? Or how would it be if Charlie were trying to help the
gentleman into the automobile, and the flower girl tried to hand the second
flower through the window? Instead she would hand it to the tramp, standing before the open door?

"Wonderful," Chaplin said, "wonderful!" He acted it out and changed
his mind. "It won't do," he said. "I couldn't act the part of a lackey
immediately after I had been overwhelmed by the knowledge that the little
girl was blind and that I was in love with her."

Sinclair and Kisch departed, but Chaplin continued at his glacial pace,
moving through his habitual parties, wanderings about town, visits, long
hours in solitude. He wandered among the sets—silent, judging, exasperated, giving orders. He was no recluse; the apartness that defined his
life was more subtle than that. He frequented nightclubs, was seen in
restaurants and on the boulevards. He went to parties, to see Marion
Davies at her beach house or William Randolph Hearst at his ranch. When
Roscoe Arbuckle opened a nightclub in Culver City it became Hollywood's meeting place, and Chaplin entertained there. Wherever Chaplin
went he was the center of attention. He acted, mimicked, played, insisted
upon being seen and upon being amusing. But he did not give himself.

He was a passionate man who loved women and food. He was tender,

and yet he seemed unable to fulfill his feelings; he could evoke laughter
and love but it was only on the screen that he seemed at home with them.
He despised the trappings of success that fascinated Hollywood, but his
mockery was cynical and merely negative. He was intact. He moved alone
through the world, unpossessed and unpossessing. And that was the theme
of all his films—the little tramp journeying through life but never joining
the world, a solitary figure. The world stomped on the little tramp's heart,
but his song and dance went on.

Once the Comte de Chasseloup showed a party of people a terrible set
of photographs he had collected in China, closeups of torture and execu-
tion. They showed men being carved alive. They saw faces black with the
horror of their pain, then white with the relief of death. Chaplin's dark
eyes looked panicked. Then his eyes and mouth slitted. "There's humanity
for you," he said. "By God, they deserve it. Cut 'em up. Torture 'em! The
bastards!" It was an embarrassing moment. Chaplin had been nearly overwhelmed. He could not give himself to it, he had to erase it, so that he
could remain untouched. He was, like the little tramp, quivering and sensitive, warm and gentle, but there was more to him than the screen image.
He could be cruel, and in his restless intensity his work always came
first.

By 1928 the motion picture had become another revolutionary technology. Otto Kahn called it a great liberating force. "It has opened up dull,
narrow lives with romance and beauty, novelty and stimulation," Kahn
told the Paramount Sales Convention Banquet that year. He predicted the
onset of a new Hollywood era. Not even mentioning the upheaval that the
arrival of the talking picture had caused, Kahn looked past such momentary phenomena to the establishment of the American film industry as a
solid institution—a development that Kahn, in tandem with his friends
Adolph Zukor and Jesse Lasky at Paramount, had helped to build. The
age of the studio had begun. "The financial position of the leading concerns is now secure beyond peradventure," Kahn said. "The credit facilities at their disposal are ample. Their securities have a ready market. The
public taste has advanced and become more discriminating." With the
opening of his Little Carnegie in New York in late 1928, Kahn became
owner of one of the first American art film houses, and in 1929 he added
sound.

The film had become a worldwide influence. It had replaced the Turkish fez with a derby. It took the queue from the head of the Chinese and
parted their hair in the middle, and introduced to them the custom of

kissing. It brought the sewing machine to Sumatra, the bathtub to Macedonia, the racing car to Brazil, the barber chair to Greece. Parisian stenographers, having seen light, ventilated, roomy offices in American films, demanded and got similar comforts. "Milka and Raina," wrote a correspondent from Sofia, Bulgaria, "promenading down our main street . . . may not be as sumptuously dressed as Helen and Mary on Fifth Avenue, but their stockings are just as transparent, their skirts even shorter and their hair bobbed according to the latest fashion created by the queens of Hollywood and reflected upon the screen of our Theatre Royale. Observing these things, one wonders if it is not the movie, more than anything else, that has brought so much uniformity of habit among the people in different corners of the earth."

The women of Japan, prior to the arrival of movies, had been taught that they were physically and mentally incapable of initiative. American films showed women making their own decisions and selecting their own husbands; some elements of Japanese society favored banning motion pictures to keep such disturbing ideas out of women's heads.

"The cinema is the most universal medium by which national ideas and national atmosphere can be spread," it was asserted in a speech before the London Board of Trade. "Motion pictures are influencing fashions, behavior, dress and housing. People all over the world are deliberately going to the cinema as to an animated catalogue to get ideas."

The movies fanned dissatisfaction, created excitement. Everything had to be youthful, plentiful, *moderne*. They fostered the public fascination with wealth and the way the rich lived. In the movies, bathrooms were breathtaking and bedrooms were boudoirs.

With the advent of sound, 1929 became the year of the musical film, and most of these concerned the rise of an unknown to stardom in show business. *The Jazz Singer*, the film that started the talkies, set the theme. In that film, the conflict lay between the hero's aspirations and the traditionalism of his father, who wanted him to limit his singing to Jewish religious services. Characteristically, the message was that the outmoded past had to be discarded, to be superseded by the new standards of success. The 1929 musicals also pursued the continuing Hollywood themes: that excitement was meat and drink to modern life and that happiness had to be pursued to extremes. However, they skirted suggestively around sexual themes.

The first step to "clean up Hollywood" had come in 1922. Will Hays, head of the newly created Motion Picture Producers and Distributors Association, had announced that Roscoe Arbuckle's films would be removed from circulation and that Arbuckle was barred from the screen.

Hays said he had met with a group that included Jesse Lasky and Adolph Zukor of Paramount, Arbuckle's studio. The studio had canceled ten thousand Arbuckle film bookings at Hays's request.

"Fatty" Arbuckle had been one of the half-dozen most important film stars, specializing in family slapstick comedy, but the content of his films had nothing to do with the Hays edict. The moralists had become more strident about the Hollywood lifestyle than about what was in the movies, for the movie stars had become emblems of new styles that clashed with American ways.

When Mary Pickford was granted a Nevada divorce, the state attorney general charged that collusion had been involved in her suit. Miss Pickford, then called America's Sweetheart, assured her fans that she intended to remain single, then married Douglas Fairbanks within a month. A top Paramount director, William Desmond Taylor, was found murdered, and the ensuing hullaballoo produced headlines about sexual deviance, a few adulteries, drug trafficking, and witchcraft, and included other Hollywood names. Paramount's major matinee idol of the early twenties, Wallace Reid, had become a hopeless heroin addict. With scandals piling one upon another, Hays was putting together a blacklist of people to be eased out of films in the cause of improving the Hollywood image, with Reid heading the list.

The Arbuckle case, however, was most damaging of all. On Labor Day, 1921, the 34-year-old, 266-pound Arbuckle was host at an impromptu party in his suite at the St. Francis Hotel in San Francisco. In disregard of Prohibition, the gin flowed. Four days later Virginia Rappe, a film actress who had become ill at the party, died of peritonitis brought on by a ruptured bladder. The hotel attempted to hush up the story, but the press learned of it and quickly came up with Maude Delmont, another party attender who did not mind flash bulbs.

Miss Delmont said Arbuckle had drunk too much and the party had become rough. Arbuckle, she said, had come into a room in which she and her friend Miss Rappe were sitting, grabbed her friend and said: "I have been trying to get you for five years." Maude heard scuffling and screaming from Arbuckle's bedroom for the next hour, and she beat on the door in a desperate attempt to save her friend. When Arbuckle emerged, Miss Rappe was badly beaten up.

When the butler opened the door at Arbuckle's home, two dozen reporters rushed past, knocking him over. When they found Arbuckle they began to fire questions about a San Francisco orgy. Maude Delmont, an instant celebrity, told the press she would rather it had happened to her than to her lifelong friend Virginia. (Actually she had only known Virginia Rappe for two days.)

"The evidence in my possession shows conclusively that either a rape or an attempt to rape was perpetrated on Miss Rappe by Roscoe Arbuckle," said District Attorney Matthew Brady. "Following this assault, Miss Rappe died as a direct result of the rupture of her bladder. The evidence discloses beyond question that her bladder was ruptured by the weight of the body of Arbuckle either in a rape assault or an attempt to commit rape." Although it was unmentioned in newspapers, word went over back fences and in service stations that Fatty had raped the woman with a bottle.

Maude Delmont filed a statement with the police embellishing her earlier charges. Arbuckle, she said, had ripped off Virginia's clothes. Virginia had screamed, "I'm dying! I'm dying! Roscoe killed me!" Bruises covered her body and there were two bites on her neck.

Shock waves quivered through the film industry. The drive for film censorship had been gathering momentum, and this appeared to doom Hollywood to regulation. The moguls began the search for a sanctimonious figurehead that ended at the office of Postmaster General Will Hays. The fiendish image of Arbuckle was unrecognizable to those who knew him as shy with women and sexually disinterested. Chaplin, asked for a comment while in London, called the charges "preposterous" and said Arbuckle was "a genial, easygoing type who would not hurt a fly."

Poor Arbuckle—whose worst crime had been that he had burned his backside on a hot stove while filming and received his guests in his pajamas—had been the victim of an extortion scheme gone haywire. Miss Delmont, a bigamist and embezzler, had sensed an opportunity that afternoon and collected Miss Rappe's clothing. She and a cohort wired to two lawyers: "WE HAVE ROSCOE ARBUCKLE IN A HOLE HERE. CHANCE TO MAKE SOME MONEY OUT OF HIM." When the story broke her plans were defeated and she decided to go for publicity instead of money.

Miss Delmont, the eyewitness who had seen and heard Arbuckle's attack on her lifelong friend of two days, never took the stand in the three trials for manslaughter. The District Attorney had found to his chagrin that she was a complete liar. She had been, as the testimony of others firmly established, locked in a bathroom with a man during the time of the alleged assault.

Arbuckle testified that he had found Miss Rappe in his bathroom vomiting violently, had taken care of her, and had placed her fully clothed on his bed. She had ripped off her clothes, screaming in pain, when he and others re-entered the room. Evidence showed that she had not been sexually violated. Miss Rappe had a long history of bladder inflammation and the rupture could have been caused by vomiting.

Nevertheless it took three grueling and devastating trials, two of them ending in deadlocked juries, before Arbuckle was acquitted. With the harrowing experience over, he headed back to movieland to resume his career. Lasky and Zukor announced the release of three completed but unreleased Arbuckle films and called him the victim of unfortunate circumstances, but the damage to Arbuckle could not be repaired.

The case against Arbuckle was not whether he had actually committed the crime, but the erosion of his image by gossip and rumor. "We find that on the afternoon of September fifth of this year," said Assistant District Attorney Milton U'Ren in his summation during the first trial, "a Babylonian feast was in progress at the St. Francis Hotel . . . And this man who . . . has made the children of the nation laugh, this man appeared in pajamas before that mixed crowd and stayed in pajamas all afternoon. My God! Make the children laugh! . . . What would the children of America think, and what would the mothers of America say, if they could have seen that man that afternoon in pajamas, surrounded by his lords and ladies, pouring wine and drinking booze?" The image lingered in the American horizon, and Arbuckle was banned.

"Does this statement mean, then, that Arbuckle is out for good?" a reporter asked Hays.

"You know as well as I do the purposes of our organization," Hays said, quoting the association charter, " 'to attain and maintain the highest moral and artistic standards.' Beyond that I cannot say anything just now."

The Arbuckle exile cost Paramount a lot of money. "But Mr. Hays is the big boss of the industry, and if the industry is to be built up and cleaned the producers and distributors must be good sports," a Fox official said. "It is costly, of course, but the whole industry will be benefited. Certainly, it means that Will Hays is on the job and that he doesn't intend to be a figurehead."

Arbuckle was reinstated eight months later, but a storm of protest was loosed, and Zukor and Hays appealed for him to bow out voluntarily. He went into vaudeville and was a hit on the Pantages circuit, but lived in fear of being heckled by the audience. He turned to direction but could not sign his own works; in 1928 he directed two feature-length films under the name of William Goodrich. He married a second time but by the end of

1928 it had ended in divorce; the bad breaks and the rejections had begun to erode his personality. In 1929 he was a nightclub owner. Chaplin and many big stars attended on opening night, and a plaque was given to him that read: "He has shown the miracle of patience without bitterness in a world of injustice."

Hollywood had put on the robes of respectability. Otto Kahn went west for an extended Hollywood visit in 1928, taking a party with him that included Ivy Lee, and became fast friends with Chaplin. They sat in restaurants together discussing art. On Kahn's return to New York, the Hearst papers called him on a story that he had given five actresses five thousand dollars each to go to Europe to study.

Kahn managed to kill the story, although it had some basis in fact. He had promised money to one actress who wanted to study with Max Reinhardt in Salzburg and to another to study for the stage in New York. A sympathetic Paramount executive cabled to Kahn: "You probably know motion picture girls will say and do anything that will get them a trip or publicity." Before arriving for the 1928 junket, Kahn had cabled the same executive, asking him to arrange a reception as splendid as the previous one, "though it is not necessary to have it 100 percent blonde, inasmuch as fortunately tastes vary."

Thus Hollywood became safe for the investments of Wall Street. One of the lingering rumors about Arbuckle was that he had been chief celebrant at a sex orgy in a brothel outside Boston during his national tour in 1917. Actually Arbuckle had not even been there. The participants, who paid a district attorney one hundred thousand dollars to hush up the matter, included Zukor and Lasky, the Paramount bosses who later banished him.

Charlie Chaplin breakfasted with his lawyer at a hotel and the two walked unnoticed through Central Park to the lawyer's apartment. It was 1927, and the crisis that had broken around his life had made him temporarily incapable of working. He was morose, abject, sunk in despondency.

"I feel completely crushed by these viperous, terrible accusations," he said when the reporters arrived at the apartment. "It's cruel and unjustified —this onslaught on me. I can't understand all this bitterness, except that I know it has been instigated by my wife's family. She must be devoid of feeling, I guess."

"Are you still in love with your wife?" a reporter asked.

"How can one be, after such horrible accusations?" he said. "I hardly think I can have any sane views on love at this time, when I'm so close to this awful experience. I see all around me happiness, tenderness, home life, sanity—all the things I love, and I am very much attached to children and home life. I like both my children—they are both very wonderful. I wouldn't say that I love one more than the other; one may be more interesting than the other, but I love them both." He heaved a sigh.

They were dark rings under his eyes. His face was taut. His wife had just filed for divorce, and for several weeks since the separation her lawyers had flayed him in the press. In Hollywood, women's clubs were taking up collections to supply milk to his two sons, since it had been widely reported that he would not give his family enough money to buy food.

"That's the tragedy of this whole thing," he said, "the stigma it has cast on their poor little lives. What I worry about most is my children—and my own self-respect." He said he would fight to the end for custody of the two boys, then back in California with their mother.

Chaplin, who had always kept his relationships with the press superficial and at arm's length, was finally talking, and the reporters eagerly wrote it all down. They had pursued him without success for days. He had managed to duck them while boarding the train in Los Angeles, and at a stopover in Chicago. A battalion of seventy reporters and photographers had been waiting at Grand Central Station when the Twentieth Century Limited pulled in, but he managed to quick-step through, into a surging crowd of the curious waiting for him in the main concourse, and strode quickly into a taxicab and disappeared, surfacing with his lawyer.

"Before we separated," Chaplin said, "I did love my wife—unfortunately. I expected a home, companionship, an interest in one another and interest in the world outside ourselves, in the world around us." A reporter wanted to hear about his penchant for marrying girls in their mid-teens. He agreed that both his wives had been rather young, but they inspired a paternal feeling in him, and he observed, "you can have the same companionship and love for them as for your children."

"Was it an intellectual companionship?" a reporter asked.

"I don't think anyone can be deeply intellectual at their age," he replied. "But I love many people, and there are some friends whom I love deeply."

Court-appointed receivers had taken possession of Chaplin Studios, seized financial records, stopped the payroll, and detectives had burst into his forty-room mansion, informing servants that nothing could be removed. Chaplin had lain slackly in bed, sending word to the studio for everyone to go home until further notice. The yellow pad on his desk was blank, even the organ was silent, and he was unable to collect his wits to think about *The Circus*, his film in production. It was rumored that he would retire from the screen.

"I have only given up work on *The Circus* temporarily," he told the assembled reporters, "until all this mess is cleared up. But I shall endeavor to work all my life. Art and affection are essential parts of every man's life. The combination of the two is what makes life—especially since art is often inspired by life." They wrote that down.

He then addressed himself to the to-do his wife's lawyers were making about Edna Purviance, one of his former leading ladies who was still on the Chaplin payroll although making a film in Cannes. "There is nothing between me and Miss Purviance," Chaplin said. "It is a terrible wrong to us both to say so."

He added: "And as for that story about the train ride, it is a deliberate fabrication, false in every detail." He was referring to the reports that he had married Lita Grey, at the time his fifteen-year-old leading lady in *The Gold Rush*, only because of the specter of statutory rape. Gossips said he had remarked to an aide while they were on a train on the way to the wedding that getting married was better than going to a penitentiary.

For years Chaplin had been establishing the image of The Little Tramp, the innocent and gentle hero of all his films. Now the nation was coming to know more of the image Chaplin enjoyed in Hollywood—his legendary standing as a womanizer. His wife's lawyers described him as miserly, bad-tempered, neglectful of his children, and a brandisher of guns. He was a depraved foreigner from the London slums who deflowered maidens, a self-absorbed satyr who viewed marriage as a burden. But they had gone even farther than that. The divorce complaint accused him of demanding that his wife submit to "abnormal, unnatural, perverted and degenerate sexual desires." His wife said he had read to her from books on the subject and had recounted his extramarital experiences with five actresses, all of whom had obliged him. Not one to deprive the public of revealing glimpses into the lives of the famous, Mrs. Chaplin contended that her husband had suggested that a woman they both knew would make an interesting threesome with them and would perform the act. The material was too raw for newspapers, but they managed to convey the throb of scandal, and mimeographed copies of the complaint were soon selling on the street in Los Angeles.

Her lawyers advised her that Chaplin had sixteen million dollars. Since he appeared to dread penitentiaries, and since the law against oral sex in California carried a maximum prison sentence of fifteen years, he might be persuaded to part with some of his fortune. It was another gold rush, and

Mrs. Chaplin and her lawyers were the prospectors. Her lawyer admitted that she had charged eight thousand dollars to his account the day before she left him. "What does eight thousand dollars worth of clothing amount to for a millionaire's wife," the lawyer asked, "particularly in view of the fact that Chaplin spent fifty thousand dollars on a recent pleasure trip to New York?"

The charges were beginning to work. The mayor of Seattle had asked the city's censorship board to decide whether to ban Chaplin films, and the League of Women Voters of LaSalle County, Illinois, asked theaters not to show Chaplin movies until the case was settled. Will Hays, in New Orleans as Chaplin headed for New York, denied reports that he and the comedian were about to confer about Hollywood's latest embarrassment. "I am, of course, not the arbiter of morals of the film industry's fifty thousand people," the Keeper of the Blacklist said. "However, there hasn't been a scandal in Hollywood since the producers and distributors organization was formed four years ago."

Chaplin was a proud and stiff-necked sort, but he now had no recourse but to talk to the press, whatever impertinences they asked him. A reporter asked when his love for Lita Grey had begun to cool.

"Cruelty kills love," he responded, "but I would rather not go into detail now. I shall reserve that for the court, and I am reserving my cross-complaint against my wife for the proper time and place. I don't understand the legalities of the thing at all. The whole case is a labyrinth of confusion."

Again and again he appealed to the American people's sense of justice. "Of course, I'm not cheerful about it now," he said, "but I am confident of the outcome. I have faith in the patience and sense of fair play of the people until I have a chance in court to tell my side of the story."

Later his lawyer took the train to Los Angeles to see him about the case. They met in a coffee shop and Chaplin asked what he should do. The lawyer said "Settle," finished his coffee, and took the next train east.

The counterbalance to Hollywood was Boston, where a 1926 issue of *The American Mercury* with an article about a small-town prostitute had been banned. Mencken, the editor of the journal, won that case, but the city's censors still kept a close watch on the printed word. Although Ernest Hemingway's editor persuaded him to tone down some of the gamier language in his war novel, *A Farewell To Arms*, it was banned in Boston nevertheless when *Scribner's* magazine serialized it in mid-1929.

The big book of 1929 was another war novel, *All Quiet on the West-*

ern Front, and, as with the Hemingway book, the language and habits of soldiers were considered too Elizabethan for twentieth-century America. Officials of Little, Brown and Company, the American publisher of the international best-seller by Erich Maria Remarque, said some alterations had been made from the English translation published in Great Britain. The controversial aspect of the affair, however, was that the Boston publishing company made further cuts upon the suggestion of the judges of the Book of the Month Club, which had chosen the book as the club's June selection. Some literary people chided the publishing house for backing down for the sake of profit.

"We made the changes entirely on our own responsibility," said Herbert F. Jenkins, vice president of Little, Brown, "and have done so in other cases. When we heard that the Book of the Month Club was going to take our book, we made a few additional changes at their suggestion. The book was not damaged. It is different only in the slightest degree." Thus the club's one hundred thousand members and other potential readers were spared the knowledge that soldiers at the front think about sex a lot, talk obscenely, and face unpleasant latrine conditions.

He had gained twenty pounds and was feeling better, and the added weight gave him a fleshy look. Thomas Edison's white hair was thinning in front and his body sagged so that he looked, as he often said of himself, as if his body were just something to carry his brains around. Sometimes as he scuffed along the corridors of his laboratories, the cold feet so far from his heart, he would feel old age creep up on him, advancing three steps and falling back two, but getting closer.

But not on that day. On February 11, 1929, he felt frisky and intended to show off by kicking his foot higher than his shoulder—he and Henry Ford enjoyed doing it together—and bragging to the young reporters of his eighteen-hour workdays. He basked in the sun at his winter home in Fort Myers, Florida, on his eighty-second birthday and thought, as he did unceasingly from the time he awoke in the morning, about rubber.

Edison stood in a grove at his Florida estate on the Gulf in a dark suit with a vest, hatless. At first glance he looked alone, but within throwing distance, in the shade, some squatting, some smoking, some chatting, were reporters, photographers, movie camera operators. He could feel his new unfamiliar false teeth chafing his gums. He could feel the sun beat on his old frame. He could smell the ocean and the orange trees. But he heard nothing. He had not heard a bird sing since he was twelve years old. The inventor of the phonograph was able to hear his invention work by biting the speaker, so that he could pick up the sound through his jaw into his undamaged inner ear. He could not hear the greetings at the pier as the *Saunterer*'s passengers alighted from the yacht and began to walk toward the spot where he stood to greet them. To the south, Havana's bars and brothels beckoned for the Yankee dollar. To the west, Lindbergh, in an amphibious Sikorsky, was an hour out of Belize on the first Central American airmail run. To the east, Italy celebrated a treaty between the Papacy and the Mussolini government.

The first to break into the clearing were Herbert Hoover, the president-elect, and Mina Edison, who watched her husband wave his hand enthusiastically as they appeared. Behind them were Hoover's friends from the yacht and more reporters. Hoover, his hat clutched in his hand, stepped forward and said "Congratulations." He saw the blaze of intellect in the old man's steel-blue eyes. Edison, watching his lips, replied "Thanks." Hoover stiffened as the photographers moved in and began to sidle out of range, but Edison, catching him by the arm, stopped him. They took pictures of the pair, then of Hoover and Edison with Henry Ford and Harvey Firestone, and finally shots of Edison alone. Then they all waited and chatted, Hoover jingling coins constantly in his pocket, while operators from Pathe Movietone News took footage of Edison for a newsreel. After some words of greeting, Edison began to talk about his rubber project while the cameras turned.

"First we are going to definitely select the best plant for our type of rubber production and then we will plant them in large quantities and spend some time breeding them up to the most efficient state possible," he said. "We will teach them to work overtime, night and day, to supply America with an emergency rubber crop. I have found over twelve hundred plants which will produce a percentage of rubber latex and about forty varieties tested to date are available for cultivation on a large scale."

Edison called it the last big project of his life and promoted it at every opportunity. He was looking for a new source of rubber, a plant that could be grown in the U.S., so that if war came the nation would be self-sufficient, even if the enemy were to capture Malaya and the East Indies. It demonstrated again that Edison's edge over ordinary mortals was his inexhaustible zeal for work, for he had known next to nothing about botany when he plunged into the work two years earlier. He had gone at it with his customary total assault—amassing a library of books, scientific articles, and clippings. He sent a dozen agents into the field to dig up plants in the United States, Cuba, and Puerto Rico. They packed the plants in peat moss and mailed them to him. His home and gardens in West Orange, New Jersey, were alive with labeled plants, as was his winter home in Florida. He had narrowed the search to goldenrod, and one of the varieties he grew in Florida was more than fourteen feet high. He thought about little else. Out for a drive on a Sunday, he would sometimes stop at a railroad siding and dig up a promising weed.

"Henry Ford has given me the use of thirty-two thousand acres of land near Savannah, Georgia," Edison went on as the cameras continued to turn, "and we are going to turn it into a vast rubber plantation and then get into actual production." He wound up the newsreel with a corny touch about how he would like to give everybody in America a slice of his birthday cake, and the moviemakers closed down their cameras.

Fort Myers had wanted to turn this day into the most festive in its history, with parades, fireworks, and picnics, but the president-elect frowned upon such un-Quakerlike pomp. Instead he and Edison took a drive through the town, waving at the black, white, and Seminole children lining the curbs. They returned for a birthday lunch, then the Hoover party sailed away for some serious fishing.

The reporters watched them leave and then typed the pleasant encounter into a story that made all the front pages, for Edison was always news. Many of them relied on answers to the interview of sorts held with Edison. Because of his deafness, the questions were written out in advance. He saw a continuation of improvements in radio. College was unnecessary for a boy with ambition. Prospects for the United States were good now that the nation would have an engineer in the White House. When asked his recipe for happiness, he said he did not know anyone who was happy.

Edison had always been accomplished at gathering a crowd. The talent had shown itself early in his career—most notably on a December morning in 1877 when Edison strode into the offices of *The Scientific American*. In his hands the thirty-year-old inventor bore a machine of brass and iron. It consisted of a cylinder covered with grooved tinfoil, two telephone speakers, and a small handle. Edison stopped at the desk of the editor and turned the handle toward him. F.C. Beach, a tough and skeptical magazine editor, looked with amusement at it and gave the handle a turn. Out of a telephone mouthpiece came a greeting: "Good morning! How do you like the phonograph?"

Edison enjoyed the joke, and basked in the attention of the crowd that quickly gathered around him as word spread through the office that the New Jersey inventor had brought in a machine that talked. "Edison was kept going for two or three hours," Beach wrote later, "but at last the crowd attained such proportions that I feared the floor would give way under the abnormal weight, and I requested the inventor to stop."

Otto Kahn at the Atlantic Beach Club, Long Island, 1927. *(The Bettmann Archive, Inc.)*

Edward Bernays in 1929.

Samuel Insull, c. 1929. (*The Bettmann Archive, Inc.*)

John D. Rockefeller, Jr., at right, with Dr. William Goodwin at Williamsburg, 1928. (*The Bettmann Archive, Inc.*)

Above: Opening session of Paris Reparations Conference, February 1929. Young and Morgan are at center. Hjalmar Schacht is fourth from right. (*The Bettmann Archive, Inc.*)
Opposite, left: Owen Young, c. 1925. (*The Bettmann Archive, Inc.*) **Opposite, right**: J. P. Morgan, Jr., c. 1929. (*The Bettmann Archive, Inc.*)

Above: Prime Minister J. Ramsay MacDonald, at right, greets Ambassador Charles Dawes at MacDonald's ancestral home at Lossiemouth, Scotland, in June 1929. (*The Bettmann Archive, Inc.*) **Opposite:** Al Capone, c. 1929. (*The Bettmann Archive, Inc.*)

Charles Chaplin, 1928. (*Wide World Photos*)

Marie Curie with President Hoover at the White House during her 1929
American visit. (*New York Public Library Picture Collection*)

Orville Wright, at left, and Commander Richard Byrd in 1927. (*The Bettmann Archive, Inc.*)

Serge Diaghilev, the Russian impresario, date unknown. (*The Bettmann Archive, Inc.*)

F. Scott Fitzgerald sketch that appeared in *The New Yorker*, April 10, 1926. (*New-York Historical Society*)

Above, top: Henry Ford and Charles Lindbergh at the Dearborn Airfield in August 1927, when Lindbergh took Ford for his first airplane ride. (*Ford Archives, Henry Ford Museum, Dearborn, Michigan*) **Above, bottom:** "Hatching," September 7, 1927: Rollin Kirby's comment as America awaited the Model A. (*New-York Historical Society*) **Opposite:** The Dearborn gala as captured in rotogravure the following Sunday.

ROTOGRAVURE
SECTION
PART ONE

The Detroit News
THE HOME NEWSPAPER

SUNDAY
OCTOBER 27, 1929
16 PAGES

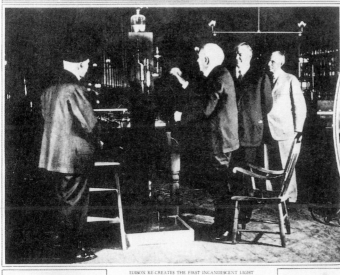

THE PRESIDENT COMES TO TOWN. Mr. Hoover on his arrival in Detroit to attend the Ford party in paying his respect to that famous American whose manifold gifts to mankind have received world wide recognition.

EDISON RE-CREATES THE FIRST INCANDESCENT LIGHT
One of the most impressive moments during the Golden Jubilee of Light at Ford's Village of Greenfield was when the great inventor stepped forward and again played the role of the pioneer in perfecting his first electric lamp. With Mr. Edison are President Herbert C. Hoover and Henry Ford, while at the left is J. M. Jehl, who was present and assisted the inventor in the original work fifty years ago.

MR. EDISON LOOKS ON. During the elaborate ceremonies at Dearborn, the aged inventor spent a busy day, going from building to building, taking in all the displays and activities with consuming interest.

MR. AND MRS. HOOVER TOUR DETROIT. Through miles of streets the President and Mrs. Hoover, in an open car and amid a downpour of rain, traveled from Dearborn to the Detroit City Hall, cheered by thousands.

THE PRESIDENT, EDISON AND FORD. This photo shows the arrival of the Presidential party at Dearborn. Mr. Hoover, with hat raised, is shaking hands with Mr. Edison, who has been escorted forward by Mr. Ford.

FIFTY YEARS AGO. One of the many scenes at Ford's Village of Greenfield, where historic buildings of other days have been rebuilt. This is a view of the General Store of the village, with an old-fashioned carriage on hitch paving by in front.

MR. FORD, THE HOST. The man who made the gigantic celebration possible, and who brought to Dearborn celebrities from all parts of the world to honor his friend, Thomas A. Edison.

THE OLD WOOD BURNER OF YEARS AGO. Part of the exhibit at the Village. Guests at the Ford party were taken for a ride on this old train, a replica of the train on which Mr. Edison served as a news butcher more than half a century ago.

Opposite, top: President Hoover greeted upon arrival at Dearborn. Left to right, Harvey Firestone, Clara Ford, Henry Ford, Mina Edison, Herbert Hoover, Mrs. Hoover, Rep. Eaton, Edison, Secretary of War James Good. **Opposite, center:** Charles Schwab at left, Representative Charles Eaton at center, and Charles Abbot of the Smithsonian at Greenfield Village, October 21, 1929. **Opposite, bottom:** Thomas Edison with President Hoover in the rain at Dearborn, October 21, 1929. **Above, top:** Julius Rosenwald at Greenfield Village on October 21, 1929. **Above, bottom:** Correspondent Will Rogers at Greenfield Village, October 21, 1929. (*All photos courtesy of Ford Archives, Henry Ford Museum, Dearborn, Michigan*)

Above: "Tail Holt," October 5, 1929. (*New-York Historical Society*)
Below: Governor Franklin D. Roosevelt at Harvard University, June 20, 1929. (*Wide World Photos*)

To the people of 1877 the news that broke in the next few days seemed fabulous. A man, it was said, had been able to capture time and play it back again. The phonograph was probably the most *unexpected* invention ever. The Patent Office admitted that nothing remotely resembling it had ever been filed before. It established Edison's reputation. Until then he had been known to scientific and business circles for his improvements to the telegraph, telephone, and stock ticker. With the phonograph, Edison became one of the most famous men in America. The acclaim was both scientific and popular. He was called the most amazing inventor of his age. The Pennsylvania Railroad organized excursions to bring out hundreds at a time to see Edison in his Menlo Park laboratory.

They met a salty and affable worker in overalls who greeted them with obvious delight. Although he had been a lonely telegrapher and had lived the secluded life of a researcher, a gift for showmanship had been waiting for an opportunity to be expressed. Edison gave the crowds a show. He would talk, sing, and shout at the machine and then have the phonograph play it back. He would turn the crank at different speeds, so that the audience first heard a series of wheezes that could not be understood, then the voice of a decrepit old man with a mouthful of water, reciting "Mary Had a Little Lamb," and then the same rhyme in the shrill voice of an excited old woman as the crank was turned quickly. Sometimes he would pat the machine and say, "Well, old phonograph, how are we getting on down there?" and the phonograph would growl back at him in Germanic curses. He took the phonograph to Washington to play before the American Academy of Sciences, then showed it to Congress in the Capitol. It proved such a hit that he was called for a command performance before President Rutherford B. Hayes, in a White House show that lasted until three in the morning.

Although he disclaimed all pretense at magic, Edison enjoyed the tales that began circulating about him. It was said that illuminations blazed in his windows at night, that figures could be seen gliding about in the fields of Menlo Park at midnight bearing lights. The farmers said Edison had a machine that could hear cows munching grass many miles away. Much of his talk of his intentions sounded like magic. One of the many reporters who came to interview him suggested that he was "something of a wizard." Edison denied it, but the remark found its way into print, and the name stuck.

Three years after the phonograph brought Edison to fame, John C. Branner, a muscular man of about thirty-five years, took a steamer to

Brazil. "The valley of the Amazon," Branner told a reporter before setting off, "is one of the greatest palm-bearing regions on the face of the globe, and contains an infinite variety of these trees. The central and western provinces have never yet been explored by the botanist and naturalist, and what their forests may contain is to this day unknown." The trip would take Branner through dangerous country, some of it navigable only by canoe, and would expose him to savage head-hunting tribes that poisoned their arrows.

These dangers would have to be faced in the name of science. Branner was an agent for the noted Professor Edison, the wizard who had startled the world anew with his incandescent lamp and was now seeking a better filament. The inventor had become convinced that it would be some sort of vegetable fiber, probably bamboo or palm. He told the press that he intended to ransack the jungles of the world, if necessary, to find it.

The task was more easily announced than done. The climate in Para, Brazil, was so dank that everything wooden deteriorated in a short time. Branner found some of his samples to be shipped to Edison covered with mold a day after they had been cut, and he feared that they would not last. Branner arranged with a baker to put them atop his furnace, but although that stopped the molding, it also split and curled them and dried them out. Furthermore, Branner found himself shaking with fever and out of action much of the time. Information on which he acted was often inaccurate, and he made fruitless trips. The natives resisted work and sometimes deserted him at inopportune moments. Seven months after setting out, a disheartened Branner found himself stranded in Matto Grosso after a wild goose chase. The merchants, he said, sent canoes down the tributary only in December when the water was high and the Indians inland. "At present," he wrote Edison, "they say that the falls are extremely dangerous, that the fevers are more so, and that the Indians come down to the river during this the dry season and are more unhealthy than the fevers."

Through his agents Professor Edison was conducting the same sort of dragnet searches that he was wont to employ in his laboratory. Other agents were dispatched to the Far East, the West Indies, Indo-China, and Ceylon. Edison justified such extravagances as having scientific purpose. His efforts at getting them into the newspapers shows he also understood their promotional appeal. The publications of the time were always willing to print details of such expeditions, the exotic dangers of which bore resemblance to the romances of Jules Verne, who was entertaining readers of the time with tales of advanced technology, balloon voyages, journeys to unknown islands, and races around the world in eighty days. Edison's men were tracking the pithless fibered palm to its lair, and although their efforts were unproductive, they kept Edison's romance before the public.

Edison had even been able to keep the public mouth agape for a year before he invented the lamp. By the latter half of 1878 he had begun confiding to reporters that, hardly winded by his success with the phonograph, he was engaged in a quest to develop electricity as a source of light and power, and that the days of the gaslighting industry were numbered. He had already worked out the principles, but was still searching for a bulb to use for illumination. He had been experimenting with various filaments and was looking for something more suitable. There was no doubting his eventual success. "I have let the other inventors get the start of me in this matter," he said, acknowledging his rivals, "but I believe I can catch up with them now."

"If you can replace gaslights," one reporter told him, "you can easily make a great fortune."

"I don't care so much about making my fortune," Edison replied, "as I do for getting ahead of the other fellows."

He said he would build a central power station for the whole downtown area of New York, and would light five hundred thousand lamps. He would produce the whole delivery system and sell electricity just as gas was sold. He would measure customer use with some metering system. It would be ready in about six weeks. He was expanding his Menlo Park shops to put this project together, and he soon intended to light up his village with a miniature exposition.

These boasts created excitement in America and England. The press, which had found him a popular subject with readers, followed his every move. The scientists braced themselves to make short work of such effrontery. Such statements, they said, were based not on scientific evidence, but on the showman tactics of a circus. Such braggadocio showed embarrassing ignorance of the principles of electricity. It was doomed to failure.

Edison was engaged, just as his detractors claimed, in the most flagrant sort of attention-getting. The campaign was conceived by Grosvenor Lowrey, a New York lawyer who was aiding Edison by seeking financial backing for him up and down Wall Street. The tireless lawyer found backers at the headquarters of American finance—the House of Morgan.

But when Edison's failures began to pile up in trying various filaments, they too were publicized. In January of 1879 Lowrey was surrounded when he entered the House of Morgan. Stockholders jokingly asked if he had any buyers for their Edison stock. Lowrey told them that every great endeavor had its setbacks, and this was the moment to stand by Edison. J. Pierpont Morgan listened with absorption, then remarked that of course Edison would be backed. "I tell you this," Lowrey wrote to Menlo Park, "because it produced a very pleasing impression on my own mind, for I saw that there was a true ring to it and that these gentlemen were likely, in a stress, to turn out—as I always supposed they would—not to be very easily frightened away from a thing once they made their mind to." Lowrey advised Edison to treat the Wall Streeters as full partners in the venture and to express himself freely when he encountered difficulties, not to be concerned that they would be frightened off.

His partners continued to worry, however, about whether he would come through on his boasts. Lowrey asked Edison to submit a report on the next stage in his work; would he require, for example, so large a work force as he presently had? The gaslight interests continued to attack Edison's competence in the newspapers. In one story Menlo Park was reported to be in despair and Edison at the point of death.

Then Edison dropped the spirits of the Morgan people even farther. He asked for more development money. By October they were crestfallen. It was just at this point—on October 21, 1879—that Edison burned the forty-hour bulb. It was the long-sought breakthrough. Lowrey, to spur investment interest, broke the story of the invention two months later in the *New York Herald*.

Edison had reasserted his magic, and the public never doubted him again. When Ford and Firestone persuaded him to take up the rubber project in 1927, he turned again to the promotional methods that had made him the Wizard of Menlo Park.

"I realize that one of the greatest needs in the United States today is an American-grown rubber of commercial value," Edison said again and again in 1929 to any reporter with a pencil in his hand. "It can be had and I am going to produce it if I have to work eighteen hours a day until it is done. The people of the nation give little enough thought to rubber production but if you will stop to think a minute you will find that we cannot get along without it. It is absolutely necessary to us every day of our lives. We depend almost entirely on it for transportation in these modern times."

Edison, the papers said, had dropped all his other work to turn to a crusade of national importance. He was rushing to re-equip his old laboratory and gearing up to get into rapid-fire action. Startling revelations about America's perilous position in the world drove him night and day. He was turning that searing genius—all the more powerful because of its isolation in deafness—into smashing the foreign hold on the rubber market. He would sweep through every library in the world on another famous Edison hunt. He would test every plant in every jungle grove, leave no territory unexplored to come up with the answers. The project was thus developed in the American consciousness not as a capital venture of Ford, Firestone, and Edison but as the highest and most devoted sort of public service. Urgency was suggested in every story—the most poignant urgency being the hovering angel over the old man. "Give me five years," he would say, "and I'll do it."

The U.S. government threw its support behind the project. The Agriculture and Commerce departments had been pursuing similar aims since 1923 and were pleased to gain Edison as a symbol. "The very fact that a man of Edison's eminence in the world of science has joined the forces engaged in the search for the answer to the rubber puzzle is in itself certain to lend impetus to the movement for the development of a rubber industry in the continental United States," said an Agriculture Department official. The Agriculture Department sent him plants and seeds and offered all cooperation, calling his project vital to the national interest.

Hoover, then commerce secretary, had secured Congressional appropriations for the rubber project. Experts had been sent to Mexico and plans were being considered to dredge the harbor of Frontera in Mexico so that crude rubber could be shipped to New Orleans, to be developed as a refining center. Britain's hold on 75 percent of the world's supply had become intolerable. If rubber could not be grown in the U.S., it could be developed in a nation over which the U.S. could exercise power within its hemisphere.

The Commerce Department was also interested in domestic production. Large stretches of undeveloped southern Florida appeared promising locations. The chief agricultural experiment station for the rubber project was near Miami, and testing was also going on in California and the southwestern states.

Edison spoke of replacing cotton with rubber as the principal southern product. Rubber, he said, would be his crowning achievement. He told American business leaders that he felt responsible to develop the new crop—for had not the nation's growing dependence on rubber all been his doing? Electrical power had brought America to this crisis. Edison announced that he was sending more than a dozen agents fanning across the nation and into Puerto Rico and Cuba, digging up plants and sending them to him. They combed the countryside from Florida to New England and as far west as South Dakota and New Mexico. The agents talked to farmers, asking them if they would please watch yonder plant and mail some seeds to Mr. Edison, just in case the specimens they had mailed him failed to produce seeds. Sometimes they promised small payments to school children to do the job. Everyone became aware that Thomas Edison was on the case. He wrote to railroad agents asking them to comb the railroad rights-of-way for plants. Soon ladies from Alabama were writing advice to Mr. Edison about where to look for cape jasmine, and the notion of domestic rubber as a grassroots effort had taken hold.

Totally absorbed in the project, Edison thought of nothing else. He read voluminously on cross-breeding. He had each plant dried, ground, and weighed. Tests were sometimes taken at different stages of growth. The exhaustiveness of the work never disheartened him. Learning the thousands of wrong ways to the goal, he said, led at last to the right way. He had made fifteen thousand tests in a year and a half. He kept telling America about his progress at every opportunity, and the country listened.

Three names in 1929 were popularly associated with scientific genius. One was Edison, one was Curie, and the third, who fled the spotlight as emphatically as Edison sought it, was Einstein.

His latest work was the talk of Western civilization. His pamphlet was a big seller in Germany, at a price of one mark, or about twenty-four cents. Much of its appeal lay in the often-repeated statement that only a dozen people could understand it.

It had taken Einstein six years to write it. The pamphlet consisted of six pages of heavy mathematical formulae in which he demonstrated that electricity and gravitation were the same thing. He called it his field theory. Einstein was attempting to show that electrical energy is the original source of existence.

On his fiftieth birthday on March 14, 1929, tributes poured in from around the world to his Berlin apartment. Cablegrams, letters, baskets of fruit, wine, and liquors filled his rooms. Checks came to him for distribution to worthy charities. Another gift was the Einstein Forest, to be planted near Jerusalem. He received a little package of tobacco from an unemployed workman, which brought him to tears.

His wife, stationed by the telephone, staved off journalists and the public. He was not antisocial or a grouch, she explained, but if Herr Einstein once began taking telephone calls, he would spend his life explaining his theories and would never be able to work.

A woman reporter cornered Frau Einstein in the elevator of their flat. "Why do you want to interview me?" Frau Einstein asked. "Why should

anyone be interested in me or in Professor Einstein?" They walked outside, standing on the street, presenting their cases to each other. One
talked about the public, the other about privacy. "To find out what our
favorite dishes are?" Frau Einstein protested. "How we dress, sleep and
live in the privacy of our home?" The voice dropped again. After a time
the reporter turned and walked away.

Far above the street, Einstein worked in a high-ceilinged room with an
iron door. He wore a sweater and slippers and smoked the workman's
mixture in his pipe. His gentle face looked dreamily out the window. A
gray halo of long hair surrounded his face. His sensuous lips contrasted
with his domed forehead. His was the strangest kind of fame, for it was
unsought. Attracting attention made him nervous. His fame rested on the
shoulders of experts who assured the world that Albert Einstein had
shaken the foundation of being; but his theory disturbed people.

"I have my own ideas about the so-called theories of Einstein, with his
relativity and his utterly befogged notions about space and time," Cardinal
O'Connell said in Boston that year. "It seems nothing short of an attempt
at muddying the waters so that, without perceiving the drift, innocent
students are led away into a realm of speculative thought, the sole basis of
which, so far as I can see, is to produce a universal doubt about God and
His creation. The outcome of this doubt and befogged speculation about
time and space is a cloak beneath which lies the ghastly apparition of
atheism."

Einstein was the most famous German in the world, but some of his
countrymen would not call him a German at all. They were enraged that a
Jew was being thus honored while their generals lived in the shadows. At a
recent scientific meeting in Berlin, while Einstein sat in a box listening to
professors discuss his theories, some young German students, their eyes
blazing with fury, had invaded his box and threatened him with their fists.
Einstein looked bemused out the window, planning the creation of additional doubt.

When the examination was over, the boys were driven up in busloads
to Glenmont, the huge Victorian mansion of the Edisons in West Orange.
Across the vast expanse of lawn a group of chiffoned and white-flanneled
guests were being served by butlers. Between them and the boys a Ha-
waiian orchestra draped with leis played plangent melodies. It was August
2, 1929, the day of the great Brain Derby—the highly publicized search
for a young successor to Edison, a youthful genius to take the Wizard's
place.

The boys looked around the lawn, flopped into chairs, and began to rehash the examination. They were washed out. They had come from all forty-eight states and the District of Columbia to find the most promising high school boy in the United States. Although the exam had included questions on Jane Addams and Marie Curie, Edison was not considering a female for the title.

Even plates of chicken salad and ice cream and the cheery efforts of Charles Edison, the inventor's son, failed to rouse their young spirits, until their interest was perked up by the sight of two butlers, followed by scrambling movie cameramen, carrying a gigantic birthday cake across the lawn.

"It's for Mr. Ford," one boy said. "See the little candy automobile."

"You're all wet. Mr. Ford's birthday was last Tuesday."

Just then Ford appeared with Mrs. Edison's niece, Nancy Miller, and since she was seven years old on the day Ford was sixty-six, they cut the cake together. That started the boys stirring again. Soon they were grinning for the cameramen. The adult guests cheered them. Anne Morrow Lindbergh, in a blue silk frock, appeared to be enjoying herself. Her husband and Edison were inside the house with the other judges working on the examinations but they came out several times during the party. Their shyness gone, the boys kidded with photographers, chatted with guests, and sent the butlers back often for more ice cream.

Anne Morrow Lindbergh was thrilled with the turn her life as a young wife had taken. She was relaxing on the lawn of one of the greatest of world figures, was the bride of an equally famous man, and wherever she went she discovered people speaking with admiration of her father, the leading light of the House of Morgan and the ambassador to Mexico. It was really a small world.

She was discovering, meanwhile, that being famous had its drawbacks. Surrounded by hubbub, she would reply to a nonchalant question without realizing that she was talking to a reporter. She had learned that she could not speak of personal matters in a crowded room. Charles had even cautioned her not to speak frankly in a hotel room while the transom was open.

Even their wedding in May had been carried out with secrecy. The people chosen to attend the service at the Morrow home in Englewood, New Jersey, had not known of it until they were assembled. Then the bride and groom had slipped past the journalists who were holding the home under siege. The unembellished announcement was made two hours after their departure. The newspapers sought them everywhere. They were rumored to be aboard a yacht near the Morgan home in Glen Cove, or seen in a Newark hotel, or driving toward North Haven. "Newspapers can never blame police forces for not finding criminals," Will Rogers chortled. "Here they have everybody from the managing editors down to the newsboys looking for Charley and Annie and can't find them. What would they do if they were looking for somebody that nobody knew?"

The bride did not find the situation amusing. Like her husband, she was appalled at the invasion of their privacy. Even newspapers opposed to such behavior found themselves drawn by the momentum. If a newspaper let the story drop, it only meant that the public would drop the paper.

Although her quarrel was with cameramen and reporters who were trampling the grass at Glenmont, those journalists were only recruits in the onslaught against privacy. The real culprits were in the house, judging the contest.

They included George Eastman, who had given the photographers their ammunition. He and Edison had developed the hardware of the motion picture. Edison had devastated traditional notions of privacy with the phonograph, the microphone, the mimeograph machine, the Edison effect that had led to the discovery of the vacuum tube and thus radio, and his improvements on the telephone, perhaps the most intrusive of all inventions. Nor was Ford blameless, for his Model T had broken down distances and isolation. And for that matter the bride's husband had played a major role in the development of the airplane. And when the newlywed Lindberghs were discovered, it was a tabloid reporter in a rented airplane who tracked them down.

Anne and Charles Lindbergh were discovering that publicity was difficult to limit. They had spent a considerable amount of their waking hours since their marriage promoting the new air-rail cross-country passenger service. With cameras flashing about them they had dedicated hangars of Transcontinental Air Transport. They had pushed buttons on the West Coast to signal the start of operations on the East Coast. They were before the cameras in Los Angeles when a movie actress cracked a bottle over the nose of a Ford Tri-Motor plane. The ambassador's daughter and tinseled actresses were allies in the enterprise. While Anne Lindbergh deplored the erosion of privacy, the people of her class could be found in the magazines endorsing beauty soaps, carpets, and cigarettes, right next to a product endorsed by her husband.

Shortly before noon the following day the boys were back on the lawn again. They had been up late on an outing to Coney Island and were tired. They watched the Edison cow chew her cud. "I'd like to flop down like that cow and take it easy," one boy whispered to a companion.

"Well, it won't be long now," said the other with a forced grin. "Here

they come." Down the front steps of Glenmont came the venerable inventor, his wife, his son Charles, and the judges. Ford and Eastman were
chatting amiably. Lindbergh looked uncomfortable. Dr. Samuel Stratton,
president of the Massachusetts Institute of Technology, looked serious.

"I want to say first," the MIT president began, "that not one of you
failed, that each of you has been a credit to your country and to the state
from which you came." The boys relaxed as he spoke. In the front row
three boys pulled out cameras and began taking pictures of the notables.
They focused on Lindbergh, who declined to smile and looked bored. One
boy fished in his pocket, pulled out another roll of film, and reloaded.
Stratton had been talking for several minutes.

"Some of the questions, we understand, gave trouble to all of you.
There was the one about the future of the automobile in one hundred
years, for instance. We thought that some of you boys might have recalled
that Mr. Ford was on the committee and would not care to discourage
him, but we believed that Colonel Lindbergh's presence might offset this.
Mr. Eastman, by the way, was greatly pleased that photography was the
hobby of so many of you." Then his demeanor abruptly changed. "I don't
want to keep you any longer in suspense," Stratton said, "and I shall
announce the winner of this contest—Wilber B. Huston of Washington."

The boys looked this way and that. The reporters scanned the group to
find him. Suddenly there was a rush toward a youth in horn-rimmed
glasses standing in a daze. The boys cheered and lifted him up on the
shoulders of two large boys, who became the head of a snake dance.
Hands were thrust toward him, and he reached out happily to grasp them.
After a few minutes of cavorting they put him back on the ground. "Much
obliged, fellows," the tanned and grinning boy said. Other scholarships
were also awarded, and all the winners were called to the front to be
congratulated and have their pictures taken with the great. Mr. Edison
looked benevolent. Ford was cordial. Lindbergh was aloof. Eastman was
kind to a boy who began to moisten about the eyes, shaking hands with
him a second time and telling him of the fine job he had done.

Wilber Huston was no longer just another boy. Pictures and stories
about the son of Bishop and Mrs. S.A. Huston of the Episcopal Diocese of
Olympia, Washington, were flashed around the world. It was reported that
he was a photography enthusiast and was interested in marine biology. He
was described as a retiring and modest lad who had to be pushed to enter
the contest. Now he was instantly and forever famous—the successor to
Edison, America's smartest boy, winner of the Brain Derby, front-page
news in every newspaper in America: Wilber B. Huston.

Just a few days after the Brain Derby, Edison caught pneumonia, and for the next several weeks the wings of Death brushed close. On September 2, for the first time since he had taken to bed, he was recovered sufficiently to sit up in a chair, conversing with his family and smoking cigars. He talked about his rubber project and looked over the reports of experiments on rubber extracted from various plants. Henry Ford visited him, expressing hope that he would be able to attend the Jubilee dinner. Ford could see that the bout with death had taken a terrible toll. Edison had begun 1929 as a hearty old man, but the year had weakened him irretrievably. The old inventor had uremia, there were indications of a kidney malfunction and diabetes, and his digestive system seemed to be wearing out. Death had flown by this time but would be back.

"Sex is simply a biological fact," Ben Lindsey had written in one of the most-read books of the decade. "It is as much as the appetite for food. Like the appetite for food, it is neither legal nor illegal, moral nor immoral. To bring Sex under the jurisdiction of law and authority is as impossible as to bring food hunger under such jurisdiction."

The book was *The Revolt of Modern Youth*, and it was prominently displayed on the bookshelves of the modern thinker of 1929. At fifty-nine years of age, hardly a youth, Lindsey had become the spokesman for the Jazz Age. His book had been translated into several languages and was selling around the world. He had followed it with *The Companionate Marriage*, which established him even more solidly as the leading exponent of sexual revolution. An Austrian churchman charged that year that Bolshevism and Lindseyism were the "two destructive forces threatening to destroy . . . European civilization." Such attacks were tonic to him, for he loved to battle the Establishment.

The battle had first been joined on a Saturday morning in 1902. The members of the Denver police board, in response to a request, filed into the courtroom of Juvenile Judge Ben B. Lindsey. They came full of curiosity, for they wanted a glimpse of the Napoleonic little judge who, at thirty-two years of age and in a short time on the bench, had so quickly acquired a reputation as a troublemaker. The judge had been harassing saloonkeepers for selling alcoholic beverages to children. This was especially bothersome to the police board because the saloonkeepers were big contributors to the political parties.

The courtroom was full of children and reporters, and the members of the police board began to feel uncomfortable. Lindsey soon made his intentions clear. He spoke of young prostitutes led to the trade in "wine rooms," as the wide-open bars of frontier Denver were called. He spoke of young boys who stole from their employers to make up gambling losses run up in saloons, and of mere children already careening drunkenly in the streets. If the children of Denver were delinquent, he said, the fault could be laid at the feet of their elders, who looked the other way while saloon owners disobeyed the law. "I therefore beg of you in this public manner, in the presence of these children, for their benefit, that you earnestly and diligently war upon these places," the judge said as the reporters wrote it all down. "I assure you that you will then have the good will and the respect that are denied you now."

In one day the little judge turned the public opinion of Denver around. The press loved the story, and the clergy praised his exposure of hypocrisy. Judge Lindsey had discovered his great talent—not being a judge, or being a lawyer, or making money, but attracting publicity, and after that Saturday he never let up.

Writing for the muckraking magazines that had undertaken the exposure of privilege and wrongdoing, he began an assault on the entrenched interests and the corrupters of power. A series of hard-hitting articles was made into a book, which he titled *The Beast*. The beast, he wrote, was like those hidden tigers in children's picture puzzles. One found its dissembled parts—a paw here, a tail there, an ear in the grass—but it was all one.

To Lindsey the enemy was a monolithic force, and he aimed at its vitals. When attacked he struck back harder, and his list of enemies grew long. At every opportunity he turned the spotlight of publicity on his murderous pas de deux with the beast. Although he failed in a campaign to become governor of Colorado, his writing made him a national figure, and a 1914 poll chose the balding judge as one of the ten most important living Americans.

By 1914 his passion was the Colorado Fuel & Iron strike, and he led a delegation to Washington to meet with President Wilson. Lindsey suggested that Rockefeller could be brought to his knees by shutting the mines, but the president seemed undisposed to follow the judge's advice. The delegation then proceeded to New York where, with Mother Jones, its members testified on the plight of strikers before the U.S. Commission on Industrial Relations. Rockefeller embraced Mother Jones and other manageable souls, but froze Lindsey out, having no intention of playing the Dragon to the judge's St. George. A congressman charged that Lindsey had "swept across the country with a troupe of vaudeville artists with the purpose of adding luster to his peculiar fame by spreading denunciation and falsehood where it will best attract attention." Chambers of Commerce in Colorado adopted resolutions condemning him. One man proposed that a committee be appointed to spit at him when he got off the train in Denver.

He conducted court without his robes and lowered his bench so as to look less magisterial and to strike a rapport with young people. He was masterful at it. A perpetual adolescent himself, he won their loyalties easily. Women confided their inmost secrets to him. He began to see a composite picture of the American family that was at variance with the pretenses of the age, and eventually he turned this material into *The Revolt of Modern Youth*.

In the book he sprinkled good advice with facile attempts to be timely, but his books came along at exactly the proper hour as an explanation of new sexual attitudes. "Thirty, forty years ago, youth couldn't have flung such a challenge with the least hope of success," he wrote. "Today, the age of the automobile, the telephone, speed, good wages and an unheard of degree of economic independence for everybody, it can." Science and its air of impersonality, he said, were teaching youth to think straight.

His books were based on case histories from his own files. They traded heavily in optimism about youth and impatience with the hypocrisy of elders, delivered in a provocative style. His latest book even dealt with birth control, which was so controversial that in many states information about it was illegal. By "companionate marriage," Lindsey meant a marriage entered with no intention of raising children; in such cases, he argued, divorce should be made almost automatic on request. His enemies called it another word for free love, and the Boston Chapter of the Daughters of the American Revolution put the book on their blacklist.

Now more a celebrity than a judge, and on tour for a time to promote the film version of *The Companionate Marriage*, he shocked his judicial colleagues with his immodesty. By the end of 1927 his colleagues could rest more easily, for Lindsey's enemies had knocked him at last from the bench.

Stopping Lindsey had become a national goal of the Ku Klux Klan, which by the middle of the decade was riding high in Colorado and was outraged because Lindsey, unlike many public officials in the state, would not accommodate himself to Klan views.

In 1924 the Klan scored victories all over Colorado. Although Lindsey appeared to have squeaked through, his victory was overturned in the courts in 1927 when some ballots were thrown out, and he was out of office for the first time in a quarter-century. The KKK moved into the juvenile court—its new chief probation officer was a Klansman—and

Lindsey departed with all his court records. A cry was raised for the return of the files, held to be the property of the state.

Lindsey, his wife, and two former employees of the court met at the Lindsey home on September 16, 1927, tore the records into shreds, and then packed them into cartons. Two days later, accompanied by friends and reporters in five cars, they set off in a caravan, Lindsey bearing the matches and gasoline. The cars pulled up and stopped at a lot at West 13th Avenue and Umatilla Street. There they sprinkled gasoline on the papers and set them ablaze.

Hundreds and hundreds of people, he told reporters, had confided in him—in him, not in the state of Colorado. They had related the intimate details of their lives. He had taken extensive notes and would be damned if he would let such records fall into the hands of the KKK. Lindsey talked as the blaze leapt, and the pencils of the reporters raced across the notebooks. Twenty-five years after his debut, Lindsey still knew how to gather a crowd.

His career as a stormy personality continued. When the Lewis and Clark chapter of the DAR in Eugene, Oregon, invited him to speak, it was assailed by the National Defense Committee, a so-called patriotic organization. Demonstrators were so threatening when he lectured in Birmingham that the police chief and detectives escorted him back to his hotel.

When the Fords invited him to Dearborn, he was facing yet another threat—ethics charges for accepting fees while a judge. He had helped a friend in a contested will and had been given a payment, which he considered a gift. His enemies claimed that he had practiced law while a judge, and he faced the possibility of being disbarred. He seemed rather unconcerned and was planning to move to Los Angeles and array himself against film censorship. He had become captivated by the glint of the place while working as an advisor for a film on juvenile reform.

History has always been full of famous people, but the famous of 1929 were famous in a new way. Their voices were heard on radio, their way of moving and walking seen in newsreels, their pictures seen in newspapers. They were the bearers of changes in social mores, fashions, and trends through news media. In the past the famous climbed a ladder and were famous in a context of neighborhood, town, hierarchy. Now they arose suddenly like bubbles in a mass. They came like Lindsey, out of the magazines; like Chaplin, out of films. They were suddenly touched with fame, or so it appeared, whereas in the old days fame grew organically. This phenomenon of a person stepping out of a mass into a sudden spotlight is the emergence of a *celebrity*.

Sometimes, as in the case of Jane Addams, a single person came to stand for a movement. Hull House was located in Chicago's Nineteenth Ward, one of the city's worst slums, but when she was called upon for help, at whatever hour of night, the legendary Jane ventured into the streets alone. When she awoke to find burglars in her room, she spoke to them calmly, and they left without taking anything. She and a band of like-minded women had opened the settlement house to be present among the city's poor. By 1929, after forty years of legend-building, Hull House was the symbol of American social work, Jane Addams had become the most famous woman in America, and the movement had become a shaping influence in American social thought. "One feels," Julius Rosenwald said of her, "that it is a benediction to have her in the home."

Rosenwald supported her morally and financially and was never admonitory, but two other supporters, Harry Hart and Joseph Schaffner, were aggrieved when Jane Addams organized a relief fund for workers in the 1910 textile strike, since many of the forty thousand workers had walked out of the Hart, Schaffner and Marx factories. Hart and Schaffner were galled by Hull House's receptivity to labor leaders during that siege. Addams went to Hart's house for dinner during the strike to explain the position of the workers to management and tried to explain management's position to visiting labor leaders. She always favored reconciliation. "Jane, if the devil himself came riding down Halsted Street with his tail waving out behind him," one of her colleagues once remarked, "you'd say, 'what a beautiful curve he has in his tail.' "

On October 21, 1929, when she was sixty-nine years old and her figure had become encircled with weight, she came to Dearborn as the symbol of progressivism in America. She spent much of her time traveling for various causes—chiefly peace in 1929—and Dearborn was another stop along the way. She and Lindsey were the two most conspicuous progressive figures at Dearborn, and they had supported many of the same causes. Youth had always been a special interest to her, and she had worked with Lindsey to reform the juvenile courts. But while he functioned as a hell-raiser, she shrank from conflict and preferred to function as a source of humane sentiment.

Their differences grew from their beginnings. Lindsey had been born in miserable poverty. His father, haunted by debts and bad health, had committed suicide. Ben was so hungry that he was unable to concentrate when he studied the law, lost his train of thought, and began to lose confidence in his abilities. At the age of nineteen he attempted suicide, but when he held the revolver to his temple by some fluke the bullet failed to fire. Overcome with revulsion, Lindsey threw himself on the bed of his locked room. From that moment on he had lived always on the alert for weakness, proving his fearlessness to himself every day. Life became a test, with himself as the center of the drama.

It was not desperation that produced Jane Addams, but the flight from privilege. She had suffered from nervousness and invalidism, and when recovering from a spine operation she found that she had a gift for taking care of children and felt better for having them in her charge. The lives of the upper classes seemed fully as destitute to her as the lives of the poor. She did not require enemies to define her identity. Her attitude toward the enemy was that found in the greatest generals: she attempted to understand them.

Jane Addams tried to understand not only why the poor people of Chicago's Nineteenth Ward kept electing a corrupt alderman, but she tried to understand the alderman as well. Sympathy was natural to her, but it was sometimes tinged with a foggy sentimentality. She could sympathize with the prostitute, but only because she believed that the prostitute was a victim, that no woman ever became one voluntarily, and above all, that none of them enjoyed it. She was as active as Rosenwald and Rockefeller in the Society for the Suppression of Vice, and like them she believed that the key to the prostitution problem was for men to suppress their illicit carnal yearnings.

That was the solution of an ingrained individualist, but unlike many of her fellow individualists at Dearborn, she had no illusions about the idyllic rural life. She saw rural life as stultifying and the city as a transforming event in the life of America. Humanity was creating its own environment and coming into control. Men were no longer dominated by the past, the extended family, codicils to their ancestors' wills, class lines, but free to make their destinies. Women were not tied to pump and washtub, but free to support themselves and make their own lives. That was what America was about, and the new arrivals to the city, from the rural areas or from other lands, had to be met and assimilated so that they could join the march.

Her influence was wide and deep. Ramsay MacDonald, the new British Prime Minister, was an old friend at Hull House. MacKenzie King, Rockefeller's chief labor advisor and a shaper of the Colorado Plan, was an alumnus, as was Gerard Swope, the president of GE.

Lindsey had used the rising national magazines to become a spokesman for his ideas, but Jane Addams used them in a deeper dimension. She became an American presence, and as much was written about her as by her. The writers invariably commented on her air of soulful calm, her melancholy eyes, the inspiring service of her life. She loved her reputation for saintliness in a thoroughly unsaintly manner; the twentieth century, with the aid of new media, had begun to produce self-conscious saints. She searched for every press clipping and article she could find about herself. She threw away the attacks and the obscene letters but saved all that praised and adored.

Businesslike, keen-minded, a fine writer, and an effective speaker, she represented all those Hull House women who had devoted their lives to projects for which Jane Addams was given credit. She hungered for the Nobel Peace Prize, which had so far been denied her. Some of her lieutenants pushed her into the spotlight, but she never protested; others resented that she was the celebrity while others were more deserving of credit. When Theodore Roosevelt wanted to dramatize his support of women's suffrage by having a woman second his nomination for president in 1912, he naturally chose Jane Addams, although others had campaigned steadfastly for the vote for years while she had given it hardly a thought.

When Yale bestowed an honorary degree on this extraordinary woman in 1909, she shared the platform with James J. Hill, one of the most shameless of the Robber Barons. The newspapers did not find the pairing peculiar; quite the contrary. "Have you noticed," one editorial writer asked, "how colleges are beginning to prize the people who do things in the world? It is only a short step from the recognition of the value of practical organization to the putting of such things into the college curriculum." Other newspapers commented that both recipients had succeeded in the real world. They got things done. Both had made names for themselves and left their mark on the times. That would have to be the criteria for an American saint. Mass communications had created its first saint, and she was a new breed. Saint Jane was the first saint to save her clippings.

Einstein and Chaplin tried to avoid the press, while Judge Lindsey and Charles Schwab tried to attract reporters. General Charles G. Dawes did neither—the press came flocking to him whenever he whirled into sight.

In June of 1929 a large crowd waited as the *Olympic* docked at Southampton to greet the new ambassador to England, the one and only Dawes. The chargé d'affaires of the U.S. Embassy boarded as head of the official greeting party and led a short ceremony. The mayor of Southampton, adding his voice to the near-unanimous opinion of the British newspapers, said that the work ahead of General Dawes was the most crucial and important ever undertaken by any American ambassador to England, and in response the new ambassador spoke of his memories of Southampton when he entered the port on a cattle ship in command of a regiment of American troops during the war.

A reporter from the local paper asked the ambassador if he intended to treat the English to some of his celebrated expressions.

"Hell's bells, no!" Dawes replied. "Now I'm a diplomat. I must don kid-glove manners. But if you newspapermen don't stop asking indiscreet questions I will be forced to break my resolutions in about ten seconds."

Ever since Hoover had nominated him, Dawes had been telling people that what he did not know about diplomacy would fill volumes, but at the dockside he demonstrated a grasp of its basics. One of his more enthusiastic friends said that America should have a better chance to improve its relations with England under the new Labor government than it would have were Sir Austen Chamberlain still the foreign secretary. Dawes gave no sign that he had heard the remark, knowing better than to comment on another nation's elections.

American and British reporters were out in force to catch the colorful ambassador, but during the train ride to London, as they sat about him in the car, he kept busy by refilling his pipe and staved off all talk about substantive matters by keeping them amused with stories. His only revelation about his activities was social.

"For four long weary years," the general said, "as Vice President I was the official diner-out for the American administration. I can assure you that for the first few months in London I want to devote all my social leisure to seeing my old English friends of the war and reparations periods."

One of the English reporters eventually came to ask him about his peculiar underslung pipe. "Do you want to know now or later?" Dawes asked, "because I assure you I am never going to mention this pipe more than once in England no matter how long I stay here."

The reporter said he would like to know immediately.

"Very well, then," said the ambassador, "I will now explain for the millionth and last time that this pipe catches all the liquid nicotine in the bottom so it cannot go through the stem and poison me. This is positively my last word on the pipe."

Dawes was a flamboyant sort, but also a good negotiator. He had shown his abilities both as head of the Board of Supply for the Allied forces during the war and as chairman of the Dawes Committee, which had started reparations payments going earlier in the decade. Hoover had sent, however, an unusual breed to Great Britain. He was after a reduction in naval strength, on both the British and American sides, and if that could be brought about by coaxing, wheedling, bullying, pounding tables, and jumping in the air, the president had sent the right man. Charles G. Dawes operated on his nerve—a quality that he showed in his contrariness, his opportunism, and his love of the spotlight.

No theater director ever had a more adroit sense of timing than he, or used it to better advantage. Although his fellow Republicans were aware of his temperament, he still managed to surprise them. That happened to a group of Republican congressmen who were checking the Wilson Administration's conduct of the war. They sent to Chicago for Dawes to make an appearance before their committee, hoping he would be of assistance in their search for malfeasance. The peppery Dawes appeared on schedule but failed to get in the swing. The committee members prodded and poked at him, while his reserve forced them to reveal their intentions more openly. When they were in their most vulnerable position, Dawes struck.

The general had been Procurement Chief for the American Army during the war and, had he chose, he must have had several morsels that would have caused the Democrats to squirm. Instead, making no effort to conceal his contempt, he told the committee that the Army had been fighting a war, not keeping books.

"Can't you understand that men were dying under shot and shell?" he exploded. "When we got a call for a carload of ether for the field hospitals, do you think we stopped to put it down in the right column of the proper ledger? Hell Maria, no—we shot it along!"

He was out of his chair. Dawes walked up and down the room, his small, wiry frame leaning into the astonished committee members as he waved his fists under their noses. His performance demolished GOP plans to make political yardage out of the war. Furthermore, it made Dawes a national celebrity—a salty midwestern banker who spouted the obscure and forgotten oaths of Ohio rivermen he had known in his youth. The phrase "Hell Maria" became closely associated with his name, and with so convenient a tag, everyone in America was aware of him.

A second outburst came when President Harding chose him as budget director. To introduce the administration to the mysteries of budgeting— the office was new to Washington—Dawes called a meeting of the cabinet. His vehement performance was even more daring than it had been before the investigating committee, for he shook his fists under the chins of some of the most powerful men in Washington. He pranced about the room with a broom to show that a Navy Department broom would sweep as well as a War Department broom and that broom buying had to be coordinated. "General Dawes is the only public speaker I have ever seen," Harding said of his find, "who can keep on talking while both feet are in the air."

When the dust settled it was discovered that Dawes had talents other than histrionic. Much in the same manner that he had used to drive and fast-talk Allied military purchases into a system that made sense, he organized government expenditures into a first-rank operation, and was one of the few dazzling stars in Harding's generally incompetent administration. Dawes performed so well that in the 1924 campaign the Republicans made economy the main issue.

Calvin Coolidge led the ticket. Dawes, following his triumph as budget director, had distinguished himself again in Europe as chairman of the committee that made the plan to begin reparations payments, and wound up as the vice-presidential candidate. When the Coolidge-Dawes ticket won, he returned to Washington to preside over the Senate.

Cantankerous as ever, Dawes had no intention of being smothered by the colorless Coolidge. He was carrying around with him, and showing to his political associates, a speech which he intended to deliver at his inauguration. The general was aware that up until then the vice-presidential inaugural ceremony, conducted in the Senate chambers, was thin gruel—a sedate business played down so as not to detract from the big show in front of the Capitol. He was about to change that tradition.

To the astonishment of Coolidge, Dawes made a savage inaugural speech in which he ripped into the Senate rules. He called them archaic and stupid, allowing a single senator to filibuster as long as he could hold out, grinding the process of legislation to a halt. In his high, rasping voice, accompanied by pounding and arm-waving, he excoriated the senators and told them to get down to business. Upstaging the president of the United States at his own inauguration was a supreme show of nerve, and it produced great notices.

It also brought the wrath of the entire Senate down upon him. But the eccentric Dawes was so lighthearted that by the end of his term he had become the most popular figure in the Senate and one of the celebrities of Washington. Upon leaving office in March, he brought peals of laughter in a farewell gesture to the Senate, gathered to hear his successor inaugurated, by pounding his fist upon the desk before him and declaiming: "I take back nothing!" He had made many friends in Washington, and in the man whose inauguration he had stolen, one enemy.

He was sent to Great Britain at a difficult moment. For the preceding century, with Great Britain expanding its empire and the United States advancing westward, they had kept out of each other's way. But with the coming of the twentieth century, the United States moved beyond its continental limits and began to develop as a world power. And with the

world war, all the old verities were shattered. Great Britain's position had
faltered and the United States suddenly usurped its place as the strongest
economic power in the world.

To make matters more irritating, Great Britain was suddenly committed to huge war debts to the United States and believed that Italy and
France had been let off much more leniently. England's export trade had
fallen off seriously. The collapse of its coal industry had left a million
workers chronically unemployed and living at public expense. It faced the
onslaught of American mass production. And as the crowning insult, the
United States was challenging the very foundation of British power, its self-
bestowed right to blockade all sea trade in the event of war—a tradition
older, dearer, and more vital to the British than was the Monroe Doctrine
to America.

The United States found the British Empire in control of much of the
world's raw materials. American industry needed cheap oil and cheap
rubber, but found British oil interests competing with American companies
in Mexico, Persia, Turkey, and Iraq, and found almost all the world's
rubber output in British hands. Led by Edison, Ford, Firestone, and
Hoover, the Americans were attempting to challenge the British rubber
monopoly.

Thus the differences between the two nations were considerable, but
Dawes was attempting to open talks with the British on mutual naval
reductions, the basis of British strength. When he arrived at Buckingham
Palace on a June night for his first presentation at court, however, he was
not thinking about sea power, but about his trousers.

Debutantes and their sharp-eyed mothers, foreign envoys, and all the
court retinue were awaiting his first appearance. The grand ballroom glittered with the splendor of jewels, decorations, nodding plumes, gold braid,
silk stockings, fans, coronets, and knee-breeches.

Before his departure from the United States, Dawes had been baited by
the press on whether he would wear knee-breeches, the standard male
attire at court. "You can go plumb to hell! That's my business!" he told
reporters. Then, before the eyes of royalty, the ambassador revealed his
preferences. Resplendent court attendants announced his name and then
ushered him into the presence of the queen. He marched in wearing orthodox evening dress, with trousers all the way down to his patent-leather
shoes.

Queen Mary, in a green and gold gown, bore the sight without fainting
and without having to resort to a fan to hide a smile. She presided alone in
the absence of George V, who was recuperating from an illness. The Lord

Chamberlain, having been duly informed that the American ambassador intended to cover his calves with trousers, had passed on the word to Her Majesty of so stunning a departure from court strictures. The Court also bore up well. Debutantes of many lands bestowed courtesies on the queen, standing before her golden throne. Her Majesty's family continued calmly —the Prince of Wales in the scarlet uniform of a colonel of the Grenadier Guards, Prince George in a naval uniform, and with them Princess Ingrid of Sweden, radiant in a pastel gown. Amid the flash all around him, Dawes looked curiously out of place in ordinary evening clothes, but he walked with determination in his stride.

The question that Dawes had raised had a long and unsettled tradition. No subject had aroused the ire of Colonial editors more than the proclivity of the Philadelphia and New York social elite to "ape the fatuities of Britain" in dress and social decorum. When Benjamin Franklin appeared in plain brown velvet before the English Privy Council he was called uncouth, but when he wore the same clothing before the king of France, he was compared to a "sturdy democrat from the age of Cato." Franklin's intention had been clear—he aimed to contrast the ostentation of Old World Courts to democratic simplicity of dress. As another gifted master of publicity, Dawes had studied Franklin well.

The British made little of it, accepting the affair as another evidence of the quirky Dawes personality. His play had not been to the British press, but to the home audience, and in the United States it was major news and greeted with approval. Dawes was lauded as a 100 percent American, a son of prairie democracy. As usual, he had managed to steal the scene.

Through much of the decade it had been an idea in currency that the United States was no place for an artist. Ezra Pound, living in Paris, said the country was lost, and many aspiring artists migrated to join him. Gertrude Stein, who presided over the most important salon for expatriate Americans in Paris, reassured them that France was the proper spiritual home for those wishing to escape the soul-stifling atmosphere that mass production and standardization was said to have created in America.

In time the voyage to France became a cliche, and in 1929, when the reparations experts were meeting in Paris, the cafes were filled with would-be artists talking endlessly about the art that they someday intended to create and tourists who strained their necks to catch a glimpse of F. Scott Fitzgerald in his cups.

When Morley Callaghan and his wife, Loretto, sailed to Paris in the spring of 1929 they especially wanted to meet two people—Ernest Hemingway, whose reputation as a serious fiction writer was rising, and the glamorous F. Scott Fitzgerald. Callaghan, himself a writer, intended if possible to find literary comradeship and enhance his own reputation as the Third Musketeer.

He was an old friend of Hemingway's, having worked with him some years earlier on a Toronto newspaper. Callaghan had never met Fitzgerald, although the celebrated novelist had helped his career by pointing out some of Callaghan's fiction to the right people, much as Fitzgerald had helped Hemingway earlier.

Hemingway was deeply involved in boxing that year, and Callaghan was good with his fists, so when he renewed his friendship with Hemingway they began to box regularly at the American Club in Paris. They would walk over carrying equipment bags while Hemingway expounded his views of literature. There was a powerful competitive streak in his nature and he talked about writing as if he were training to take on not only his contemporaries but the supreme masters of the past. When they went out for beer and continued their discussions, Hemingway would drink his quickly, as if challenging Callaghan to keep up. Hemingway expressed himself slowly and precisely and admired men who did things expertly, with courage and a cool head. He was handsome and moustached, and his natural warmth and sweetness saved him from undue severity.

It rained one afternoon on their way to the club. The rain was so gentle—it was one of those soft early-summer Paris rains—that, although Callaghan lacked a raincoat, they decided not to take a taxi. Hemingway held his raincoat like a tent over his friend and himself.

The club had no boxing ring, but there was a room in the back downstairs, with mats and parallel bars, for working out. They went down there and stripped down to their shorts and shirts and put on their gloves. Callaghan had heard so much of Hemingway's prowess as a boxer that at first he had been intimidated, but soon discovered that he had little to fear. Hemingway's form was perfect but his timing was bad. In an alley fight the tall, brawny Hemingway could have taken him, but in the ring Callaghan, although overweight and four inches shorter, could outbox him.

When they began to fight Callaghan flicked away at his mouth and nose, counting on his quick hands. Hemingway kept his brown eyes riveted on his opponent, waiting for an opening. When Hemingway threw a left, Callaghan slipped it and stepped in, catching him with a left to the mouth. Hemingway's mouth began to bleed and his tongue curled along his lip, wiping off blood. Again he was hit on the lip, and sucked in the blood. He took a third punch on the mouth, then, as Callaghan prepared to slip in again, he spat a mouthful of blood into Callaghan's face.

Callaghan dropped his stance. The blood dripped from his face to his shirt, staining it red. The two men stared at each other for a moment. "That's what the bullfighters do when they're wounded," Hemingway said. "It's a way of showing contempt." He smiled winningly.

Callaghan tried to laugh. The two had to stop boxing while he wiped the symbol of Hemingway's contempt for injury from his face and shirt. Neither mentioned the incident again, and they went out to drink at the Falstaff. Hemingway's cut and swollen mouth didn't deter him from being as jolly and talkative as usual.

Every time Callaghan would mention his desire to meet Fitzgerald, Hemingway would shrug and say he had no word about him. Puzzled by Hemingway's lack of enthusiasm, Morley and Loretto went out one night to call unaccompanied on the Fitzgeralds. No one answered the apartment buzzer but as they turned to leave a taxi drew up and the handsome couple, a street lamp illuminating their matching golden hair, alighted in the street. Soon all of them were in the Fitzgerald apartment talking.

Fitzgerald was interested in anything Hemingway was doing and asked about him promptly. He had a copy of Hemingway's new novel, *A Farewell To Arms,* in manuscript and read a segment to his guests. Zelda, however, scorned the passage and Scott was injured when Callaghan failed to share his enthusiasm.

Zelda did much of the talking. Callaghan, who had expected to meet a carefree and flippant woman, was surprised at her solemnity. She talked on for a while, until Scott announced that his wife was tired and would go to bed immediately. As she left compliantly, he explained to the guests that she had to get up early for her ballet lessons.

Fitzgerald crisply and correctly poured himself another drink and lifted the glass to his fine-featured face. He asked Callaghan's opinion of several American writers, and in each case Callaghan dismissed their work as of minor significance. Fitzgerald smiled, listening closely. Leaning forward, his face suddenly colorless as a corpse's, he said, "Let's have lunch tomorrow, Morley."

"I'd be glad to have lunch," Callaghan said.

"Whom would you like to have lunch with us?" Fitzgerald asked.

"It doesn't matter, Scott."

"Clive Bell, the art critic, is in town. Do you know his work?"

"I've read his book."

"No," he said. "No, I don't think he impresses you enough."

"I'd like to meet him, if you'd like to have him along," Callaghan said. Loretto stirred uneasily. Fitzgerald kept smiling.

"No," he said, "I don't think Clive Bell impresses you, Morley. Who does impress you, Morley?"

Callaghan could feel his face burning, but before he could set the customary goodbyes in motion, Fitzgerald stood up slowly and said, "Would this impress you, Morley?"

He got to his knees, put his head on the floor and tried to stand on his head. One leg came up, but he was unable to get the other one up and remain balanced. He waved and swayed at Callaghan's feet, then lost his balance and sprawled on the floor. Callaghan got up and helped him to his feet. "You're a little drunk," Callaghan said.

"No, not at all," Fitzgerald said, and pulled himself together as he rose to his feet. They exchanged goodbyes and the Callaghans left.

The next day he told Hemingway the story. Hemingway only commented, "Well, that's Scott."

"Standing on his head!" Callaghan said. "It might have been better if I had punched him on the nose."

"There's no distinction in punching Scott on the nose," Hemingway said. "Every taxi driver in Paris has done it."

The Fitzgeralds through the 1920s had been embodiments of characters from his books. They rode down Fifth Avenue in New York on the top of a taxi, arriving at a party with Zelda cheering on the roof. Scott was escorted out of George White's *Scandals* for undressing in an orchestra seat. Once he drove his car into a lake because it seemed like fun. Zelda danced on tabletops and dove into fountains. They were full-fledged celebrities, in the newspapers for fights with waiters and detectives. They established themselves, in the words of *The New Yorker*, as "the best-looking couple in modern literary society." They were approached to star in the film version of his first novel, *This Side of Paradise,* but Scott turned it down—to Zelda's great disappointment—because his editor warned him that it would destroy his reputation as a serious writer. He continued, however, to court publicity, standing on his head in the lobby of the Biltmore when he discovered that he had not been mentioned in the newspapers for a week.

They were more than celebrities, however. Like Dawes they used their incandescent personalities to advertise themselves, but like Mussolini and Jane Addams they used their public image and their writing to foster a set of attitudes. Zelda was regarded everywhere as the high priestess of the Jazz Age. In the middle of 1929 the beautiful and quirky woman wrote an article about the flapper. The flapper, she said, was an important new personality type: the woman who experiments with life, who does things consciously to create effects. The flapper created herself as a product and advertised it. As flappers, she wrote, women learned "to capitalize their natural resources and get their money's worth." The article had something in it of a hall of mirrors, for Scott Fitzgerald had created and popularized the flapper out of his wife's personality.

The Fitzgeralds had become Twenties celebrities, but they had wrecked a lot of parties and dispatched many apologies. The day after their first meeting the Callaghans received a profuse apology and the next evening the four of them went out to dinner. As they left the restaurant and walked in the night, Zelda began to laugh. She asked several times about finding something to do. She stopped on the street, laughing. "I know," she said, "let's go roller skating."

"Where do you go roller skating around here?" Callaghan asked.

"We can find a place. Don't you want to go roller skating, Loretto?"

"I'll go," Loretto said. "I'm game."

"And you?" she asked Morley.

"I've only roller-skated two or three times," he said, laughing. "I'll go along, though, if you want to."

Fitzgerald had been losing his patience. Grabbing Zelda by the wrists, he said: "I'm putting you in a taxi. You go home now and go to bed." His tone was vehement. Zelda's manner changed, and she consented to be whisked away in a passing taxi. Scott dismissed the incident. "Zelda has to get up early in the morning," he said. "She's taking those ballet lessons." He added that Zelda had begun ballet training late in life and it was especially exhausting for her, then asked if Callaghan might suggest to Hemingway that all six of them have dinner together.

Callaghan called for Hemingway the following afternoon. He told Ernest that Scott and Zelda had had dinner with them and that he liked Scott a lot.

"You didn't tell Scott where I lived," Hemingway asked, "did you?"

"No, I didn't."

"If you're going to be seeing a lot of Scott, don't tell him where we live, eh?"

"Why not? What's the matter?"

"The Fitzgeralds will come walking in on us at all hours."

Morley suggested that they should be told that the Hemingways' new baby shouldn't be disturbed.

"It won't stop them." Hemingway shrugged. "And besides, Zelda is crazy."

"How do you mean?"

"She's just crazy. You'll find out."

Living up to their composite image had been fun for a while, but also wearing. By 1929 the public image of the Fitzgeralds was lagging behind the facts, for the last wisps of romantic haze had blown away from their lives. Although Scott was making more money than ever, they had slid more deeply into debt. His work had never been more popular and sought-after, yet he feared his decline as a serious writer. The *Saturday Evening Post* was paying four thousand dollars each for what he considered trifles, but he needed the money to feed his own and his wife's ever more prodigal tastes. The marriage was sunk in extravagance and dissipation. Zelda was absorbed in her dancing, was often tired, and had to be watched for erratic behavior. She was struggling to make a name for herself independent of him, and he found it difficult to bear. He mocked her lessons. His health suffered in the grip of alcohol, and she complained that he preferred drinking companions to her. She accused him of a homosexual attachment to Hemingway. Scott, who had been Hemingway's champion and had become almost a hero worshipper, began to doubt himself and fear that it might be true.

One day Scott told Morley of how Ernest had been a sparring partner in the United States and a bouncer in tough bars. He told of how Heming-way had been hit with mortar fire while serving in Italy during the war, and then of how he was hit again with machine gun fire in the legs while carrying a wounded comrade. He told several bawdy Hemingway adven-tures, filtered through the magical Fitzgerald sensibility. Then he told a story that Callaghan had heard before—of how Hemingway had become annoyed at ringside one night while the middleweight champion of France pummeled an incompetent opponent and had climbed through the ropes and knocked the champ out.

"Do you really think Ernest is that good?" Callaghan asked.

"Ernest is probably not good enough to be the heavyweight champion," Fitzgerald said, "but I would say that he is about as good as Young Stribling."

"Look, Scott, Ernest is an amateur. I'm an amateur. All this talk is ridiculous. But we do have fun."

Not responding directly to the remark, Fitzgerald asked if he might watch the two authors box, and Callaghan suggested he ask Hemingway.

Fitzgerald seemed worried that Hemingway would rebuff him, for Hemingway's feelings for Fitzgerald had changed. He continued to respect Fitzgerald as a writer but had lost respect for him as a person. He noted with scorn that Scott could not handle alcohol, and he had tired of Scott's and Zelda's shopworn hijinks. Hemingway had instructed his American editor not to give Fitzgerald his address and was willing to meet him only in public places. Worst of all, as he had told Scott, he believed that Zelda had caused Fitzgerald's slide into dissipation by her continuous need to be amused.

Hemingway said that Zelda was crazy, but he did not know her as Scott had known her. He had not seen her as the belle of Alabama, her skin the color of a rose petal dipped in cream, her hair gleaming like spun gold, as the young doomed officers stationed near Montgomery watched her at dances. She had been so bewitching that a specific Army directive was issued forbidding stunt flying over her home. When Lieutenant Fitzgerald and Zelda Sayre found each other they discovered a kinship almost of brother and sister, for both believed that no price was too high if one hungered for the extravagant. And now the bill had arrived at the table.

Fitzgerald had chronicled the new life of roadsters, petting, and hip flasks, a generation "grown up to find all Gods dead, all wars fought, all faiths in man shaken," as he had written in *This Side Of Paradise*. If he was "the laureate of the Jazz Age," it was not just because of the high burnish of his prose, but because his work proclaimed that there was no ceiling on aspirations, that anybody could do anything, that life was romance. Hemingway's preoccupations were more mordant and violent. Like Fitzgerald, his work helped create an image of the man—as if his prose helped to prove that he was not weak like his father, who had been dominated by his mother and had committed suicide.

These two men, the bear and the centaur, walked together one summer afternoon in 1929 on a Paris street. When Callaghan responded to the knock at his door, the two men he had hoped for so long to bring together stood side by side smiling and in good spirits. Hemingway, carrying the bag with the boxing gloves, said they had eaten lunch and decided to stop for him rather than wait for him to stop by.

They joked in the taxi on the way to the American Club. When they arrived, Hemingway asked Fitzgerald to take out his watch and act as timekeeper. Scott seemed thrilled. He moved off the bench, squatted, and called time.

During the first round Hemingway chased his opponent. He kept an eye on Callaghan's left, which had stung him so often in the past. Fitzgerald called time, and then signaled for the second round.

Hemingway came in fast, his left down, and was smacked in the mouth. His lip began to bleed. Callaghan had been drawing blood all summer, and the two had sometimes joked about it, but this time it obviously disturbed Hemingway, who came lunging in with reckless punches. Callaghan circled him, jabbing at his mouth. The heavier and stronger

Hemingway began to proclaim by his movements that although he was being jabbed often, all he needed was to land one punch and the fight would be all over. Wiping the blood from his mouth, he leapt in, and Callaghan beat him to the punch. He hit Hemingway on the jaw. The big man went down and sprawled on his back. He shook his head to clear it, rested a moment on his back, and then rose slowly.

"Oh, my God!" Fitzgerald cried. He shook his head helplessly. "I let the round go four minutes."

"Christ!" Hemingway yelled. He stood fuming for a few seconds while Fitzgerald continued to stare at his watch. "All right, Scott," he said, "if you want to see me getting the shit knocked out of me, just say so. Only don't say you made a mistake." He went to the shower room to wipe the blood from his mouth.

The crestfallen Fitzgerald whispered anxiously to Callaghan that he had not done it on purpose but had become so interested in the bout that he lost track. He seemed ready to fall apart, but moved away from Callaghan as Hemingway returned to the workout room. Hemingway, his face washed, looked calmer. Callaghan suggested they get back to boxing and he and Hemingway squared off.

They fought a crisp round, both keeping out of trouble, as Scott sat pale at the sidelines. A young English student who had been playing billiards in the next room intruded with advice to Hemingway on how to box. "Do you think you could show me?" Hemingway asked. When they fought, Hemingway smiled, spread his legs, stuck one arm straight out and the other defiantly on his hip. He remained in that attitude, turning slowly as the young man cautiously circled him. The humiliated student left without throwing a punch. After his departure Hemingway brightened and the three men began talking agreeably. Fitzgerald continued, however, to appear ill at ease, and Hemingway did not offer an apology.

Soon the literary world buzzed with stories about the fight. Hemingway said that, benumbed with lobster and wine and hardly able to keep his eyes open, he had slipped and fallen down. Another version was that Callaghan had challenged Hemingway after an argument about the authenticity of the boxing lore in Callaghan's fiction, and that a large crowd had witnessed Callaghan knock Ernest cold. In a third version, Callaghan rushed for the shower, dressed quickly, ran to a telegraph agent and cabled his publisher: "JUST KNOCKED OUT ERNEST HEMINGWAY."

That was the end of the Musketeers. Fitzgerald continued to defend Hemingway from a growing list of enemies, including virtually everyone who had helped him become recognized. He defended his friend from

Zelda, who called him a pansy with hair on his chest. The camaraderie of Scott and Ernest, however, was becoming a memory.

When the Fitzgeralds began to drive south that summer, they argued about where to stay in Beaune. He wanted to stay at a hotel Ernest had recommended. Zelda refused, and they drove all night. She laughed in bursts that summer, so that there seemed nothing of simple human pleasure in her laugh but something suppressed and ecstatic. In Cannes they went with friends to see a documentary film about underwater life. When an octopus was shown on the screen, Zelda shrieked and threw herself into the arms of a friend, screaming, "What is it? What is it?"

All about him Fitzgerald saw signs of crackup and collapse. One of his classmates killed himself and his wife on Long Island; another fell accidentally from a skyscraper in Philadelphia; a third committed suicide leaping from a window in New York. One was fatally wounded in a New York speakeasy; another, confined to an insane asylum, was killed by a maniac with an ax. Ring Lardner, one of his best friends, was killing himself with drink. Edmund Wilson, his literary mentor since they had been at Princeton together, suffered a nervous breakdown.

In October, as the Fitzgeralds were returning through the mountainous and steep roads of southern France to Paris, Zelda grabbed the steering wheel and tried to steer them off the cliff. She said the car had taken over and was swerving by its own will and that she had to hold it in place.

While the Fitzgerald fortunes ebbed, *A Farewell To Arms,* Hemingway's great novel of the war, was published in September to enthusiastic reviews. Although not a political book, it summed up much of the prevailing mood of 1929 about the war—the pervasive sense that everyone, even the victorious nations, had been defeated. His long struggle, fought on an empty stomach in chilly apartments, was over. The book began to sell extremely well and Hemingway seemed on the way to popular success.

At the age of five, Hemingway had attempted to convince his grandfather that he had stopped a runaway horse. As he grew older he became more successful in his incessant self-promotion. Whenever he bought a huge fish, he managed to convey the impression that he had caught it, and his animal charm, his pride in strength, and his courage helped to embellish his exaggerations. As one legend faded, another took root.

"I have heard of him, both at various times and all in one great bunch," Dorothy Parker was writing of him that fall for *The New Yorker,* "that he is so hard-boiled he makes a daily practice of busting his widowed mother in the nose; that he dictates his stories because he can't write, and has them read to him because he can't read; that he is expatriate to such a degree that he tears down any American flag he sees flying in France; that no woman within half-a-mile of him is a safe woman; that he not only commands enormous prices for his short stories, but insists, additionally, on taking the right eye out of the editor's face; that he has been a tramp, a safe-cracker, and a stockyard attendant . . . and that he also writes under the name of Morley Callaghan. About all that remains to be said is that he is the Lost Dauphin, that he was shot as a German spy, and that he is actually a woman, masquerading in man's clothes . . . For it is hard not to tell spectacular things of Ernest Hemingway; people are so eager to hear that you haven't the heart to send them away empty." She ended by praising his courage through pain and poverty and his uncompromising vision. The legend had blossomed. Ernest Hemingway was on his way to the heavyweight championship.

Celebrity was fame in a world of diminishing privacy and it grew out of the same sources as the new form of capitalism—which, as was so often proclaimed, was integrated and humane, based not on profits but on service. In the old days of capitalism by Divine ordinance, when Providence tapped on the shoulder those who were to be given the nation's industrial and financial leadership, a Great Personage could say with impunity: "The public be damned." What did he owe the public? But the interlocked system of Tender Capitalism, aided by the new networks of communication, had ended all that. Now all were in service to one another, and those more highly placed were merely in more strenuous service. The public, therefore, had a right to examine its servants, to invade their trysts and check their linen for soil. Heroes were even more vulnerable. Where, after all, would Charles Lindbergh be without the public? He could not have sold his book or his lucrative *New York Times* pieces or have become a figurehead consultant for airlines without public enthusiasm.

Progress had consigned privacy to the dust bin of history. Once the customary mode of living, privacy was now the exception, and for those in the mostly strenuous service, elaborate precautions had to be made to secure privacy—as Lindy and Anne demonstrated when they wed in May. In subjecting celebrities to scrutiny, the public merely levied a legitimate tax—a sharply graduated tax—on fame and riches. Those more completely created by publicity were more tightly in its grasp, but even business leaders were not shielded from the searchlights that overtook Arbuckle, Chaplin, and Lindbergh.

With this direct connection between the new integrated capitalism and

the decline of privacy, it was fitting that the key move of capitalist consolidation, the formation of U.S. Steel, led directly into the first great
twentieth-century act of public burning by publicity—the grilling of steel-
master Charles Schwab in 1902.

Schwab had been a key figure in the delivery of Carnegie's steel holdings to Morgan and, as the president of U.S. Steel, had become an instant
celebrity and a wealthy man. Having subdued his tastes for many years
under the stern watch of his boss, Carnegie, he sailed abroad to shake
loose, bought an impressive roadster and drove off to Monte Carlo. Soon
his escapades were keeping the cable wires humming.

Wall Street bristled with the news. The steel trust was controversial
enough, the financiers grumbled, without its president gambling heavily in
the pleasure spots of Europe and providing newspapers with lurid copy.
Editorials scolded Schwab for his behavior, which created doubts in the
popular mind about the caliber of men in control of American business.
The most outraged person of all was the man who had shepherded the
mellow-voiced Schwab to the top—Andrew Carnegie, who although retired was a major stockholder in U.S. Steel. "He shows a sad lack of solid
qualities of good sense," he wrote to Morgan, "and his influence upon the
many thousands of young men who naturally look to him will prove pernicious in the extreme."

Schwab began to receive cables warning him of the stir he had created
in the United States, and was distraught by Carnegie's hectoring. He feared
the reaction of the House of Morgan, wherein his masters dwelt.

The elder J.P. Morgan was a devout supporter of the Episcopal
Church but was also a solemn adherent to the double standard and was
tolerant of weaknesses of the flesh, being susceptible to most of them
himself. A Morgan aide passed on the word to Schwab not to be overly
concerned and just to deny the stories.

Now a man about town, Schwab was traveling with a fast set. His
companions included notorious figures like Diamond Jim Brady, who kept
the stage entertainers, the Dolly Sisters, as mistresses—both of them.
Some Steel Trust financiers clashed with Schwab on other issues, too, and
not sure of his future, Schwab purchased Bethlehem Steel, a faltering
Pennsylvania company that was not part of the trust.

Carnegie's continuous attacks threw Schwab into depression. He was
irritable, suffered fainting spells, was unable to sleep, and lost feeling in his
limbs. His health began to slide. His doctors advised complete rest away
from the controversy, and in the latter half of 1902 he sailed for southern
France, running from news stories that he would soon announce his
resignation.

The press continued to bedevil him, and stories were published stating that he was about to die. A Paris newspaper reported that the dying Schwab planned to distribute his wealth, and his hotel was besieged with fortune-hunters. At home, pressure mounted against him within U.S. Steel. He came home in early 1903 not fully recovered and told Morgan that he might have to cease all business activities for a time. Soon he was gone, and had begun to build Bethlehem Steel into the second largest steel company in the nation.

Schwab had caught the public imagination for good, and was seldom out of the limelight. He was much praised, but his career was marked by recurring public controversies. The controversy had nothing to do with his manner, for he was no Ben Lindsey. If Schwab ever said anything controversial it was by mistake. He intended to please everyone, and he spread a layer of steaming optimism upon the American soil.

By the time Wilson called him to government service during the war, Schwab had made Bethlehem the largest American armaments company. Monte Carlo was forgotten as he became regarded as a national hero for his shipbuilding efforts. Then the audit of the Emergency Fleet Corporation, the government agency he had headed during the war, raised issues that clouded Schwab's record.

In 1921, a witness told a House committee that near the end of Schwab's eight-month stay in the government post, Schwab had submitted a personal expenses bill of a quarter of a million dollars, and that the Bethlehem Shipbuilding Corporation had charged one hundred thousand dollars of it to the government in a bill for ship construction.

The witness was Colonel Eugene Adabie, former general controller of the U.S. Shipping Board. The colonel said an accounting firm had made the discovery during an audit of Bethlehem. Three days after the voucher was discovered, operatives of Perley Morse & Company, the accounting firm, were barred from Bethlehem's books.

Bethlehem Steel struck back, charging that government money was being wasted on expensive audits. Bethlehem officials met with the Shipping Board, and eventually the colonel was summoned to a conference that included Schwab. "Mr. Schwab was very much put out when the chairman insisted on retaining the original auditors that I had selected," the colonel recollected to the committee, "and he wanted me to reconsider my refusal to have them substituted. He expressed the belief that he could not get a fair audit from Perley Morse & Company. He said he did not believe they were in this for any purpose except sensationalism."

When Eugene Grace, the Bethlehem president, took the stand, he admitted that Schwab had been repaid for all of his expenses while occupying the government post, but denied that the burden had been passed on to the government. The committee asked Morse, president of the auditing firm, whether any part of the two hundred sixty-nine thousand dollars paid to Schwab for expenses actually came out of ship construction.

"All I can say," Morse replied, "is that the voucher was there and it appeared in the books. I have the pages of the book. The voucher was seen by one of my accountants who had it in his hands. Another accountant saw the entry in the books. There is no question as to the voucher. The only question in my mind exists as to the procedure that took place after we were refused access to the Bethlehem books." He said his accountants were told that the voucher had been "disallowed," but had seen no documentary proof.

Witnesses reminded the committee of how indispensable Schwab had seemed only three years earlier in the spring of 1918, when the Germans were making a final drive and the U.S. needed to transport three hundred fifty thousand troops a month to France. "That meant increased tonnage," one witness said, "and we saw the need of bolstering up the construction end of the Shipping Board. We needed a man of Mr. Schwab's experience, ability and enthusiasm. Mr. Schwab explained that firms in which he was interested had contracts amounting to five hundred million dollars with the government. He was positive he would be subjected to unfair criticism, but finally agreed if the situation were outlined to President Wilson, and the president insisted."

It was said that Schwab, sure that scandalmongers would try to impugn his motives, had objected strongly to the pressures exerted on him to take the government post. He took it only when he made it clear that, because he was still Bethlehem board chairman, he would separate himself utterly from any business transactions with Bethlehem.

Schwab told the committee that he had never taken a penny from the government—not even the one dollar annual salary to which he was entitled. In the most dramatic moment of the hearing, he described a meeting set up with the auditor Morse through a third party. He said that at the meeting at the St. Regis Hotel he told Morse "that the facts which I had related were true, and that I was now at the end of a long forty years' business career, and that it was a matter so indescribably deep in my heart to be charged with something of that kind that I hoped he would correct it. He would not do it. He said there were explanations and reasons . . ." Schwab began to cry in the witness chair. "I hope you will excuse me, Mr. Chairman and gentlemen of the committee," he said, the tears rolling from his brown eyes.

"I can't help making this reflection at this time," one congressman broke in. "As a member of this committee I want to express on the record my appreciation of the manner, Mr. Schwab, in which you have introduced evidence concerning this voucher; and aside from my membership on the committee I want to express my appreciation as an American citizen of the service you rendered in the recent war." Applause broke out through the room. "There is no jury to affect, or court to be influenced," the congressman continued, "but I say that out of an appreciation of the situation I feel that I am compelled to give expression to it."

"I thank you very much," Schwab said. The committee chairman bit his lips, betraying his feelings with moist eyes and flushed cheeks. Several of Schwab's friends were crying. He had completely won the day.

The committee report completely exonerated Schwab, and three months later the Bethlehem board chairman showed himself as a master of self-promotion. He was presented with a large bronze plaque at a meeting of the New York State Chamber of Commerce in appreciation of his efforts in winning the war. While there he told a story which, although it was six years old, brought headlines all over the nation and glory that surpassed his wartime plaudits.

In 1915 the United States was still a neutral in the war, but Schwab had heavy contracts to build ships for the British, as well as supply ordnance and munitions. His performance of the contract was astounding and the most stunned were the Germans. They sent an emissary to offer him one hundred million dollars to break his British contracts. In the meantime, the British Secret Service had been shadowing the German intriguers and learned of their proposal. The British called their American financial advisor to Washington and gave him authority to offer anything up to one hundred fifty million dollars for the Bethlehem plants—five times what they were worth—to keep them from falling into German hands. Schwab turned him down, as he had the Germans. "There is not enough money in Germany and Great Britain combined to buy the Bethlehem Steel Corporation until it has executed its obligations to the British government," he replied.

Schwab was asked why he had not told this story when he testified before the Committee on Shipping Board Operations. He smiled and said that he had never felt comfortable relating incidents of his life to support his reputation. He thought a man should leave his reputation to find itself out. It was a master play, and for the next few years Schwab was again affectionately regarded as a hero.

But in 1925 Schwab was again beset by lingering questions about his government service. The government filed suit against Bethlehem for fifteen million dollars which it claimed were excess profits earned by various subterfuges. While Schwab served as director general of the Emergency Fleet Corporation, the suit charged, he had held other companies to a maximum of 10 percent profit while failing to hold Bethlehem. Schwab's response was obvious: he had made it clear when taking the office that he did not want the slightest contact with Bethlehem contracts. Bethlehem filed a countersuit for nine million dollars that it claimed the government still owed on contracts, and in 1929, at the time of the Jubilee, the case was still dragging through the courts and creating chagrin for Schwab.

So the story of his wartime service was dusted off for another play. The nation again was told of his reluctance to take the job; of the critical point that had arrived in the war; and of how he had thrown himself into the work with ardor and energy, infusing the workers with spirit, getting two million doughboys to France and saving the world for democracy.

Schwab justly deserved credit for his work with the government. But the image he attempted to convey did not tell the whole story of Charles Schwab. It took digging to get at that.

In 1894, when he was still with Carnegie Steel, Schwab was in charge of a huge contract with the U.S. Navy to build armor plate for fighting ships. The Navy had placed resident inspectors on the premises to insure that the terms of the contract were followed, but they went home at the end of the day, while the plant remained in operation around the clock. There was more furious activity than ever when the inspectors left. The imperfections in the metal, caused by uneven cooling, were plugged up.

"Do you know," Schwab was asked when he appeared before the House Committee on Naval Affairs, "whether the company really did conceal the fact of blowholes in the plate?"

"I think likely that was done," Schwab said.

"Was it done with your knowledge?"

"Well, the concealment was not, no; but I had knowledge of this fact, that they did not make any plates that did not have blowholes."

"You had knowledge that these blowholes were plugged in many instances?"

"No, sir, I did not say that. I said I had knowledge that the plates had blowholes, and that I should not be surprised if they were concealed."

Schwab said that the inevitable blowholes did not harm the effectiveness of the plate in the least. Yet he would never argue a point if he could use subterfuge instead. The same trait was shown in another aspect of the case. Naval inspectors chose plates to be shipped off to the Naval Testing

Grounds. The plates they chose were surreptiously moved and given a special treatment. The treatment, however, damaged the plates rather than improving them.

A congressman asked Schwab to explain: "Then in fact they expected and the intention was to improve the plate?"

"The intention," Schwab said, "was to discover a method of improving the plate."

"Right there I want to ask a question. I want to know why you could not tell the government about that?"

"That was a mistake," Schwab said. "I admit that. They should have done it; but on the other hand, as you know these government people . . . I could readily understand why they did not tell them because as I say to you they [the inspectors] were not practical men and they would not have understood the thing."

That was Charles Schwab's image problem. Although he hired Ivy Lee to work on it, there was always so much he wanted to leave out. Early in 1929 Lee sent out a set of rules, as formulated by Schwab for making prosperity last. They consisted largely of Schwab truisms about dealing fairly with people. "Conduct business in the full light of day," was one of the rules. "Public confidence and public suspicion may be separated only by a door."

Schwab used words not to reveal but to conceal. Every diamond brooch and emerald bracelet he brought to his wife was a concealment, and she knew it. He was forever praising his marvelous marriage, but by 1929 he and his wife were living apart, a state that can be maintained without public notice if one has several homes.

The public was startled by the Chaplin divorce case because the beloved comedian as a sexual experimenter was so at variance with the image he projected on the screen. But Chaplin's tramp was only a role that he played and he conjured it up out of a part of his real personality. The problem that Ivy Lee had with clients like Schwab was that their public role was a denial of their real nature and not part of their personalities at all. Schwab professed to love the workers, but he depised them; he pretended to have a marvelous marriage, and it was said in print that he had, but his marriage was barren and pointless.

During the war, Schwab had been called to a meeting in Washington at which he was asked to re-allocate some of his contracts to other companies. In the presence of the secretary of war, he began to cry. He said that he would not mind giving up the contracts, but that taking them away would be a reflection on his company, and that would be excessively painful to him, for he had no children, and the company was the only thing in his life, and it would break his heart to have anything said against it. The scene was so affecting that he kept all the contracts. They called him a supersalesman, and he proved it often. It was a role that required dishonesty, for how far could he get by talking to the press in praise of marital infidelity, or advising Kiwanians to lie to the public frequently, or how many tears could he well up in the eyes of the secretary of war with references to his illegitimate daughter?

The man who came to the presidency in 1929 was another product of the pervasive new emphasis on promotion and propaganda that had grown since the war, during which it was first discovered how the new network of communications could mobilize public opinion. Herbert Hoover was a pioneer in shaping opinion and had been adept at it for more than a decade, yet he shunned the spotlight and lacked the temperament to be a celebrity.

He was a new departure in presidents for that decade—a world citizen in a period of isolationism, proud of his ties to Europe. Hoover had been through the Suez Canal so often that he had lost count, and had written a textbook on mining during the leisure of long voyages. When his activities as an engineering consultant were at their height, he had permanent homes in London, St. Petersburg, and San Francisco.

For fifteen years he had been a world-famous personage. A decade before becoming president he had been regarded as a great humanitarian and a glamorous personality. He had won wealth and renown as a mining engineer in Australia by the age of twenty-five. He had burned with fever in China, waded through hip-deep mountain snow, squatted in a tent while a dust storm threatened to bury his expedition, and could tell stories about dozens of other adventures, with which he regaled his friends. He had traveled with his spirited bride through the Far East to restore the mines and railway systems of an oriental empire, journeying through brigand-infested remote China with an escort of cavalry. Later he became interested in tales of ancient silver mines hidden in the Burmese mountains back of Mandalay. The rich deposits discovered once supplied both India and China with silver. Hoover liked to tell of the time he crawled into an abandoned Burmese mine in search of precious metals and found fresh tiger tracks. He caught a fever in the jungle and lay shivering for weeks in Mandalay, but got up and completed the mine project. It took five years of labor, including the construction of a railway into the interior.

Perhaps his greatest adventure, however, was his work during the war as head of the Commission for Relief in Belgium, and in January of

1929 the world was pointedly reminded of it. Hugh Gibson, the U.S. ambassador to Belgium, was in the royal box with King Albert in Brussels when President-elect Hoover addressed them from the United States by radiotelephone to Belgium. At the Palace of Academies almost the whole Belgian governing class, more than one thousand people, gathered to hear him on headsets and over loudspeakers.

"Belgians may well rejoice in anything I say in Mr. Hoover's honor," said the ambassador, a close friend of Hoover's. "For the first time in history, an honorary citizen of Belgium has been elected to the presidency of the United States. Of his many honors, he values none higher than the royal decree making him a Belgian citizen." King Albert called Hoover "the soul of our relief amidst the greatest political, maritime and economic difficulties."

Hoover had convinced the British during the war to remove the food blockade—a difficult step, since British control of the seas was its key to winning the war. He had matched wits with kings and premiers, generals and diplomats in delicate negotiations. He introduced the Germans to a new concept, world opinion, which he said would hold Germany responsible if it let Belgium starve by refusing to admit food supplies. He convinced the British that if their Navy did not allow the supplies through, the Germans would not be hurt; it would be the Belgians who would starve. In the long view, he said, stunted bodies and mental retardation in the coming generation were not secure foundations upon which to rebuild civilization. He asked the belligerents to look beyond the war. Living a charmed life, he crossed time and again through mine-planted waters, through closed frontiers. He crossed the Channel forty times, sailing into danger every time. On one occasion his ship was captured by Germans who released it just as the ship became the center of a French bombing raid.

Hoover, as the Washington reporters knew, was enormously talented at influencing public opinion—and public opinion was particularly important to him because of his philosophical taste for "voluntarism." After the United States entered the war, he became President Wilson's Food Administrator, and worked on elaborate and far-reaching campaigns to make it patriotic to conserve food. "That is one place where we could use our women to great advantage," he said of his plan. "We are great advertisers. A few phrases, too, would turn the trick—and the world lives by phrases, and we most of all perhaps. We need some phrase that puts the stamp of shame on wasteful eating, dressing and display of jewelry . . . We could not bring the law to bear on this, only educate and direct public opinion." He resisted advice to use punitive measures on retailers who violated American policy, preferring what he called "the club of public opinion"— the same club he had shaken to get food to the Belgians.

Hoover had gathered field representatives in Washington, instructed them on the food situation, and sent them out to organize community pledge campaigns. A measure of his public relations canniness was that he had a black administrator, unheard of in 1918, to work on the campaign among black Americans. Housewives were asked to sign pledge cards to carry out the requests of the Food Administration in their households, and the signers received a window emblem and kitchen poster. At Hoover's urging, President Wilson proclaimed "wheatless, meatless and porkless days," all of them voluntary and successful. The Food Administration set fair ceiling prices and published them in newspapers, advocating boycotts and popular pressure rather than the prosecution of retailers. To Hoover, democratic methods of mobilizing opinion were slower but ultimately more effective than strong-arm methods.

Hoover, even in his college days, was masterful at influencing opinion, and he practiced it for eight years as commerce secretary, but he preferred behind-the-scenes work and often used the president or another figure as a cover. Nevertheless, over the years a blurry and unfinished image of Hoover emerged, and it had considerable public appeal: the image of a blend of Quaker humanitarian and efficient engineer. He was, it was said, eager to lighten the world's burdens, a man of peace, but unlike the abstract and idealistic Wilson, Hoover was a nuts-and-bolts man of scientific know-how. He was also, of course, a successful businessman. The parallels to Ford, Edison, and the other business-technological heroes of the age were unmistakable.

In 1928 the Republican Party produced a film that it distributed across the country for the presidential campaign. It was called *The Master Of Emergencies*, and it was made up largely of old flood film footage. It showed Hoover as the secretary of commerce taking in hand the human and engineering difficulties flooding presented.

In February of 1929, the month before he became president, he again visited a flood scene, riding in the lead automobile in a two-hundred-mile tour over the muddy roads of the Florida Everglades. He asked questions as they rode, but gave no indication of his reaction. Thousands of acres of sugarcane waved as the caravan zipped past.

Glenn Skipper, the national Republican committeeman from Florida, had the sinking feeling that things were not going right. He looked out the window and hoped for desolation. Although the Everglades had been ripped by wind and water, at a cost of two thousand lives, in two horrendous floods in 1926 and 1928, they did not look ravaged. The swamp had covered its wounds. Palmettos, scrub pines, and weeds had sprung up to hide the evidence. The party had been treated to bucolic scenes of green sugarcane, gardens of beans, peppers, and tomatoes, and orange groves. Except for the ruinous condition of the roads and the wreckage of scattered homes and barns, there was little to convince the president-elect that this was the greatest disaster in Florida's history. Skipper bumped along morosely through the Everglades hoping for some kind of sign from the master of emergencies.

Hundreds of army tents housing farm families were scattered across the countryside, with wives cooking and washing as best they could in the rough. Others were lodged in hastily built frame cabins. Along the route signs had been placed indicating the high-water marks in the floods. Near Moorhaven one sign testified that more than three hundred lives were lost near the spot. At Hoover's side was Major General Edgar Jadwin, chief of the Army Engineers, who was in charge of the Mississippi flood control project.

Hoover had been president-elect for three months and remained an undefined figure. He had visited Edison on his birthday and lunched with Colonel Lindbergh. Mostly, though, he had been fishing on a friend's yacht and staying at the Belle Isle estate of J.C. Penney, not far from the Capone mansion. He had, in three months, generated little news. The press, with the newfound ability that it learned in the 1920s to make news out of a lack of news, dwelt on his Sphinxlike qualities, on how mysterious he remained.

Skipper grew more nervous as the day went by, and hoped that Hoover might commit himself during the dinner. Hoover had asked for no speeches, but Skipper knew that was almost impossible with so many politicians at one table, including the governor and a ranking Congressman. Hoover would be forced to respond to comments. Hoover had been the first Republican to carry Florida since the Civil War, and Skipper had helped bring that off by making flood control a major issue. Now he had to deliver.

The dinner was held in Clewiston, a little settlement in the Everglades. Intimates of Hoover knew that he had an invincible resistance to committing himself if he chose not to, and that he embarrassed easily, but Skipper was no intimate. As General Jadwin was introduced and began to speak, Hoover slouched in his seat and turned red, aware that his turn was coming. General Jadwin explained the processes of applying for federal aid. He said he had recommended to Congress that the federal government help the state of Florida and that he expected the federal share would end up to be about four million of the estimated ten million dollars in flood and reclamation costs.

The general received hearty applause. The chairman of the House Committee on Flood Control then raised the ante. He told the group he thought the federal government ought to pay the entire bill. That brought tumultuous applause. Glowing, the governor offered to rename the flood area the Hoover-Skipper district if the Republicans came through on such promises.

Hoover was not there, however, to hear much of it. During General Jadwin's remarks, a Secret Service agent came into the room and whispered in Hoover's ear. He immediately rose and left the room. While the congressman and governor heightened the enthusiasm, he failed to return. Skipper glanced anxiously at the door, wondering what kind of telephone call would take Hoover so long. Hoover did not return. Apparently embarrassed, he had gone to the home of his host and retired early.

This sort of behavior as president-elect raised questions about the master of emergencies. A few weeks before the Florida trip he had been traveling through Latin America on a highly publicized goodwill tour. He and his wife, Lou Hoover, were on the cruiser *Maryland* in the Pacific. They were about to cross the Andes and to board the *Utah* in the Atlantic, and the crew of the *Maryland* held a farewell party. When a chief petty officer concluded a pleasant little speech on their behalf, the party waited for Hoover, standing far back on the deck, to step forward and respond. He did not move. Eventually his handsome, white-haired wife saved the moment with a gracious response.

As secretary of commerce, he would receive visitors in his office by rising awkwardly from his chair, extending a hand diffidently and proferring a half-hearted shake. From there interviews would proceed so uneasily that the visitor invariably became uncomfortable. Hoover would never initiate conversation but would wait for questions, which he would answer tersely, volunteering nothing, often while looking at his shoes.

When he ran for the presidency, his aides complained that he was liable to be outcharmed when photographed with a pillar. He could not unbend enough to slap backs or exchange pleasantries. Nevertheless he won the election of 1928. He was not the favorite of Republican political leaders, but the business community, after eight years under his guidance as commerce secretary, was solidly for him, and his supporters included Edison, Ford, Rosenwald, Lindbergh, and Jane Addams. Schwab, who had pledged the steel industry's support to Hoover, put it plainly in early

1929 when he said he was sure nothing would be done during the Hoover term "to disturb the sound business structure upon which our prosperity is founded."

An important nucleus of support had been the old staff of the Commission for Relief in Belgium. Over the years the staff had maintained a long campaign to bring him to the presidency, and on March 3, 1929, on the eve of the inauguration, four hundred of them met in Washington. Some had not seen each other since Hoover had dispatched them with a safe-conduct and they had sped over the frontiers of Europe to feed the Poles, the Germans, the Czechs, the Montenegrins, and a dozen other peoples demoralized and sickened by the war.

The place of honor at their pre-inaugural dinner was Hoover's, but he was not there. A lit candle was set at his place. It reminded Americans of the "invisible guest," one of the devices Hoover had used to raise money to feed Europe's starving people. The empty place setting represented the presence of the hungry.

"The memory of what he has done is a cause for great Christian fervor," a speaker said. "It's very curious how we people here tonight are tied together by such a service. None of us ever expected a reward, and it was Hoover who organized everything that was done. It was his genius for leadership."

It had taken this entire decade, the speaker went on, to appreciate how close to collapse the whole of Western civilization had come after the war. The world had been feverish and hysterical. Disease swept Europe. In Germany, money became worthless. Men stood on soap boxes and shouted. The Four Horsemen of the Apocalypse had galloped through Europe. If Hoover had not acted, if he had not insisted upon feeding conquered enemies and had not restored stability after the war through his food campaign, the history of the 1920s would have been different.

Votive candles were still lit before the Virgin for Hoover in Germany. In Russian villages the peasants still thanked Hoover for the food he had sent them. In the remote steppes of Central Asia, Mongol tribes sat at the campfire and told stories of Hoover, the legendary giant who brought food to the hungry. Hoover had subdued the Four Horsemen: Famine, Pestilence, Death, and the fourth, which he hated above all others. Some called it War; Hoover tended to think of the Fourth Horseman as Revolution.

The American people were impressed with the prospects of his administration, but the rest of the world, and especially Europe, was more impressed. After two presidents of limited talents, Hoover loomed as the perfect American leader for a new phase of greater United States involvement in world affairs. He was cosmopolitan, humanitarian, brilliant, and devoted to peace. Hopes for his administration were so high that he told friends he feared he would never live up to his advance notices. All the auguries, according to *The Times* of London, were good, and Hoover took office "at the moment when the strength and prosperity of his own country never stood higher." Another London newspaper, hoping for improved relations with the United States, called the Hoover presidency "a piece of good luck of which the fullest use should be made by any British statesman worthy of the name."

With no drastic domestic problems to face in 1929, Hoover was free to bring his wide experience in world affairs and his promotional talents to bear on disarmament. The main priority of his first year in office was to reduce military expenditures. He intended to appeal not to the idealistic repugnance for war, but to the scientific disapproval of waste. His image would thus be that of the careful engineer measuring disarmament—not the zany jack-in-the-box image that had sprung up about the last major promotional adventure for peace, the 1915 fiasco called the Peace Ship.

Three principals at the Dearborn dinner—Henry Ford, Jane Addams, and Ben Lindsey—had been involved in that effort, which began late in 1915 when Ford became determined to keep the United States out of the war in Europe single-handedly. "New York wants war," he said at a press conference, "but not the United States." He denounced J.P. Morgan for his loans to France and England and said the Morgan partners "ought to be tin-canned out of the country." He would burn his factory to the ground, he threatened, before he would accept a single order for cars that might be used for military purposes.

There was another will as determined as his—a Hungarian Jew named Rosika Schwimmer. Earlier in 1915 she had been at the International Congress of Women at the Hague supporting the concept of a people's congress of peace delegates from neutral countries. With Jane Addams she gathered evidence that mediation would find a friendly reception even in the warring nations. She went to Detroit to see Ford, and in a single meeting convinced him that she had the answer. A contest for his allegiance began, with Madame Schwimmer pulling him toward Europe and Mrs. Ford and his secretary, Liebold, attempting to keep him out of antiwar activity.

Ford met with Madame Schwimmer and Jane Addams in New York. Over lunch at a hotel someone suggested, why not charter a ship and take the delegates over in it? Ford leapt upon the idea. Jane Addams hung back, concerned about the flamboyant characters of her allies. They argued that a gay and hearty move was valuable. Why should peace be a gray, negative quality? Why concede all the verve to the militarists? Madame Schwimmer, who had begun to grow weary of Miss Addams genteel ways, called her "Slippery Jane" because she was so hard to pin down on principle. The ship, Madame Schwimmer was convinced, would rivet the world's attention and give her the leadership of the women's peace movement.

When the ship, the *Oscar II*, was chartered and ready to sail, the celebrities balked. William Jennings Bryan was too busy; Julius Rosenwald sent regrets. Jane Addams continued to get in the way, trying to tone down Ford and Schwimmer, while Ford called for "the people" to take matters in their own hands if necessary and for soldiers to stage a strike. The biggest celebrity Madame Schwimmer was able to attract was Judge Lindsey. Miss Addams begged off because of illness. Ford found himself instead surrounded with single-taxers, anti-vivisectionists, and others with various favorite theories. One woman, with the press at her heels, stopped on board to offer a miracle medicine that would heal the wounds of war casualties. Another man visited the ship prior to departure to declaim against tobacco. He was usually haunting public parks, where he would snatch cigars and cigarettes from the mouths of passersby.

The Peace Ship became the press joke of the year. On the afternoon of sailing, December 4, 1915, someone at the Hoboken, New Jersey, dock handed Ford a package. When the wrapper was opened, Ford found a cage with two squirrels inside. The reporters roared. An actor among the passengers commandeered a megaphone and established himself on deck as master of ceremonies. At his signal the crowd of ten thousand honored Ford with a salute: "Hip, hip, hooray."

Ford awaited the arrival of Edison, hoping he could convince his friend to come, and that Edison's prestige would still the ridicule. Pulled in opposite directions by his wife and Madame Schwimmer, he was becoming denunciatory. He blurted out on one occasion that the war was the doing of the Jews and, tapping his pocket, he said that he had the papers to prove it. At other times he was convinced that drinking had made the French and Germans quarrelsome and distrustful, or that the improper mixture of foods had been responsible. He was out of his depth.

The actor with the megaphone called out, "Here's the fellow who makes the electric light for you to see by. Three cheers for Edison." Ford decided to make a gamble. He would offer Edison a million dollars to come along, forthwith, without luggage.

Mr. and Mrs. Edison came up the gangplank with Edsel Ford and Clara, Henry Ford's wife. They greeted Henry and talked. Later Ford and Edison stood together by the rail. Ford spoke with a quizzical, intense expression. Edison shrugged. Ford leaned closer and spoke into his ear. Edison shook his head. In a few minutes he left with his wife, Ford's wife, and Edsel, and the ship was on its way to Europe. The crowd cheered. When the steamer was a few hundred feet from the pier, a man who called himself Mr. Zero dived in and began swimming after it. The crew of a river boat pulled him out. Mr. Zero said he was following behind to ward off torpedoes.

Ford and Madame Schwimmer were embarked on one of the most disastrous publicity misadventures of the century. Four days after they sailed, President Wilson made a forceful plea for preparedness, with specific demands for increasing the size of the Army and adding new ships to the Navy. On board, Ford authorized the appointment of a committee to respond to the president. Madame Schwimmer and her disciples dominated the committee and drafted an anti-preparedness statement. Lindsey felt that he was being herded along and was having none of it; he supported Wilson on preparedness. The rumor began that those who refused to sign would be dropped ashore at the first opportunity, to get back to America however they would, and that produced more fuel for a blowup. The press began to send back stories of mutiny on the Peace Ship, and the affair was made to appear a farce. Ford returned and began to take orders for war contracts.

Nineteen twenty-nine, however, provided a far different climate. The havoc of the war, the destruction and upheaval it had created, and the widespread disillusion over the peace terms had created considerable sentiment for peace and disarmament. Disillusion pervaded Ernest Hemingway's war novel, *A Farewell To Arms*, which by midyear was being serialized in *Scribner's* magazine and stirring up controversy. Horror dominated the year's biggest international best-seller, *All Quiet on the Western Front*, a novel by a former German foot soldier.

The German Officers Club considered the book, by Erich Maria Remarque, "an insult," and the Austrian defense minister forbade soldiers to read it. The uproar about the book was furious, especially among the German military. They charged that the author's name was actually Kramer, as if writing under a pseudonym were a crime; that he was a French Jew; that he had never been in the war; that he was fifty-five and too old for service; that he had served not on the German side but on the

French; that he had been stationed in Germany and had never seen action; and that he had first written the book as a glorification of war and had changed the emphasis when a publisher rejected it. Remarque was actually a thirty-one-year-old semi-invalid who had been gravely wounded in the German army in combat, and despite all the accusations—and perhaps in part because of them—by October the book had sold a million and a half copies around the world.

Bankers, businessmen, and opinion-molders were preponderantly for peace and disarmament. Thomas Lamont, the House of Morgan partner, led a campaign at the International Chamber of Commerce meeting in Amsterdam that summer to endorse the Kellogg-Briand Pact against war. What had seemed folly in 1915 had been transformed, in a play showing in German and Polish cities, into a historic quest by 1929. In the drama, called *The Peace Ship*, Henry Ford attempts to intervene in the European war by sailing from America with a shipful of peace advocates. In one scene he is fettered by a mob of angry passengers who have been stirred up by newspapermen. As confusion and discord grow aboard the vessel, Ford becomes unsure of his project, but he is inspired by talks with a female anti-war leader. On landing in Norway, she dies. Ford reads the U.S. newspapers, in which he has been made to look ridiculous, and abandons his search for peace.

Weapons development also created sentiment for disarmament. "It is not necessary to dwell upon the appalling results of the last war, but with the discovery of science, improvement of the means of destruction on sea and land, nobody can look upon another war without shuddering at the inevitable results," said Frank Kellogg, Coolidge's secretary of state. "It is my opinion that Western civilization would not survive another such calamity. World opinion has been changed largely by its results."

In May of 1929, a twin-engine plane with a crew of three flew over the Army post at Governor's Island in lower New York, then headed north and flew over Broadway. Turning south again at Central Park, it headed for its objective—Fort Jay, the Army base on the island. Suddenly the windows in the skyscrapers on Wall Street reflected the glare of a sudden flash. A second flash and a third followed.

When people called the newspapers to find out what was happening, they learned that it was an Army flight test and that flares had been dropped in lieu of bombs. The plane had flown six hundred miles from Dayton, Ohio, where war games and a salute to Orville Wright were being held, and into Manhattan to demonstrate that a plane could strike far from its base, that it could thrust deep into every territory and return without stopping. The plane landed in Washington a little over two hours after its strike.

The duty officer at Fort Jay said it was impossible to sight the plane in the murky sky, since the fort had no searchlight, and that the anti-aircraft guns therefore would have been ineffectual.

The bomber carried navigation and radio equipment that enabled it to fly over the Alleghenies through thick fog. The refueling ship and the bomber were in telephone contact and at one point the bomber was apprised of conditions from a station on the ground. American editors were taken aback by the failure of air defense to repel a lone plane about which the defenders had been warned in advance.

An even more stunning demonstration had been held nine months earlier over London when seventy-five planes, each capable of carrying five hundred pounds of bombs, swooped upon the city from the northeast. Despite a matched defense force and batteries of anti-aircraft guns, the mission was accomplished in a half-hour. Power houses, water works, the Air Ministry Building and other government and strategic buildings were the targets. In the opinion of military observers, there would not have been a single loss for the raiders.

The writers who commented on the demonstration noted that no nation engaged in total war would hesitate to use poison gas. Two hundred planes carrying fifty tons of diphenylaminechlorarsine could wipe out London; a thousand planes in a lightning raid could add Liverpool, Leeds, Manchester, Bristol, and other key British cities, and British civilization could be wiped out. Deadly plague or bacilli bombs could be dropped to infect and wipe out nations with disease. Bombs were being developed that could obliterate a city block; planes would eventually be developed, it was claimed, capable of flying at the incredible speed of three hundred miles per hour. "There is no doubt that all the safeguards heretofore adopted by nations on sea and on land," Edison wrote, "no longer give protection against great fleets of large airplanes provided with explosives and death-gas bombs, which undoubtedly can destroy nearly all of the inhabitants of a city." Eventually planes would be flown automatically by radio and would drop their bombs by remote control. Every living thing in a major city, even the rats and cockroaches, would be wiped out in an hour.

But the end of Western civilization was not bothering William Randolph Hearst in 1929 and so little of this material was in the Hearst papers. The two things that most bothered Hearst were his waistline and the British. Whenever he lost a few pounds the weight would creep back upon his sixty-six-year-old frame, handicapping his tennis and his horse-back riding and making him a less than natty companion for his extra-marital interest, the movie actress Marion Davies.

As for the British, the United States had failed to heed his editorial counsel and had lined up with them in the last war. This annoyed Hearst, who had pushed the nation into the Spanish-American War and was used to getting his way. There were no national newspapers in 1929, but Hearst had a national empire of more than a score of local papers. He consumed the most newsprint of any operation in the world and all his people said what he wanted them to say—that the British were sneaky and self-serving and that Marion Davies was a great, great actress.

Hearst suspected British intentions and saw no reason to improve the foul relations that had been growing between the two English-speaking powers. The United States was now a rich nation and had inescapable trade rivalries with Great Britain. Leon Trotsky, exiled from the Soviet Union, ventured a clanging prophecy. "England made war on France dur-ing the Revolution of 1789, she made war on Germany, and she will make war on America," he told a correspondent in Constantinople. "Every country that suddenly becomes prosperous automatically becomes the irreconcilable enemy of England. A terrific struggle for the dictatorship of world capitalism is under way. England and her colonies include three-quarters of the globe. But wherever she goes she encounters the United States. The antagonism between these two countries will dominate the world for a decade, perhaps for a quarter of a century."

The most tawdry expression of anti-British feeling came from Mayor Bill Thompson of Chicago, who warned King George V to stay out of the city or he could expect a punch in the royal snoot. But suspicion of England could be found during Senate sessions on the Kellogg-Briand Pact, a pledge to renounce war as a means of settling disputes. Senator James Reed of Missouri waved a map showing the British possessions in the Western Hemisphere colored in screaming red. At what are the cannon of Bermuda aimed, asked the Senate's foremost Big Navy man, if not at the heart of America?

While the Senate was debating the Kellogg-Briand anti-war pledge it was preparing to follow it with a bill to construct fifteen cruisers and an aircraft carrier. If both were adopted the Congress would lend its senti-ments to disarmament and its purse to preparedness.

"Would you hear the voice of the world, oh, you dreamers of dreams?" Reed orated against the Kellogg-Briand Pact. He described the roar of furnaces forging plates of warships, the chorus of mighty hammers shaping the keels of great battleships, the hum of myriad lathes shaping rifles and machine guns, the whirr of airplanes, the thump of armies on the march. "In face of that, the imbecile cry of safety is raised. We are told to put our faith in paper treaties. Paper treaties will not arrest the force of explosive shells; paper treaties will not hold back invading armies; paper treaties will not save our commerce upon the seas."

Reed failed to stop the Kellogg-Briand Pact. With that out of the way, however, Congress adopted the Fifteen-Cruiser Bill, and President Coolidge signed it, leaving the Kellogg Pact for Hoover, his successor, to sign. "There has been quite an argument over whose budget will pay for the new cruisers just voted," Will Rogers wrote in his column. "Coolidge has offered to split the cost fifty-fifty. He will pay for the blue prints if Hoover will pay for the cruisers."

Whenever questions of naval strength were being discussed, the figure of William Shearer was invariably lurking just around the corner. The scarlet map that Senator Reed waved had come out of Shearer's briefcase, along with other supporting data. Taking a break from his Washington lobbying early in 1929, Shearer took a train to California. He showed Hearst the map, explaining how the British controlled every trade route in the world and had the United States surrounded. Hearst ordered that every one of his papers publish the Shearer map.

Shearer had first surfaced as a major publicist in 1927, a crucial year for issues of peace and disarmament. That summer of 1927 the Naval Conference at Geneva, with the United States, Great Britain, and Japan in attendance, had fallen apart. French Foreign Minister Aristide Briand in that same year made the initial proposal to outlaw war that grew into the Kellogg-Briand Pact. Late in the year Jane Addams, president of the Women's International League for Peace and Freedom, presented Coolidge with a petition bearing thirty thousand signatures urging him to take a serious look at Briand's proposal. Since then she had pressed for another naval conference, contending that the Geneva meeting had failed because admirals controlled it.

Others suggested that the true conference-wrecker had been Shearer. Although a publicist and thus by designation a background figure, he had become the most vivid personality at the 1927 conference—entertaining lavishly, living in the best residential area of Geneva, and able to get into any conference activity by flashing phony press credentials from the *New York Daily News* and the *Chicago Tribune*.

Ambassador Hugh Gibson, head of the American delegation, disapproved of him, but the naval members of the delegation hovered about Shearer. The British complained of Shearer's presence, but there was little the Americans could do about him. Whenever a British spokesman looked through a crowd at a press conference, Shearer, his slicked hair parted sharply in the middle, was standing in the midst of reporters. He did not ask questions, but he prompted others to do so and afterward would pull reporters off to the side to give his own interpretation of what had been said. Wythe Williams of *The New York Times* and Henry Wales of *The Chicago Tribune* had checked in with him first thing upon arrival in Geneva and stayed with him much of the time. They made so inseparable a trio that some reporters believed Shearer got to read their stories before they were cabled off to America. Wales, who had written a faked "interview" with Lindbergh when the pilot had landed in Paris on his triumphal flight, had provided Shearer with the press credentials.

The main subject at Geneva had been cruisers. It had been called to complete unfinished business left over from the Washington Conference. The earlier conference in Washington in 1921—the first successful arms limitation conference in history—had ended in an agreement to limit battleships. Great Britain and the United States had agreed to parity, or equality, in battleship tonnage, with Japan agreeing to limit herself to three-fifths of the tonnage of the other two, in an agreement called "5-5-3." The cruiser question, however, had been unresolved.

On the day that the three powers first presented their proposals at Geneva, Shearer invited the press corps to his apartment where he immediately impressed them with his expert knowledge of the subject and his air of knowing more than he told. After that he was frequently to be found in the dining room of Geneva's best hotel, holding forth and buying rounds of drinks. American admirals and reporters surrounded him night after night. His dark hair glistened under the chandeliers and his precise staccato voice captured and held the attention of his listeners. On one night he might muse aloud on Ivy Lee's work in lobbying for the naval parity agreement and speculate about the true aims of Rockefeller and the international bankers in sending Lee to Geneva. Another night he would tell of how a German submarine of less than six hundred tons had crossed to the United States shores, operated on its coast, and then sailed back to Germany under its own fuel. That was, he said, a point to remember when the Japanese recommended no limitations on "small submarines."

He and his wife entertained well and often. The British did not attend. Nor did Ambassador Gibson, who steered clear of Shearer, but his Navy men went. To the distress of the British, they consorted freely with Shearer and largely shared his opinions and attitudes. Like him, they regarded the Washington Conference as a disaster for the United States, during which American strength had been sacrificed for political purposes. They were determined that it would not happen again. Around the hotel dining table at night they twisted the British Lion's tail, and scarcely bothered to conceal their hope that the conference would fail.

For seven weeks Shearer prepared daily reports and handed them out every morning. They were well-documented background sheets, filled with data about gun calibers, tonnages, armor plating, and elevations. Even reporters who disliked him read it and occasionally fell back on his data. They threw away his diatribes but kept the information sheets. Pressed to send out daily stories, they came to rely on his work, and thus he influenced what millions of Americans read about the events in Geneva.

The information had come out of Navy files. Before leaving for Geneva, Shearer had looked in on his friends in the Navy Department. "What am I to be loaded with?" he asked. Soon afterward a package bearing a Navy frank arrived at his address. When he opened it he found a large Blue Book full of confidential information on the various navies and conjectures as to proposals that Britain and Japan might put forward. It was excellent ammunition and often, in Shearer's apartment at the end of a conference day, the reporters Wales and Williams would dip into it.

When the conference ended in debacle, Shearer was exultant. The following day one of the Geneva newspapers devoted an article to him, called "The Man Who Wrecked the Conference."

The admirals never asked Shearer what he was doing in Geneva. Wales, at what seemed a sufficiently informal moment, one night asked him for whom he was working. "Well," Shearer said with a smile, "if you have battleships, you will have doors, and if you have doors, you must have doorknobs." He said he worked for the Pittsburgh Doorknob Company.

"War is kind of like meat," Will Rogers wrote. "You can't have it because you can't afford it." Hoover had Quaker sentiments against war, but was more appalled by the thought of uniformed men sitting around in barracks with nothing to do. Nor did he want any of those fifteen cruisers his predecessor and the Congress had forced upon him.

A startling development, however, promised a new opportunity to change the tide of events. The Labor Party in Great Britain had turned out the Conservatives, the party of the admiralty. Hoover sent General Dawes as his ambassador to Great Britain with instructions to move quickly. The meeting of the new ambassador with J. Ramsay MacDonald, head of the new Labor Government, was, according to the *London Daily News,* "the greatest event marking Anglo-American relations in our time." The two men opened a new era in diplomacy—a drive to re-establish the momentum of disarmament that had been stymied at Geneva.

On July 24 Hoover signed the Kellogg-Briand Pact and ordered that construction of three cruisers be held up pending further news in naval negotiations. Prime Minister MacDonald ordered the suspension of construction of two cruisers, a submarine depot ship, and two submarines.

Hoover loved fishing and horseshoes and had an unpretentious mountain retreat he called Rapidan Camp where he relaxed. The weekend after signing the pact he repaired to his retreat in the Blue Ridge Mountains of Virginia, bringing some of his military leaders along. While they lounged in stout boots and old clothes in the open air, Secretary of War James Good held out against Hoover's demands that ways be found to reduce army expenditures. The cavalry, he said, how can we do without it? Look around you; what else but cavalry would you send into these mountains?

Meanwhile, Shearer kept the patriots simmering. He took heart when the U.S. Supreme Court refused to permit citizenship to Ford's old shipmate, Madame Schwimmer, because she would not take up arms for the United States. He visited the D.A.R., whereupon that august body protested pacifism as a foreign import. The Illinois American Legion condemned Hull House as a den of radicals. The American Legion, which admired Mussolini and strutted around in a pastiche of fascism, called for investigations of anti-war groups and claimed that powerful foreign organizations were paying for pacifist activities. The veterans' conventions rang with resolutions for more cruisers, not less. Congressmen said Hoover had no authority to suspend cruiser construction without a definite agreement on naval parity. Union leaders reminded the president of the hardships that shipyard workers would suffer from loss of work.

Shearer was mounting a counteroffensive. He spoke against the League of Nations and the World Court, a project for which he was secretly in Hearst's pay. In July he told a Kiwanis Club meeting that Great Britain was creating propaganda for the cancellation of all war debts. He called for the British to abolish her naval bases at Halifax, Bermuda, Trinidad, and Jamaica, four bases which he said controlled American trade routes and the strategic approaches to the Panama Canal.

At fifty-four, Shearer had the back and shoulders of a boxer and an unlined face; he was a backslapper who swaggered into rooms to take complete charge of the conversation. J.P. Morgan's English secretary, he boasted, had once accused him of being a spy and he had replied that it was hard to be a spy while playing a big bass drum. He had arrived just in time, his bearing suggested, to save the nation from pacifist emasculation, and he cited figures to prove that Britain and Japan were far ahead in ships, guns, fuel, and armaments. He carried his genealogy around in his briefcase and pulled it out to show that his forebears had fought in every war from the Revolution onward.

He fended off all efforts to ascertain the sources of his employment. "I am well known, and well disliked," he replied when the Church Peace Union asked him directly. "I fight internationalism, pacifism and communism. I make many enemies and many friends. I hate pink, red and yellow. I claim nothing and expect less, but whatever I represent, it is all-American—which seems to arouse suspicion as well as curiosity."

Then, overflowing with confidence, Shearer made a slip. In August he filed a suit in New York Supreme Court, claiming that the three biggest companies in warship construction owed him a quarter of a million dollars for services rendered at the Geneva Naval Conference in 1927 and other services. One was the Newport News Company, which had built the ten-thousand-ton cruiser *Houston* launched that same month. Another was American Brown Boveri, which had built the great aircraft carrier, the *Saratoga*. Third was the company that had built the *Lexington* aircraft carrier and was the most important maker of ship armament and fighting vessels in the world—the Bethlehem Shipbuilding Corporation. Shearer was working for Charles Schwab.

President Hoover moved in. He held a press conference on September 6, and, in the most dramatic moment of his administration, he attacked the shipbuilding companies. He said it was against the public interest for companies having contracts for building naval vessels to make secret attempts to sway the public in favor of larger expenditures by means of propaganda. Furthermore, he said, the propaganda had spread distrust and hate on a world scale, and he called upon his attorney general to see what action could be taken.

All the facts on which he based his remarks had already been printed, as a back-page item, when Shearer filed his lawsuit. The newspapers had not even sought comment from the shipbuilding companies. But when the president pointed a finger, it became news. The Shearer affair became the front-page sensation of the month and the Senate hearings suddenly were listed on news desks as a must-cover.

Shearer swaggered about, calling a press conference in New York to bask in publicity. The main point of interest of his remarks, however, were his boasts that he had received the Blue Book full of private information from somebody in the Navy who had mailed it to him. His apparent purpose in revealing this help was to make himself appear important, but the public effect was that Hoover had just what he wanted—evidence that Navy officials had plotted to scuttle the Geneva Conference. Now both the shipbuilding companies and the Navy were in an embarrassing position. In front of scores of reporters at the hearing the shipbuilders admitted that Shearer had been in their employ and that they had funneled money to him through their trade association, the Council of American Shipbuilders.

All that was left to the shipbuilders was to decide whether they wanted to look like fools or knaves, and they chose foolishness. They said they never had a formulated notion of what they sent Shearer to do in Geneva, but probably just wanted him to gather information. He had talked them into it. They were "jazzed off their feet" by a supersalesman, they claimed. Nevertheless it was shown that they had been posted on his activities, for his reports were full of boasts of how he had become "leader of the unofficial fight" in Geneva. They were also aware of the Navy's approval of Shearer's work. "If Shearer were paid three million dollars for his services at Geneva, he would not have been paid too much," one Navy commander told them.

The room was packed for the appearance of the Bethlehem chairman of the board. Charles Schwab described himself as "a homely steel puddler from Pittsburgh." He said he had never known that any agreement had been entered into with Shearer, and that had he known he would have advised against that "most unwise undertaking." Shearer was terminated, he said, as soon as he and Bethlehem president Eugene Grace learned of his activities. It was clear, however, that no one had been reprimanded. Schwab took the occasion to renounce Shearer and all his works.

"At a great meeting of all the iron and steel interests," he said, "at a dinner given in honor of Marshal Foch, it was my privilege and honor to have spoken for the American iron and steel people; and I said that as controlling the greatest ordnance works in the world I would gladly see it scrapped and sunk to the bottom of the sea if it would bring peace and lack of this work to the American people. That was long before the Geneva conference."

Shearer completed the devastation with an erratic, accusatory appearance in which he tried to put the committee on the defensive for attempting to smear a great patriot with scurrilous material from old Scotland Yard files, which charged him with involvements with jewel thieves, "swell mobsmen," and bootleggers. It was a nasty picture, made nastier by the testimony of the shipbuilders that suggested that the suit filed against them had come when they had called Shearer's bluff after he asked for a quarter of a million dollars. If not amply paid, they said, he had threatened to destroy them by making the case bigger than Teapot Dome.

Shearer claimed that Schwab, who denied ever having met him, had been the first contact that led him into the work, although he had never talked with Schwab about the specific Geneva project. It had come out of previous promotional work he had done for the companies.

He denied their testimony that he was to be paid only twenty-five thousand dollars for the work. He said he was to receive a bonus, just as Bethlehem president Eugene Grace "got a bonus of one million dollars from Mr. Schwab for his activities during our short engagement in the war." That remark was not picked up at the time, but later would have important consequences.

Even before he left Geneva, he said, his enemies were at work. He had learned, he said, that Frank B. Kellogg, Coolidge's secretary of state, "had called the Bethlehem crowd on the mat and instructed them to get rid of me, and, as I have had it interpreted to me, if they did not, they might proceed against Mr. Schwab on this suit of fifteen million dollars pending at the Department of Justice." He was referring, of course, to the government charges that Bethlehem had made excess profits during the war, and several times during his testimony Shearer suggested that the suit was being used as leverage by the government.

At last, he said, the shipbuilding representatives told him that it would have to appear as if his services had been discontinued until the storm blew over. This feint, he explained, would get "Nervous Nellie"—his nickname for Secretary of State Kellogg—off Schwab's case.

After a check by Ivy Lee, who did public relations for Schwab, cleared Shearer of rumors that he was a German spy, he went back to work for the shipbuilders (still concealing for whom he was working) and campaigned for the Fifteen-Cruiser Bill. But his demands for more money, and personality difficulties, led to a stormy meeting during which he was fired. When he asked for an explanation, he told the committee, one of the shipbuilding executives said his conscience would not permit him to keep Shearer on. "I hope," Shearer riposted, "your conscience will not trouble you so much that you will not build any of the cruisers."

By the time it ended, he had torn the shipbuilders to shreds and exposed himself in the process as a sneak, a bully, and a fool. Every person he mentioned in his testimony sent telegrams denying or disavowing his testimony. He had become anathema; even Hearst sent word that he had terminated Shearer's services. Some regarded him as a menace, others as a windbag. "If Shearer is as important and can do as much as the Senate and our whole government seems to think he can, why don't we just hire him ourselves to keep us out of any other wars?" Will Rogers asked in his column. "It's the cheapest peace insurance I know of, for he is certainly not high-priced if he has done what they think he has." Whatever one thought of Shearer the effect was much the same. Hoover had demolished his opposition, just by pointing in their direction. Once again he had shown how well he could set forces in motion to get the desired effect while staying behind the scenes. Now he was ready for the next move—but this one would take his personal involvement.

It had been a chilly night in early October 1929, but the day was balmy and brilliant, and both President Hoover and Prime Minister MacDonald were dressed in old clothes. They sat about on the porch at Hoover's Rapidan retreat, Secretary of State Henry Stimson with them, and then the two went for a walk. The sumac foliage was crimson and the waters of the Rapidan swollen with rains. They walked down an old path and then followed the river back. The two world leaders talked, smoking briar pipes and sitting on a log beside the mountain stream, the dumpy, round-faced Hoover a strong contrast to MacDonald, who was tall and loose-limbed, with a mass of gray hair, dark and glowing eyes, and an ample moustache.

The two men were as different in temperament and experience as they were in appearance. When Hoover was living in London representing great mining interests, MacDonald had been working on a socialist newspaper. One represented the social and economic discontent of postwar Britain, the other the political conservatism and technological radicalism of America.

MacDonald was the crusading journalist come to power, a professional agitator who arose from obscure poverty by the force of his personality. His friends called him a mystic. He was a poet, an intellectual, a doctrinaire with the religious zeal of the Scottish Covenanter. He was on familiar terms with God and regarded himself as a missionary for peace. Like Wilson he was a political preacher, but mellower, more attuned, more physically attractive.

Hoover had the detailed and unromantic mind of the engineer. He once said that engineers could construct waterfalls far more lovely than those accidentally created by nature. He liked standardized housing and exercise on electric horses. His Quaker faith was mild and practical, almost Confucian. The mystical he left to others. He understood graphs better than poetry. As might be guessed, they liked each other. Hoover found the prime minister frank, whimsical, delightful; MacDonald found in the president a quiet and unassuming strength of purpose, a man who dealt with admirals not by kicking their behinds but by learning more than they knew about their subject.

MacDonald, the first prime minister ever to visit the United States, had come to continue with Hoover the fruitful work begun with Dawes. The object was a five-power naval conference of the U.S., Great Britain, Japan, France, and Italy, to be held in London early in 1930. The deadlock created at Geneva in 1927 had been sprung. A secret the government had known for a couple of years—the interests behind Shearer—had been used at the precisely right moment. Nothing stood in Hoover's way. He would be remiss if he did not place the U.S. delegation under the firm control of civilians, led by Secretary of State Stimson and including Ambassadors Morrow and Dawes.

The prime minister was surprised by Hoover's impatient fervor for disarmament. By the time they stood up and left the log for a midday dinner, they had welded a comradeship.

Returning to Washington, MacDonald addressed the Senate. He visited New York to make major speeches and to dine on various occasions with Thomas Lamont, Edsel Ford, and Otto Kahn. He went on to Toronto for the AFL convention. AFL president Green, who had opened the meeting by calling MacDonald's visit "a holy mission," declared that labor in the U.S. and Canada would mobilize public opinion in support of the prime minister's peace program.

The finely chiseled MacDonald, a proletarian with the look of an aristocrat, was a great hit. Countless sermons praised the efforts of the two leaders; speakers referred to MacDonald as "a saint." The *Literary Digest* article on the visit was entitled "Why America Likes the MacDonalds— And How!"

Dawes and Young believed the prime minister would be equally charming at Dearborn, and considerable efforts were made to get him to attend. Just before MacDonald had sailed for the United States, Ambassador Dawes had again urged him to include the dinner on his American itinerary, but the prime minister said he was afraid he would be in Quebec by then. Young urged that the Fords make the invitation "both cordial and emphatic," as Napoleon Boynton, a GE executive, put it, but the Fords may never have followed up.

When the time came for the two heads of government to say farewell, Hoover broke the rule against informal social invitations and went with MacDonald to a stag dinner given by Stimson. Later in the week he was still keeping up with the prime minister by radio. Fiddling with dials and inclining his ear to the loudspeaker, he listened to MacDonald from New York. When a call came from a close friend during the broadcast, Hoover said, "Tell him I'm busy."

Hoover and MacDonald had introduced a new personal diplomacy into the world and a new spirit in foreign affairs. No power had ever before voluntarily agreed to parity when it could be supreme. Yet Britain, which had naval supremacy, and the United States, which was capable of becoming supreme, were willing to forego such a contest.

The president's term was bursting into full flower. Statesmanship had returned to the White House. When he and his wife attended the fifth game of the World Series in Philadelphia, a victrola attached to an amplifier played "Hail To the Chief" and the crowd gave him a wild ovation. He had the pulse of the nation, and the little uncertainties that pricked the stock market seemed minor.

A few days later he left on his first extended trip as president. The train wound its way up along the Potomac, zigzagged through the Alleghenies and rolled down across level country to Dearborn, the first stop in his midwest tour.

On the day in mid-October that Madame Curie and General Dawes arrived on the *Ile de France* in New York, a new presentation opened at the Roxy. It included talking newsreels of the prime minister's visit, and the main feature was *They Had To See Paris,* Will Rogers' first talking film. The stage presentation was *Scheherazade,* with Léonide Massine in the lead role of the Negro slave. More than a decade earlier Massine had replaced Nijinsky both in his roles and in Diaghilev's affection, and had danced the scandalous first American performance of *Afternoon of a Faun.*

When first produced in 1910, *Scheherazade* had staggered Europe with its barbaric passions. Marcel Proust said he had never seen anything as beautiful. Its voluptuous spirit had also bestirred America, and American police. The Catholic Theatre Movement had been particularly shocked at the orgiastic dance that ensued when the sultan's wives persuade the eunuchs to liberate the black slaves from their golden cages. The scene in which the sultan's men slaughter the wives and slaves had been danced with a shocking blood-lust.

But the Roxy production had been entirely reworked and was almost unrecognizable. Its cruelty and passion had been smoothed and domesticated into a charming and decorative production. In this version the narrator interrupted the story to explain the proceedings to a small child, and the revenge scene was done with a tactful sense of moderation and good taste. The children of Diaghilev, the New York homosexual population, flocked to the Roxy to see it. Diaghilev had not lived to see Massine's betrayal.

Every age is stamped with a particular variety of crime, and in the twenties the fashion was forged documents. The Hearst press gave wide promotion in 1927 to the "Mexican Documents," which purported to show that the Mexican government had distributed 1.2 million dollars to a number of United States citizens, including U.S. senators, to act as agents for Mexico. Once again Hearst was bidding to make foreign policy, but he was frustrated when it was shown that the papers were fakes.

In 1928, however, another batch of sensational documents was in the news. These purported to show that various Americans were paid to propagandize for diplomatic recognition of the Soviet Union. In addition to U.S. senators William Borah and George Norris, the documents also implicated Ivy Lee, who had long favored United States recognition of the Soviet government. A close inspection revealed that these papers, too, were fraudulent.

In early 1929, Hubert Knickerbocker, Berlin correspondent for the *New York Evening Post*, was offered another group of documents. According to these documents the earlier discredited papers had been faked by the Soviet secret police to conceal even more incriminating evidence against Borah and Norris. This enterprising attempt to reverse a setback ended when Berlin police, acting with Knickerbocker's help, arrested two anti-Soviet Russian emigrés. In the apartment of one of them police found hundreds of rubber stamps, passports, official Soviet stationery, seals, a chemical laboratory, and hundreds of pictures of communist leaders. The czarist agents went on trial in July and got off with short terms.

Evidence linked the men with a trans-European network of forgers, most of them Russian emigrés, who had been manufacturing false documents since the Russian Revolution. One of their earlier products had brought down Ramsay MacDonald's Labor government in 1924. They had planted a faked letter that purported to give instructions from G.E. Zinoviev, head of the Communist International, to British communists for engaging in subversion. It had been created to defeat MacDonald, whose government was in the process of establishing diplomatic relations with the U.S.S.R. And the same network, in what amounted to its masterpiece, had produced a document that became world famous. It was sold to Henry

Ford who had used it for one of the most bizarre promotions of the twentieth century.

The big event at the Dearborn airfield on an afternoon in 1926 was so packed that Ray Dahlinger, the airfield manager, called for volunteers to help control the crowd. An intelligent-looking young man who said he was a reporter was deputized for crowd control. The young man fidgeted as he watched for the arrival of Ford. Soon the great engineer was spotted riding to the scene in an open Lincoln. It was a big day for Ford, and he was in excellent spirits, having just arisen from a luncheon of soybean steak and carrot juice. He was issuing orders to remove all smokers from his vicinity. The young man edged in close to Ford. He felt in his pocket, grasping a small package. When an airplane left the runway for the sky, as all eyes followed it, he reached again into his pocket and pulled something out, leaned into the open auto and dropped it into Ford's lap. "I am serving a subpoena," he announced, "for the United States Circuit Court in the case of Sapiro versus Ford." He turned and fled.

Over his shoulder he could hear the great Ford agonizing: "No, no, no! Take it away!"

Guards chased the lawyer who had pierced their defenses and cornered him. "You think you're pretty smart, don't you?" sneered the tough airfield manager Dahlinger. "Well, you didn't serve a subpoena on Mr. Henry Ford at all. You served it on Mr. Ford's brother, John Ford."

The lawyer looked at the men surrounding him. "Then what's all the fuss about?" he asked, and walked away unharmed.

The fuss was about Ford and the Jews. Ford was more than just an engineer. He was a social theorist and a visionary. He understood the drift of the world; he knew who his enemies were. The Jews controlled Wall Street and all the money-lending interests that preyed upon the productive. Otto Kahn, who stood to make a profit, had helped get the U.S. into the war. His partner, Paul Warburg, controlled the Federal Reserve System. The Jews ran Washington.

Once the role of the Jews was understood, history became intelligible. The Jews were behind the rise of cabarets and chorus girls. They had corrupted the Chicago White Sox into throwing the 1919 World Series. Their agents sold the liquor and nicotine that poisoned America. They fostered the naughty novels, the Broadway sex farces, the shocking Hollywood morals, horse racing, flashy jewelry. When rents went up, it was the Jewish landlord gouging the working people. They filled the airwaves with the savage jungle rhythms of erotic, moaning jazz. On Seventh Avenue they shortened skirts and made rolled stockings the fashion.

Ford had grown up in the Midwest, where Wall Street was often depicted as a gigantic Jewish pawnshop, and the Jew was the villain of Populist sentiment. But as Ford fought U.S. entry into the war and as the U.S. became the great lending nation of the world, he began to see more clearly the immense proportions of Jewish global ambitions. Thomas Edison had helped show him that. The commercial rise of Germany, Edison said, had been the cause of the war, and the Jews had been behind German business success. War, Ford said, was just a way of making a profit, and as the Gentiles blew each other up, it was with Jewish explosives and poison gases.

Ernest Liebold, his personal secretary, had awakened Ford to the full implications of Jewish plotting. Liebold had been in touch with former czarist agents, driven out of Russia by the Revolution. They had a full dossier on Jewish activities. One of them, a member of a monarchist group called the Russian Black Hundred, had come to Liebold with a colossal document that detailed the particulars of a Jewish plot by seven all-powerful leaders of that accursed race. They intended to destroy the Aryan world by fostering all sorts of social maladies. This key document showed that the usurious Jews lay behind war, unrest, class conflict, avarice, vice, decadence.

Liebold purchased a copy of this document, called *The Protocols of the Learned Elders of Zion*, and rushed back to Detroit with it. He intended to inform the world about the Jews through the *Dearborn Independent*, a weekly newspaper Ford had begun to publish. The articles Liebold prepared for the next year and a half on "The International Jew" brought the paper worldwide attention. The outcry from the Jews confirmed Liebold's conviction that he had plumbed the truth.

"Few thinking men have given any credence to the charges offered against the Jews," said Rabbi Leo Franklin of Detroit, speaking of his next-door neighbor Ford. "But his publications have besmirched the name of the Jews in the eyes of the great majority, and especially in the small towns of the country, where Ford's word is taken as gospel. He has also fed the flames of anti-Semitism throughout the world."

Non-Jews were also disturbed about Ford's newspaper campaign. President Harding enlisted Edison to talk to his friend about letting the matter drop. Edsel Ford was pained by his father's publications and made his unhappiness known. In 1922 the word came to the staff to drop the International Jew stuff.

But once one gets hold of such material there is no letting go. Liebold reopened the case. This time he unmasked Aaron Sapiro, a Chicago lawyer and promoter. Sapiro, mobilizing the bitterness of farmers about their lot, was attempting to form a huge new wheat-marketing organization. He claimed it was a cooperative and that it would provide solidarity for farmers. Liebold saw it as a Jewish cabal. Julius Rosenwald and other Jews were rushing to help Sapiro with contributions. Otto Kahn lent his influence to obtaining credit.

Sapiro brought a million-dollar suit against Ford for defamation of character. Ford was besieged. The other auto companies were beginning to use the Jewish issue against him. As the Model T began to show its age, Ford sales had undergone their first serious slump, and its replacement, the Model A, was about to come out. A second Jew had filed a libel suit against him. Most of all, he was in terror of appearing in court.

The day he was scheduled to be a witness, the word came out that he had been in a severe auto accident and was in his private hospital where he was unable to speak with anyone. It was a bizarre accident. He had been forced off the road, it was reported, and over an embankment by a mysterious motorist who had lain in wait for him at the gates of the Ford plant and then vanished without a trace. It was called an assassination attempt. Dahlinger, it was reported, had quickly removed the wreckage—thus leaving it an accident without witnesses, police report, or other tangible evidence. The trial ended in a mistrial before Ford recovered.

Then Ford learned, apparently all at once in a flash, that *The Protocols of the Learned Elders of Zion* were a fraud. Everyone, he noted, knew they were fakes; they had long been discredited, he pointed out, as the work of czarist agents who had fabricated them to stir up anti-Semitism in Russia and divert people from revolution. Ford had an agent contact the American Jewish Committee immediately to negotiate peace terms.

He capped his reversal with a six-hundred-word statement that was not just a retraction but a denial. He said he knew nothing of what had appeared in the *Dearborn Independent* and never read it. He had turned its operation over to others in his organization. He said he was deeply mortified to learn that his newspaper had given currency to such forgeries and slanders. The Jews accepted the explanation with a straight face. Mr. Ford, said Rosenwald of Sears, Roebuck, "will find that the spirit of forgiveness is not entirely a Christian virtue."

Two thousand people attended a dinner in May 1929 at the Commodore Hotel in New York to honor David A. Brown, the national chairman of the United Jewish campaign. Cablegrams came in from all over the world. Henry Ford was in attendance, and although he did not speak, he issued a statement that was published in the newspapers.

"I am happy to come here tonight to pay a tribute of admiration to my good friend David A. Brown," the Ford statement said, "and through him to the great race which is proud and fortunate to count him among their own. David A. Brown is a shining example of the great benevolence of the Jewish people, their philanthropy, their eagerness to make this world better, to educate the untutored, to heal the sick, to care for the orphans; their intense and intelligent participation in all that makes for civic righteousness and social justice stamps them a great people—and David A. Brown is one of the greatest and finest sons."

Henry Ford was laying the aberration to a deserved rest, and so it was all over—or was it?

"The German people are a slave people," said the recording played over the loudspeakers of Nazi headquarters throughout Germany. "From the standpoint of international law they trail behind the last Negro colony in the Congo. All the rights of sovereignty have been taken from us, and now we're just good enough so that the stock exchange capitalists can fill their sacks of gold with interest, money and percentages." The voice, crackling hysterically from the phonograph, belonged to one of the rising masters of promotion—Joseph Goebbels, the Nazi propagandist.

The German people were voting on October 21, 1929, on the Liberty Law—a proposal that Nazis and other rightist groups had forced on the ballot. The Liberty Law proclaimed that the admission of war guilt was a lie forced upon Germany in defeat, and that those recommending the Young Plan to Germany were traitors. The Nazis needed the approval of only 10 percent of the voters to get the proposal to the Reichstag, the German parliament, but if the Reichstag rejected it, only a majority vote of the people could make it law.

Government and moderate forces believed the Young Plan would be accepted. Reduced payments to the victors and financial autonomy for German parliament, but if the Reichstag rejected it, only a majority vote evacuation of all occupied German territory. The British were already preparing to leave, and the French would be out early in 1930.

The Nazis patterned themselves after the Italian Fascists, sang the praises of Mussolini, and had their own strong man in the wings. Adolf Hitler, they said, would lead Germany because he would seize the Young

Plan as the central German issue and would break the shackles of the Treaty of Versailles.

They had another hot issue, though, and were exploiting it all over Germany. They promoted the desecration of Jewish cemeteries. In Wiesbaden they encouraged agitation against a medical congress to be held there that included Jewish physicians. The Masons, under attack for having Jewish members, had become defensive, and some Masonic leaders explained that quotas were set for Jewish membership. "We ask every applicant for membership in our order if he knows if he has Jewish blood in his veins," one Masonic officer said.

In Bavaria, an old favorite of anti-Semites had returned: the ritual murder story. When a five-year-old boy was found dead early in 1929, his throat cut, the Nazis said the Jews had been out again in search of Christian blood for their ceremonies. One weekly proclaimed in its headlines, "Blond Boy Slaughtered, Passover Blood Drawn."

Much of the Nazi material and techniques could be traced back to the *Dearborn Independent*. The Ford newspaper had stirred up emotions about a southern factory girl supposedly murdered by a Jew, and had suggested that it was not difficult to understand why the Ku Klux Klan was riding again across America. A few years earlier the Dearborn paper said that Rosenwald had encouraged blacks to settle in Chicago and thus had caused the 1919 race riot; in 1929, anti-Jewish newspapers in Germany were writing that Rosenwald was helping blacks arm against whites in the U.S. Ford's newspaper had admonished the "white man" to smarten up and push the Jews out of America, had called the Jews the inveterate enemies of the white man's civilization; the Nazis had merely embellished the message.

Above all Ford had brought the *Protocols* to the world. Hundreds of thousands of copies of that discredited work and "The International Jew" series of the *Dearborn Independent* were spread all over the world, including Palestine. One German publisher had reissued them in a dozen languages. Hitler had copied paragraphs of "The International Jew" verbatim and pasted them into his own demented writings. A large photograph of Ford hung on the wall in Hitler's private office. It may have been taken down by 1929, when Ford was being assailed as "an artificial Jew"; in April a German journal reported that he had joined "the Palestine lodge" in Detroit.

Despite Ford's history of virulent lies against Jews, several had been invited to the dinner and, surprisingly, had come. Rosenwald, never one to stir up trouble, had been anxious to make amends with Ford. It was easy to forget that Otto Kahn, with his clipped British accent, was a Jew at all, although the events in Germany were beginning to remind Kahn himself of it. Perhaps the most interesting presence of all the five hundred guests was Rabbi Leo Franklin. The rabbi was Ford's next-door neighbor and at one time annually received a new free automobile. When Ford's attacks on Jews had begun, their relations cooled. The rabbi was nonplussed one day to find a chauffeur at his door, a new custom-built Ford parked in his driveway, and the keys dangling from the chauffeur's hand. When he re-covered his speech, Rabbi Franklin told the chauffeur to take the car away. Later Ford called. "What's the matter, Dr. Franklin?" he asked in a puzzled tone. "Has something come between us?"

On October 21, while balloting continued in Germany and GE chair-man Young served as toastmaster in Dearborn, the Nazis and their allies staged street demonstrations against the Young Plan which brought about a series of clashes between demonstrators and police in various parts of Berlin. The largest occurred in North Berlin, where three hundred Nazis attempted to march against a synagogue and ignored orders to disperse. Mounted police used their clubs. Another confrontation occurred in Potsdamerstrasse, where Nazis attempted to break through a police cordon.

Once the head of a poor and despised party, Hitler had begun to do well. The Nazis had new paymasters, a number of large industrial organi-zations, who were playing down their former anti-capitalist stance. Hitler had just acquired a nine-room home in one of the best neighborhoods in Munich. He had a valet, a housekeeper, and two big bulldogs.

The age of the celebrity had arrived by 1929. It was the age in which one made news, like Lindy and Anne, by trying to avoid making news; when one said nothing, like President-elect Hoover, only to be written about as a sphinx and an enigma; when a public figure, such as General Dawes, was chased by reporters who wrote down quotations in which everything of substance was skirted. It was the age in which the celebrated made news by standing on their heads in hotel lobbies. Celebrity stamped the age with a whacky flavor, for it raised the possibility that anyone could become famous overnight by climbing up a skyscraper, sitting on a flag-pole, swallowing goldfish, or being chosen to succeed a great inventor.

The Lindbergh flight brought in the floodtide of celebrity, and celebrity at once became the most effective form of promotion. Long, reasoned arguments went out; the ten-second glimpse, the personal appearance, and the immediate effect came in. Sometimes this promotion was only an endorsement of products, and sometimes it was only self-promotion, but sometimes it heralded a new personality type. People, as Zelda said of the flapper, became statements. That, far better than a manifesto, explained the rise of Mussolini; and Hitler was quick to learn by his example. Like a new weapon in warfare, promotion became compelling whether one liked it or not. Lindbergh hated the newspapers but continued to sell articles to them; Chaplin attempted to live the life of an old-fashioned artist in a new medium, but when his estranged wife used publicity he had to defend himself with the same weapon and promote himself as the lovable fellow of his films.

Nineteen twenty-nine opened new levels in promotion. Hoover took office to become the first president to have four White House secretaries— earlier presidents had been satisfied with one—and each of the four was concerned with promotion. One was in charge of the press and public engagements (that was George Akerson, who went with Hoover to Dearborn); another was in charge of relations with Congress, essentially a lobbyist; a third was a speechwriter, since modern presidents did not speak their own words anymore, but the more effective prose of others. The fourth, a secretive sort, undertook investigative assignments; he had once worked for *Everybody's* magazine, sleuthing for the muckrakers, including Ben Lindsey.

The theme most often promoted through 1929 was that this new American system that had been created, this capitalism with a heart, this America Model 1929, was devoted not to private gain but to service. Every member of local business organizations, which were called service clubs, heard that at the weekly luncheon, even to the extent that parallels were drawn with the example of Jesus. Jesus, it was said, was the first Rotarian. Edison conveyed a similar message in promoting his rubber project. Schwab delivered the message to any reporter who would listen. It was picked up by William Shearer and every other operator. It became necessary to claim that what was being promoted was not on behalf of some selfish interest, but for the public good and, if possible, as in Shearer's case, to hide the particular interests for whom the promoter worked. Shearer's method was just standard operating procedure.

The American economy of 1929 was a fascinating system: ebullient and cocky on the surface and riddled underneath with bad conscience. Capitalism was always attempting to overcome its selfish base and declare itself for some higher purpose. Beneath Owen Young's lectures on stewardship and Henry Ford's pronouncements of altruism lay that haunted conscience. Justification was originally, according to theologians, an act of God in which the sinner is restored to favor; by 1929, although God had moved well into the background of modern life, the need for justification had not lessened. Guilt gave capitalism much of its vitality.

Justification explains the histories of at least some of the great promoters of 1929. In search of justification Jane Addams left her cocoon of privilege for the impoverished Nineteenth Ward of Chicago; Ben Lindsey threw aside the revolver that failed to fire and plunged into battle with The Beast; Otto Kahn donated generously to cultivate an American civilization; socialite Marie Meloney found a cause for her life in Marie Curie. The same impetus for justification drove the man whose name is synonymous with modern capitalism.

When most folk were abed in the drowsy Virginia town of Williamsburg, Dr. William A. Goodwin was on the streets. In 1927 he and a young architect were working with a map of the town, believed to have been drawn by a French army cartographer in 1782. If the Frenchman's map were accurate, it was the key to the whole colonial arrangement of Williamsburg, for it showed not only the general plan, but the shapes, sizes, and positions of all the buildings as they appeared near the end of the Revolution. Eager to check its accuracy, Goodwin and the architect stole out at night and worked with the aid of a flashlight so as to avoid attracting attention.

The midnight hour was a pleasant time on the streets for Goodwin, an Episcopal clergyman. He believed that when the town was quiet, he could sense the spirits of former Williamsburgers, could hear their comings and goings, and could feel their presence around him. It was, he said, the most interesting place to live in all the world.

The clergyman had a ruling passion—a restoration of Williamsburg. He hardly saw the seedy backwater town around him, with its peeling paint, gas stations, and telephone poles, and the stores with the cute phonetically spelled names. Goodwin saw into things, and Williamsburg to him was the old Tidewater town that had been the cultural and political center of the vast colony of Virginia, where royal governors had ruled in the Palace until revolutionary fervor forced them to flee. "I am convinced," Goodwin said, "that from a historical point of view this is the greatest teaching opportunity which exists in America."

He was the sort who never recognized defeat and bounced away from rebuff. By 1928 it appeared that his far-fetched dream had taken on substance. He was buying land all over town and had a staff working for him. Newspaper reporters began to show up in his office, joining the stream of agents, property owners, and lawyers continuously waiting to see him. The rich yellow color that indicated purchased property began to spread all over Goodwin's office map. Goodwin held off the curious. He promised that he was not seeking real estate profits, and said that revealing too much about the restoration might wreck a project that could be the making of the town. Newspaper editors grudgingly agreed to stand off for a while. But all over the buzzing town, people were wondering where Goodwin was getting his money. Some said it was Otto Kahn; some said it was the Kodak camera man, George Eastman; some said Henry Ford.

Goodwin's wealthy benefactor wished to remain anonymous, even to the staff. He did not want to send real estate prices soaring and was uncertain how far he wanted to commit himself in what would be the most ambitious restoration ever conceived in America. Because he had once signed himself "David's Father," he was referred to in the office as "Mister David" or just "Mister D."

In June of 1928 the citizens of Williamsburg were called together for a mass meeting. The plan was laid out to them; the terms of the contract transferring city property to the restoration interests was explained; and Goodwin spoke of the benefits that would come to Williamsburg from the restoration. "It is now my very great privilege to announce," he concluded, "that the donors of the money to restore Williamsburg are Mr. and Mrs. John D. Rockefeller of New York." The audience broke into applause.

By 1929 the overhauling of Williamsburg had begun. The sounds of demolition were heard, and houses were seen moving down the street to another site. Plans were being formulated for a modern water and sewage system, underground power lines to replace the poles, new provisions for fire prevention, sidewalk improvement, preservation of old trees. In May the Fords visited the restoration; Ford was interested in pointers for his own Greenfield Village.

The detective work began. The mysteries of a life that had been overlaid by paint did not yield up their secrets immediately. Forgotten graveyards remained to be found. Research assistants pored over wills, histories, diaries, inventories, newspapers, town maps, tax and court records, letters, prints, paintings, insurance policies. Architects studied walls, floors, stairs, mantels. Houses were stripped down to the framing to trace their changes.

At the end of the town's main street stood a high school, and, over a twenty-acre area of surrounding land, lay an elementary school, a dry-cleaning plant, and the main line of the Chesapeake and Ohio Railroad. But the extraordinarily attuned, as Goodwin was, could see that this was the site of the Palace and its lavish formal gardens. Here had been elegant entertainments attacked for their wastefulness. Here, after the royal governors had been driven out, Patrick Henry, the first revolutionary governor, and then Thomas Jefferson, who succeeded him, had conducted affairs of state.

The Palace had burned to the ground in 1781 and had been effaced and forgotten. But underneath, the partition walls were intact. Some of the chimney bases and wine bins were there. The foundations of some outbuildings were buried in the ground. Indications of old gates, walls, steps, and details that showed the design of the garden waited beneath the soil. Fragments of china, sections of mantelpiece and panels, fireplace facings, hearthstones, ornamental bricks, wall copings—all lay under the surface like a giant puzzle.

On the night of October 21 at the banquet hall, Rockefeller sat at the head table with Madame Curie and President Hoover, Ford, and Young. On one side of Rockefeller sat Gerard Swope, president of GE; on the other side, Clara Ford. He could see Otto Kahn, his partner in relocating an opera house. He could see Schwab, whose hireling had worked against Rockefeller's aims at Geneva; and Secretary of War James Good, seeking ways to cut the military budget. He could see Rosenwald, who had aided him in the Standard Oil of Indiana proxy fight; and Lindsey, who had fought him in the Colorado mine strike; and Dr. Samuel Stratton, the president of M.I.T., who had announced the winner of the Brain Derby on the Edison lawn in August.

There had been a time when Rockefeller had questioned why he was so rich, why so much had been given to him. The question shaped his life, tied so closely to the veneration he bore his father. The only answer he had found was in the immense fabric of society. It could not be, as the simplifiers said, that all that money was just grabbed and consolidated for the enrichment of a single family. It had to be part of a plan. Over the years Rockefeller had decided, based on his own religious views, that his wealth had to do with stewardship. It was a new idea, although not exclusively his. All this money had not been given to him for his own glorification but for service. Although he sometimes found satisfaction in power, it was often a burden that furrowed his brow. To Rockefeller it explained the whole vaulting capitalist system—that those to whom were given great advantage and privilege were to repay it in service. Otherwise, he feared, the free enterprise system was nothing but red meat and a pack of hungry dogs.

When he returned from the Near East at the end of March, he caught up on all his projects. There was Prohibition to support, international peace, Negro colleges, medical research, missions to convert the benighted to Christianity, redwoods in the Yosemite Valley to save from the predations of loggers, the midtown New York project that an aide had suggested calling Rockefeller Center, and Williamsburg—especially Williamsburg.

He was as absorbed in its restoration as if he had been its creator, and he snatched up details of the plans like a vacuum cleaner pulling in debris. Goodwin was impressed by Rockefeller's grasp of details; he appeared to understand situations, even about individual buildings, down to the nails. On the site, Rockefeller would pull out the four-foot rule that he always carried with him and measure the width of a door. He was involved in every important decision and always came down on the side of accuracy. Rockefeller's grasp of his own enterprises was more absorbent than was Ford's. Ford was forever overflowing with ideas but was blurry on details and left them to others. Rockefeller was a detail man, with a mind honed for intense concentration and capacity, and he moved methodically from one pile of papers to the next, not leaping back and forth like Ford. Goodwin would watch how in spare moments Rockefeller would break out a pile of correspondence and begin to read letters. He appeared to be a man without salt, but one could see behind that appearance—the square jaws, strong chin, and firm mouth all clenched—a driven Puritan. Rockefeller had been to see the pyramids that year, and whatever it was that had obsessed the Pharaohs was also building Williamsburg.

In 1929 it also chanced that the name of Rockefeller was linked not only to Williamsburg and its evocation of the traditional and patriotic but to modern art—the iconoclastic spirit that Diaghilev had brought to America. Mrs. Rockefeller was interested in Matisse and Van Gogh and Seurat. When they were in Egypt that year she met like-minded women and on the return trip began frequent talks about a more lively museum in the city to supplement the staid Metropolitan, which would exhibit only works that had been adjudged classics. The opening of the new museum was, on October 21, only weeks away. "It is not unreasonable to suppose," said a prospectus for the Museum of Modern Art, "that within ten years New York, with its vast wealth, its already magnificent private collections and its enthusiastic but not organized interest in modern art, could achieve perhaps the greatest modern museum in the world."

So Rockefeller was destined to become one of the great patrons of modern art. Yet he detested it. He could not stand what he saw as the adolescent scratching and dabbling of such painters. To him the beautiful was impersonal—the glazed, flawless, almost featureless perfection of

Chinese porcelain. Never again, he believed, would any artistry surpass the craft of the seventeenth-century artisans whose porcelains had once filled the palaces of Imperial China. It was a rarefied passion, for to the untutored eye, one K'ang Hsi porcelain looked much like another. Rockefeller, fascinated by the subtleties of detail, lost himself in them.

He had been collecting for many years, but his major plunge came in 1915 when J.P. Morgan abruptly put his late father's Chinese porcelains, on extended loan to the Metropolitan Museum, up for sale. Rockefeller took a look at them, and when he added up the purchases he wished to make, the bill came to over a million dollars. He wrote to his father asking for a loan. "Such an opportunity to secure the finest examples of Chinese porcelain can never occur again," he wrote, "and I want to avail myself of it."

The old man was not sure he liked the turn his son's tastes were taking. The family ethic was based on work and thrift, and, within the limits of mountainous wealth, a comparative simplicity. Life was an earnest business to the Rockefellers. To be sure, his son was almost too serious in his sense of mission, and never touched alcohol, but the boy had embraced various worldly things like theater and dancing. At some point one slid over into voluptuousness. The son replied to his father's hesitancy with passion.

"I have never squandered money on horses, yachts, automobiles, or other foolish extravagances," he wrote. "A fondness for these porcelains is my only hobby—the only thing on which I have cared to spend money. I have found their study a great recreation and diversion, and I have become very fond of them." He admitted that they were costly, but noted that they were an investment. The old man sent the money. When his son initiated a talk about the terms of the loan, the old Rockefeller dismissed it, calling the porcelains a gift.

The Morgan purchases only whetted his appetite. He continued buying over the years, moving into Ming porcelain, trading off inferior examples for better. He had all his porcelains photographed and, in his personal inventory, he described them in the most intimate detail.

When he returned from the land of pyramids, Rockefeller was able again to repair to the inner sanctum that held his heart's desires. They were beautiful. The passions of human figures had been formalized there, and the flowers and symbols expressed restraint and centuries of tradition —not something by a modernist that looked as though it had been painted with the hot and wet tongue of self-expression. He would steal time from the strains of service to examine his beauties, sitting on the floor, feeling the heft of a vase in his hands, peering at it on hands and knees, rolling it about, examining it from every angle and under every slant of light, checking again against imitation, imperfection, forgery, wily repairs. Locked in his chambers, on his well-carpeted floor, Rockefeller gave himself over to the worship of proportioned beauty.

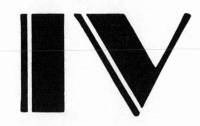

PART IV

Light's Golden Jubilee

IN THE WINTER of 1929 it was apparent in the theatrical district of New York, for an observer who noticed the longer skirts and longer hair of the women, that the age of the flapper was over. For blocks in every direction, as the crowds left the theaters, the streets were congested with automobiles. On February 11, 1929, which by coincidence was Edison's birthday, a new play by Eugene O'Neill opened at the Martin Beck Theatre. The play, *Dynamo*, was, according to its author, "the first play of a trilogy that will dig at the roots of the sickness of today as I feel it—the death of an old god and the failure of science and materialism to give any satisfying new one for the surviving primitive religious instinct to find a meaning for life in, and to comfort its fears of death with."

This time America's foremost playwright, according to the reviewers, had failed to produce another masterpiece. A plot about a spiritual journey through atheism to the worship of electricity, ending with self-immolation on a dynamo, struck them as contrived and silly. The redeeming feature of the production was the set design. A dynamo dominated the stage, and in accordance with O'Neill's directions it was "huge and black, with something of a massive female idol about it, the exciter set on the main structure like a head with blank oblong eyes above a gross, rounded torso." The oil switches seemed "like queer Hindu idols tortured into scientific supplications."

The play's protagonist had become obsessed with the dynamo when his mother died. "Listen to her singing," he proclaimed, "the hymn of electricity . . . if you could only get back into that . . . know what it means . . . then you'd know the real God! Oh, Mother of Life, my mother is dead, she has passed back into you, tell her to forgive me, and to help me find your truth." The concept was intriguingly tangential to Einstein's new theory that electricity was the basis of all being.

The set was designed by Lee Simonson, who, following a suggestion of the playwright, prepared for the project by visiting the General Electric plant in Stevenson, Connecticut. He heard the water rush through the sluices and the dynamo hum in a constant monotone. He saw the transformers that changed the river's current into a current of thirty thousand volts. The transformation generated such temperatures that water could not cool the transformer, which was jacketed in cylinders of heavy viscous

257

oil. At a switchboard of blinking red and green lights, Simonson saw load-changes signaled that released enough energy to turn the wheels of factories or light small cities. He stood in front of condensers on an upper story where the thirty-thousand-volt current was fed to the main transmission line. He watched from ten feet behind the protecting rail. The energy coursing through a copper wire at that point was so powerful that a static spark could jump across the gap and burn him severely. No insulation could withstand the copper wires, which would ignite anyone who touched them.

"Here was water that became fire, energy that sang a monotonous tune, that did croon like a lullaby and then became incandescent light," Simonson wrote in his notebook. "Here was power that could give man the strength of a god able to move mountains, the source of blind energy that could execute his commands over a network of metallic nerves beyond the reach of his eyes, that could light his way through darkness, reclaim him from toil and, if not propitiated, consume him with flame. As I left a commonplace bare brick and steel powerhouse, I was touched with a terror and a veneration for the invisible forces controlling modern life that are potentially its salvation and its destruction, its heaven and its hell. I have left many cathedrals less awed and humbled. I had been at a shrine where an invisible miracle was daily performed, a transubstantiation no less miraculous than that of the Mass. And the purely mathematical calculation of engineers had given porcelain insulators the same beauty of form that ancient artists had given to temple vessels."

By 1929 key figures of the American business technology had come to believe that great cities had reached the limits of their growth, and that the future belonged to smaller suburban and rural communities. The traffic jams of big cities and the increasing costs of supplying urban populations with water underscored the growing technological difficulties of urban life, while the proliferation of electricity could decentralize the population. They saw a future in which electrical labor-saving devices in the home would eliminate the servant class, work would shrink to two hundred four-hour days a year, and one hundred enormous powerhouses would provide the nation's entire electrical supply, replacing small power stations scattered about the country.

Samuel Insull, a transplanted Londoner who began pooling electricity early in the century and providing it to rural areas of the Middle West, was one of the practical pioneers in the movement. One of its theoreticians was Henry Ford, who thought that electrical power, by reinstituting small-town values, would overcome the moral decay that urbanization had created. Another outstanding advocate was Owen Young, the board chairman of GE. He spoke continuously before farmers' associations on the extension of power and light into rural areas. "Electricity has within itself the possibility of giving all the service that steam and water power can give and it can give it anywhere," Young said. "It could be so managed that it distributed industries and so distributed men and women."

The new development in electricity that heralded this historic reversal was called superpower—the construction of huge interconnected electrical delivery systems that would create a deep reservoir of electricity.

"Now the second industrial revolution is already marked by the wide distribution of electric energy and the substitution of comparatively few central stations for hundreds of thousands of individual factory power plants," Waldemar Kaempffert wrote in 1929, in an expansion of the Ford-Young thesis. "Power is no longer confined. Already we are immersed in a vast, unseen ocean of it that can be tapped by the farmhouse or steel mill. Industry is responding. No longer is the huge city, with its swarming hordes lodged in tenements, its huddled factories, its disgraceful subways and street cars, to dominate society. Industry is migrating or establishing itself anew in the small town. The current of emigration which has been steadily flowing to the city for decades is now flowing back to the country. Unlike the first industrial revolution the age of superpower, of energy shot with the speed of light into thousands of small towns and villages, was foreseen. President Hoover foresaw it and welcomed it. As central stations grew in size and it became possible to flash energy at more than three hundred thousand volts up and down the Pacific Coast, engineers began to plan the second electrical revolution—the revolution which was to free energy from time and space."

Nor did this historic moment lack a symbol—although the symbol was not yet built. By early 1929 the area around the nondescript little desert town of Las Vegas, Nevada, was filling with the poor and dispossessed, hoping to be near the front of the line when hiring for the construction of Boulder Dam would begin. About one hundred fifty miles away the cities of Los Angeles, Pasadena, Glendale, and the rest of Southern California waited for the water and electrical power to begin flowing.

Boulder Dam was also the focal point of a national argument about the control of electrical power. Its champions had been advocates of government-owned power, its opponents the private power companies led by their trade association, the National Electric Light Association. These companies had contended through the debate that Los Angeles would not need water for another half-century and that there was no need for electric power in that part of the world—but now that it was coming, they planned to convert it to private power control.

Superpower was not just a technological change, but a political issue entwined with the struggle for popular control of electrical power. In this struggle Light's Golden Jubilee was born. The Jubilee celebrated Big Business, but above all the big business of private electrical power. It was staged in praise of American technology, but above all the technology of electrical power, including the improved casings and increased voltages that would deliver superpower. In an age of promotion, it was an elaborate promotion for private power interests.

Light's Golden Jubilee was intensely appropriate for 1929, for, more than any other single factor, the electrical power companies were the indicators of what was happening to the American economy. The pyramiding holding companies that they had created, which, by piling one upon another had hoisted the economy to such unprecedented heights, were the leading cause of the sudden instability that was trembling so discernibly on October 21, when the notables gathered at Dearborn.

In the spirit of ballyhoo, General Electric, with some financial help from Westinghouse, had conceived and financed the Jubilee as a way of using Thomas Edison to promote it own interests. To bring it off GE went to one of the rising young public relations figures of the day, a nephew of Sigmund Freud whose knowledge of mass psychology was unequaled, the brooding, introspective Edward L. Bernays.

Edward Bernays was in the same line as Ivy Lee but had a different clientele. Lee's office was in the Wall Street area, near Rockefeller and Kahn, two of his major clients. Bernays' luxurious carpeted offices were in midtown Manhattan. His clients were people like Bernarr Macfadden, a health enthusiast who also published the *Daily Graphic*, New York's greasiest tabloid; and George Harrison Phelps, the beleaguered head of a Detroit advertising agency.

In 1927 Phelps had been given the unpromising task of promoting the new Dodge Victory Six against the gargantuan publicity that had been used to advance the Ford Model A. The Dodge company had fallen into the hands of bankers, inexperienced in marketing and advertising, who drove Phelps to insomnia with complaints. He enlisted Bernays to succor him.

Bernays found the Victory Six an interesting design concept, low-slung and sturdy. He became convinced that the debut of the Victory Six could generate enormous interest by using radio instead of newspapers as the basic advertising medium. Radio was still new enough to be startling. Until then, radio advertising had been local, but NBC was building a chain of stations around the country. Bernays recommended nationwide radio advertising.

The radio draw would be a spectacular cast of characters with Will Rogers as master of ceremonies. NBC liked the idea and added an innovation of its own. The network was gradually developing the ability to switch from one broadcasting point to another and, wishing to show off its technology, suggested that the various entertainers perform not in a single studio, but from various places around the nation. Rogers, then stomping around Mexico with Ambassador Morrow, would go home to Beverly Hills. Al Jolson would perform from a hotel room in New Orleans. Another act would play from Chicago. Paul Whiteman would lead his orchestra from the NBC main studio in New York.

It was the most ambitious hookup yet attempted, and a radio first—forty broadcasting stations working together to put on a performance for a large audience around the nation. NBC used twenty thousand miles of wire. Bernays introduced another idea to Merlin Aylesworth, the NBC president: he convinced Aylesworth to plug the program and generate advance interest. NBC discovered that several additional stations joined because of the advance publicity. In a publicity ploy, Bernays announced that Dodge was considering "SOS insurance" to cover possible losses if the show were interrupted for an emergency.

The program went on at 10:30 P.M., East Coast time. Rogers kidded with Graham McNamee, the NBC announcer, imitated President Coolidge, and joked about the contest between the new Ford and Dodge cars. He also introduced the various entertainers. An hour later the show went off the air without a single hitch.

It was the talk of the country. "This achievement in broadcasting proves that science has brought all Americans into one neighborhood," said the president of Brown University. "Prophecy as to the future possibilities of radio development seems utterly futile when confronted by the astounding achievement of this evening," another public figure said. Lee De Forest said that the American people had become so familiar with the daily miracles of radio that "few except communications engineers can even remotely appreciate the immense triumph of engineering and science which the broadcast hour signalizes tonight."

It was estimated that thirty-five million people listened. The president of Dodge Brothers was thrilled to tell the glories of Dodge construction over the air with big stars and was impressed by the size of the audience.

Phelps began to sleep again at night. Ford had spent 1.3 million dollars for newspaper advertising for the Model A; the radio show cost sixty-seven thousand dollars. It was front page news in newspapers all over the nation, including the *New York Times*, which proclaimed: "All America Used as a Radio Studio." It was nearly a perfect campaign, with one exception. The car didn't sell. The postmortem judgment was that the lines were too advanced and the car was too low-slung.

Bernays' work for the American Tobacco Company was more successful. George Washington Hill, the company president, had introduced women into cigarette advertising in an effort to open an untapped source of new customers. "Reach for a Lucky instead of a sweet" was one of the first advertising slogans to be heard on the NBC chain, and it was especially aimed at women, for whom slimness had become the mode in fashion.

But thinness, Hill contended, was not only fashionable but a sign of good health. Luckies could promote good health by keeping people slim. Celebrities were singing testimonials about how good inhaling a Lucky made them feel. "In the athletic world, men study every method of maintaining physical fitness," wrote Damon Runyon, a noted sports expert. Runyon had a simple rule for weight maintenance: "Light a Lucky when you crave the things which make you fat." The celebrated songwriter, George M. Cohan, testified, "Lucky is a marvelous pal—the toasted flavor overcomes a craving for foods which add weight."

Bernays was not an advertising man but a public relations counselor and so he promoted not Luckies, but slimness. He arranged to have a commercial photographer send a letter to other photographers praising trim women who lit cigarettes instead of eating sweets. He also promoted moderation. Ziegfeld beauties were enlisted in the cause of moderation, pledging themselves to the "modern figure with its tantalizing, sinuous curves."

A furious enemy soon entered the fray. "We are marshaling together the big guns of the industry and steps are being taken to protect its interests," wrote *Candy Weekly*, the candy trade publication. The candy trade association organized a protest that reached the Federal Trade Commission, the Radio Commission, and the Better Business Bureau of the Associated Advertising Clubs of America. The industry succeeded in getting the War Department to rebuke Lieutenant General Robert Lee Bullard, retired, for stating that Lucky Strike helped keep Army men fit as a fiddle.

The candy industry struck back with material about candy's medicinal properties in weight control and saving body tissues. "Do not let anyone tell you that a cigarette can take the place of a piece of candy," warned an advertisement of a New York confectionary chain. "The cigarette will inflame your nostrils, poison with nicotine every organ of your body, and dry up your blood—nails in your coffin."

Bernays convinced Hill that by way of a counterattack he should finance a scientific study of the harmful effects of sugar. The published work, signed by a physician, concluded that "sugar is undermining the nation's health."

Hill, not the least interested in how tobacco was grown or cigarettes made, devoted all his time to marketing. One day he asked Bernays to try to change the prejudice against women smoking on the street, in order to increase their cigarette smoking.

The problem suggested his Uncle Sigmund's theories of psychoanalysis, and so Bernays, for the first time in the history of marketing, took the matter to a psychoanalyst. A.A. Brill, a well-known figure in the field, told Bernays and the American Tobacco Company that cigarettes were identified with men, and that women, as a result of their emancipation, were suppressing their femininity—doing the same work as men and having fewer children than before. Cigarettes were therefore symbols of freedom.

Bernays' secretary sent out thirty telegrams to debutantes inviting them to join a march for freedom "in the interests of equality of the sexes and to fight another sex taboo." On Easter Sunday, 1929, a group of young women, their smoke curling skyward, strolled up Fifth Avenue in the Easter Parade, militantly smoking cigarettes.

That was the kind of twirl Bernays put on his work. During the first week of February 1929, Bernays—a slight, boyish, well-dressed man of thirty-seven years with luxuriant black hair—was visited by Napoleon Boynton, a young General Electric executive. "I hear that you are very able," Boynton began, as if to suggest that he had chosen Bernays himself. Boynton explained that GE wanted Edison to receive a lot of public attention in 1929, to be capped with a huge gathering in his honor.

Drumming his fingers occasionally and blowing into his hand, Bernays listened intently, already beginning to work out the psychology. Boynton told Bernays he wanted him to produce a public relations plan and issue press releases.

Bernays already knew generally how to do it. First, he explained to Boynton, was to set a goal of highest exposure. That would be, obviously, the culminating event of October 21. Around that date would be built a curve of public interest rising continuously over the months from February to October.

Eager to take the assignment, Bernays accepted on the spot. He began to tell Boynton his immediate reaction. This age, he said, is essentially technological and scientific, and a scientific figure ought to be its hero. Lincoln and Washington were political heroes for an era of nation-building; Carnegie and Frick had been heroes of the industrial age; Lindbergh and Babe Ruth had been news-created heroes; now it ought to be technology's turn.

It promised to be a lot of work. Considering the amount of time to be put into it, a nine-thousand-dollar retainer for eight months' work was not easy money. For Bernays, however, the project had other attractions. It gave him an opportunity to shape an event—to show how an event, rather than just words, could produce an immense public effect. This could be, he thought at once, the most important assignment of his career.

Within a few days he had two items ready to go. One was a letter to the Post Office Department, suggesting that the fiftieth anniversary of the invention of the incandescent lamp be commemorated with a special stamp. The other was a press release prepared in advance. "Edison Pioneers Propose World-Wide Celebration of Light's Golden Jubilee," the headline read. "Birthday Celebration by Inventor's Old Associates—Take Action to Institute 'Greatest Living Tribute' On Occasion of Fiftieth Anniversary of Incandescent Lamps."

Nobody suspected that the smoothly laid plans were about to be upset by the mercurial personality of Henry Ford and the ruffled feathers of Thomas Edison.

The previous fall, Edison had received the nation's highest honor, the Congressional Medal of Honor, and the entire electrical industry had taken the occasion to promote a huge advertising campaign with Edison cast as patron saint. Yet while all this glorification was going on publicly, the same people were hindering efforts of the Edison family to get into radio manufacture. RCA, which controlled the entire field through its grip on the patent pool, had refused Edison a license to make radios.

His son, Charles Edison, ran the family business as president of Thomas A. Edison, Inc. A product of Edison's second marriage, Charles, still a young man, lacked any talent for invention but helped his father ably in business. After painful delays, he had finally persuaded RCA to let the Splitdorf Company—which had been granted a radio license—make the sets for Edison. Charles Edison soon learned to his chagrin, however, that Splitdorf was in extreme disarray, and the supply problem soon became acute. The radio trust had pushed Edison into a mess.

In the midst of that situation, Charles Edison asked what seemed a small favor of two of the leading Edison Pioneers, one of them a GE executive. He asked for a free plug. Somewhere in all the snowstorm of tributes to his father, he asked, it might be mentioned that Edison made radios. The two Pioneers had promised to come through but had not, and this failure, or "double cross," as Edison called it, was yet another rebuff for the old man to resent.

Charles eventually came up with a solution to the Splitdorf problem. He contacted Charles Schwab, who had a large interest in Splitdorf, and offered to run the company for a management fee. By January of 1929 the offer was taken and Charles Edison began working Thomas A. Edison, Inc., out of a troublesome situation. Nevertheless father and son were both peeved by the shabby treatment they had received at the hands of GE, which basically controlled RCA.

Thus Charles Edison, on his father's birthday, February 11, attended the annual luncheon of the Edison Pioneers in New York with something less than a feeling of camaraderie. He maintained close contacts with the Pioneers, who met every year to honor their old boss on his birthday. Sentimental memories bound the old associates in a fraternity, and they loved to tell stories about the tobacco-spitting cuss they had worked for, but the Pioneers also had business implications. Many of Edison's former employees had risen to positions of authority in electrical manufacturing companies and power and light companies, and were thus important to Thomas A. Edison, Inc.

As Bernays' press release stated, the Pioneers announced plans for the Jubilee as a tribute of the Edison Pioneers, but the particulars did not develop as GE had intended. Henry Ford knew of Edison's treatment at the hands of RCA. Once he heard of GE's huge plans for a celebration, which had been undertaken without even consulting Edison, he decided to "kidnap the party" away from GE headquarters at Schenectady. He promptly decided to rush the work of Greenfield Village, reshape the Dearborn project as an elaborate tribute to Edison, and hold it on October 21, upsetting GE's plan to hold it at Schenectady. Before February was out, Ford informed the newspapers of his own plans for observing the birth of the incandescent light.

GE found its patron saint stolen from under its nose, and Swope and Young were reportedly upset. Edison was delighted, for he believed that GE was more interested in exploiting than honoring him. GE reluctantly agreed to leave the dinner in the hands of the erratic Ford. And so Bernays suddenly found himself working with Ford, although not for him.

The name of General Electric did not appear on that initial press release that Bernays sent out for Light's Golden Jubilee, nor on any others. Bernays was not in the business of advertising products. He sold concepts, and to sell the Jubilee he carefully avoided the mention of GE.

Instead he organized a Light's Golden Jubilee Committee, a group of famous citizens that included John D. Rockefeller, Jr., Charles Schwab, J.P. Morgan, George Eastman, William Green, Dr. Charles Mayo, Julius Rosenwald, Jane Addams, Will Hays, Otto Kahn, and Ambassador Dwight Morrow. All it took was a telephone call to get permission for the use of their names on a letterhead. The fictitious committee, a process some called "stuffing the shirt," was a Bernays invention that he had been using for more than a decade and that by 1929 was widely imitated.

Bernays worked almost totally by indirection. A few years earlier Venida, a hair net company, had hired him when the fashion for bobbed hair began to hurt sales. He did not, in all his efforts for Venida, mention the company name. He wrote to the New York City health commissioner, suggesting that he contact his counterparts around the nation in support of a rule that women who cook and wait on tables should wear hair nets, and other letters went to other parts of the country. Soon the health commissioner in Seattle decreed that milkshake mixers must wear hair nets. The need for women working around machinery to wear hair nets for greater safety soon attracted public attention. In some states bills were introduced to make hair nets an industrial requirement, and in others labor commissioners established it as an industry rule. Never did Bernays mention his relationship to Venida. On another occasion, when a group of importers hired him to fight high tariffs, he put together a letterhead committee of women consumers and fought high tariffs in what appeared to be the consumers' interest. Bernays called these methods "the conversion of selfish private interests into the public interest." William Shearer could have called his indirections by the same name.

The indirect delighted Bernays, and he was happiest when influencing the public in ways it never suspected. To Bernays, life was a billiard game, and everything was hit off the cushion.

Business had discovered by the 1920s that it needed men like Bernays. The networks of communication had produced an information speedup never before experienced in history. Fashions came and went in a season. New trends sprang up suddenly and were then swept away. These currents and tides held perils for a business. There was potential for quick success but also for being shipwrecked. Businessmen found themselves at the mercy of a whim—the Prince of Wales could decide to go bareheaded and wipe out the hat industry in six weeks.

That was where Edward Bernays could help. Since so much depended upon the right image, of riding a trend, business needed an analyst of mass psychology. Bernays had been studying the mass mind for years. He had seen the effect of his own work with Diaghilev's Ballets Russes, and in 1917, when he did publicity for the national tour of Enrico Caruso, the great Metropolitan Opera tenor, he had been amazed at the reception Caruso received in the hinterlands where they were impressed by his name although they had never heard him sing.

With the entrance of the United States into the war, Bernays joined the Committee on Public Information and here saw the massive use of propaganda on an unprecedented scale. It was a total assault on the American people to shape attitudes and foster sacrifice on the home front. Some, like Hoover in the Food Administration, were adept at it, but Bernays saw that President Wilson was inept. Wilson never knew which stops to finger, and his efforts were counterproductive. Bernays studied the mistakes Wilson had made in trying to sell the League of Nations to Americans. "It was the war," Bernays later wrote, "which opened the eyes of the intelligent few in all departments of life to the possibilities of regimenting the modern mind."

Bernays, the first person to teach the new science of propaganda as an academic pursuit, sometimes found a student in his classes at New York University who might be concerned about the malevolent use of communications outlets. He might argue that it was an unequal match because the citizen was disorganized and at the mercy of powerful organized forces. Bernays' answer was based on his experience with Venida.

Some years before, he said, Irene Castle took a fancy to cut her hair short. Mrs. Castle, a famous dancer, looked lovely in short hair. No one had put her up to it. Within weeks women were storming the barber shops. The makers of hair nets were reduced to panic. Hairpin manufacturers laid off workers, and hats had to be remodeled, and the hair comb industry was in confusion. Barbers, poverty-stricken by the coming of cheap replaceable razor blades, were back in business again, and beauty parlors sprang up everywhere. Eventually even the conduct of women was affected. Shorter hair seemed allied with emancipation and soon they were wearing makeup and shortening their skirts. The cosmetics industry was happily surprised and cloth makers were taken by despair. Thousands lost their jobs and thousands of others were put to work. "Would this have been better or worse," Bernays asked, "if Mrs. Castle's decision had been influenced by a propagandist?" The new technology had already created the channels and people were being influenced. If they were not guided by some overseeing intelligence, they would still be at the mercy of invisible influences. The only differences would be that the influences would be the vagaries of chance, and Bernays preferred direction.

Deep thinkers saw through to essences by ignoring surfaces, but to Bernays the surfaces affected the soul. Sometimes the effect was intentional; when a French nobleman threw away his powdered wig and knee breeches and began wearing natural hair and trousers, he had joined the Revolution. Sometimes the effect was seductively unintentional; when women began to wear fashions inspired by the Ballets Russes, their attitudes about themselves and their sexuality changed.

Bernays sold the Jubilee for the next eight months without any concern about whether anyone heard a mention of General Electric. In April Ford succeeded in getting President Hoover himself as general chairman of the Jubilee Committee. The electric power and light industry prepared to spend over a million dollars in newspaper advertising. GE presented the old Menlo Park laboratory to Ford. The New York Edison Company gave Ford an 1891 electrical generating plant, which Ford thereupon used to supply current to his museum. Golden lamps were placed in the torch of the Statue of Liberty, and steamship captains and pilots promptly notified of the change in the landscape.

In early June, the Light's Golden Jubilee stamp went on sale. Henry Ford, then in Atlantic City, had to borrow two cents to buy one—an incident that made the newspapers all over the country. He repaid by check, and an autograph dealer bid one hundred dollars for the two-cent check. When the offer was rejected, it became another national story. The Jubilee had taken hold and picked up a momentum of its own. Bernays still worked, however, at creating events. He suggested that Commander Byrd somehow mark the Jubilee and Byrd obliged: the long-distance airplane beacon and emergency light mounted atop one of the radio towers in Little America was named the Edison Beacon.

Although he was regarded as a mass psychologist, Bernays never directly worked on the mass mind. He preferred indirection and the employment of the Barnum method.

When Phineas T. Barnum, the Prince of Ballyhoo, wanted to induce the people of England to swarm to his presentation of General Tom Thumb, he used a roundabout method. The run-of-the-mill promoter would have hit the dock landing at full speed, papering the newspapers with publicity and plastering the fences with announcements promising a rare delectation. Barnum said not a word and printed not a broadside.

Instead he moved quietly into a posh mansion in Grafton Street with

his midget attraction and hired a brace of elegant servants. Then he un-
folded a select list of nobility to whom the General would be at home, and
sent tastefully engraved invitations. He also invited some of the more
important English editors. The novelty of seeing a midget so sprucely
appointed was almost irresistible, and the carriages arrived daily. In time
Edward Everett, the U.S. ambassador to England, called to pay his respects, and arranged an audience with Queen Victoria.

Barnum never attempted to entice the English masses directly. He
merely created circumstances and events that piqued the interest of the
British ruling class and press. Those two mighty shapers of opinion fired
the popular imagination, and presently everyone from Shoreditch to May-
fair was eager to see the amazing miniature man who had intrigued the
queen and the nobility. When Barnum opened in Piccadilly, every performance played to a full house.

Bernays used the same method and discovered that Ford understood
the method as well. Together they concentrated on attracting important
people, the American equivalent of the British nobility, to the Jubilee
finale. Bernays placed little stock in direct attempts to reach the masses
and regarded that as a wasteful use of his energies. He relied instead on
intermediaries, elite groups through which the desired effect would perco-
late downward. In the guest list of "group leaders and opinion molders"—
a phrase Bernays had originated—lay the proof that the Jubilee was an
event of enormous significance. Ford understood scarcity value and advised Bernays to hold the press invitations down.

Thus they worked together, two masters of the industrial democratic
society with deep anti-democratic impulses, the absolute monarch of the
River Rouge and a mass psychologist with a dreary view of the capacity of
the people for self-government. Thomas Jefferson had believed that universal literacy would foster popular control of American institutions.
Bernays regarded that as a delusion. Literacy had produced predigested
advertising slogans and tabloid newspapers with an unvarying fare of sex,
crime, and sports. People in the mass did not think; they relied on stereotypes and formulas. "Each man's rubber stamps are the duplicates of
millions of others," Bernays wrote in a book published in 1928, "so that
when those millions are exposed to the same stimuli, all receive identical
imprints." Bernays had the same contempt for the American boob that
Mencken had fostered in his writings.

Democracy, Bernays thought, was an invalid. Power had passed from
kings and royalty to the people, but the people were unaware of what to do
with it. The intelligent minorities continued to rule as before, though not

by whip and rack. They took control of communication and with it directed the mass mind, and this rule, although hidden, was total. "The conscious and intelligent manipulation of the organized habits and opinions of the masses," Bernays wrote in his book, "is an important element in democratic society. Those who manipulate this unseen mechanism of society constitute an invisible government which is the true ruling power of the country . . . It is the intelligent minorities which need to make use of propaganda continuously and systematically. In the active proselytizing minorities in whom selfish interests and public interest coincide lie the progress and development of America."

Selfish interests and public interest, and whether they coincided or clashed, was the theme of the debate about electrical power that seemed unresolvable in 1929. For several years Henry Ford had tried to work his powers of persuasion on group leaders and the masses on just this issue, focusing on Muscle Shoals.

Built by the War Department to produce nitrates for the war effort, the Muscle Shoals development, on the Tennessee River in northern Alabama, lay abandoned in 1929. To the east stood the half-completed Wilson Dam, potentially a source of electrical power for the Tennessee Valley, and a second dam had been mapped out but never begun. Ford had failed to get Muscle Shoals for himself.

Henry Ford had made his first bid for the Tennessee River project in early 1922 when he led a delegation to the Washington office of Secretary of War John Weeks. Ford's assistants explained the terms of the contract that he was offering the government. Weeks said he would discuss it with President Harding and the proper congressional committees.

As the Detroit entourage departed, Ford sent one of his men back to tell Weeks that he would have no public statement on the meeting and that the Secretary of War should make any statement that seemed appropriate. Weeks was therefore annoyed the following day to find that Ford had not only decided to speak to the press, but had chided the Secretary of War in print for delaying the project and losing precious time.

"We didn't want Muscle Shoals for selfish purposes in the first place," said Ford, who was usually more combative in print than across a table. "Hanged if we care very much whether we get it now. It was an industrial philanthropy which we offered—an offer based on a desire for great public service. A subsidy means getting something from the government for nothing. We're not asking the government for a nickel. Instead, we are giving the government an offer unprecedented for its generosity."

That rocked Weeks back on his heels. It would be no easy task to convince Congress that Ford's proposal was an act of philanthropy. All the so-called generosity was in Ford's public statements and promises, not in the carefully drawn contract. Once again Ford was playing to the grandstand.

Weeks responded to Ford's attack with an unfriendly reply. He had not delayed the proposal, he said, which had only just come into his hands. Ford had been quiet during the discussion and had not shown a single sign of displeasure. By the time Ford reached his hotel, Weeks said, he had apparently forgotten that he had asked Weeks to be the sole source of a public statement. "I regret," Weeks added, "that Mr. Ford, by this action, seems to have put himself in the class of those who go to the press with that kind of sentiment rather than saying it to the individual involved."

Although Ford on that particular day affected an offhand air about Muscle Shoals, he had been telling friends and interviewers that he regarded this opportunity as his destiny. There was nothing he wanted more, not even another billion dollars. He wanted it so much, and was so avidly in search of allies, that he had even voluntarily given up attacking the Jews in his newspaper.

Ford had offered less for Muscle Shoals than its value as scrap, but many people were picking up war surplus at bargain prices; it was a sideline of the Harding administration. Opposition developed among senators who charged that selling to Ford under the terms offered would be a giveaway. Ford was convincing, weaving his spell with masterful publicity. He said it would be one of the greatest undertakings ever seen. He would build a seventy-five-mile-long constellation of cities along the river. He would show that industry could be decentralized and placed in a humanistic setting that preserved rural values. And, although the contract called for a one-hundred-year lease, he would turn over the finished product to the people in fifty years, in such a way that neither he nor his heirs could profit from it.

Eventually it would become a greater industrial center than Detroit. He would begin by operating the nitrate plants to make fertilizer. Then he would complete the Wilson Dam. Thousands would be put to work. It was a shame, he said, that rising water levels would soon make it necessary to put construction off to 1923, when so many men needed work in 1922. When the dam was completed, the valley would become a demi-paradise. Ford did not intend to sell any of his power to anyone, but would use all of it for his own projects, including the manufacture of auto parts to be shipped to Detroit for assembly.

This, Ford determined, would be his magnum opus—the work that would set his mark upon history. He would develop Muscle Shoals as a gift to the people of the United States.

Ford always had a talent for capturing the mass imagination. The countryside of northern Alabama soon began to look like the Klondike, with wayfarers arriving every day. Real estate was changing hands rapidly. Alabamans began to plant orchards, convinced they would make their fortunes selling fruit to the incoming throngs. A letter described the area as "one seething mass of excited humanity." Employment agencies sent flyers around the nation, hustling industrial workers to get in line with them for employment at Muscle Shoals and soliciting an enrollment fee of one dollar. The chief of the Army Engineers recommended that persons exploiting the jobless be prosecuted. The itinerant who came found nothing. Even the limited government operations in the vicinity had been closed down for a year.

But people were confident that Henry Ford would soon have it humming. He was regarded as a seer and a genius. Organizations began to rally to his support for the Muscle Shoals bid, including farmer groups, realtors, newspapers, Southern politicians, and the American Federation of Labor. Rallies to support Ford were held in Montgomery and Atlanta. The secretary of agriculture came out for Ford.

Much of the interest centered on fertilizer. Objections were raised that the proposed contract Ford had submitted did not even require him to make any, but Ford's agents assured everyone that his word was good and that he had a secret way of doing it. "It has been his dream," said William B. Mayo, one of his chief engineers, "to make fertilizers so low that everybody can use all he wants."

Responding to Mayo's testimony, a Mississippi congressman deplored the doubts raised about Ford's intentions. "They have just been gutter fishing around," he said. "Is not it a fact that Mr. Ford intends to make fertilizer so easy that a plain free nigger could mix it in the ground?" The Ford emissary smiled in agreement. "We have great respect for Mr. Ford in our country," the congressman continued. "We call him Uncle Henry, and we believe he will give us cheap fertilizer just like he has given us automobiles to ride around."

Ford faced opposition from various quarters. Rival proposals were submitted. Proponents of public power said it would end the best chance for public power in America and that Ford's operation would be beyond regulation. Army officers thought Ford's offer too low. A minority report out of the House Military Affairs Committee called Ford's campaign a propaganda masterpiece, "a rosy picture of the great activity that is to be started overnight at Muscle Shoals, where they promise a million men will be given employment." The fertilizer interests moved into busy opposition. The National Fertilizer Association sent out circulars entitled "Cost to Taxpayers of Ford Muscle Shoals Offer." The byproduct coking interests, the air nitrogen fixation interests, and the fertilizer interests were all lined up against him through the House of Morgan. Ford said the fertilizer trust was afraid that its prices would be undercut.

His fertilizer expert was Thomas A. Edison. "I'm not a chemist," Ford said, "but Edison has been down there and knows every detail of this proposition. He is working on this thing right now in his laboratory at East Orange. He says that with Muscle Shoals we can give the people a better fertilizer at a much lower price than they have ever had before." Edison testified to the same before the Senate Agriculture Committee. Despite his abrasiveness, it looked as if Ford might bring it off, especially since the partnership of Ford and Edison gave it an almost mythic dimension.

But the two men may have overreached themselves and doomed the project with their preaching of monetary freethinking. Ford had proposed to complete the Wilson Dam for the government at a cost estimated at thirty million dollars, but instead of raising the money by bond issue, he proposed that the government issue "energy dollars" to be paid to the workers for their labor. Taxes would, he said, be unnecessary. It was time to put away childish things such as the gold standard and to issue money based on the nation's resources. Money would then be based on "the real actual wealth of the country." Edison joined by sending out similar monetary theories to fourteen prominent economists and financial experts.

"Once more, the raucous voices of the promoters of economic, social and political quackeries and the vendors of tickets to Utopia are being heard in the land," Otto Kahn told the Association of Stock Exchange Firms in New York. "Even the dead bones of greenbackism and fiat money are being taken from their unhallowed resting-places and an effort is being made to breathe life again into their skeletons."

The uproar among bankers and economists chastened Edison, who dropped "the energy dollar," calling it "a complex question." Ford also retired and said nothing for months. When he spoke again, he was unrepentent.

"During the war," Ford said, "the country turned its every resource to help free the world from militarism—a militarism bolstered by an international money power. Now, in the same way, we are going to fight to the last ditch to free American industry and American agriculture from that same money power. If the American people can once catch the idea of what waterpower means—how it can be put to service in a thousand ways, cutting the cost of industrial power to a minimum and thus, through better service, make possible a higher standard of living for all people, at a greatly reduced cost—they never again will submit to the proposition that to get power they must pay tribute to Wall Street. All the people need to catch the idea is an example. A potential example lies at Muscle Shoals. In a sense the destiny of the American people for centuries to come lies there on the Tennessee River, because whoever controls a nation's power controls that nation's people."

Ford said he put his faith in the people—that they would not allow Wall Street to defeat them. Muscle Shoals was more than a single project, he said, it was a model. All electrical development that followed would be based upon it, with cheap power to run plants, light homes, and operate farm machinery. The government would obtain so much revenue from these power projects that all taxation would be ended.

"American power today is dependent on the steam power of coal," Ford said. "The great private financiers own the bulk of the nation's coal mines. The financiers, centered in Wall Street, have a stranglehold on the industry and transportation of the country. If Muscle Shoals is developed along unselfish lines, it will work splendidly and so simply that in no time hundreds of other water power developments will spring up all over the country and the days of American industry paying tribute for its power would be gone forever. Every human being in the country would reap the benefit. I am consecrated to the principle of freeing American industry. All I want is a chance at Muscle Shoals and, if it's the last thing I do on this earth, I'll fight for that chance."

In succeeding years the Alabama Power Company and other private interests attempted to take over Muscle Shoals without success, fighting not only among themselves but against the proponents of public power. In 1928, after years of struggle, Senator George Norris, a Nebraska Republican, got his bill for public development of Muscle Shoals through Congress only to see President Coolidge thwart his aims with a pocket veto.

The outraged Norris abandoned his party in the 1928 presidential campaign and threw his support to the Democratic candidate, Alfred E. Smith. Norris charged that the Coolidge administration was in the hands of a power trust, and that Hoover was a willing accomplice. The power trust was such a menace, he said in a stunning address in Omaha, that its defeat was more important than party loyalties. His defection drew a rare political response from Thomas Edison.

"Waterpower seems to have been adopted as the shibboleth of politics in this campaign," Edison said in a statement released through the Engineers' National Hoover Committee. He blandly went on to declare that waterpower alone could not furnish all of the nation's electrical energy needs and sidestepped the more controversial issues. The statement suggested, however, that Ford's grandest scheme was not yet totally abandoned.

By 1929 Ford's attacks on Wall Street had ceased. Instead he deplored politicians who, he said, were roadblocks to progress who could never develop anything themselves. He told an interviewer for *Electrical World*, a trade magazine, that Light's Golden Jubilee was more than a celebration of the birth of electrical power—it was also a promotion for its wider use.

"People talk about a power trust," Ford said. "I only wish that there actually were a power trust, a central directing organization for the development and use of every power source in the country tied into one operating and business unit. It has got to come as the one necessary and economic method of power production. Our national power system will become a unit, just as our postal system is. This would mightily speed the day when electric power would fulfill its destiny as the bearer of mankind's burdens." The rhetoric had changed, but Ford was the same.

In electrical energy in the 1920s, the name of Samuel Insull stood first. Insull had electrified rural America by pooling power. He had made his electrical stocks into high-flying rivals to RCA and General Motors. In the Midwest, Insull, born a Cockney in London in 1859, was Mr. Big Business. Generous with gifts and gentle with underlings, he had a white, neatly clipped moustache and white hair that set off a pair of eyes that nevertheless brimmed in a flash with hostility. He had become a social arbiter in his adopted Chicago and it went hard with those who failed to respond to his calls for public service or contributions to his charities. The women of Chicago's wealthy district, the so-called Gold Coast, especially disliked him, but they were careful to complain of his rudeness only at night in their bedrooms, where only their husbands could hear. He could be ruthless, and his ire was directed most against those who had been his social superiors and against the bankers of New York.

Under the sooty skies of Chicago in 1929 his monument was going up. The forty-two-story building resembled a giant's chair, with arms and a seat, and was called Insull's Throne. The ground floor would contain a new opera house, and with it he intended to make Chicago the musical capital of America.

Perhaps Samuel Insull was not as arrogant as people thought. It may have been his appearance that put them off; as a young man he had grown a moustache to cover an upper lip that tended to curl into a sneer when his emotions were stirred, and he had hyperthyroid eyes that popped and glared. At sixty-nine years of age he was ruler of a huge public utility empire stretching through thirty-two states from Lake Michigan to Texas. It included three hundred steam plants and two hundred hydroelectric plants and comprised one-eighth of all the electrical power in the United States. It was said that he loved power—electrical, political, and financial. He never hesitated to use any kind of power at hand. There was in him utterly nothing of the crusader. He dealt with men as he found them and was never disappointed in them because he expected so little.

One day late in 1925 a political functionary stopped at Insull's office. He was campaign manager for a Republican politician named Frank L. Smith. Smith wanted to be the U.S. senator from Illinois, but to make it he had to win the Republican primary election from the incumbent, a man with the unlikely name of William McKinley.

Sitting with Insull, the functionary explained Smith's qualifications and platform. Insull promptly responded that he did not think McKinley had made a good senator and that he liked Smith's views. He reached into his drawer, counted out fifty thousand dollars in cash, and gave it to the campaign manager.

In March of 1926 the two men met a second time. Insull asked how the campaign was going. Not so well, the campaign manager said. We've been having trouble raising money. The McKinley people have been spreading the rumor that you made such a large contribution that we don't need any money. Insull nodded in understanding and made another fifty-thousand-dollar cash contribution. The two chanced to meet a third time. Once again the campaign manager complained of difficulty in raising funds. From the funds of the Commonwealth Edison Company, one of his utilities, Insull gave him another twenty-five thousand dollars, which made him virtually the sole support of Smith. It was helpful for Insull to be in his good graces, however, for Smith was chairman of the Illinois Commerce Commission, the agency that set rates for all the utility companies in the state.

Smith won easily and began to plan the fall campaign against his Democratic opponent. Then he ran into a problem. A Senate colleague of McKinley's revealed that utility baron Sam Insull had contributed huge sums to Smith's campaign and charged that a twenty-million-dollar utility deal was involved. A Senate committee swept into Chicago to hold hearings and national publicity was generated. Insull took the stand and admitted that he had paid for the Smith campaign. He was so open about it that editorial writers and University of Chicago reformers called him brazen. Insull refused, however, to reveal his contributions to other Chicago political figures. The case was soon being cited in editorials around the country as a classic example of the corrupting influence of money in politics.

Chicago was, furthermore, legendary for its corruption. It was said that the gangsters bombed each other from airplanes; that fifteen men with tommyguns surrounded Capone at all times; that Capone's doors and shutters were armored, and that a great vault beneath his floor contained a treasure of champagne and emeralds.

The real Chicago was wilder and grittier than the fables. The stench of blood and ordure from the slaughterhouses rolled in with the smoke; a judge, concerned about the criminal court load, advised grand juries to vote fewer indictments; Chicago newspapermen broke into homes to steal photographs; bootleggers made their deliveries openly without the least fear of being questioned by police; witnesses in criminal cases were sometimes found floating dead in the lake; and scandal upon scandal made it obvious that the whole city was for sale.

The ex-mayor, Big Bill Thompson, came out of retirement in 1927 to run for his old post in a campaign punctuated with gunplay, fist fights, and the theft of ballot boxes. Thompson was a braggart, a swaggerer, and a loudmouth who played to the worst elements of any crowd. Rather than develop any issues, Thompson, who hated England, charged that the Chicago superintendent of schools was plotting with King George V to take Washington's portrait out of the schools. Mayor William Dever replied that grand juries had helped take some of Thompson's school board out of the schools when Thompson last administered the city government. "Of course none of Mayor Dever's board were indicted," Thompson shouted. "The King of England wouldn't let 'em be indicted. You take a chance when you're 100 percent American."

The Thompson candidacy on top of the Smith scandal had the forces of clean government, including Hull House and Julius Rosenwald, aghast. Rosenwald, who had warned in an earlier campaign that the city would go to hell if Thompson were elected mayor, found himself drawn into a political campaign in which Insull was on the other side. Thompson avoided public attacks on Rosenwald but cursed him in private as a wily Jew who posed as a great philanthropist while he underpaid the fine Chicago citizens in his employ. With his attacks on England and on the utilities, Thompson hardly sounded like Insull's man. Insull, however, was a Thompson contributor. A utility man survived by living with the political facts and paid little attention to what candidates boomed from platforms. Thompson won the election.

Insull had been silent before the Senate investigating committee about his contributions to other Chicago figures because he was protecting a major deal that was brewing. Insull already had control of the city's elevated trains. He had been invited to take over the streetcar lines as well, and the city also planned to build a subway for his operation. At first Insull was reluctant to take on these transit utilities and said he would dictate his terms if he accepted the burden. The streetcars, he pointed out, needed major improvements. The lines needed extensions, new cars, and repairs. The subway construction work would be a great responsibility. The streetcar lines had to be refinanced. Insull began collecting political debts, and almost every politician in Chicago owed him a favor.

I want receiverships, he told the Thompson administration. I want extensions to give me the transit franchise for many years into the future. I want fare increases. The politicians were concerned about the expected public reaction. Mayor Thompson, after flailing the utilities in his campaign, could hardly agree to fare increases and franchises measured in generations. The members of the Illinois Commerce Commission protested to Insull that it would not look good, so soon after the Smith affair, to give him what he wanted.

Insull and the Chicago and Illinois political powers came to an understanding. The City's Corporation Counsel would oppose the Insull proposals and the Commerce Commission would reject them, but it would only be a rain dance for public consumption. They would throw the contest in a manner that would make it easy for Insull to get a reversal in the courts. Then it would look as if they had taken up the cause of the consumer and opposed the utilities but Insull would still get all he wanted.

The plan to give Insull the city transit system stalled, however, in the State Legislature. A cabal of downstate legislators, assuming that this was a big Insull steal for which he was willing to pay, sent him their terms. Insull did not intend to get into the business of bribing the entire State Legislature and refused to pay anything.

Early in 1929 a revised plan was proposed, with the city maintaining ownership of the subway and Insull managing it. Insull had been excoriated for his silence before the Senate committee but had something to show for his ordeal. The other part of the affair, the contributions to Smith and the uproar they had caused, was a waste. The contributions had not only been too conspicuous, but unnecessary, since McKinley died right after the campaign. McKinley had been a streetcar magnate himself and he and

Insull, in various territorial wars, had become enemies. Blinded by spitefulness, he had thrown money at McKinley's opponent and had been kept on the grill for two years in numerous appearances before the committee. And it had all grown out of the self-indulgence of a pink-cheeked, ruthless old Cockney with pop eyes.

Furthermore, Smith had never made it to the Senate, although he had won the election. Julius Rosenwald had been partly responsible for that. A stalwart Republican, Rosenwald was determined to rescue his party from men like Frank Smith. During the 1926 campaign he told the newspapers that if Smith were elected in November the Senate would not seat him because of the taint of Insull money. Since Rosenwald had conferred with President Coolidge, he appeared to speak with authority. If Smith would not step aside in gentlemanly fashion, Rosenwald said, the Republicans should come up with an unbought independent candidate for the November election. The reformers eventually did field an amateur who, because of Rosenwald's influence, was labeled "the mail-order candidate." When he was urged to back the candidate with a large contribution, Rosenwald refused to become an "insullator" and to fight with the same tactics the enemy employed. Publicly he was above using money as influence; privately, his civic virtue led him to an unusual proposal.

A month before the 1926 general election Smith and Rosenwald met in a hotel room in Chicago. Rosenwald took off his coat, threw it across the back of a chair, and sat down in his shirtsleeves. "May I talk plainly?" he asked.

"You sought the interview," Smith said, "so, of course, you can say what you came to say."

"I do not want to hurt your feelings," Rosenwald said.

"They have already been hurt about as deeply as possible, so speak your mind."

"You know that if you are elected United States Senator you can't be seated, don't you?"

"No, I don't know that. I don't think anyone knows that, because the only persons who have anything to say about that are the members of the United States Senate and I do not believe that they will prejudge the facts or deny a sovereign state its rights under the Constitution."

"I have it from one very high in authority," Rosenwald replied, "that you can't be seated."

"I don't know anyone high enough in authority to make such a statement, when the matter has not yet been brought to the attention of the Senate in a proper way."

Rosenwald then spoke of his own belief in modest expenditures for political campaigns, but said that he had considered spending five hundred thousand dollars to elect an alternative to Smith if that were possible. While taking a siesta, he said, he had thought that if he would pay that much to elect his candidate, why not give it to Smith to withdraw? He then made one of the greatest philanthropic offers of his career.

"No one knows what I am about to say to you except my wife, whose consent I had to get before I could make the offer, and no one else will know from me," Rosenwald said. "If you will withdraw from the Senatorial race I am here to offer you ten thousand shares of Sears, Roebuck stock the moment you sign your withdrawal notice. In a few months that stock will be worth three-quarters of a million dollars. You can give as your reason for withdrawing that your health won't permit you to make the campaign or any other reason you want to give. The ten thousand shares of stock will be deposited in escrow in any bank you name, to be turned over to you when your withdrawal occurs."

Smith commented on the hypocrisy of reformers who thought they could buy in secret what the Illinois voters had given in their sovereignty.

"Oh, you do not put it fairly," Rosenwald said. "You have a perfect right to withdraw if you want to."

Smith brought up the matter of his integrity.

"I think you will be elected," Rosenwald said, "but that will not be vindication. You will always have a feeling of hurt which will be accentuated by the continuous attacks upon you. These attacks will ruin your health. Your re-election will not be worth the effort and the suffering. You can live more happily by not being a candidate; you can enjoy life and have plenty of money to do it with."

When Smith declined the offer, they sat looking at each other for a moment. Then Rosenwald got up, put on his coat, and walked slowly to the door. As he opened it, he said, "If you want to see me before it is too late, you have my telephone number."

"I shall not want to see you on this matter at any time," Smith replied.

Smith won the election but, as Rosenwald had predicted, was excluded by a vote of the Senate because the utility commissioner had been financed by a utility magnate in his political campaign.

They met again in 1928 at the Republican convention in Kansas City, where Hoover was being nominated for the presidency. Smith, staying with the Illinois delegation, heard a voice greet him in a dark hotel hallway. He saw someone sitting in shadows in a chair at the end of the hall. "You remember me, don't you?" Rosenwald asked. "We came very near being partners once."

"We did not even come close. I don't do business with sordid-minded people," Smith said and passed on.

When he stopped at the door of his hotel room Smith felt a tug at his coat and turned to find Rosenwald. "What did you mean by what you said out there?" Rosenwald asked. "Why, you don't think I had any sinister motive in trying to get you out of the race for United States Senator, do you?"

Smith said he had as much right to assume the worst as had Rosenwald to assume that there was something dishonest about the Insull contribution to his election fund.

"Why, I want nothing from any United States Senator," Rosenwald said.

Smith said he wondered what Rosenwald would do if he were to tell the story of the offer made two years earlier, and Rosenwald responded that he would have admitted it, but hoped Smith would not find that necessary. He looked closely at Smith. "Well," Rosenwald said, "everything happened to you that I told you would happen, didn't it?"

"Yes, as per schedule," Smith said.

"You are the first man I have known to refuse a million dollars," Rosenwald said.

"No, the woods are full of them, and most of them would have been less courteous in refusing you than I was," said Smith.

In February of 1929 a University of Chicago political science professor undertook a book called *The Case of Frank Smith*, with Rosenwald financing it at a cost of sixty-two hundred dollars. Rosenwald planned to have it sent all over the country—to members of Congress, the Illinois State Legislature, newspapers and publicists, and civic organizations—as a case study in the fight against corrupt government. The most interesting wrinkle, however, would not be in the book, for Rosenwald told his subsidized author nothing of his offer to Smith.

In January the stock market had taken another of those breathtaking leaps that characterized the Big Boom. The public utility stocks, which were leading the way, rose half as much in January 1929 as they had through the boom year of 1928, and the rise continued through the spring, keeping lights burning through the evening on Wall Street in an effort to catch up with the furious trading. To a considerable degree this superadded boom within a boom was due to a single development: the House of Morgan had embarked on its greatest venture yet—the United Corporation, an electric power supercorporation with a capitalization twenty times that of U.S. Steel, regarded since its 1900 formation as the giant merger of all time.

The United Corporation was announced with all the stops out. "Yesterday's announcement was therefore hailed in public utility circles as the most important step ever taken in modernizing the public utility structure in the East," the *New York Times* reported in a front-page story of January 11. "Further steps in this direction are expected." The fundamental purpose of the United Corporation, the announcement stated, would be "the fostering of closer relations among the great public utility systems in the East."

The House of Morgan had begun collecting utility stocks the previous year with the Mohawk-Hudson Power Company of upstate New York. In the summer of 1928, Gerard Swope, the GE president, stopped by to meet with Thomas W. Lamont, the patrician mastermind at the House of Morgan. Swope came with a large bloc of GE-owned shares of Mohawk-Hudson. The agreement eventually signed over the stocks to Morgan for 23.6 million dollars in December, only weeks before Lamont, Morgan, and Young left for the reparations conference in Paris.

Morgan continued buying a controlling interest in major utility companies in Pennsylvania, New Jersey, and New York and placing them in his holding company. In financial terms the United Corporation was nothing but a large box to hold the stocks of these companies, but the public announcements described it as much more. The United Corporation, it was said, would develop a talent pool of engineering, operating, and financial experts that smaller companies could not provide. It would diversify risk for the investor; instead of having all his money riding on a single electrical company that could be wiped out in a disaster, it would be spread over many companies. Most important, the United Corporation would develop the eastern superpower system that electrical engineers had been advocating for years. With a turn of a switch it would be able to push power from one city to another. Power would flow south from the St. Lawrence, Niagara Falls, and the streams of northern New York over transmission lines to connect with other regional systems and create a reservoir of power. These new power sources would produce declining rates, because of the economies that could be created through merger. Visionaries could picture it as a step along the way to Ford's notion of a national power system.

In financial terms, the House of Morgan had the base of a gargantuan monopoly—the collection of the gas and electric business of the Mid-Atlantic region and eventually over a wider area into a single company.

The United Corporation would be to utilities what American Telephone and Telegraph was to the telephone industry. The Mom and Pop days of the electrical power industry were over.

It was no wonder that speculators beat the drums. To that accompaniment other companies began to drop into the box. They submitted without a struggle. Some joined formally, while others imperceptibly donned the Morgan collar, for the House of Morgan operated by stealth, in transactions that involved directorships, somebody's old college roommate, someone's brother-in-law.

The excitement thus generated boosted Samuel Insull's stocks to new heights, although they hardly needed help. His companies' shares, even in the biggest of booms, outperformed the rest of the market. With his stocks doing so well and the transit deal taking shape again, Insull should have been overjoyed. Yet he was not pleased about what was happening in the east. His old foe, the House of Morgan, was on the march, and he watched for a sign of Morgan Superpower. On Sundays he took auto drives into the rich farm countryside around Chicago, looking at his transmission lines and listening for a footfall from the east.

Insull had a forty-two-hundred-acre estate at Libertyville where electrical gadgetry sheared the sheep, milked the cows, fed the stock, and heated the barns, but he paid little attention to his farm in the spring of 1929. He smoked cigars furiously and counted shares in his head. He was buying his own stocks as quickly as possible and recapitalizing his companies to come up with more money, for the attack had begun. Insull had been expecting the House of Morgan, but this assault came from an unexpected quarter—from a raider in Cleveland who suspected and feared New York as much as he did.

Even as a boy, Cyrus S. Eaton had been a secretive sort. He had worked in utilities in the Canadian West until a great wave of public ownership of power in Canada sent him retreating to the United States. By the 1920s he had amassed a large investment bank and a holding company and operated his varied activities out of Cleveland. The secretive boy had grown up to become a man without intimates, a one-man operation who worked in mystery. He moved silently, like a great shark, masking his acquisitiveness behind a soft-spoken demeanor.

Eaton had covered his purchases carefully, and they were at first unnoticed, but they were wide-ranging, systematic, and obviously involved in a takeover scheme. By late 1928 his holdings had grown several times as large as Insull's own.

During the late summer of 1928 Insull and Eaton had chanced to make an ocean crossing together and were frequently in each other's company. While Eaton's agents in the United States were buying up Commonwealth Edison, Middle West, and other Insull properties, Eaton conversed affably with Insull without mentioning a word about it. With blue-eyed innocence he discussed his farm outside Cleveland and his interest in foxhunting. By 1929 Insull had discovered Eaton's acquisitions and had become obsessed with stopping him.

In addition to Morgan, other investment bankers had invaded utility companies and Insull saw operators and managers losing their grip on their own companies. He was particularly worried because his stocks were sold so widely. He had been, for that matter, a hawker of stocks, selling them from door to door and especially to his electric customers. The Insull stamp was on his companies by the force of his personality, not by tight ownership.

Insull already presided over a tangle of companies. His defense, he decided, was to entangle them further. His trusted friends exchanged their utility holdings for stocks in a new investment trust called Insull Utility Investments. With this weapon the Insull family could maneuver itself into a position to control the empire through manipulation of a complex maze of companies pyramided one upon another. There were eight steps in the intricate structure between operating company and Insull Utility Investments. Through it Insull could buy enough of the voting stock of the four major operating companies to control them. Insull was planning to preserve his empire by evasive action.

The only way to deal with bankers, according to Insull, was to call them over to your office when you wanted them. Bankers had to be kept in their place. They had never been allowed to tell Insull how to operate his businesses, although, when it involved his affairs, Insull instructed them on how to run theirs. That was how he had done business in Chicago for many years.

New York was something else. Nobody behaved with such insolence toward bankers in New York. The House of Morgan expected deference and gratitude and preferred that mere businessmen keep their uninformed opinions to themselves. They guarded their prerogatives and in their limited dealings with him over the years had found Insull intolerable.

Insull despised the New York money gang. He saw Wall Street as an octopus, its tentacles reaching into all the major American cities, through countless boards of directors, across select lists of special club members who were invited to share in its gains, into Washington, London, and Paris, manipulating much of what happened in the world. The head was the House of Morgan and its tentacles the companies and banks it controlled. Allied to the Morgan operation was the Jewish investment banking community, led by Otto Kahn. The other allies were the two gigantic Rockefeller banks, the Chase National and the National City. These three elements—the Morgan circle, the Jewish circle, the Rockefeller circle—shared the government bond business. Morgan dominated the financing of industry; the Jews were in charge of railroad financing; Chase dominated oil.

The House of Morgan had a differing view of its role. Morgan and Lamont loved power, profit, and privilege and intended to amass all three in the way they knew best—banking. The House of Morgan did not regard itself as part of a conspiracy to run the world, only to operate the world's financial services. The House lent money and marketed and traded securities. It stood for no interference in those pursuits, but it did not operate companies; there was no money in it. There was no need to work that hard when providing financial services was almost no work at all, merely a matter of always dealing from a strong monopolistic position. Of course the House of Morgan placed its men on important boards of directors all over the nation. How otherwise could it protect its investments? Someone had to be on the spot to insure that the company was competently run. And that, in their view, was all there was to their conspiracy.

Morgan and Eaton, the two men that Insull most feared in 1929, shared certain attitudes. Both were buccaneers who were not interested in operating utilities but in money. Eaton had raided Detroit Edison without being able to take it over, but he had come out of the raid with some of the utility's bond business. The House of Morgan had the same aim, and that was what the United Corporation was all about—capturing the bond business of the utilities. Morgan's principal target was Halsey, Stuart, the Chicago bonding house that had Insull's bond business.

Halsey, Stuart had jumped into public utility financing when it was still a despised sideline of the bonding-house small fry. By 1929 the house was in an excellent position for the sudden expansion of central power stations and transmission lines that had so quickly made electrical power financing such a major factor in the American economy.

Thus J.P. Morgan set his sights for Insull's bonds, the largest bond business in the nation outside the grasp of the Wall Street forces, for financing public utilities was much more lucrative than operating them. For the House of Morgan, however, which never admitted to selfish reasons for its operations, it was embarked on a crusade against the Forces of Disorder. Morgan's wall-mottoes were Consolidate, Rationalize, Control.

He lived by the tenets of a High Church God whose commandments were Catholicity, Stability, Integration. The best assurance of these conditions was that the world be financed out of a few square blocks in Lower Manhattan. The forces of disorder took many guises. Placing some other value above profit was a sign of the insidious intrusion of disorder. Embezzlement was Disorder within a company, competition was Disorder among companies. In 1900 Disorder had taken the form of people believing that man could fly; in 1929 it took the form of prophets of doom predicting that the boom would end. Almost every innovation was seen in the House of Morgan as Disorder. Morgan moved slowly but unerringly to put all this Disorder under control. One day, early in the century, an automobile manufacturer seeking backing in the House of Morgan predicted that a day was coming when three hundred thousand autos would be sold every year in the United States. One Morgan partner was so exasperated that he had to get up and leave the room.

In the middle of February of 1929 two men visited Charles O'Malley in his Boston office. The two self-assured men asked him to help them buy one or two Boston newspapers. They would not disclose for whom they were working, but, they said, if the newspaper proved initially receptive they would be willing to get down to names.

"What amount of money do you intend spending?" O'Malley asked.

"Well, we are inclined to go as high . . ." The man looked at his cohort. "As high as twenty million dollars for each newspaper in Boston."

That seemed high enough to O'Malley. He asked some more questions.

"The interests which I represent," one of the men said, "intend buying fifty or sixty newspapers in the United States from Maine to California. They will probably have five in the New England states, and in other places they will purchase the key newspaper in respective towns throughout the country. At the present time they are negotiating for a large newspaper in Indianapolis. I think it is the *Indianapolis News*."

O'Malley liked to get involved in big dealings, although some people took him less seriously than he took himself. When he dropped in on the managing editor of the *Boston Post* less than a week later and brought up the subject of a purchase, the editor was unconvinced that anything was behind it. Nevertheless the next day he wrote a memorandum to the *Post* editor and publisher in which he related that O'Malley claimed to represent the Insull interests, who had authorized him to enter into negotiations for large newspapers, and that the deal could be put through in a month.

"I think what he says is nine-tenths bluff," the managing editor wrote in the memorandum. "It isn't likely the Insull people would pick him to engineer these twenty-million-dollar deals. He may have some sort of string with them. For some years he has been a sort of press agent for the gas and electric people.

"It may be these power people are foolish enough to go around paying wild prices for newspapers. According to Charlie, they expect to round up fifty to sixty of the biggest papers. But such a scheme would become public and react terrifically on them.

"Already the clouds are gathering over their heads. The people simply won't stand for such a bold scheme. Of course, so far they have acted in such utter contempt of public opinion and seem so absolutely sure of themselves that they may believe they can rope in the papers as easily as the independent gas and electric companies."

Three months later, in May, the *Post* editor and publisher told about the episode in an appearance before the Federal Trade Commission. Samuel Insull was on an extended European visit, but his brother denied ever hearing of O'Malley and said the Insulls were not interested in buying newspapers. O'Malley also denied mentioning the Insulls. He said he was negotiating for two men who represented banks in New York and Chicago.

The story soon faded without being resolved. But it had made its point. By coincidence or by design the people who were buying newspapers, buying a share of a newspaper, lending money to publishers, or otherwise getting a foothold in the print media were people who had made their fortunes in public utilities.

To Senator Norris, the enemy of the power trust, this sounded suspicious. He singled out Insull for an attack, citing his financing of the Smith campaign and noting that he had moved out of the Midwest into Maine, where he had control of public utilities through the state. The incident fit Insull's behavior, he said.

The president of Cities Service admitted that he had bought the *Kansas City Journal-Post* so he could use it to publish his views on gas rates, and it was becoming clear that electrical interests were making a huge effort to influence newspapers. Light's Golden Jubilee was part of that effort.

For a decade the owners of electrical utilities had made good publicity a concerted effort through their trade association, the National Electric Light Association. The nation had never before seen so extensive a campaign.

They had organized clergymen, hired lecturers to speak at farmers' clubs and service organizations, sent women to speak at teas, subsidized professors, furnished free editorial material for newspapers, set up courses in public utilities in universities, and raised large sums for national programs to defeat public power programs like Muscle Shoals and Boulder Dam. The man who oversaw and coordinated this massive propaganda campaign was Merlin Aylesworth, managing director of the trade association. Aylesworth said the National Electric Light Association, called NELA, used every means at its disposal except skywriting to get its message to the public. Eventually he left at Owen Young's call to become president of NBC, but he kept up interest in NELA, was sympathetic to its views, and helped put radio programs together. He was one of the links between the power trust and the radio trust.

"I would advise any manager who lives in a community where there is a college," Aylesworth once told an electrical convention, "to get the professor of economics, let us say, interested in your problems. Have him lecture on your subject to his classes. Once in a while it will pay you to take such men and give them a retainer of one or two hundred dollars a year for the privilege of letting you study and consult with them."

One of the jobs Aylesworth undertook was establishing committees of inspection to look over how public utility issues were presented in textbooks, working with other utility trade associations, including gas, streetcars, and railroads. What they found, NELA officials said, was "poisonous." It was discovered in Missouri, for example, that 97 percent of the textbooks in use were written by socialists and advocates of public ownership. These textbooks depicted a scene that included corruption, greed, folly, subterfuge, and inefficiency in public utilities. This bit of scurrility, for example, was found in a Michigan textbook:

"Franchises were very valuable and were frequently secured by corrupting the city council. Attempts to limit the privileges of public utility corporations often have been resisted by similar methods. Privately managed public utilities have, therefore, been a very potent cause of public corruption."

Insull, working on the delicate streetcar deal, was doubtless distressed at this brazen passage from a textbook for elementary and junior high schools:

"The reason why street car companies in some cities cannot reduce fares is because the company has 'watered the stock.' By this is meant that a company, for example, builds and equips a car line at a cost of say, $100,000. Instead of issuing exactly this amount of stock, which is the honest procedure, the company doubles the amount by issuing $200,000 in stock and sells it to the stockholders, many of whom do not know that it is half 'water.' The men who organized the company pocket the difference between the cost of the road and the amount of stock sold. It would be an easy matter to pay a good interest on the $100,000 honestly invested in the road and still give the people cheap fares. But the company insists that the fares must be kept high enough to pay dividends on the entire $200,000, consequently the fares are double what they by right should be."

Insull doubtless must have been even more upset to find himself referred to in a textbook in this way: "As late as 1926 a man then serving as the president of a number of electric light companies in the Middle West gave in a single primary campaign over $200,000 to the campaign funds of candidates of both parties." This referred to the Smith affair; Insull had also made a small contribution to the Democratic candidate.

NELA objected to the tendency in many of the books to show public ownership of power and other utilities in a favorable light. They were even annoyed by statements that some streetcars were noisy and gave poor service and that these conditions could be remedied if the city authorities insisted upon it. And they were appalled by the cavalier manner in which some textbook authors assumed that regulatory commissions were weighted in favor of the utility owners and against the taxpayers.

They did not, however, storm into publishing houses and demand changes. They approached textbook companies with broad grins and handshakes, suggesting that they were a little surprised to find their textbooks so out of date. Their authors, they said, were obviously theorists who were out of touch with the vital changes coming about in public utilities. They suggested that their own committees—consisting of authorities like Mr. Insull and Mr. Aylesworth—look over these books and suggest changes.

They also worked the schools with a delicate hand. "Working the schools," a NELA official explained during a workshop at a convention, "is something which must be handled very carefully. A misplay in that will do a lot of harm. You cannot afford to let the public think or the politicians to come out and say that the electric light and power companies, water, gas, and telephone companies are trying to circulate propaganda through the public schools. Your approach is through the superintendent of schools in each city, in the form of pamphlets which are put in their hands merely for the purpose of giving them proper information."

The themes that should be stressed in those pamphlets, he said, are that the public, in a sense, already owns the utilities, since much of the stock is held by widows and orphans and people of small means.

Government-owned utilities, he said, should be shown as socialistic. Adverse criticism of utility services, the pamphlets warned, retarded a community's growth.

The textbook revision project was well on its way to success by 1925, as the chairman of the NELA Education Committee reported to Aylesworth:

"While this is a big task, the results so far would indicate that the method followed is correct, and I am told that after the larger publishers are straightened out and are working with us, the small publishers will naturally fall into line. I feel that we have made a good start in getting the largest schoolbook publishing house, who printed over twelve million books last year, with us, which will be a tremendous leverage on any other house should opposition occur, which I doubt."

NELA's approved textbooks gradually swamped the schools. Insull no longer had to face embarrassment at mentions of his contributions to the campaign of Frank Smith, and students could go all the way through twelfth grade without hearing a word about what to do about noisy streetcars. Instead they heard that regulatory commissions were very effective and that utility rates were fair.

The private power companies subsidized objective-appearing studies showing—despite considerable evidence to the contrary—that publicly owned power did not work, and they formed committees to block speakers who favored government-owned power on the grounds that such ideas were Red-tainted. Much effort was put into producing "studies" to be printed in newspapers and then buying thousands of copies of the paper at many times the regular rate to send to other editors.

All of this work was done surreptitiously. "We never mention it except confidentially in our committee for this reason," one public relations man explained. "We were told by editors that if we were going to brag about the amount of column inches we were able to obtain free in their newspapers they would take good care that we should not get any." Even records of the number of column inches were not kept in the fear that such material could be misunderstood if it fell into the wrong hands, but Aylesworth said privately at a convention that one regional organization was "getting thousands and thousands of columns of news space without cost, and getting the kind of news they want."

The propaganda work was also free in another sense. It actually cost a lot of money, when the hotel bills, conventions, expense accounts, and lobbying in Washington against public power projects were totaled. It was free, however, for the electric companies because the money did not come out of profits but out of operating expenses, so it just went on their customers' bills and the customers paid for being deceived. "All the money being spent is worthwhile," Aylesworth said at one of the utility conventions. "And may I leave this thought with you executives. Don't quit now. At the next convention have more young ladies here so as to do the job right, and let off more men from the departments so they may come here. Don't be afraid of expense. The public pays the expense."

All went well until the project was discovered. The Federal Trade Commission, looking into various aspects of electric power, began turning up evidence bit by bit. It was learned that a college professor in Alabama had been hired by the power companies to travel about the state, speaking at clubs, churches, and teas, praising private power interests and condemning municipally owned electric light plants. He was introduced as a director of extension at the university, but the FTC investigation disclosed that power interests were subsidizing him at six hundred dollars a month.

Early in 1929, Mrs. John D. Sherman of Estes Park, Colorado, testified before the FTC. Mrs. Sherman, former president of the Federation of Women's Clubs, had been paid six hundred dollars per article by NELA to prepare material planted in various magazines designed to promote the sale of electrical appliances. The articles were part of the "Better Equipped Homes Campaign." Even the views of Hoover as secretary of commerce had been sent out in news releases by agencies that were actually controlled by private-power interests.

Many newspapers did not make much of the FTC hearings, although the Hearst press gave it considerable play. Insull's alleged offer for a Boston newspaper, however, became a headline all over the nation when it came out of an FTC hearing in May 1929.

"It has been shown," Senator Norris charged in September, "that four hundred thousand dollars was raised by this trust to control the action of the federal Congress. In the main, this particular attempt was to defeat the Muscle Shoals bill, the Boulder Dam Bill, and the Senate resolution directing an investigation of the subject." He ran down the list of propaganda activities of the electrical power companies and then noted that it all had been done in secret. "No one would have any right to object and no one would object if these private corporations would advocate openly their viewpoint and their method of supplying electricity to the people," he said. "But these emissaries were not known by the people who heard them or the people to be influenced by them to be in the pay of this monopoly."

Atlantic City, an oasis of hotels, ocean breezes, taffy, kewpie dolls, and a long boardwalk, was a favorite convention city in 1929. In June NELA convened there as electrical executives drank from the same bowl, swore eternal friendship, and strolled from the hotel dining room arm in arm singing that one of their number was a jolly good fellow.

The convention was the opening event of Light's Golden Jubilee. It attracted important personages, including the British ambassador, the Speaker of the House, eleven U.S. senators, many congressmen, and the vice-president. On opening night, Preston Arkwright, NELA president, pushed a button that turned on a searchlight on the auditorium roof. In the night sky a small plane that had been hovering in wait for the signal swooped downward. On the side of the plane was a siren driven by wind, and when it began to wail the sound was picked up by a device connected to the auditorium's light control. The siren's wail flashed on all the lights of the building. It was a rather complicated way to get the auditorium lit, but the crowd roared in appreciation. Outside a battery of field pieces on the beach fired a nineteen-shot vice presidential salute. At sea, the battleship *Wyoming* returned the salute and then turned on its searchlights in a flashing drill for the boardwalk crowds, including hundreds who could not get into the packed auditorium.

In the days that followed the gathering got down to more serious trade association business. The theme of the year, judging from most of the emphasis, was the reduction of rates in 1929. Reduced rates, it was said, would increase volume and thus use the plant equipment to its full capacity, would stimulate expansion and would increase electrical use so that electrical manufacturers could sell their appliances. The chief reason for higher rates, it was said, was people who refused to use enough electricity. "Sales Increase or Rate Increase" was the title of the address of Matthew Sloan, president of New York Edison. Sloan urged an "inducement rate" —a drop in rate after the customer exceeded a number of kilowatt hours per month. There were the usual component of anti-socialist speeches, some of them coming through the miracle of movietone films. The major accomplishment of the year, according to Awkwright, was "weathering the assault of those who would nationalize the industry."

On the day that Henry Ford visited the convention, most of the speeches were about Edison as an inventor and pioneer in electricity. The presentation included a sound film of Edison made at his Fort Myers home earlier in the year. Ford sat on the platform, smiling as the tributes to his friend were offered.

Ford hated to speak before audiences and in such situations sometimes suffered a total loss of calm. It had happened most notably in a Washington theater a few days before the sailing of the Peace Ship. "We want

Ford!" the crowd had yelled over and over. Petrified, he hunched his shoulders and tried to slide down in his seat. He told the rally organizer seated with him that he could not do it, but as the crowd grew more insistent he was forced to acknowledge the cheers. On unsteady legs he mounted the stage. "I simply want to ask you to remember the slogan," he said, raising his fist, " 'Out of the trenches before Christmas, and never go back,' and I thank you for your attention." Flushed and flustered, he dashed from the theater.

Fourteen years later, in Atlantic City, he contained his impulse to bolt as he walked to the speaker's platform. The applause subsided as he set himself to speak. "We build at Dearborn eight thousand complete electric light plants every day," Ford said, referring, of course, to his automobiles. "This being an electrical meeting, I thought I'd like to tell you that." He started back to his seat, then stopped, said "Thank you," and continued to his seat.

For a moment the crowd was taken aback with the realization that Ford, whose prophecies were bound in books, at whose door reporters waited for pithy observations, had come one thousand miles to make a speech only a bit longer than a bracelet inscription. Then the program moved on to more selling—electricity, light bulbs, appliances, the profit motive, regulation, and publicity to counterattack the attacks on the power trust.

But the best of the Jubilee opening event was not its dull addresses on free enterprise. It was to be found on the Boardwalk at night. The ordinary boardwalk lights had been replaced by special golden lamps, faceted like pomegranates. An arch of glittering jewels spanned States Avenue, and over it, from several angles, searchlights played continuously. Red steam issued from lighted urns. Farther up the boardwalk two huge aviation searchlights, one throwing orange light and one white, swept continuously across the surf so that the incoming waves, diffused in foam, took on all the colors of the rainbow. An electric fountain at Indiana Avenue and the Boardwalk threw water that changed color under lights, and far out on the Million-Dollar Pier searchlights oscillated and rolled into the sky. Multi-colored lights flashed on and off up and down buildings in continuous sequences, as if they were climbing to the top, and to watch it was like watching the syncopation of a jazz tune.

One of the songs the men sang at the seaside that year was a parody of "Yes, We Have No Bananas." It went:

Yes, we've no excess profits,
No overgrown surplus today,
We've interest unceasing,
And taxes unceasing,
And all of the help to pay.
We've an old-fashioned Commission
That holds rates down with precision,
But yes, we've no excess profits,
No overgrown surplus today.

The leaders of the electrical power industry, as indicated in their jingle, felt cozy with regulation and their far-reaching propaganda never complained that free enterprise was being shackled by governmental controls.

In 1898, when Samuel Insull had first proposed regulation, he had found himself regarded as a crackpot. But a strong wave of enthusiasm for public ownership early in the twentieth century gradually changed the industry's attitudes. In bringing the rest of the industry along, Insull played upon the fear of public ownership, but that was largely a ploy. The real problems of electrical utilities, in his view, were competition and short-term franchises, and he was willing to be regulated to eliminate them.

"If you want to do the largest possible amount of business on the smallest possible capital investment in any line of public service," Insull preached, "the best way to achieve that is to prevent duplication of investment; and the only way you can prevent duplication of investment is by the refusal of competitive franchises which naturally leads to absolute monopoly on the part of the particular utility operating in that particular territory. It is an economic, fundamental condition of our business that it should be a monopoly business."

By 1929 most electrical utilities were regulated. Public commissions, supposedly, set the limits of their profits. As their business expanded and their efficiency increased, they were not supposed to reap larger profits, but to pass the savings along to customers through lower rates.

The stocks, therefore, should not have increased sharply in value. Yet around the nation, the holding companies specializing in electrical utility stocks had become the cutting edge of the frenetic financial news of 1929. Several holding companies would compete to buy up a small power plant in Georgia, and in the process drive up the plant's value. The securities were in such demand that they were being rationed; speculators waited in line to drive the value farther up. Promotional activity fanned the boom. Light's Golden Jubilee had stimulated major increases in the electrical industry's national and local advertising. RCA pushed radios, GE pushed appliances, Westinghouse tripled its advertising budget for the year. The Duke power companies advised northern firms in advertisements to forsake the land of labor unions and come south to the land of cheap white labor; Commonwealth Edison, one of Insull's companies, advertised the attractions of Chicago in national magazines.

Insull rode the crest. The Lincoln Printing Company, which he owned, was doing a good business with job orders to print more stocks of his own holding companies. The presses hummed, the stock rolled out into the hands of salesmen, who sold it door-to-door.

His holding companies, worth one hundred million dollars a few months earlier, were now worth four times that amount; apparently so, since they had sold four hundred million dollars' worth of stock. Even the knowledge that it was watered failed to hurt sales.

"Watering the stock" is a phrase that came from a cattleman who used to bring his livestock down from upstate New York to sell to New York City. Just before he was to meet the metropolitan purchasing agents who were to weigh the cattle, he would lead them to the trough and let them drink their fill. He called this "watering the stock." Later he became a speculator and manipulator of railroad stocks. When he discovered how much money could be raised by printing extra stock and selling it, he was aware of the analogy to his old trade, and he called this also "watering the stock."

Nobody seemed to care that Insull had sold four times as much stock as his companies were worth. In his competent hands, it was assumed, they would eventually be worth that much anyway, so Insull was just selling in anticipation of coming certainties.

He kept himself posted on the hourly changes, the ruddy pink flesh of his British cheeks flushed with the news of his advances. They were not occurring entirely spontaneously. Insull had people on the floor of the Chicago Stock Exchange whose sole purpose was to "maintain the market" by timely buying and selling. He and his family had thus been able to accomplish a formidable killing on Insull Utility Investments, driving up the prices when they were virtually the only ones with stock to sell. Insull had become more of a stock speculator by mid-1929 than he was a utility president. He was grabbing opportunities and that was what the market was all about.

Banks called him and asked him please to borrow their money, for Chicago had lurched into go-getter banking. "Say, I just want you to know," the new president of the Continental Bank told Samuel Insull, Jr., at a party, "that if you fellows ever want to borrow more than the legal limit, all you have to do is organize a new corporation and we'll be happy to lend you another twenty-one million dollars."

But the flurry of paper printing and stock watering created problems. As the school textbook that NELA so disliked had pointed out, stock watering makes it more difficult to pay dividends. To come up with the profits, Insull used some creative accounting techniques, chiefly the parrot-birdcage approach.

It worked this way: A woman owned a parrot and her husband owned a birdcage. One day they struck a profitable deal. He sold her the birdcage for one hundred fifty dollars more than he had paid for it, and she sold him the parrot for one hundred fifty dollars more than she had paid for it. Together the family made three hundred dollars.

One day in 1929 one of Insull's biggest holding companies, Middle West Utilities, sold securities to National Electric Power, another of his companies, for three million dollars more than he had paid for them. At the same time National Electric Power sold stocks to Middle West Securities for three million dollars more than it had paid for them. Both companies made three million dollars. Since Middle West was a holding company that owned National Electric Power, it siphoned the three million dollars from its offshoot. Thus Middle West gained six million dollars in assets on securities that it still owned.

The summer of 1929 was filled with paper profits for Samuel Insull. Middle West Utilities rose from $169 a share to $529. Commonwealth Edison of Chicago rose from $202 to $450. Most vital to Insull was the fortune of his new superholding company that he had created in January. He and his family owned all the shares of the high-powered company, Insull Utility Investments, when it was created. They had purchased them for $7.54 a share. By the end of July each share was worth $126; by August each was worth $150.

In January he had estimated his worth at five million dollars; by the end of the summer Insull was worth one hundred and fifty million dollars. It was as though he had discovered a way of printing money. "My God," he said to his broker, "a hundred and fifty million dollars! Do you know what I'm going to do? I'm going to buy an ocean liner!"

One man, however, was skeptical about the Insull empire. In the midst of the greatest prosperity the world had ever known, Paul Douglas, an economics professor at the University of Chicago, was asking questions that suggested all might not be sound with the utility genius. Such skepticism was odious to good Chicagoans. In the summer of 1929 Douglas and Harold L. Ickes, a Chicago lawyer, were driving to an appointment when the economics professor voiced his concern. He said he had received reports that a number of important Chicago businessmen were disturbed by his views and were pressing the University of Chicago to muzzle him or fire him. He thought that he was being followed as well. For several days he had seen a man who appeared to be trailing him, and every time he turned, the man seemed to try to hide his face or would duck into a doorway.

Ickes warned Douglas to be careful. Like others among the city's reformers, he was reluctant to meet Insull's power head-on. Everybody knew that Insull had powerful connections, and it was whispered that his influence extended even to the Capone mob.

As they talked, Douglas and Ickes were on their way to meet with Fred Lundin at his summer place at Fox Lake. Lundin, the former Republican boss of Chicago, had indicated that he might be sympathetic with their aims. Once an ally who had aided in the rise of Chicago's buffoon mayor to prominence, he had broken with Bill Thompson because the mayor had fallen completely under the Insull influence.

Lundin had run with the pack in Chicago and, like Insull, had accepted the general level of the city's politics, but he was an intelligent man who hoped for something better. During the course of the afternoon he spat venomously accurate remarks about Chicago's rulers. Near the end of the afternoon, Douglas said that after hearing so much of chicanery and corruption he had to ask Lundin: whom would he trust?

Lundin always wore tinted glasses, which gave him a sinister appearance, and behind them his eyes squinted and his lenses steamed in the sun. The most incorruptible force he knew was the enemy of the power trust, Senator George Norris. "You can't buy him, you can't bully him, you can't frighten him. Douglas, I would give anything to be just half as good a man as George Norris."

The visitors left, however, somewhat disappointed. Lundin had been frank and friendly but had not committed himself to their cause. He played another brand of politics. The only way to defeat Insull, he told them, was to play with the weapons of Chicago politics. Forget the issues, the facts and figures, and go for Insull just as Thompson went after an opponent— with irrelevancies, lies, rumor, slander, bombast, and plays to the resentments of the electorate. Douglas responded that his Quaker faith taught that it was dangerous and self-defeating to use evil means to attain an end. Lundin listened politely, but he would not throw in his lot with babes in the wood. Let them go to Rosenwald for support, he concluded.

Douglas was a tall, shaggy, harmless-looking professor, but underneath his threadbare clothes and within a rugged frame—he kept in shape by swimming along the coast of Lake Michigan—beat the heart of a fighter. He was a man without frivolousness, and at night the thirty-seven-year-old professor relaxed by reading the federal budget.

He could absorb data at breathtaking speed, and he needed that skill in investigating the financial affairs of Samuel Insull. It was a time-consuming and confusing account, and he sometimes wondered whether Insull himself understood the edifice of pyramids he had built. In time, however, he had found some of the ways that Insull managed to make large profits despite regulation.

He had been examining the streetcar deal for some time and had become an opponent. His appearances before committees and public bodies had caused consternation among the businessmen of Chicago, because they were afraid Insull might back out of it.

Insull claimed that the streetcar companies he was taking over were worth two hundred sixty-four million dollars, but the assets did not stand up to examination. They included old horsecar systems that had long vanished from city streets but were still carried on the books as assets. They included a twenty-two-year-old decrepit trolley system that, according to Insull, had not depreciated but doubled in value since 1907. They even included tracks that had been dug up and abandoned, cars that had been sold for scrap, and horses long dead.

Yet Douglas could get nowhere against Insull's power. The streetcar deal had not even been slowed up by his testimony. The State Legislature accepted Insull's valuations without question and adopted an enabling law for the takeover by a four to one margin. The city council had accepted Insull's package with a single dissenting vote. The only hope for the reformers was to defeat the proposal in the 1930 referendum.

The glimpse that the streetcar deal provided into how public utilities were actually valued was a revelation to Douglas. Watered stock made it necessary to create imaginative assets that included neckties, cigars, and dinners. So many stocks had been issued to politicians and speculators that the ghosts of horses had to be resurrected to help pay dividends.

Electrical companies had become experts at creating imaginary assets because the regulating commissions allowed them to base their profits on a percentage (usually 8 percent) of their investment. Being able to double their assets allowed them to double their profits. The commissions invariably accepted whatever value the companies forwarded to them. If rate payers challenged the company on assets or anything else they had to pay the legal fees out of their own pockets, while the company charged its legal fees to operating expenses—and thus to the very customers they were fighting in the courts. It was little wonder that NELA had come to favor regulation. The Insull empire rested on a fragile and unquestioned set of imaginary assets. It never entered Douglas' mind, however—not in the summer of 1929, at any rate—that much of the prosperity of the United States was based on the same elaborate fantasy.

Insull's huge system of holding companies had lost contact with reality. For three years he had been expanding, buying paper and textile mills, real estate development companies, and shoe factories. He paid almost any price for them. "What in hell would you do," responded the president of one electric power and light company, when asked why he had sold to Insull, "if someone came along and offered you three times as much as your company was ever worth?" Buying at a high price or at any price increased the value of the property and made larger profits possible, since the amount of profit allowed was based on the value of the assets. Owning anything was an advantage to Insull now. It gave Insull's companies, as it gave so many others during the great boom of 1929, an opportunity to issue more stock.

Juggling all those properties had created a precarious financial operation of pyramids. Insull Utility Investments was the apex. One of the companies it owned, Middle West Utilities, was itself a large holding company. Holding companies were controlling holding companies which in turn controlled lesser holding companies that controlled still smaller holding companies. The Tidewater Power Company in North Carolina was controlled by the Seaboard Service Company, which was controlled by the National Electric Power Company, which was controlled by Middle West Utilities, which was controlled by Insull Utility Investments. The Androscoggin Electric Company in Maine was controlled by the Androscoggin Corporation, which was controlled by the Central Maine Power Company, which was controlled by the New England Public Service Company, which was controlled by Middle West Utilities, which was controlled by Insull Utility Investments.

But by midyear Insull had decided that even Insull Utility Investments was not a safe enough device. He was preparing to create a co-equal superholding company called Corporation Securities Company of Chicago. This new company and Insull Utility Investments would, in part, own each other. They would buy each other with each other's money. Once again stocks would come raining out of the Lincoln Printing Company and investment bankers would grow fatter selling the paper to the public.

Despite the almost incomprehensible scheme of two superholding companies clutching each other, the public never doubted Insull. He was the backbone of Big Business in the farming states. It was worth money to be seen talking to him outside a bank. People invested their life savings in his enterprises. He was chairman of sixty-five boards of directors and president of eleven companies.

But Insull was haunted by Cyrus Eaton's blue eyes fixed softly upon him as he talked of his farm and of anything else except the raid he had begun on Insull's properties. What the public considered financial wizardry was principally a maze to keep Eaton out. Insull was caught in a dilemma. He needed more money to fight off Eaton and Morgan, but when he issued more stock to get the money, he made himself more vulnerable to raiding, because more stocks were on the market. Even the fantastic rise in the prices of his own stocks was a curse—for he had to pay the same prices as everyone else when he bought them back. It would cost several fortunes to get them out of Eaton's hands.

Powerful muscles rippled in his shoulders and chest as he paddled about the pool, with his chin jutting slightly forward to keep his aristocratic features out of the water. But as he was helped out of the pool to lie in a chair in the bright Georgia sun, an incongruous pair of legs emerged beneath that strong torso—withered and weak legs that could barely stand under him.

Franklin Delano Roosevelt loved Warm Springs. When the rain fell on Pine Mountain a few miles away, it ran down 3,800 feet to a deep pocket of rock where it was warmed by the inner earth and then returned to the surface at 88 degrees Fahrenheit. The Creek Indians had known of its properties and used to bring their wounded warriors to the springs for healing. FDR, something of a wounded warrior himself, had been going to Warm Springs for eight years to be invigorated by its miraculous restorative waters.

He was there for a respite from his duties as governor of New York, and as he lay in the summer sun, reading the magazines and New York newspapers that had come in the mail, he was pained to find an account hinting that he was alarmingly run-down from the work and lacking energy. He read everything, the political news and the advertisements, and made mental notes as he read. It seemed to him that electricity was his big issue. He knew from his conversations with GE board chairman Owen Young, who often advised him on electrical matters, that a major attempt was being made to get people to use more electricity, and he could see the advertisements for appliances in every publication. The increase in electrical customers, which had been mounting by the millions every year, had slowed to a halt in 1929. Most of the available customers already had electricity, and those who were not customers lived in inaccessible back-country areas.

The business pages had the same familiar news of rising stocks. With special attention FDR watched the United Corporation, the giant holding company that the House of Morgan had been putting together. When electrical utilities were supposed to be limited to a modest return by regulation, it was hard to fathom why they were climbing so high on the stock market. One would expect them to have, like bonds, almost a fixed value.

Young said it was the move toward consolidation that made the stocks so attractive. Superpower, he had advised, would make tremendous savings possible. Young argued that it was a misnomer to call this benign consolidation a power trust. The classic trust was formed to limit production and raise prices, but the power consolidations would increase output and lower prices.

FDR was extremely interested in waterpower. His destiny was bound up with water. It had been in the waters at Campobello that he had first experienced the inhuman chill that had been the onset of polio; his recovery, such as it was, had been accomplished in the buoyant mineral waters of Warm Springs; and waterpower on the St. Lawrence was the issue that was about to make him, he was convinced, a national figure and would lock him in struggle with the insiders who were aiming to clean up on utilities monopolies.

He had been pressed into running for governor. His first priority, he believed, was to recover as fully as he could from polio. He was determined to walk again, and had made considerable progress. His strength had returned, although not to his legs, and at forty-six he was a vigorous man. He had always been anxious that the day would come when he would have to choose between his political ambition and further recovery. He owed it to his family, he believed, to see his therapy through to the end, to become as able as possible, and to accomplish that was full-time work in itself.

He had accepted his disability and took the nomination in order to become a national political force ahead of his own timetable. "I am ready," he announced on leaving Warm Springs, "to carry on the duties of governor of New York and to remain constantly on the job during the entire legislative period."

The emerging issue in New York, he believed, was waterpower. With Young in Paris, he looked elsewhere for counsel. He found that rates to consumers for electricity were much lower on the Ontario side of the St. Lawrence, where the government operated the power plants. He found that regulation in the United States was a sham. The holding companies, which were technically not in the power business (but in the holding business) were beyond the reach of regulation. Obviously truckloads of concealed profits could be piloted through such a gap in the law. Insull had been doing that for years—charging his operating companies whatever he chose for imaginary services by the holding companies, and siphoning out most of the profits before they reached the company that was actually subject to regulation. The holding company was another prodigy of that master of the fantastic, the American corporation lawyer. Will Rogers put it pithily: "A holding company is where you hand an accomplice the goods while a policeman searches you."

Shortly after inauguration FDR called the first of a series of informal conferences of state officials to discuss matters slated for legislation. The meeting was held in the Executive Chamber in the Capitol. At one end of the long room stood a huge desk behind which the governor sat during hearings. At the opposite end was the door by which he entered from his private chamber. No one realized what a problem the walk would present for FDR.

He came in, holding his secretary's arm for support, his cane in his right hand. Everyone stood when he entered. The floor was polished and FDR had to put the tip of his cane down with extra care so it would not slide. The group, intending to wait for him to reach his desk and sit down before they resumed their seats, watched with growing tension as he moved through the room with his awkward, dragging walk. The moment seemed interminable.

He was not halfway across the room when he sensed their mood. He looked up and smiled and in a carefree gesture threw back his head, his strong chin jutting out, and he waved his cane. "That's all right," he assured them, "I'll make it!" The crowd laughed and the tension was dissipated immediately.

A few moments later they were at work, and one of the first items on his agenda was his plan for developing the St. Lawrence. The dams and power plants would be developed by the state. The state would sell the power to private companies, which owned the transmission lines and de-livery system. He had no intention, however, of letting the Morgan trust, which had all the power in New York State under its control, make runaway profits. He would sell the state's power to the utilities only under contract, and bypass the regulatory commission completely. The contract

would spell out the rates that the power companies could charge to consumers, and if the companies did not like that arrangement, he was prepared to take the state into the transmission business and deliver the power
to the customers' homes. The fight against the power trust—conducted for
a few years by a few lonely voices—had broken open, and was being led
by the governor in the leading state in the nation and the emerging leader
of a powerful political organization.

It was a good issue for him. The St. Lawrence Seaway was an important item on the national agenda. Boulder Dam would present an opportunity for public power. Sentiment for public power at Muscle Shoals was
high in Congress. In New York, the Republican legislators were closely
identified with power interests as directors and stockholders; the State
Republican chairman was an organizer of the huge merger that was deep-
ening and widening through the year, with more companies falling into the
Morgan net.

FDR believed the Republicans were vulnerable. He returned from his
rest in Warm Springs ready to do battle. He intended to embarrass the
Republican-dominated state legislature at every turn, goading the GOP to
social action or exposing it as lacking empathy with ordinary people. FDR
began to concentrate on state hospitals. He found himself under a disadvantage, since he could not tour them. When his car arrived, the superintendent and he would drive about the grounds inspecting the exterior
while he was told of the exemplary conditions inside. As former assistant
secretary of the navy, he knew how much stock to put in such reports. He
decided to make his wife his inspector. Eleanor Roosevelt was trained on
the job. He answered her naive reports with tough questions. Had she
looked for beds put away in closets or behind doors? Had she checked the
distances between beds? Had she looked into the pots in the kitchen? Had
she watched people's eyes and lips as they spoke for signs of cynicism?

In the same way the foxy Roosevelt examined the power companies as
they came before regulatory commissions. He watched their trick of lower-
ing rates, with great fanfare, when close inspection showed that the rates
had been too high and were still too high. He had experts explain to him
how the utility companies, which were entitled to 8 percent profit on their
investment, jacked up the value of their properties with bookkeeping
tricks. He learned that the real reason why electrical power cost so much
was watered stock and high profits to Wall Street insiders.

That year the statehouse newspaper reporters built a skit in their annual show around a parody of *Show Boat*. They mocked FDR by depicting
him touring state waters in "Captain Frank's Show-Off Boat" and losing

the power fight to the Republicans. FDR, however, did not intend to lose. He knew the GOP-controlled press would not favor his plan for the St. Lawrence, but he planned to talk directly to the people—over the radio. The Democrats had contracted for an hour of radio a month, and Roosevelt was convinced that American politicians had failed to realize its possibilities. He began to talk to his audiences about their electric bills and how the Morgan monopoly would increase them. He told farmers at state fairs that their rates were outrageous and invited them to check what Canadian farmers paid. He sent letters to officials in the conservative towns of upstate New York, inquiring about local power rates, and found he had touched a nerve. The House of Morgan began to suspect that Roosevelt might have the popular side of the issue. Roosevelt knew, as the yachting enthusiasts of Wall Street did not, that this was not a land of prosperity for millions of farmers who were having increasing difficulty making ends meet.

He was beginning to attract national attention. He was concerned about what he described as the unholy alliance of big business and big government—the alliance that Hoover had forged through the 1920s. FDR expressed alarm at the concentration of power in Washington and the nation's drift into centralized federal control. "If there is failure on the part of a state to provide adequate educational facilities for its boys and girls, an immediate cry goes up that a department of education should be established in Washington," he said. "If a state fails to keep abreast of modern [health] provisions, immediately the enthusiasts turn to the creation of a department of health in Washington. If a state fails adequately to regulate its public service corporations, the easiest course is to ask the Interstate Commerce Commission or the Federal Trade Commission to take jurisdiction."

These two major concerns—that political control was centralizing and that Morgan was producing an electric monopoly—came together in a Fourth of July speech that made him a figure to reckon with. "We may well ask," he orated from the rostrum of Tammany Hall's new home on Union Square, "are we in danger of a new feudal control that we may have to bring forth a new Declaration of Independence? It is not that these great industrial and economic mergers are necessarily bad from the economic point of view but the fact is that independence in business is a thing of the past. Can a man today run a drug store, a cigar store, a grocery store as an independent business? The doctrine of the separation of Church and State has been pretty well laid down and I believe universally accepted in this country. I want to proclaim a new doctrine: a complete separation of business and government."

Fifteen hundred Democrats cheered as he was hailed as the next president, and Will Rogers commented from Los Angeles that he had just about thrown his hat in the ring. Some political analysts, however, thought his showboat had run aground. Attacks on bigness were quaint and passé and nobody cared about them. Even for socialists, the issue was not bigness, but in whose interest bigness was organized. Mergers, Heywood Broun wrote that year in *The Nation*, could be a useful way to unify and organize American industry and eliminate the evils of competition.

As Ickes and Douglas went after Insull in Chicago, FDR had thrown down the gauntlet to Morgan in New York. He had lawyers working on the legality of the Morgan holding companies. He was not concerned about being out of step. When his cousin, Theodore Roosevelt, had opened his attack on the trusts, that had been an unfashionable view. Conditions in time would catch up with him. Hoover was leading the fight for private power in one party and GE's Owen Young was allied with the power interests in the other party. FDR had staked out a boldly different position. It was out of synchronization with the decade, but the decade was almost over. His speech, he wrote to a friend, had stirred up quite a breeze. And by the way, he added, do your rich friends still think the stock market boom is going to last forever?

When Governor Roosevelt received a letter from his Attorney General, he was touring on a state-owned yacht. Unable to read it on the run—it was late July and he was inspecting state facilities—he stuffed it in his pocket for later perusal. Before he got around to that, he could read its effects in the stock market quotations.

The Attorney General, a Republican considered FDR's likely gubernatorial opponent next time around, said he found no violation of anti-monopoly statutes in Morgan's holding companies. Though peeved at the fact that it had already been released to the press, FDR was unsurprised. And even though the gist of the opinion had been anticipated on Wall Street, it gave the market a little upward nudge. All the companies involved in the power merger were strong. Mohawk-Hudson, which included Owen Young as a director, went up ten points. The increase spilled over into firms eventually expected to be gathered into the Morgan nest.

The decade was ending much as it began. Business was still untrammeled, and attempts to regulate were circumvented by the inventiveness of corporation lawyers. Legislatures were still packed with the friends, and often the partners, of utility magnates; the state governments seemed little affected by attempts of a few reformers to bring electrical power companies under control.

But the American business psyche had changed. In 1922, at the onset of the seven fat years, it could be assumed that the House of Morgan would steady Wall Street against overzealous speculation. By 1929 the firm, under the influence of Lamont, had not only joined the pack of frenzied speculators but was elbowing forward to lead the pack. The stocks Morgan had gathered together in the United Corporation were worth sixty-nine million dollars. They were marketed as one hundred twenty-two million dollars' worth of stocks. It was a highly diluted watering. Yet on the day they hit the market they were already worth one hundred forty-one million dollars. By early September they were worth two hundred sixty million dollars.

General Dawes, Colonel Lindbergh, and Owen Young all had a personal interest in this astounding success. They were all substantial stockholders in at least one of the House of Morgan's three huge holding company creations of 1929: the United Corporation, for power utilities; the Allegheny Corporation, for railroads; and Standard Brands, for foods.

Creating stocks—to own, to sell, to distribute to one's allies—was the key to riches. Any speculator could buy and sell stocks, but only investment banks like the House of Morgan could create them, and the real money was made by controlling stocks from the moment of their creation. Some of the common stock of these three Morgan creatures went into the Morgan coffers. Some of it was distributed—not sold on the open market, but parceled out to a select list of people, at great bargains far below market value.

The people who received this rich opportunity were not just lucky lottery winners, but carefully selected people. Lindbergh was the prospective son-in-law of a Morgan partner; Dawes was influential in banking circles and a loyal promoter of Morgan interests in Chicago. Young was chairman of the board of GE and RCA, two companies that banked millions of dollars; the money did not belong to Young, but he had pivotal influence as to where it would be banked. Other presidents and board chairmen were presented with similar bonanzas, and Morgan used the money of these companies to carry on his operations.

The political leaders also received a stock offer, including former President Coolidge, U.S. senators, members of the Hoover cabinet, and the national chairmen of both major parties. The Democratic national chairman, John J. Raskob, wrote in thanks that he hoped "the future holds opportunities for me to reciprocate." The House of Morgan also cut in some financial writers.

The stocks that Morgan watered and issued were supposed to produce greater efficiency, but they did the reverse; they strained operating companies to produce dividends and they skimmed off the cream for the insiders. They did not build factories, or put Americans to work, raise wages, lower electrical rates, or improve electrical service. They prevented factories from being built, put Americans out of work, lowered wages, raised rates, and impeded electrical services. Just as completely as if it had been extracted by Tammany Hall and used to pay political bribes, they were a huge charge against the public—but in the summer of 1929, the reckoning had not yet been made.

Summer came, and autumn, and Bernays helped put together the huge American pageant called the Jubilee. Back and forth between Dearborn and New York, conferring with Boynton of GE and Ford, helping with advertisements and displays and offering guidelines and instructions to local units in arranging floats, Bernays made the Jubilee into a celebration not only of Edison, but of the spirit that he was supposed to represent.

Bernays continued to turn out releases. He even wrote one on Edison's favorite flowers, sent it to garden editors and in most cases saw it in print. Out of that effort a New Jersey nursery named its new dahlia the "Thomas A. Edison" and sent it to the annual show of the American Dahlia Society in Madison Square Garden.

Forty-two vaudeville acts and bands around the nation adopted a new song by George M. Cohan:

> Oh say can you see by the light that he gives you and me
> What a man he is, what a grand old 'Wiz!'
> Mo-ping, gro-ping in the dark, without him we would be,
> There's a light tonight that's shining,
> It's his light so bright that's shining,
> O'er the land of the free and the lands o'er the sea,
> Oh, he lights the way, Mr. Thomas A. —
> Edison, miracle man, oh man.

Cohan had written it in time for the National Air Races in Cleveland on August 31, called Edison Day. Airmail pilots raced from the Cleveland airport to Milan, Ohio, Edison's birthplace, and back in the Light's Golden Jubilee Derby. The Cohan song was played there and at the American Legion convention, which opened with a tribute to Edison; and the Shriners played it in Kansas City in a show that also included fireworks that produced a realistic battle effect; and in Buffalo they played it at a festival called "Main Street Fifty Years Ago." City after city put golden globes over the streetlamps, suffusing the nation in an amber glow. The country teemed with parades, fireworks, lighting festivals, the floodlighting of public buildings, and tableaus in which children depicted the stages of light from the campfire of the Stone Age to the invention of the bulb. There were many oversized pictures of The Wizard, and mile upon mile of red, white, and blue bunting. In some cities, the lights would be left on. In others, they would be turned off.

"On the day of the jubilee celebration of his invention of the electric lamp," Emil Ludwig, the celebrated biographer, wrote from Europe, "all the electric lights on earth, or at least in America, should be turned off at a given moment at night so that by means of complete darkness the present generation might realize for a minute what it owes to this second Prometheus." Ludwig's idea was rejected—it would create disruption all over the world to go without light.

Mayors and governors issued proclamations in honor of the occasion. Libraries displayed books about Edison and electricity. Museum heads arranged exhibits to illustrate the discovery of light. In Cincinnati, where it was discovered that Edison once dwelt obscurely as a nocturnal telegrapher, various relics including bulbs, lamps, phonographs, telegraphic instruments, and various electrical devices were displayed in an exposition. Educational groups conducted essay contests. Women's clubs held events to mark the Jubilee. Dining car menus on the nation's trains—Bernays overlooked nothing—mentioned the Jubilee.

It was much the same around the world. The great cathedrals of Europe were floodlit. Albert Einstein in Berlin wrote a short address to send by cable and radio hookup across the Atlantic to Dearborn. In Antarctica Byrd did the same. In Amsterdam the canals were bordered with lamps to reflect in the waters. Bridges spanning the canals were festooned with lights and garlands of light swung from tree to tree.

There was even a measure of suspense as the world waited to see if Edison would be recovered sufficiently to attend the grand celebration in his honor. On October 16, only five days before the affair, Edison made his first visit to his laboratory since he was felled by pneumonia in August. He made the trip in his Model T Ford and spent an hour at his desk, going over his correspondence and reports of his laboratory assistants on their rubber experiments.

In Jubilee promotion Edison was presented as an American archetype —rough of dress and manner, contemptuous of theory, a genius who denied the existence of genius, democratic to the core, feverish and insomniac with work, the American go-getter.

He was, one electrical executive said, "the spirit of America incarnate," typifying individual enterprise and daring. Some people, he added, wanted to supplant this spirit with paternalistic government, a development that should cause the nation to ponder whither it was drifting.

The Jubilee also sold consumer goods. "Light's Golden Jubilee" was emblazoned in letters about the Grand Central Palace in New York when the National Electrical Exposition opened in October. Ten thousand golden light bulbs glowed upon a scene of acres of toasters, washing machines, electric clocks, vibratone massage machines, a machine that cleaned, waxed, and polished floors, a bulb that emitted ultraviolet rays, electric sewing machines, vacuum cleaners, refrigerators, electric oil burners, and car radios.

As a promotional gimmick, GE's bulb-making subsidiary reproduced tens of thousands of copies of the original news article that had broken the story of the invention of the lamp. "Be sure and have a copy of the newspaper story of Thomas Edison's great invention where everyone may see and read it," a trade publication advised. "This story, which appeared in the *New York Herald* fifty years ago, will be a sensation now just as it was then. Copies of this reprint can be bought from the Sales Promotion Department at Nela Park, Cleveland. They sell for one dollar a hundred and make a great and inexpensive interest creator to distribute to your customers. Another little thing that will swell the Jubilee Gospel." Bernays was disturbed to find, however, that GE had doctored the *Herald* article, crudely inserting its "Mazda" trade name wherever the lamp was mentioned. At his recommendation, the sheets were destroyed.

Advertisements with a picture of Edison and the lamp appeared in almost every American magazine. The most elaborate was a nineteen-page, four-color advertisement in the nation's largest magazine in circulation, the *Saturday Evening Post*. The advertisement, the most expensive in history, cost a quarter of a million dollars. A preprint package called it "the greatest testimonial ever written into an advertisement." The package included a page for Thomas A. Edison, Inc., to sell its radios and other products.

National business leaders and editorial writers proclaimed Edison as the genius who had provided the underpinning of the modern age and had created American prosperity. "The distinctive production methods that have made the United States what it is are the direct result of Mr. Edison's inventions and discoveries," Ford said. "We are ahead of all other countries, simply and solely because we have Mr. Edison." Figures substantiated the Ford view. The United States used as much electricity as the whole rest of the world. New York State used more electricity than any foreign nation except Germany. There were more telephones in Chicago than in France. Power and labor-saving machinery produced high wages; lack of power and machinery in other nations kept wages low.

President Hoover called electrical energy "the greatest tool that has ever come into the hands of man." Most important, articles pointed out, the Edison invention was producing a continuous acceleration, which could be seen in the stock quotations. As C.M. Ripley pointed out in a trade magazine, it had taken fifty-three years to introduce nineteen million telephones, but only forty-six years to get twenty-four million electric customers, only thirty-four years to get twenty-five million automobiles in use, only seven years to sell thirteen million radio sets, only four years to establish twenty thousand miles of airways, only one year to triple the airplane manufacturing business, only one year to triple the amount of air-mail carried, and only two years to double the number of electric refrigerators. "The output of electricity by the utility companies has trebled in the past ten years," Ripley wrote, "and according to Roger Babson it will be trebled in the next ten or fifteen years." Electricity had set off an unprecedented spiral that had eliminated business downturns forever. In mid-October the purchasing agent for GE's Edison Lamp Works in New Jersey introduced Yale economist Irving Fisher at a New York gathering. Fisher told the group that stock prices had reached "what looks like a permanently high plateau." The Jubilee was, more than any other event of the year, the distillation of the spirit of 1929.

As expected, the Jubilee was an enormous success celebrated all over the nation and around the world. For the culminating event at Dearborn, the notables, led by the president, made their pilgrimage to Edison. At the appointed hour the buses pulled up at Ford's bigger and better Independence Hall for the testimonial dinner, and when they were all assembled in the banquet hall, a small party left for the re-enactment of the experiment in the same laboratory in which it had been done a half-century earlier. Ford had all the lights cut, and the banquet hall was lit by candles and oil lamps, so that the grounds were full of brooding shapes as Ford and Edison and the president rode through the misty rain. Francis Jehl, the assistant who had been with Edison when the incandescent lamp was perfected on October 21, 1879, waited for them in the red brick laboratory. As Edison bent over the table at work, Ford and Hoover stood by his side. Flickers played over his strong grave face and gleamed in his silver hair, catching glints on bottles on a shelf behind them. Jehl turned the pages of an old notebook in which he had recorded the 1879 test results. A photographer hovered in the background, and announcers for NBC and CBS spoke into microphones.

In Independence Hall a short distance away the guests were seated around the tables listening to the account of Graham McNamee of NBC over loudspeakers. Millions of people around the nation also listened on their radios to a dramatization intended to recreate the birth of electric power and light. It was impossible to capture in such a scene, however, the totality of Edison's achievement. He had invented not just the first practical light bulb but an entire range of electrical apparatus. To make his lamp usable, he had invented new power sources, the most efficient dynamos ever created at that point in history; he had invented literally scores of components in a delivery system, from cables to meters to sockets. Then he had created a manufacturing industry to make these goods and an engineering organization to install them. He had even created his own customers—an industry of central generating plants to buy the products of his manufacturing plants.

The Edison genius was embodied not so much in a lamp as in the series of research buildings in which he worked, for he had founded the modern technological-social matrix. His social and commercial senses were perfectly integrated. Before he had undertaken his first lamp experiment he had formed a notion of what he expected to achieve and, with utter modernity, had stated it in purely economic terms. He was interested in producing not a toy but a new world. He knew all this from the very outset.

When he began his work on the lamp, he started not by studying filaments or bulbs, but in a way then completely novel, and since become commonplace. He began by studying the gaslight industry. From the beginning, he attacked the problem at its social and economic base. Edison became an expert on gaslighting—its operations, its finances, its demography, its dangers and inconveniences, its seasonal curves, its logistics, its geography. When he understood gaslight thoroughly he knew how to replace it. He even knew what the bulbs would cost to manufacture and what he would charge for them, before he ever set hand to an experiment.

The networks had picked up the orchestra playing "Oh, Susanna" in the banquet hall during a lull in the laboratory proceedings, and switched back as Edison rose from his chair to test the vacuum. Then he told Jehl to seal it. Slowly the party moved downstairs to the dynamo room. The crucial test was coming. McNamee, who sometimes ran before he went on the air to put a breathless quality into his voice, described the scene with enough vividness so that the Byrd party could hear it through the Antarctic static. "The lamp is now ready, as it was a half century ago!" McNamee shouted. "Will it light? Will it burn? Or will it flicker and die, as so many previous lamps had died? Oh, you could hear a pin drop in this long room. Now the group is once more about the old vacuum pump. Mr. Edison has the two wires in his hand. Now he is reaching up to the old lamp. Now he is making the connection. *It lights!* Light's Golden Jubilee has come to a triumphant climax!"

At that moment, through a signal from Ford, thousands of golden globes glowed all over the site. Searchlights flashed on into the air, playing on a Goodyear blimp that said " '79 and '29." Like a tall skeleton in the night, the tower at the airport was illuminated by beacons and lights running up and down it. Half a continent away, at Menlo Park, New Jersey, thousands cheered as a light went on in the Edison Tower, built at the site of the old laboratories. McNamee, his voice burbling with excitement, said: "And Edison said—let there be light!" Ford's own exact replica of the Liberty Bell began to peal. Two airplanes, flying under dangerous conditions, took off from the Dearborn airport. One circled over Independence Hall and the other, covered with red lights, flew in circles over Detroit. In the Motor City, bells were rung and whistles blown.

As the great inventor walked out the door of his laboratory fireworks were whizzing into the sky. His body registered their dull thuds. The party was preparing to return to the banquet hall and play out the celebration to its end—a tribute to a glorious career. But one of the most fascinating facets of public ceremonies, perhaps the most fascinating, is what they conceal, for what they deny gives them their resonance. The Jubilee was a story of how Edison had restructured the world and thus a story of fabulous and unqualified success. But to tell the story of Edison and electricity in its full dimensions would also include the distasteful subject of failure. There was no interest in 1929 in stories about failure, and it would have proved embarrassing to some of the people in the room, so the Jubilee blazed with light to celebrate a tale without shadows. It might have been told, however, from 1881 on, if Samuel Insull had been among the speakers.

After nightfall on a winter day in early 1881, Edison was waiting for the arrival of an employee from England. Edward Johnson, his chief engineer, had gone to fetch the Briton at the dock and bring him back to the New York headquarters, where Edison was spending virtually all his time. Johnson filled the new arrival in on his duties, which, since an emergency had arisen, were to begin immediately. The lad was only twenty-one years old but was said to be exceptionally sharp and had made a good reputation for himself in Edison's London office.

The young Briton knew Edison only through magazine accounts and was taken aback at the first sight of his hero. Edison was wearing rumpled black pants that looked slept in, a seedy Prince Albert coat, a brown overcoat, and a large sombrero. His hair was long and shaggy and his face was stubbled. His shirt was dirty and a soiled white handkerchief was tied around his neck.

His recruit from London was equally a shock to Edison—skinny, pop-eyed, fuzzy-cheeked, very formal of manner, with a Cockney accent so thick that the half-deaf Edison could barely understand him. That was the first encounter of Thomas Edison and Samuel Insull.

Insull was shown his sleeping quarters and was rushed out to bolt down some food. By eight o'clock they were back in Edison's office, ready to work all night if necessary. Edison explained the situation to him. He was building a central electrical station in Pearl Street, a demonstration to show the world the future course of electrical power. It would cover approximately a square mile in lower Manhattan. His financial backers, the House of Morgan, had refused to throw any more money into his project, so he was using his own resources. He told Insull that he had $78,000 in credit with Morgan. Johnson was sailing for London before dawn to dispose of various holdings and come up with more cash. Now, the question for Insull was, what should be sold, how should it be sold, and how much could be realized on each property?

Insull felt luck touch his shoulder. The first task he encountered on landing in America happened to be the one about which he knew more than anyone else in the world—Edison's European holdings. While working in the London office he had practically committed all that information to memory. When Johnson left at four o'clock for the ship, he was completely prepared. Insull had sweepingly impressed Edison.

From that moment on Insull signed Edison's checks, answered his mail, bought his clothes, and generally functioned as his secretary. He took charge of canvassing—sending men from door to door through the Pearl Street district asking people if they would change from gaslight to electricity; learning how many homes had gas and how much each used; and the number of establishments using small engines that could be replaced by electric motors. He took charge of Edison's office, assumed duties as he saw fit, and increased his authority whenever possible. Edison was a sloppy administrator, caring nothing about the running of an office, the day of the week, or the hour of the day. Much of the work was done at night, when Insull was able to catch up with Edison, and sometimes the inventor would spend the night explaining the technology of electricity to the young Englishman. He listened avidly. At first the other men regarded him as a young misfit; they learned quickly that he had to be respected. He was intelligent, tough, and—most impressive of all—Edison's favorite.

In those days Edison was not only an inventor but an engineer, builder, and manufacturer. He had developed the most efficient dynamo yet to power his central station and was the world's first manufacturer of electrical equipment, including bulbs, light fixtures, sockets, switches, fuses, fuse blocks, meters, voltage regulators, and the like. They were exciting days for Edison and his protégé. They were also difficult days, for Edison's Wall Street backers—the people who had lent him the money to get the experiments started and now owned a share of the business—could not be shaken for anything more. Edison needed money chronically, he needed millions, but the House of Morgan did not regard Edison as a creative force; he was an impetuous promoter who appeared to disrespect money and was willing to throw all that he had into equipment and even into research. This view was encouraged by the gas interests, who tried to depict Edison as slightly ridiculous.

Insull had known a lot about the business, but as the months went by he learned something startling—that the money was not in manufacturing equipment and building central stations. For those who wished only to profit, the money was in holding the patents. They sat upon perhaps the most valuable patent rights in history. All Morgan and company had to do was wait, and the patents would reap wealth without any outlay. Without selling, making, or investing anything the patent holders could issue licenses and earn royalties.

Edison, however, was interested in glory. He intended to show the world the immeasurable significance of electricity by lighting up entire cities from central stations. If his backers would not support him, he would scrape up the money himself. This made it necessary for him to sell many of his shares in the Edison Electric Light Company—the company that held the patents. Insull realized that Edison was playing a dangerous game; he was losing his grip on the Edison Electric Light Company, the key to the whole enterprise. And—this must have seemed amusing on Wall Street—Edison had to pay them for the right to use the inventions he had created.

Furthermore, he and his backers had completely opposite views about the development of electrical power. The Wall Streeters, led by Morgan, who had a plant in his own home, believed that its future lay in individual self-contained plants in each building. Edison was building them for the hotels, office buildings, and factories, hoping that they would stir further interest in electric power. Nevertheless he believed that the future belonged to central stations, with conduits and cables providing electricity over large areas. The difference between the two views was profit. The Edison way required large capital outlays and slow returns. The Wall Street preference provided quick profits.

The Pearl Street station was Edison's main chance to show the central station's potential. Like so much of what Edison attempted in those days, it was crowned with success—the prototype of all that would occur in electricity over the next half-century. It was an engineering success. It was not—and this was rather a new experience for Edison—a promotional success. Everyone marveled at it, but no one put money in central stations.

Edison decided to send Insull out to foster central stations around the country. For the next eighteen months Insull traveled the nation around, taking canvasses, and selling the Edison central power station. Sometimes salesmanship failed to work. Insull quickly discovered that municipal officials were less interested in compelling argument or sound engineering than they were in cash in unmarked envelopes. Insull learned the knack quickly, and soon various cities in New York, Massachusetts, Ohio, and Pennsylvania had central stations.

In time the manufacturing companies—the industry making equipment for the stations—began to show a profit and the Wall Street speculators, operating from the base of the Edison Electric Light Company, moved in. Insull, by now adept at such maneuvers, fought off Morgan and the raiders. He had worked up a baneful dislike of the hidebound and predatory bankers, especially New York bankers, and particularly one New York banker. There were times, he told a friend, when revenge was sweeter than profit.

With the coming of the electric streetcars, the electrical manufacturing industry suddenly zoomed, and by the end of 1886 unfilled orders were piling up on Edison's desk. Insull found an abandoned locomotive works in Schenectady and some of the manufacturing was moved up there, with Insull in charge of operations. Its rapid expansion created more money problems, but the Wall Street bankers still refused to assist. Insull spent half his time borrowing money and rushing from bank to bank to cover checks. He learned another skill that would serve him later in his career—money juggling.

With the problem of how to meet a three-thousand-worker payroll preying upon his mind, a solution appeared through the agency of Henry Villard, a transportation magnate and speculator. Villard suggested a consolidation of all Edison companies, including the Edison Electric Light Company, into a single corporation and refinancing the lot.

Villard, who represented German interests and had notions about creating a worldwide electrical cartel, was an old friend of Edison's. Reorganization soon became caught between the interests of Morgan, who represented the patent-holders, and Edison, representing the manufacturing. When an arbitrator attempting to determine the values of each component asked in August of 1888 for a balance sheet of the Machine Works, Insull coached Edison on an answer. "I do not want to give any such statement," he wrote to Edison in a confidential message. *"In other words, I do not want you to give me your permission to give such a statement.* That is not until you can have a thorough discussion and understanding as to the matter in New York." Insull wrote in the memo that a proposed arrangement had collapsed because it favored Edison to the disadvantage of Morgan and that the revised deal was an attempt to reverse the scales for Morgan. If the earlier arrangement were not going through, he continued, "it is because the Villard and the Drexel, Morgan people [the name of Morgan's firm] think that it is too good a deal for the shops. Now they can put the present proposals in any form they like, but you may be sure that when you sift the thing right to the bottom it will be no such advantageous deal as that previously proposed." It would be one that favored the financiers, not the "shops."

Edison wanted the consolidation, preferably before any patent suits were decided in favor of the Edison Electric Light Company. Any such victories, he thought, would puff up the patent-holders even more. In January 1889 the reorganization was completed. Edison had lost majority control, but had come out of it with 1.7 million dollars in cash and stocks, and for the first time in twenty-two years was financially at ease. Insull was second vice president and a member of the board of directors. Villard, though he spent most of his time seeking mergers, was listed as president. The new company was called the Edison General Electric Company.

The chief rival to Edison General Electric in those days was the Thomson-Houston Company of Lynn, Massachusetts. It was run on completely different principles from Edison's company. It spent next to nothing on research and development and as little as possible on machinery. Occasionally it purchased ideas from impoverished inventors, but more often it stole—through spying, learning trade secrets, copying the work of others. In February of 1891, Charles Coffin, the president of Thomson-Houston, called the plant to tell the manager that Mr. Villard was about to be shown through it and that his identity was not to be revealed. Villard was still seeking an electrical trust. Morgan smiled on the prospect of a merger with Thomson-Houston, but Edison, who hated trusts, was upset to learn of Villard's scheme.

"The statement that they ask no favor from the Edison company might be met by the fact that, having boldly appropriated and infringed upon every patent we use, there is little left to favor them with, except our business, which they are now after," Edison wrote to Villard. Edison added that he needed competition to be creative.

In June 1891 the Edison companies won a devastating court victory over Thomson-Houston on patent infringement. With Thomson-Houston blocked from manufacturing and in danger of going out of business, Villard and Coffin met more frequently. Selling the Massachusetts company to Edison General Electric was seriously discussed through the fall, and Villard expected soon to have Thomson-Houston in his grasp. He had not reckoned, however, with the treachery of Morgan.

Morgan commissioned a study and received an enthusiastic report favoring the acquisition of Thomson-Houston. When representatives of both companies met in Boston, however, Coffin's men announced in a last-minute surprise that he had decided not to sell. "We don't think much of the way that the Edison company has been managed," one of Coffin's men said. Morgan, fascinated, asked for further information. Coffin came to the House of Morgan in December to claim that Thomson-Houston was the more efficient company, netting half again as much on its capital as did Edison General Electric. Morgan, examining the figures, quickly agreed.

Morgan understood nothing of mass production and mass sales. He had always regarded electric light as a luxury item for the wealthy. Few customers at high rates meant a small outlay; lower rates and more customers meant more equipment. Edison's view was completely opposite. "We will make the lamps so cheap," he once remarked, "that only the rich will be able to afford candles." Under Insull's guidance, light bulbs had decreased from one dollar in 1886 to forty-four cents by 1891. "Fact is, Mr. Villard," Edison once wrote, "that all electrical machinery is entirely too high now. These high prices hurt the business. With the leaden collar of the Edison Electric Light Co. around me, I have never been able to show what can be done. The ground of cheapening has scarcely been scratched."

The House of Morgan did not see Thomson-Houston's lack of research facilities as an unwise economy, nor did Morgan realize that his own stock-watering operations and empty capitalization had kept Edison General Electric profits down. He decided for the balance sheets and against Disorder. If he could not sell Thomson-Houston to Edison General Electric, he would sell Edison General Electric to Thomson-Houston. In either case he would have banking and financial control.

The final decision was to consolidate the two firms completely, an alternative that Coffin suggested, with Thomson-Houston as the dominant element in the merger.

Villard was told that his resignation would be courteously accepted. Edison was notified that the company had been sold out from under him. MR. EDISON FROZEN OUT HE WAS NOT PRACTICAL ENOUGH FOR THE WAYS OF WALL STREET, one newspaper summed up in a headline. With the exception of alternating current, which he spitefully had opposed, Edison had created the electrical industry and plotted its social and economic force, but lost it to a predator who knew nothing about electricity but knew when to swoop for the kill.

In the settlement, Edison was consoled with five million dollars—but it had been glory, not money, that he had always sought. "I am going to do something now," he announced a little later, "so different, so much bigger than anything I've ever done before that people will forget my name was ever connected with anything electrical." He was talking about the elephantine machine that he took into the New Jersey woods to mine iron ore by magnetic separation—and on which he lost millions of dollars. He and an assistant developed the motion picture, but his genius for recognizing and understanding social and economic evolution had been lost, and he regarded it as a toy and a passing craze, and left its development to others. He had produced cement houses that nobody wanted, and had developed the storage battery—a respectable work, but hardly fit for a figure who intended to transform the world. For forty years he had been announcing great discoveries just around the corner and now the rubber project was his last chance, but he knew after his brush with death in August that it was too late.

As for Insull, he had been asked to stay on with the new company, which shortened its name to General Electric, but had remained only briefly. When he left the new top people gave him a farewell dinner, a silver punch bowl, and fulsome praise at a large dinner at Delmonico's in New York. When the time came for him to respond he had arisen, and in an address stripped of all graciousness he promised that he would make his Chicago central station bigger than General Electric. His hyperthyroid eyes glowed and his upper lip, under his moustache, was curled in a sneer. He vowed to himself that nothing would ever take his world away from him, that nobody would do to him what had been done to Edison.

Edison and the others reached the banquet hall on their return from the re-enactment. The president preceded Edison. The inventor looked in and saw a sea of faces, turned, and collapsed on a davenport just outside the door. "I won't go in," he said.

Mrs. Edison bent over him. "What's the matter?" she asked.

"I can't go in," he said. He looked tired and frightened.

"You are the whole show, you know," she urged. "Do come in. Shall I get you a glass of milk?" She went to the kitchen and came back with it. He drank the milk thoughtfully, a gulp at a time. Then he rose and walked into the banquet hall. Like an old vaudevillian, his face snapped into a professional smile as he hit the doorway and the crowd broke into applause as he walked past their tables and back to his seat at the main table.

The smile had to be consciously maintained. Beneath it was a waxen and sick face. Edison was suddenly an old man wearing the face of defeat, and Insull recognized it, for he had been there when the battle had been lost.

The room decorated in gilt palm leaves was swarming with reunion, full of partnerships and rivalries. Many of the electrical executives had been associates of Edison. Ford waved to his neighbor, Rabbi Franklin; chatted with Chrysler; and greeted Secretary of War Good, who as a congressman had opposed his Muscle Shoals proposal. Charles Edison met the GE executive who had not come through with the plug for Edison Radios, and met Schwab, who had helped him manage Splitdorf Company. The guests included William Mayo, who had testified before a congressional committee on Ford's plans to make cheap fertilizer; and nearby stood Kahn, who had opposed the energy dollar that would pay for Muscle Shoals. Lindsey met Jane Addams, who had put him up at Hull House when he was on his way east to tell of the miners' plight in the Colorado strike. Merlin Aylesworth, NBC president, met Missy Meloney, in whose magazine, *The Delineator*, he had planted stories by the woman's club president when he was NELA director. Swope of GE met Green of the AFL, who still had not come up with a proposal to organize GE workers. Insull saw his adversary in Chicago politics, Rosenwald, at another table.

The sight of Charles Eaton reminded some guests of the intricate connections among people in the room. As Rev. Eaton he had been pastor of the Euclid Avenue Baptist Church of Cleveland, the church of the Rockefeller family. As Congressman Eaton, Republican of New Jersey, he was preparing an eyewitness story to send back to a New Jersey newspaper in his district. As Charles Eaton, GE executive, he had worked on promoting the Jubilee. He had accompanied Charles Schwab on his shipyard tours during the war when he stirred the workers to greater efforts as a dollar-a-

year man. And he had introduced his nephew, Cyrus Eaton, to the Rocke-
fellers and provided his entree to the world of power and privilege—until
Cyrus Eaton had developed enough leverage to attempt a takeover of
Insull's companies. The two Eatons were united at the dinner.

Good food and old-time music enhanced the banquet. Young, the GE
board chairman and toastmaster, was applauded five times, most enthusiastically when he commented graciously on the presence of Madame
Curie. His equally gracious speech, without much substance, dealt with
Edison's vitality and passion for work. He did not mention how GE had
disposed of Edison in 1891 and how, as a last vindictive step, Coffin had
torn Edison's name from the company, renaming it General Electric.

The president of the Edison Pioneers spoke briefly, and Will Rogers,
looking pained after his accident, amused the people at his table with
comments. Messages came from Byrd at Little America, Ambassador
Morrow in Mexico City, Marconi, the Prince of Wales, the President of
Germany, and Einstein by radio-cable transmission from Berlin. Ford
when introduced turned scarlet and bowed three times, but did not speak.

The audience rose to applaud and cheer as Edison stepped before the
microphones. He read from a typewritten sheet in a trembling, high-
pitched voice and became inaudible near the end. His voice faltered, his
head bent slightly forward and he had difficulty with his pronunciation.
When he finished his brief remarks he turned and rushed out the door.
Undisturbed, Hoover made the closing address.

Great as the lamp and Edison's other inventions have been, the president said, "there is perhaps one less noticed, but maybe even greater; and
that was the discovery of the method of invention. That method today is
that highly equipped, definitely organized, laborious laboratory research . . .
Mr. Edison was the pioneer in the determination of the new method of
applied science, and nowadays a thousand applied sciences laboratories
have followed upon Menlo Park, supported by the industries of this country. They yearly produce to us thousands of inventions." Ford, he said,
had honored Edison "in a manner which appeals to our sense of fitness"
by "founding an institution dedicated to education and scientific research."

The guests departed in a renewed fusillade of fireworks, while Edison
was treated for collapse.

The president, who had led the caravan into Dearborn, led it back out
in triumph. His appearance in downtown Detroit, despite heavy rains, had
rung with cheers. The press reaction to his Dearborn speech was gratify-
ing, and some points were given him, for possibly the first time in his

speaking career, for pithiness of expression. His train continued to Cincinnati, where he would mark the opening of the Ohio River to water traffic and speak about the further development of inland waterways.

Naturally he must have been concerned about the palpitations of the stock market, but when weighed in the balance the indicators were still tipped toward a glorious administration. It looked as if the long and troublesome question of reparations had been resolved and the world could begin to recuperate from the devastating war. His predecessor had sent several thousand Marines to Nicaragua to set matters in order, but by October all had been pulled out but a tiny force. On the day of the dinner the White House announced the appointment of two senators, a Republican and a Democrat, as delegates to the London Naval Conference the following January. On Armistice Day he intended to make another humanitarian bid—a proposal that food ships in time of war be exempt from capture. Unrestricted submarine warfare had pitched the United States into the last war, and both Britain and the United States favored an absolute ban on subs. The food ship proposal if adopted would help reduce armaments, for the fear of hunger and starvation stimulated nations toward a larger navy.

The Japanese, however, were concerned with British and American partnership in the Pacific. A small island incapable of self-support, Japan needed raw materials and food from the Asian mainland, and regarded the submarine as its principal defense. On October 21, while the dinner was being celebrated, the Japanese began annual naval maneuvers, with their movements as veiled in secrecy as in wartime. Beginning in July, a series of industrial mobilizations had been run to see how Japanese factories could perform with intensified production demands on a war footing. In that same month they had secretly reconnoitered Manchuria. They had converted a battleship and a battle cruiser, both slated for destruction as a result of the Washington Conference, into aircraft carriers, which were not limited by the Washington accords.

They were aware of the suspicions of a few Americans. "Japan is increasing with feverish rapidity every type of warship not included in the Treaty," William Shearer, to become famous in 1929 as the big bass drum, had warned in 1924 in a speech before the National Security League. Two years later Shearer had fictionalized his forebodings in a thriller called *Pacifico*, in which an American naval commander discovers the plans of a half-German, half-Japanese count to establish a Japanese world empire, which was thwarted in the nick of time. The Japanese were undoubtedly glad that Shearer had turned his suspicious nature against the British.

They were more seriously interested in the views of Hector Bywater, a British naval expert. In his book, *The Great Pacific War*, Bywater had forecast in 1925 that Japan's growing industrial needs and population and its limited island resources would propel it into conquests on the Asian mainland, including Manchuria, and would throw it into war with the United States—a war marked by fanatical Emperor-worship.

The Japanese Navy translated the book, without Bywater's knowledge and without paying him royalties, and published it with a Japanese commentary. The Japanese were at once fascinated and insulted. The book ended with the United States fighting its way back island by island across the Pacific and turning the tide in a decisive naval battle. In desperation the Japanese tried everything, including attacks by fanatical pilots who would attack American ships in suicide crash dives, but were forced to negotiate for peace near the end of 1932 when the Chinese joined as allies of the Americans.

Tota Ishimaru, a lieutenant commander in the Imperial Navy, wrote a rebuttal to these insults to the Emperor, but was intrigued by Bywater's plan to begin the war with a sneak attack on the American Pacific fleet. Commander Ishimaru wrote "that by making a good use of this publication the people of our country may turn a misfortune into a blessing."

But all this was unknown to Hoover as he left Dearborn, and he was gratified by the Japanese reaction to the Hoover-MacDonald talks of October and by Japanese eagerness to participate in the upcoming London Conference. Japan had signed the Kellogg-Briand Pact to renounce war, and the Japanese minister of naval affairs said his country shared the spirit of Rapidan and welcomed reductions in shipbuilding. Like Hoover, Japanese leaders appeared interested in curtailing the waste of armaments so that the nation could accomplish the technological prosperity that had been established in the West. Even in the Orient technology was triumphing, and it was expected that peace would follow.

No other nation seemed as taken with Light's Golden Jubilee. The Japanese marked the date with enthusiasm. Four representatives of Japanese power companies attended the dinner at Dearborn. The president of the Japanese branch of the Jubilee suggested that a monument be erected at the site where one of Edison's agents seeking the perfect filter had found the bamboo he wanted. On October 21, in Tokyo, three scout planes of the Imperial Air Corps, flying at a height of two thousand meters, dropped eight flare bombs, each lasting five minutes. The surrounding district was brilliantly illuminated for miles. Three hundred engineering students paraded with balloons and electric lanterns, ending at the main entrance to the Imperial Palace. Led by Mayor Horikiri, they shouted "Banzai!" three times and dispersed on signal.

Bernays rode back to New York on the train with Owen Young, thinking about Edison's collapse and worrying that the old man may have been pushed too hard. What he said, however, was that Edison had apparently enjoyed himself thoroughly and had loved poking around the Ford project. Fortunately, the aged genius was apparently all right. Hoover's personal physician had attended him and there appeared to be nothing wrong that could not be remedied with a little rest. He was staying at the Ford home.

Bernays was returning to New York to take up a suddenly more promising career. His new clients included Amtorg, the Soviet trade agency that had become so busy in the United States. He had already made a decision to rid himself of his mimeograph machine. Bernays was through writing press releases that ended up in wastebaskets. Public relations, as he had demonstrated, was a matter of deeds rather than words. He would counsel his clients on how to build goodwill, not just disseminate statements.

He knew that the Jubilee had been a triumph. He did not realize that he had created the quintessential event of 1929. He had taken the dominant tone of the decade of ballyhoo—an age of flagpole sitters and goldfish swallowers, of daily sensations and stunts performed in front of newsreel cameras and photographers, announcers, and reporters and had subdued it to a refined amber tone. He had conferred importance upon it and made it a headline in every newspaper in America.

The Jubilee finale was thus an appropriate climax to a year in which the Brain Derby found a successor to Edison; a year in which Ford and Edison sat at a table in a field, surrounded by reporters and, to accept the old Menlo Park glass-blowing plant, read the words printed for them on placards; a year in which new holding companies were created to hold smaller holding companies while press releases were issued to tell of the marvelous effects that would follow from such tricks of prestidigitation.

Man had created a world of technology superimposed upon the world of nature, and it seemed to follow that the new network of communications could create a world of engineered events. If textbooks could be changed to replace old history with new, if speculation could be taken in hand so that stocks became malleable to rises and falls, if trends could be created so that they did not occur spontaneously but according to the will of tobacco companies, it followed that important events could be conceived and manufactured—and that manufactured events could be important.

Near the beginning of the decade many Americans had become followers of the French psychotherapist, Emile Coué, and had been taught to get up in the morning and say: "Every day in every way I am getting better and better." Science taught them to believe that everything was possible, that expectations were unlimited. Business leaders taught them that a new form of economic justice could be created not by pressures and struggle but by the good sentiments of business commanders. They were told that the appearance of regulation was much the same as regulation itself. They were told that Big Business could not be dishonest. And when the stock market faltered, especially in September and October, it was believed that nothing was structurally wrong, but that there was a crisis of credibility and that doubt and fear were the only problems of the market. Those who did not boost were held to be perverse. Ample evidence lay about to dispel all of these sentiments, but it was not looked for. And so the illusions and images lingered into late October, to be celebrated at Dearborn. All illusions last but for a time and are at last dispelled. As the actors left Dearborn they were not aware that the illusion was evaporating, and that their snug world had already disappeared.

EPILOGUE

Something new came to America that fall: the dramatic radio program. NBC picked up a Chicago show called *Amos 'n' Andy* and began to broadcast it over the network in August of 1929. Late in October, nine days after the Jubilee dinner, the story concerned Lightning, an out-of-work young black, who asked Andy for a job with the taxi company.

"Well, Lightning," Andy said, "course I would like to give you a job but de bizness repression is on right now."

"What is dat you say, Mr. Andy?"

"Is you been keeping yo' eye on de stock market?"

"Nosah, I ain't never seed it."

"Well, de stock market crashed."

"Anybody get hurt?"

Among the injured were holders of RCA stock, the glamour stock of the age and the owner of NBC. RCA plummeted along with U.S. Steel, General Motors, Sears, and hundreds of others. The newsreels were calling Otto Kahn to ask him for a ninety-second segment. He went to the opening of the fall season at the Metropolitan but did not get to see the third act of *Manon Lescaut*. He was in the lobby, talking rapidly, as the market drop raised the pitch of voice from baritone to soprano.

Few people, however, were talking about a repression, a recession, or a depression. Morgan was in Europe, but Thomas Lamont organized support to arrest the crash and sounded the dominant theme for months to come. "There has been a little distress selling on the Stock Exchange," he told reporters in the name of the House of Morgan, claiming that it was merely "due to a technical condition of the market." Ford, Lamont, Young, Insull, and Rosenwald were summoned to Washington to meet with President Hoover and to look optimistic. Financial writers said the problem was psychological and had nothing to do with the country's economic structure. Hoover told the press that "the fundamental business of the country, that is, production and distribution of commodities, is on a sound and prosperous basis." At the end of October, Ivy Lee released a statement from John D. Rockefeller, Sr.: "Believing that fundamental conditions of the country are sound . . . my son and I have for some days been purchasing sound common stocks." In November, Henry Ford cut

325

his retail prices as "the best contribution that could be made to assure a continuation of good business." In December, Schwab said that the business conferences the president was calling were the "most constructive peacetime effort which the nation has ever seen" and that American business had never been better emplaced than in 1929. As the New Year arrived the secretary of the treasury predicted "a revival of activity in the spring." In February the secretary of commerce said there was nothing to be disturbed about. In March the president said unemployment would clear up within sixty days. Month followed month and the salesmen went on dispensing sunshine, as the 1920s receded into memory.

Samuel Insull and his son slipped out the servants' entrance of the Paris hotel in which they had been staying. It was an October night in 1932. Carrying only a light handbag between them, they turned the corner and hailed a taxi, then caught a train across the border into Italy.

Three hours before their departure they had received a telegram from Chicago informing them that Insull had been indicted on charges of embezzlement and larceny of more than five hundred thousand dollars from their ruined electrical utility empire. The state attorney of Illinois asked the State Department to request extradition from Italy and called the flight "an overt act" that made Insull "a fugitive from justice."

Insull had already left Italy. By a roundabout train and plane route through Milan, Rome, and Albania, he had reached Athens, leaving his son behind. Greece was a haven for fugitives from extradition and it appeared that he might be settling down for a long stay. Money was cabled to him from Chicago. His confidential secretary in Chicago, visited by law enforcement officials, admitted having sent coded cablegrams to Insull but refused to disclose the text, even under threat of indictment as an accessory.

A few days later at the Grand Bretagne Hotel in Athens at noon, several cars were parked outside while their occupants watched Insull standing at the balcony. He had been under surveillance for several hours. A detective stepped out on the balcony and announced his identity. Insull could be seen hesitating for a moment, then following him without resistance.

"I have committed no crime and there is no warrant out for me," he told the Greek press. "The failure of my company was not fraudulent. I have come to Athens purely as a tourist. I find the climate delightful."

It was said that his papers were not in order and that he would be detained until the question of extradition was settled. The police station staff prepared the best room in the lockup for him, with an adjoining bath.

He turned down the offer of a meal, taking only a sandwich and a glass of soda water and thanking the police for their attentions. "This whole affair is a result of a thirst for vengeance on the part of my enemies," Insull said. "The truth will out finally." He said that he and his wife had lost one hundred fifty million dollars in his business failure. Although he tried to look jaunty and insolent, he was frightened of being assassinated. He was the central figure in the most important and devastating business failure of the Great Depression. Thousands of investors had been affected; banks had been left in chaos. Corporations, tied by a thousand strands to other parts of the American economy, had been pulled down with him. Insull's crash had shaken the earth.

Back in the United States, people no longer spoke of him as the Great Businessman of the Middle West. Many stockholders believed that he had protected himself at their expense.

Even after the crash the private Insull boom had continued. The Insull companies seemed immune to the problems that had flattened the rest of the economy. But behind the apparent prosperity lay desperation. They overvalued their companies, and when they announced a stock sale they included the expected proceeds from the sale itself as money on hand. They pushed out dividends as bait, announcing far in advance that Insull companies would pay a hefty dividend for the year. Although the two superholding companies were losing money, the reports for two years were juggled to show profits. Frantic activity was maintained in the sale of stocks, including a merry-go-round of sales from one Insull agent to another to keep up a semblance of heavy trading. By late 1931, the second superholding company, Corporation Securities Company, was insolvent, yet Insull continued to take money out of it and sell shares in it. The "service charges" that the Insull holding companies charged their operating companies increased as more cash became imperative.

Late in 1931 the sliding became rough. When the huge Corporation Securities Company went into bankruptcy, its assets amounted to only sixty thousand dollars. Notes were called, extensions were asked, more borrowing was attempted. The Insull companies, all seventy-five of them, had become tangled. Money was shifted around from one company to another in a desperate attempt to stop an avalanche. Mistakes were made and the record became disorganized and disorderly.

The government called it a swindle. They said the Insulls had sold forty-nine million dollars in stocks merely to pay off loans, buy other stocks, and pay fees. Franklin Roosevelt, the Democratic candidate for president in 1932, made a symbol of "the Ishmaels and the Insulls, whose hand is against every man's." Harold Ickes, one of Insull's old Chicago foes in the fight against the streetcar deal, had become a speechwriter for FDR. Candidates and editorial writers used Insull through the campaign to personalize the business duplicity that had brought on the Crash and the Depression.

Insull made a long fight of it. For a year and a half he warded off attempts to extradite him. Meanwhile other indictments as well as civil suits piled up in the United States. The Greek government notified Insull that he would have to leave when his residency permit ran out at the end of 1933. After a delay on grounds of ill health, Insull slipped away on March 15, 1934, on a tramp steamer, his hair and moustache dyed and his eyebrows pencilled. On March 22 the U.S. Congress adopted a bill authorizing the arrest of Insull in any country in which it had extraterritorial rights by treaty. When the tramp steamer landed at Istanbul for provisions, the Turkish authorities took him forcibly from the vessel, detained him in a proceeding apparently devoid of any legality, and he was sent back to the U.S. in American custody.

He returned determined to teach manners to photographers and protesting his innocence. He admitted making mistakes but said that he made them in an attempt to save his companies, not wreck and raid them. When he arrived in Chicago he ran a gauntlet of scores of reporters and photographers and about three thousand people who lined both sides of his path from Union Station. The national sensation of his return in the midst of the Depression brought some out to boo and curse him, while others cheered the man who had been such a hero.

In October he went on trial in federal court for using the mails to defraud. He said he had left the country because he was broken in health and had been through a great ordeal when his two superholding companies went into receivership. He said he decided not to return when indicted because he believed the trial would be political. When he told his life story on the stand, the weary but defiant seventy-four-year-old man brought out the handkerchiefs, especially among his associates.

In the summations Insull's lawyers pictured "Old Man Depression" as the culprit and pointed out that Insull had not bilked stockholders for his own gain but had been wiped out with them. "The thing on trial here is a period in American finance," one orated. "Crazy? Certainly. Wild? Yes. That was the free public market that the prosecution loves so well. They say we lost for the public one hundred forty million dollars in this scheme. I don't know how many millions were lost, but it was a great many. Who got it?" The jury found Insull and his co-defendants not guilty. He won acquittals in other criminal trials that followed as well.

A character witness showed up at Insull's mail fraud trial: his old blue-eyed traveling companion Cyrus Eaton, who had once sailed the Atlantic with him on a liner without once mentioning his purchase of Insull stocks. The Cleveland financier described Insull as a fine businessman and said Insull stocks were of high value at one time; he had bought a lot of them, he said.

He did not add, however, that when he sold them to protect himself from a raid by Schwab, he had set the Insull edifice to tottering. Charles Schwab had come storming into Ohio in 1929 to attempt a takeover of Youngstown Sheet & Tube, one of Eaton's holdings. Schwab offered Bethlehem Steel shares for Youngstown shares. Eaton, fighting against the takeover, looked for reasons why Youngstown shareholders should be advised against such a trade—and he found a convincing argument.

The Senate testimony of William Shearer had brought out the information that Schwab had paid a huge bonus to Eugene Grace, the Bethlehem president, while Schwab, the Bethlehem board chairman, was off working for the government during the war. Eaton knew that Schwab was deceptive by nature and would not tell his stockholders anything he could hide from them. He discovered that Schwab had a tricky way of giving Bethlehem executives high salaries while keeping the facts from the stockholders: He paid them in bonuses that did not appear in the annual reports. Bethlehem executives had received large bonuses between 1925 and 1928, when the Bethlehem stockholders had received no dividends. Grace, listed in 1929 at a salary of twelve thousand dollars, had been paid 1.6 million dollars as a bonus for that year alone. In comparison, the president of Standard Oil of New Jersey, one of the most highly paid executives in the nation, made one hundred twenty-five thousand dollars in 1929.

Eaton thus had a good argument, but he needed money fast to make his fight against the takeover. In 1930 he offered to sell all his Insull stocks back to Insull, but the price he named was millions of dollars above the market value. When Insull said it was too high, Eaton threatened to dump them, probably in New York among Insull's enemies. Insull managed to bring the price down, but he spent fifty-six million dollars for his orphans of the storm.

Now Eaton had the funds to fight Schwab, and he made a successful fight of it, finally winning in the courts. But Insull found his finances strained to the breaking point in buying off Eaton. When the Chicago banks failed to come through with promised loans, Insull was desperate. He went to the hated New York banks and so went into debt to the people that he was no longer able to avoid. Morgan had waited patiently, biding his time, until he had the leverage he wanted. There was a touch of irony in Eaton's appearance at the trial as a character witness for Insull, for Eaton had unwittingly pushed him into the grasp of Morgan.

Morgan still had his homes in France, England, Manhattan, and Glen Cove, his hunting lodge in Scotland, his private railway car, and when the Depression began he launched his new yacht. In October of 1929 it had still been under construction at the Bath Iron Works in Maine. The four-million-dollar yacht, the most costly ever built, was launched early the following year. It sat low in the water and had an unprecedented amount of deck space. Most of the woodwork, beams, and deck were teak. It included two separate living quarters for Morgan, many other staterooms, a laundry, and a lounging room with an open fireplace. It had a crew of fifty-eight. A turbine and generator provided light—enough current to furnish electric light for a city of fifteen thousand. It was equipped with refrigeration for Morgan's gourmet tastes in oysters, lobsters, and wines. It included an elevator and a thermostat system that maintained a constant temperature.

Neither the crash nor the resulting depression had cramped his style in the least. Business had of course decreased, but Morgan compensated for that by paying no income taxes in 1930 or 1931.

Morgan had moved against Insull to secure financial control of the electrical companies at precisely the proper moment, when Insull was most vulnerable. His instinct in such matters was unerring. The House of Morgan had spread rumors that Insull was in difficulties and let it be known that Morgan had taken umbrage. "They were out to do me up, were the reports," Insull testified during the mail-fraud trial, "and these things weren't doing the market any good. These false reports gained tremendous circulation and it was necessary to support the market in our stocks." By supporting the market, Insull meant various manipulations were used to keep his stock prices up.

There were also rumors about Insull's health during the trying period, and it was commonly believed that Insull's enemies at the House of Morgan were whispering them. "One time when I was going to Europe in 1931," Insull said during the trial, "there was a report at Southampton that I was dead. I don't recall whether I was buried."

In lending money to Insull the New York banks insisted upon the best collateral, and such was their power that with only a twenty-million-dollar loan they managed to shut Insull down. He went to Owen Young to cash in on a favor—he had put Young on his "select list" for cut rates on his holding company stocks—but a two-million-dollar loan from GE and

Young's attempt to use his influence with Morgan failed to stop the banks. They called the loans at the unerringly proper moment and, under Morgan's leadership, they lined up for the receiverships and refinancings; the money made on shipwrecked companies was usually the easiest money of all.

And so, in one of those twists of history, Insull had ended up in the grip of Morgan, the son of the Morgan who had taken Edison's companies. Edison had fallen with the inevitability of heroic saga; Insull fell in melodrama, with a tale of intrigue on the Orient Express, coded telegrams, disguises, and fresh trails in the Mediterranean.

Insull, the genius of central station power, was out of his element in high finance, and the whole shaky structure—in which holding companies owned each other, in which everything was overvalued, in which dead horses were listed as assets, in which stock was diluted to the color of a mineral spring—could not sustain hard times. Too many overvalued companies, trading on a future of perpetual growth, had brought the boom down with a mighty crash. Some said Insull's fall was a result of the Depression; but there were more and more people in America who felt that Insull, and others like him, were its cause. Morgan, even in peaceful Glen Cove, tilling his late wife's tulip corner, could hear in his mind the reawakened forces of Disorder—their voices shouting at rallies, their fists raised as if to punch through the seamless garment of God's Plan. They were oddities to him. On his black-hulled yacht, or in his tapestried private railway car, insulated by servants, he had no conception of what they said in barbershops, what women discussed over bridge tables. He had never tasted potlikker; the sharp ozone smell of the subway had never penetrated his fine nostrils. He had always regarded aloof ignorance as good taste, and disdained the prophylactic skills of an Ivy Lee or a Bernays to doctor his image. His stare had forced whole congressional committees to avert their gaze, and he had sat in majestic contempt of photographic flashes. But when the New Deal began to glare unblinkingly back at him during the Depression, he was at last forced to capitulate to the press; at a hearing in Washington, Morgan posed for photographers with a sardonic midget sitting on his knee.

It all passed. Secretary of War Good died a month after the dinner. Lindsey was disbarred in December of 1929. Edison never recovered his stride and died in 1931; his last words were: "It is very beautiful over there." He left his rubber project unfinished. Hoover lived on and on, but without his reputation; he was booed at the 1931 World Series. Mussolini's reputation also ended in a shambles. Al Capone's Florida home became evidence when the Internal Revenue Service put together a tax evasion charge that sent him to prison, and he died in the throes of advanced syphilis. Zelda Fitzgerald spent much of the rest of her life in mental institutions beginning in 1930. The New Deal subdued Morgan.

Ford's rubber plantations came to naught. The "Lindbergh Line" air-rail service was among the casualties of the Depression, but Transcontinental Air Transport merged with another airline and is now Trans World Airlines. President Roosevelt's administration brought public power to the Tennessee Valley. Insull's Chicago foes, Paul Douglas and Harold Ickes, went to Washington, the former as a U.S. senator and the latter as Roosevelt's secretary of the interior. The Japanese invaded Manchuria in 1931. The first Lindbergh child was kidnapped and later was found dead. Hitler renounced reparations payments, and only Finland ever paid back all its World War I debts to the United States.

The Metropolitan Opera stayed at Broadway and 39th Street until 1966, when it moved into Lincoln Center. Nevertheless, the midtown project was built without an opera house, attracted RCA and NBC as tenants, and was called Radio City for a time, although its official name became Rockefeller Center. Jane Addams won a Nobel Peace Prize in 1931. Henry Mencken became as ardent a foe of the New Deal as he had been of Prohibition. Sinclair Lewis in 1930 became the first American to win a Nobel Prize for Literature. The union movement was resuscitated in the Depression, and, after bloody struggles, the United Auto Workers organized Ford plants. In 1934 Marie Curie died of pernicious anemia caused by long exposure to radioactivity. Julius Rosenwald remarried. Cyrus Eaton became a strong promoter of increased trade with the Soviet Union during the Cold War, won a Lenin Peace Prize, and was called before an anti-communist investigating committee. Hemingway and Eastman committed suicide when overtaken by poor health. The scheme of Young and Swope to give sweeping powers to trade associations later became known as the Swope Plan, and, although never adopted in full, some of its aspects became New Deal policies during the Depression.

General Electric was forced to divest itself of RCA. In 1948 GE was found guilty of conspiring with Krupp for twelve years, including during the Nazi era, to fix prices, eliminate competition, and pool patents in tungsten carbide. Will Rogers, the aviation promoter, died in a plane crash in 1935. Damon Runyon, who smoked Luckies for his health, died of throat cancer. Wilber B. Huston, the winner of the Brain Derby, went to work for Theodore Edison, the inventor's son. The two worked on a point-of-purchase display that included recorded sales pitches.

The Jubilee was later praised by a Yale social psychologist as "one of the most astonishing pieces of propaganda ever engineered in this country during peace time." A few days after the dinner a GE advertising executive asked Bernays to count the inches of editorial space Thomas Edison had received in the past year. "I think you will agree with me," Bernays wrote back to a company official, "that this can be listed under 'foolish questions of the year.' It is impossible to estimate the amount of space Mr. Edison received or the amount of attention the event attracted." Bernays did not hear from the advertising executive again.

Sixteen years after the Jubilee, Hitler was overcome and his war machine dismantled. When the hostilities ended, the commander of the U.S. Army of Occupation and his deputy drove to the chalet of Hjalmar Schacht to arrest the financier for war crimes. He had been indicted at Nuremberg as an agent of the Nazi apparatus, and few knew that he and Sarnoff had formulated the Young Plan to bring peace to Europe.

Schacht, whose parents had lived in America, insisted that he was neither an anti-Semite nor an anti-American. He pointed to the only picture on his wall. "Look at this," he told his captors, "if you don't believe me." It was a signed photograph of Sarnoff to his Hebrew-speaking friend Schacht, inscribed in Paris in 1929.

APPENDIX 1

Sources and Obligations

This account of the events preceding the crash of 1929 has been taken from a great number of published magazine and newspaper accounts of the period, which are listed in the bibliography of periodicals. The bibliography cites, however, only a small and arbitrary sampling of unsigned *New York Times* articles actually used as sources; a complete listing would make a small pamphlet in itself. A number of books, separately listed in the bibliography, were also used as sources. The Otto H. Kahn papers at the Firestone Library, Princeton University, were valuable, as were the Edison papers at the Edison National Historic Site in West Orange, New Jersey. Edward L. Bernays was interviewed in his home at Cambridge, Massachusetts, on November 1, 1976, furnishing additional material. Bernays also provided press releases of the Jubilee, and others were found in the Edison papers. While at the Henry Ford Museum at Dearborn the author was shown motion pictures of the Greenfield Village gathering of October 21, 1929.

In one instance, at the outset of the book, a quotation is used without any authentication that it was actually said at the moment indicated in the text. If the reader chooses, he may regard this as a fictionalization. The quotation is Edison's comment on his restored laboratories: "Well, we never kept it this clean." Sources, including the Josephson biography, indicate that he and Ford actually had this conversational exchange but do not indicate that it was said at that moment, or at any other particular moment. It has been placed at the end of the scene for its effect.

The remainder of the prologue material comes from newspaper, magazine, and trade journal accounts, press releases, Bernays' memoirs, and the interview with Bernays. The remarks of Edison's old cronies were printed in a Detroit newspaper (clipping in Edison archives). The story of Edison's tour of his old laboratories appeared virtually word for word in various newspapers, indicating that it was adapted from a press release.

Mencken's views are from his signed articles in 1929 issues of the *American Mercury*. The account of his meeting with Sinclair Lewis is recounted in the Mayfield memoir.

PART I The Businessmen

Capone's party is told in Kobler. The Young sermon on Big Business was a front-page *New York Times* story. The Rosenwald material comes from Werner and contemporary periodicals. Schwab's career is told in Hessen and in the Winkler ("Steel") and Strawn profiles. Tarbell and the Pringle profile provided the portrait of Young, and the reparations issue was widely covered in newspapers and magazines. The role of Sarnoff, not printed in contemporary accounts, is told in Lyons.

Gammack, McMullen, and Wamsley articles provide examples of stock-market behavior, and a ship-news reporter furnished Schwab's views in the *New York Times*. The RCA stock story is told in Brooks; the taxi scene with Kahn and Cravath is from Bernays's memoirs. Allen's two books also furnished stock-market material.

Fordlandia was described in Nevins-Hill and Naylor. Material on Ford comes from Nevins-Hill, Sward, and Bradford. Ford's struggle with changing styles and the Model A are found in Merz, newspaper accounts, *The Literary Digest* and Kaempffert ("The Mussolini of Highland Park").

Sources for the Rockefeller material include Fosdick, the *Literary Digest*, and the *New York Times*, as well as Pringle's profile of Ivy Lee in *Big Frogs*. The proxy fight was as widely covered as any event of the century. For the Colonel Stewart sketch, see Speers ("A Baron of the Petroleum World"). Rosenwald's role was recounted in Werner.

The formation of U.S. Steel is an oft-told story. Walker and Winkler furnish a picture of Morgan *fils*, and the description of the *Bibliothèque Nationale* book show was found in the *New York Times*. The Bank for International Settlements is outlined in newspaper articles and the *Literary Digest* ("A World Bank for Financial Peace").

Pringle in *Big Frogs* is again useful for a portrait of Will Hays. Material on the films came from newspapers and magazines, and the Hays role in the formation of an aviation trade association from his memoirs. The history of the Colorado Plan is developed in Fosdick. The changing rhetoric of capitalism is copious in newspapers and magazines, and David Brody's article, "The Rise and Decline of Welfare Capitalism," in Braeman was helpful. The meeting of Green with Young and Swope is described in Loth. Young's attitudes are outlined in Tarbell. Rothbard provides helpful comments on trade associations. Mussolini is described by Cortesi and Ybarra; Diggins comments on American attitudes, as does the *Literary Digest* ("Why Our Bankers Like Mussolini"). Kahn's book provided examples of his thinking. The *Literary Digest* ("Philadelphia Justice for Chicago's Al Capone") gives a complete account of his arrest and conviction, and Kobler was also consulted.

PART II   Machinery, the New Messiah

The opening scene of the donation of the glass-blowing plant comes from news accounts, Bernays's memoirs, and the Bernays interview. The museum project is described in Wood and was supplemented by Bernays' memoirs. The outline of the then-proposed Chicago Museum is from Kaempffert ("Museum Will Depict Upward Climb of Man"). Owen Young on the age of science is from the *New York Times*, as are the Archbishop's cautionary note and Ford on prohibition and flying. Congressman Clancy's comments are from transcripts of House Merchant Marine and Fisheries hearings. The description of the bootleggers' operation is from the *Literary Digest* ("Zero Hour in the Rum War"). The RCA Communications proposal is from the *New York Times* and *Business Week* ("World Battle Starts in Air and Under Sea"), as well as Gammack. RCA's formation is told in Tarbell. Other material comes from hearings and from Anderson. The Firestone tire order is mentioned in Lief. The role of radio in the Hoover inauguration was covered in the *New York Times*, which also printed Young's comments on the coming political influence of broadcasting. Aylesworth's comments are from House Merchant Marine and Fisheries Committee transcripts. The Goldsmith television demonstration was described in the *New York Times*, and the animated cartoon commercial was in *Business Week* ("Selling—With Sound Effects").

Magazines and newspapers covered the RCA acquisition of Victor and RKO. The Antarctic activity is covered in Owen, Speers, and Byrd. The Wright material is from Hodgins, Kelly, and the *Literary Digest* ("Aviation's Twenty-Five Birthday Candles"). In his book Walsh attempts to show that Wilbur was the true inventor of the airplane and Orville only his assistant, and that Orville muddied the record to present himself as co-inventor. The case, at least concerning Orville's motives and acts, appears to be overstated.

Lindbergh's engagement and the Havana landing are from the *New York Times*. The air-rail decor is from the *Literary Digest* ("All Abroad the Lindbergh Limited!"). Ford's growing role in aviation is from Nevins-Hill, newspaper articles, and magazines. Rogers on aviation is from Ketchum and Clancy. The crashes were covered in daily newspapers. Numerous magazine sources speculated on the technology of the future. Rocketry and Goddard are covered by Duffus ("A Great Rocket For Exploring Outer Space"). The I. G. Farben and Krupp stories are from newspaper accounts, Borkin-Welsh, Straight, and Reimann. Trade with Russia is described in *Business Week* ("Blueprint of a Nation—in Red") and Mitchell. The discovery of the Mayan ruins and Lindbergh at Teterboro and Roosevelt Field are from the *New York Times*. The Curie material comes from Reid, the *New York Times*, the *Literary Digest*, Lescarboura, the Bernays memoirs, and a letter to the author from Bernays.

PART III   The Promoters

Coverage of Ivy Lee and the Rockefeller Plaza plan combines material from the Pringle profile of Lee, the *New York Times*, and Brock. The Kahn material comes from Kahn's papers and Matz. The sketch of Nijinsky in the asylum and visiting the Ballets Russes was found in the Lifar book. Material on the American tours was covered in the Kahn papers, the *New York Times*, and the Bernays memoirs. The death of Diaghilev is told in Lifar and Kochno.

The Chaplin material is from Kisch, the *Literary Digest*, Frank, and Lita Grey Chaplin. Kahn's Paramount speech is among the Kahn papers. The influence of film around the world is from several sources, especially Wilstach. Newspaper accounts and Yallop furnished the Arbuckle material, and Yallop also developed the evidence that Maude Delmont was attempting to frame the comic. Kahn's Hollywood pastimes come from his papers.

Edison at Fort Myers was researched through photographs and Speers ("Edison Forecasts 'Hoover Prosperity' "). The phonograph invention story is from Josephson. The tale of his agent in Brazil comes from the Edison papers and the *New York Times*. The note from Lowrey on J.P. Morgan's attitude toward Edison's progress on the incandescent bulb is from the Edison notes, as is much of the material on rubber. Other material comes from news clippings in the Edison files.

Einstein on his fiftieth birthday was covered in the *Literary Digest*, and the Cardinal's warning is from the *New York Times*. The Brain Derby material came from the Edison files and the *Boston Globe* account found in the files. Anne Morrow Lindbergh's attitudes are in her published diaries, *Hour of Gold, Hour of Lead*. Edison's illness was covered day by day in the newspapers.

Much of the Lindsey material is from Larson. The Addams material was found in Davis, Linn, and Conway. Dawes is depicted in Callender, Pearson, Selden, and Williamson. Dawes at court is described in the *Literary Digest* ("The Mystery of the Ambassador's Calves").

Fitzgerald and Hemingway material was found in Milford, Callaghan, Baker, Parker, and Mosher. The Schwab story is found in Hessen, Winkler, Strawn, the *New York Times* coverage of hearings, and the *Literary Digest*. Hoover was depicted in Pringle's profile in *Big Frogs*, Duffus ("The Most Traveled President"), and Lloyd. The Everglades scene is from Speers ("Florida Flood Need Impresses Hoover"). The Peace Ship account comes from Larson and Sward.

Attitudes in 1929 on war and arms limitations come from various periodicals. The Fort Jay bombing is told in the *New York Times* and the *Literary Digest*, and the London raid is described in Chase. The *Literary Digest* concentrated on the cruiser controversy through early 1929. The Shearer material comes from daily *New York Times* coverage, McCoy, and *The Nation*.

The Hoover-MacDonald meetings were widely covered, but the McCormick piece added an analysis of their differing personalities. The *Literary Digest* account of the visit was also helpful. Attempts to get MacDonald to the Dearborn dinner are documented in the Ford archives. For the changes in "Scheherazade," see Martin. The *New York Times* accounts of the trial give particulars of the forged Soviet documents.

Ford's anti-Semitic activities and his retraction are found in Sward, the *Literary Digest* and the *New York Times*. Anti-Semitism in Germany and the vote on the Liberty Law were covered in the *Times* (especially "Anti-Semites Busy Again in Germany"). Hoover's White House staff was profiled anonymously in the *American Mercury*. The material on Rockefeller is from Fosdick and the *New York Times*.

PART IV   Light's Golden Jubilee

The story of *Dynamo* can be found in Simonson and the *Literary Digest* ("O'Neill Wrestles with God"). Young's quote is from Tarbell. The Kaempffert article is included in the bibliography. The Dodge Victory Six broadcast is from Bernays and the *New York Times*. The Lucky Strike advertising copy can be found in advertisements in the *Literary Digest* and elsewhere. Other material on advertising is from Wallace, Wagner, the Bernays memoirs, and the *New York Times*. The Boynton visit to Bernays is from Bernays' interview of 1976. Edison's rancor about his treatment by RCA is preserved in Edison files. Ford's decision to take over the October 21 celebration is reported in the Josephson biography. Material on the Light's Golden Jubilee committee is from press releases. Bernays' views are reported in profiles by Flynn and Pringle ("Mass Psychologist"). Ford's purchase of the Edison stamp was reported in the *New York Times*. Flynn first developed the comparison of Barnum's and Bernays' techniques. Bernays' quotation on propaganda comes from his 1928 book.

The Muscle Shoals and waterpower material is from the *New York Times* and Ford's article in *Review of Reviews*, reprinted from *Electrical World*. The Insull material is from McDonald, Werner, and the *New York Times*. The portrait of Chicago is from Josephson's article. The encounter of Smith and Rosenwald is based on Smith's own account of the conversation, found in Werner. The formation of United Corporation was reported in the *New York Times*. Insull's defense against Eaton is from newspaper accounts of the trial and McDonald. The description of Eaton is from Sheehan. Insull's financial entanglements are covered in McDonald, Allen (*The Lords of Creation*), and Flynn. The alleged attempt of Insull to buy the *Boston Post* was reported in Federal Trade Commission hearings and covered in newspapers of the time. NELA's propaganda campaign was covered in the newspapers and can be found distilled in Gruening and Thompson. The Norris quote is from Norris's article. The Atlantic City convention was reported in trade magazines, the *New York Times*, and Bernays' press releases. Insull's comments on the virtues of utility monopoly are from a 1916 address to the Iowa section of the National Electric Light Association, the Iowa State and Interurban Railway Association, and the Iowa District Gas Association and is printed in his book. The daily press reported the soaring stock prices of utilities. The quotation from the Continental Bank president is from McDonald. McDonald and Allen report Insull's mid-1929 fortune. Douglas reports in his memoirs on the meeting with Lundin and his researches into Insull's finances. Allen explains Insull's intricate holding companies. The portrait of Roosevelt in 1929 is from Gould and Freidel, and his fight with the power trust is from the *New York Times*, the *Literary Digest*, and Freidel. Allen reports that the House of Morgan was encouraging the stock frenzy. Material on the select list and how it was selected is found in 1933 hearings of the Senate Committee on Banking and Currency.

Material on the Jubilee is from Bernays' memoirs, the Edison files, news clippings, and trade journals. The Ripley article, from an unidentified trade magazine, was found in the Edison files. A transcript of the NBC broadcast was found at the Ford museum. The description of the banquet comes from various newspaper sources, chiefly the *New York Times* and the *Philadelphia Inquirer*. Congressman Eaton's own account was published in the *Daily Home News* of New Brunswick, New Jersey.

The meeting of Insull and Edison is reported in the Josephson biography and in Silverberg. The confidential message from Insull is from Edison's files in West Orange. The description of the dinner at Delmonico's is from McDonald.

Edison's fear of returning to the banquet was reported in the *New York Times*. The Japanese interest in the Bywater book was reported in Honan. Other material was reported in the *Literary Digest* and the *New York Times*. Also useful was Nicholas Roosevelt's review of the Bywater book. The thoughts of Bernays on returning to New York came from his memoirs and the interview.

Epilogue

The Amos 'n' Andy dialogue was reported by Wertheim. The Kahn material is from the Kahn papers. Lamont's quotation is from Galbraith. Insull's flight is from the *New York Times* stories. The Eaton-Schwab proxy fight is reported in Sheehan. Insull's fall into Morgan's hands was chronicled in McDonald.The description of the Morgan yacht is from the *New York Times*, and Morgan's moves were also reported in trial testimony. The request for Bernays to count inches is reported in his memoirs. The closing anecdote about Schacht is from Lyons.

A Final Note

No definitive list of attendees at the Dearborn dinner exists, but staff members at the Henry Ford Museum were engaged in 1979 in putting one together. Whether Ambassador Dawes attended remains a mystery. He was listed in advance publicity as an expected guest, and the *Detroit Free Press* places him at the head table, but this may be a case of mistaken identity. It is possible that he arrived late and attended only the dinner, and that his name was not included on any list. For the purposes of this book I have not placed him at the dinner.

Years later Henry Ford ordered a mural painted of the dinner showing all the guests. Among those visible are Mr. and Mrs. Edsel Ford and their sons Benson and Henry. Actually a childhood disease of one of the children kept them all in quarantine that night and they missed the dinner. As history, then, to paraphrase Henry Ford's most famous quotation, the mural is more or less bunk.

APPENDIX 2

Biographical Notes

Addams, Jane, 1860–1935. Graduate, 1881, of Rockford Seminary. Formed interest in social work after visiting Toynbee Hall, a London settlement house. With Hull House, located in Chicago's slums, as base of operation, she became most important figure in reform in U.S. Became pacifist under influence of Tolstoy's writings. Target of attacks by Daughters of the American Revolution and like-minded groups which lasted through the 1920s for her anti-war activities. Shared Nobel Peace Prize with Nicholas Murray Butler in 1931. Prolific writer of books and magazine articles. Most famous work, *Twenty Years at Hull House*, published 1910.

Alexanderson, Ernst F.W., 1878–1975. Swedish native. Began forty-six-year career with General Electric in 1902. His alternator made possible first voice and music broadcast in 1906. Held 322 patents. Gave first home television demonstration in his home in Schenectady, 1927. Television systems later developed were based only partly on his work.

Arbuckle, Roscoe Conkling (Fatty), 1887–1933. Began film career with shorts for Mack Sennett, eventually released films through Famous Players Lasky. Made a thousand dollars a day until his arrest in 1921 on charges of manslaughter of a young actress. Tried three times, acquitted at third trial. Directed comedies under pseudonyms, opened nightclub. Making shorts and trying for comeback at time of death. "Those who demanded their pound of flesh finally received their satisfaction," said Will Rogers. "Roscoe 'Fatty' Arbuckle accommodated them by dying, and from a broken heart."

Aylesworth, Merlin Hall, 1886–1952. Graduate of University of Denver and Columbia University. Practiced law in Colorado. Chairman of Colorado Public Utilities Commission, then executive with Utah Power and Light Company, then managing director, National Electric Light Association. Became president of National Broadcasting Company, 1926, active in formation of network radio and development of program content. President of Radio City Music Hall, 1934–1935. President and chairman of the board of RKO, 1936. Publisher of *New York World Telegram*, 1938–1939.

Bernays, Edward L., 1891–   . Born in Vienna, Austria, nephew of Sigmund Freud, moved with family to New York as infant. Father a successful grain merchant. Received bachelor's degree at the agricultural college of Cornell University but moved instead into public relations. Represented Enrico Caruso and the American tour of the Ballets Russes. During World War I served on Committee on Public Information. Public relations counsel for Light's Golden Jubilee. During Depression, served on Hoover's Emergency Committee for Employment. Public relations director of New York World's Fair, 1939. Co-chairman of Victory Book Campaign, 1943, and headed Treasury Department's national publicity advisory committee for the third war loan. Now retired and living in Cambridge, Massachusetts.

340

Byrd, Richard Evelyn, 1888–1957. Member of one of the oldest Virginia families, graduated from Naval Academy, 1912. Lost the race to Lindbergh, 1927, in attempt to fly from New York to Paris nonstop. Edsel Ford and John D. Rockefeller, Jr. supported his 1928–1929 Antarctic expedition, which included flight over South Pole on November 29, 1929. Expedition led to his promotion to rear admiral. Other Antarctic expeditions in 1933 and 1939. Named in 1946 to command Navy's Antarctic Developments Project and placed in charge of Operation Deep Freeze, 1954, which was sent to establish permanent bases in Antarctica.

Callaghan, Morley Edward, 1903–   . After stint with Toronto newspaper he became highly regarded writer of fiction with publication of a novel, *Strange Fugitive*, 1928. Twentieth book, published 1977, was also a novel, *Close to the Sun Again*. Lives in Toronto.

Capone, Alphonse, 1899–1947. Born in Naples, Italy, raised in Brooklyn. Studied under Johnny Torrio, whom he joined in Chicago as a lieutenant. Eventually became boss of gang involved in various rackets. His enterprise included men on East Coast; trucks criss-crossed the nation providing Midwest with illegal alcohol during Prohibition. Involved in gang wars for control of liquor trade. Strong supporter of William Thompson as Chicago political leader. Arrested in Philadelphia in 1929, served a year. Went on trial in 1931 for tax evasion, served eleven years in federal prisons in Atlanta and at Alcatraz. Released 1939, admitted to Union Memorial Hospital in Baltimore for treatment of paresis which eventually caused brain damage. Died at Miami Beach.

Carnegie, Andrew, 1835–1919. Applying technological advances, he raised the quality and lowered the price of his steel; came to control the industry. Schwab his protégé. Sold out to Morgan, devoted remainder of life to philanthropy.

Chaplin, Charles Spencer, 1889–1977. Grew up in slums of London. Signed to appear in Keystone films in 1913, became quick success. In 1918 completed his own studio, joined with Mary Pickford, Douglas Fairbanks, and D. W. Griffith to form United Artists. Became delight of serious critics as well as public. Most important films: *The Gold Rush* (1925), *City Lights* (1931), *Modern Times* (1936). Politically vocal during Depression, later investigated and assailed for "communist" views. Left U.S. in 1952 and, because still a British citizen, denied re-entry. Welcomed back in 1972 to receive special Academy Award. Author of *My Autobiography*, 1964.

Curie, Marie Sklodowska, 1867–1934. Born in Warsaw. Involved as student in nationalist and progressive movement against Russian rule. Studied in Paris, met and married Pierre Curie, a French scientist. Together they discovered two new elements—polonium and radium—and explored her theory that radioactivity is a consequence of activity within the atom. Jointly received the Nobel Prize for physics, 1903. After Pierre was killed in a street accident, she received a second Nobel Prize—the first person ever to be so honored. Came to United States, 1921, to receive a gram of radium and returned, 1929, to receive funds for the Warsaw Radium Institute. In the year after her death, her daughter and son-in-law, Irene and Frederic Joliot-Curie, won a Nobel Prize.

Dawes, Charles Gates, 1865–1951. Born in Marietta, Ohio. Educated, Marietta College and Cincinnati Law School. Active in business as a utility executive and banker and in Republican politics. Controller of the Currency in McKinley administration at age of thirty-two. Organized Central Trust Company of Illinois. Served in World War I in France as a general, remained as member of Liquidation Commission. First director of the budget, Harding administration. Chairman of Dawes Commission on Reparations, awarded Nobel Peace Prize. Vice-president in Coolidge administration. Considered a presidential candidate at 1928 GOP convention. Ambassador to Great Britain, 1929. Delegate to London Naval Conference, 1930. Negotiated ten-million-dollar loan to assure opening of Chicago World's Fair during Depression. First president of Reconstruction Finance Corporation. Interested in archeology and music. One of his compositions, "Melody in A Major," was adapted as a popular song, "It's All in the Game," a hit in the 1950s.

De Forest, Lee, 1873–1961. Developed triode vacuum tube; also worked in sound films and television. Called "the father of radio broadcasting."

Diaghilev, Serge, 1872–1929. Born Novgorod, Russia. Graduated from Conservatory of Petrograd and became director of the Czar's ballet in Petrograd. Chosen as manager when the Ballets Russes was sent outside Russia, to Paris, for first time, 1909. In 1910 the ballet company became the rage of Paris with *Scheherazade*, settings by Bakst, music by Rimsky-Korsakoff. Became a focal point for iconoclastic artistry—Picasso, Matisse, Stravinsky, Prokofieff, Nijinsky, Pavlova, Fokine. Spent lavishly for settings, costumes, orchestra, dancers. Toured United States under sponsorship of Otto Kahn, 1916.

Douglas, Paul Howard, 1892–1976. Bowdoin College graduate; doctorate, Columbia University. Taught economics at University of Chicago, became opponent of Insull. Elected Chicago alderman, 1939. Enlisted for combat service in World War II at age fifty and became war hero. Elected as Illinois Democrat to U.S. Senate, 1948, and served three terms, a champion of civil rights. Defeated for re-election, 1966; joined faculty at New School for Social Research, New York.

Eaton, Charles Aubrey, 1868–1953. Born Nova Scotia. Ordained Baptist minister, ran dairy farm and industrial relations firm; then General Electric executive. Congressman (Republican, New Jersey) for fourteen terms. As chairman and ranking GOP member, House Foreign Affairs Committee, he supported European recovery program after World War II and became a power in postwar foreign policy.

Eaton, Cyrus Stephen, 1883–1979. Born Nova Scotia. Graduated McMaster University, Toronto. Became associated with Rockefellers. Began extensive activity with utilities, 1912; became interested in Insull properties in late 1920s. Also active in steel, rubber, paints. Organized Republic Steel Company, 1930. After World War II became promoter of Soviet-American friendship, financed meeting of Soviet and American atomic scientists in 1954.

Edison, Thomas Alva, 1847–1931. Little formal education. Learned telegraphy and at seventeen was on the road as telegraph operator. First successful invention was a stock ticker. In 1876 devised a significant improvement for the telephone transmitter. Opened Menlo Park laboratory in same year, vowing to produce "a minor invention every ten days and a big one every six months or so." There invented the phonograph and the incandescent lamp. Became a manufacturer by necessity, and in 1882 began operation of the Pearl Street Station in New York. Moved to larger quarters in West Orange in 1887 where he continued to develop inventions, including the motion picture machine. Had become one of most admired American folk heroes: the self-taught go-getter whose genius was of a practical bent. During World War I directed research on armaments as president of Naval Consulting Board. Last project was working with Firestone and Ford to develop rubber from goldenrod. He produced the business-technology link that has characterized the modern world and developed the power source that made it possible. Upon the death of Edison, President Hoover considered having the nation's electrical power system turned off as a tribute but discovered that such a step would produce catastrophe.

Einstein, Albert, 1879–1955. Born in Ulm, Germany, of Jewish parents. Graduate of Polytechnic Academy, Zurich, Switzerland. Published special theory of relativity, 1905. Published general theory of relativity, 1916. Awarded Nobel Prize in physics, 1921. Published unified field theory, 1929. Fled Germany, joined staff at Institute for Advanced Study, Princeton, New Jersey, 1933. Revised unified field theory, 1949.

Fitzgerald, Francis Scott Key, 1896–1940. Educated at Princeton University. A highly popular writer in the 1920s and a symbol of the new spirit of the times, his critical reputation was established in 1925 with *The Great Gatsby*. With the coming of the Depression, time appeared to have passed him by. Writing gave way to alcoholism and poor health and he wrote to sustain Zelda's lengthy stays in asylums and rest homes. He moved to Hollywood to work on movie scripts and died there at forty-four. Since his death his reputation has been restored.

Fitzgerald, Zelda Sayre, 1900–1948. Born Montgomery, Alabama. As wife of F. Scott Fitzgerald, became embodiment of the flapper. Admitted with symptoms of extreme anxiety to mental hospital outside Paris, 1930. Published a novel, *Save Me the Waltz*, 1932. Spent remainder of life in and out of mental institutions. Died in hospital fire.

Ford, Henry, 1863–1947. Educated, Dearborn public schools. Disliked assisting father in farming, always interested in machines and had uncanny knack with them. Joined Edison Illuminating Company, Detroit, 1891, and eventually became chief engineer. Worked on internal combustion engine in spare hours. Advised by employers to pay more attention to job, give up experimenting. First person to encourage him was the great inventor Edison, in Detroit for a dinner. Ford told his plans, Edison responded that he should keep at it. Ford came to idolize the inventor and they later became close friends. At forty, formed the Ford Motor Company. Revolutionized motorcar industry, 1908, with Model T, a cheap auto for the masses; introduced mass-production techniques. Announced five-dollar workday, 1914. Fought Selden patent trust, establishing reputation as foe of monopoly. Ran for U.S. Senate, 1918; widely supported as an undeclared candidate for presidency in early 1920s. Accumulated more than one billion dollars. Ford Foundation endowed in 1936. One of the most paradoxical and influential figures in history. "Ford runs modern society," F. Scott Fitzgerald wrote in 1924, "and not the politicians who are only screens." Aldous Huxley's *Brave New World*, published 1932, depicted a future society in which "Our Ford" was deified.

Hays, William Harrison, 1879–1954. Graduate of Wabash College. A lawyer who rose through Indiana politics to become chairman of Republican National

Committee, 1918, then presided over Warren Harding's presidential victory in
1920. Became Postmaster General in Harding cabinet. Left in 1922 to become
president of Motion Picture Producers and Distributors of America. Regarded
through much of 1920s as a possible presidential candidate. Called to testify in
1924 Teapot Dome investigation. When called back in 1928, it became clear
that he had misled Senate committee in earlier testimony. Promulgated Motion
Picture Code, 1930. Resigned from film post, 1945.

Hearst, William Randolph, 1863–1951. Expelled from Harvard, 1885. Took
over editorship of *San Francisco Examiner,* 1887. Began building a newspaper
empire, relying heavily on stunts, crusades, and siding with the working people.
Helped push United States into Spanish-American War. Expanded into magazines and movies, owned more than a score of newspapers. Delivered delegate
votes that won FDR the Democratic nomination, 1932, but turned against him.
Heavy spending brought papers near bankruptcy by 1937, when empire began
to decline.

Hemingway, Ernest Miller, 1899–1961. No college. Began writing as newspaper reporter, attracted attention as expatriate in Paris, where he met James
Joyce and Gertrude Stein. *The Sun Also Rises,* his first novel, established him as
a writer to be watched, and *A Farewell To Arms,* published in 1929, catapulted
him to the front rank of American prose stylists. Bullfighting, big-game hunting,
and the Spanish Civil War became the subjects of later works. In 1954 he was
awarded the Nobel Prize for literature. He was seriously injured in a plane
crash in Africa that same year and never fully recovered.

Hoover, Herbert Clark, 1874–1964. Stanford University graduate. Mining
engineer and partner in London firm. Russian oil and Burmese tin projects
helped make his fortune. Became head of relief efforts in London when World
War I broke out. Named chairman of Commission for the Relief of Belgium,
1915. In 1917 President Wilson appointed him head of Food Administration
Board. Took charge of providing food and help for war-torn Europe after the
war. Secretary of commerce in Harding and Coolidge administrations. Elected
president, 1928. His administration, begun with bright hopes, was engulfed in
Depression. Advocated public works programs, sought voluntary wage and
price maintenance. Franklin D. Roosevelt defeated his bid for re-election, 1932.

Insull, Samuel, 1859–1938. Studied stenography and bookkeeping in London, came to United States as assistant to Edison, helped formulate Edison
General Electric. His views on mass use of electricity paralleled Ford's on mass
production. Chairman of Illinois State Council of Defense during World War
I. A pioneer in promoting public sale of utility stocks, which helped produce remarkable financial growth of his companies; his key companies eventually failed.
Acquitted on all charges of fraud, embezzlement, and violation of bankruptcy
laws. Never recovered financially and in the Depression became a symbol of
frantic financing.

Jones, Mary Harris (Mother), 1830–1930. Born in Cork, Ireland. After yellow fever wiped out her family in Memphis she became Chicago dressmaker,
but great fire of 1871 destroyed her business. Devoted remainder of life to the
cause of labor. Opposed child labor. Organized marches to close down mines in
hard-coal strike of 1900. Became organizer for United Mine Workers, arrested
as agitator during Colorado Fuel & Iron strike, 1914. Made last speech to a

group of labor leaders in Silver Spring, Maryland, on her one-hundredth birthday. A few days later received congratulatory telegram from John D. Rockefeller, Jr.

Kahn, Otto Hermann, 1867–1934. Born in Germany into a cultured Jewish
family. Went to his first opera at eleven, was enthralled. Dreamed of an artistic
life but launched career as executive in London branch of the Deutsche Bank.
Became British subject. Took position in American bank and eventually became
partner in Kuhn, Loeb investment house. Became known as a cultural entrepren-
eur and a patron of the arts, knew most of the important figures in the arts in
his time. Revitalized the Metropolitan Opera Company by bringing Arturo
Toscanini and Giulio Gatti-Casazza from La Scala to be conductor and general
manager, respectively. Introduced Nijinsky and Ballets Russes, Stanislavski, the
Abbey Players, and the Moscow Art Theatre to America. Resigned as Met
chairman, 1931.

Lamont, Thomas William, 1870–1948. Harvard graduate. Was journalist for
the *New York Tribune* before entering banking. Became Morgan partner, 1910.
Served on peace commission, 1919. Specialist in international loans and currency. Served on reparations commissions in 1924 and 1929. Worked on establishing Bank of International Settlements, 1931. Corresponded with literary
figures, supported the *Saturday Review of Literature*. Upon death of Morgan,
1943, became chairman of the board, J.P. Morgan & Company, Inc., and held
chairmanship until his death.

Lee, Ivy Ledbetter, 1877–1934. Princeton University graduate. Founder of
the business of public relations, he was the first important publicist for business
firms. Became associated with Pennsylvania Railroad, then helped Rockefeller
during Colorado Fuel & Iron strike. Clients also included firms of Otto Kahn
and Charles Schwab. An advocate of increased trade with U.S.S.R. and of U.S.
recognition of Soviet government, was falsely accused of being in pay of Soviets.
He did represent foreign interests, however, including German dye trust, I.G.
Farben. Died at St. Luke's Hospital, New York, of a brain tumor. His associates
had to put obituary together; the great publicist had never prepared one for
himself.

Lewis, Sinclair, 1885–1951. Career as a novelist of social criticism zoomed
with *Main Street*, 1920, continued with *Babbitt*, 1922. Other significant fiction
included *Elmer Gantry*, 1927; *The Man Who Knew Coolidge*, 1928; *Dodsworth*,
1929; *It Can't Happen Here*, 1935. Won Nobel Prize for literature, 1930.

Lindbergh, Anne Spencer Morrow, 1906–   . Smith College graduate.
Author of several successful books, most notably *Gift From the Sea*, 1955. Lives
in Darien, Connecticut.

Lindbergh, Charles Augustus, Jr., 1902–1974. Father served in Congress.
Became world-famous figure upon making nonstop flight from New York to
Paris in 1927. On a later flight to Mexico City he met Anne Morrow, daughter
of Ambassador Dwight Morrow. Their engagement was announced in 1929 and
they were married that same year. In 1929 he also became technical advisor to
Pan-American Airways and Transcontinental Air Transport. The Lindberghs'
two-year-old son was kidnapped and murdered in 1932. Became convinced in
1930s that Nazi airpower was invincible and British were soft. Nazis awarded
him Service Cross of the German Eagle, 1938. Accused British and Jews of

pushing United States into war with Germany. During World War II worked with Henry Ford on aviation at Dearborn. In late years he embraced environmental concerns, campaigned against supersonic transport jet.

Lindsey, Benjamin Barr, 1869–1943. On bench in Denver for a quarter-century. Ran unsuccessfully for governor of Colorado. His books, especially *The Beast in the Jungle* and *The Companionate Marriage*, aroused great controversy. Ruled the loser in a judgeship election, he left the bench in 1927. Disbarred, 1929, for accepting gift as mediator on behalf of two children in contested will. Ejected from Cathedral of St. John the Divine, New York, 1930, when he disrupted service; his sexual views had been attacked from pulpit. Arrested and charged with disorderly conduct. Nazis burned his books on Berlin University campus, 1933. Elected judge of Los Angeles Superior Court, 1934. Granted Mary Pickford a divorce from Douglas Fairbanks, 1935. Regarded as founder of juvenile court system.

MacDonald, James Ramsay, 1866–1937. Born in Lossiemouth, Scotland. Joined Fabian Society after reaching London. Pursued political career, lost his seat in Parliament and was denounced as traitor for pacifism during World War I. Became Great Britain's first Labor prime minister, 1924; government fell with Zinoviev letter. Second MacDonald government took office, 1929. Reorganized cabinet in coalition with Liberals and Conservatives, 1931. Resigned, 1935. Died on shipboard seeking rest; his doctor had advised that he leave strife-torn Europe and its problems. His retort: "I cannot believe this war talk."

Meloney, Marie Mattingly, 1876?–1943. Trained as concert pianist, turned to journalism after suffering horseback accident. Began career in 1900 with *Washington Post*, worked in Washington for various newspapers; bureau chief for *Denver Post*. Editor of *The Delineator*. Interviewed Mussolini four times, turned down an interview with Hitler after he broke an appointment. Editor of the *Herald Tribune Magazine* and later of *This Week*. Organizer, Marie Curie Radium Committee. Founder, Better Homes in America. Organizer, Forum on Current Problems, 1930.

Mencken, Henry Louis, 1880–1956. Lived all his life in his native Baltimore. After high school he wrote for newspapers and was associated most of his life with the *Baltimore Sun*. In 1908 wrote first important study of Nietzsche in America. Co-editor of *The Smart Set*, 1914. Editor of the *American Mercury*, 1924–1933. Now best remembered for his memoirs and *The American Language*, his massive philological study.

Morgan, John Pierpont, 1837–1913. Put together General Electric, American Telephone & Telegraph, International Harvester, and United States Steel, making him a leading figure in the age of trusts. Most important and most legendary financier of the age. Important art collector.

Morgan, John Pierpont, 1867–1943. Graduated from Harvard, 1889. Became partner in father's private banking firm at age of twenty-four. Became head of firm upon death of his father, 1913. During World War I organized syndicate of twenty-two hundred banks to handle Allied loans, launching modern era of international finance. Served as member of the Reparations Committee and helped design Bank of International Settlements, 1929. During Depression the House of Morgan was investigated several times, and in 1933 the Banking Act forced the House to choose between investment and commercial banking, thus curbing its enormous power. Morgan chose commercial banking.

Mussolini, Benito Juarez, 1883–1945. Born in Dovia, Italy, of poor parents. Became prominent Socialist agitator and journalist, then switched politics to found Fascism. Took power in Italy, 1922. Invaded and conquered Ethiopia, 1935. Proclaimed alliance with Hitler, 1938. Suffered heavy reverses from the first in World War II. Killed by Italian partisans.

Nijinsky, Vaslav, 1890–1950. His mother succeeded in getting him into the Imperial Ballet of St. Petersburg when he was nine years old. Professional debut, 1907. Joined Diaghilev for Paris appearance, 1909. First United States appearance, 1916. Final performance in Montevideo in 1917 when mental disorder began. Entered private hospital for mentally disturbed two years later. Lived during World War II with wife in Odenburg, Hungary, and settled in Surrey, England, in 1947.

Rockefeller, John Davison, 1839–1937. Organized Standard Oil Company of Ohio, 1870. By 1881 had taken over 90 percent of petroleum industry. U.S. Supreme Court demanded breakup of Standard Oil Trust, 1911. By 1895 he had ceased active participation in company, devoted time to philanthropy.

Rockefeller, John Davison, Jr., 1874–1960. Educated at Brown University. Heir to huge Standard Oil fortune. Turned from business to become his father's principal agent in philanthropy and eventually came to hold most of the vast Rockefeller estate. Administered four great corporate philanthropies: the Institute for Medical Research, the General Education Fund, the Rockefeller Foundation, and the Laura Spelman Rockefeller Memorial Fund. Championed and aided the cause of Prohibition; his 1932 announcement that he had changed his mind was an important factor in repeal. Contributed, according to *New York Times*, a total of six hundred million dollars to various causes; they included restoration of Williamsburg, California redwoods, Yosemite National Park, Palisades Interstate Park, Palomar Mountain's two-hundred-inch telescope at California Institute of Technology, Lincoln Center for the Performing Arts in New York, and a seventeen-acre site for the United Nations building along the East River in Manhattan. Respected if not loved in America; a 1956 *Time* magazine cover story (entitled "The Good Man") called him "an authentic American hero."

Rogers, William Penn Adair, 1879–1935. Partly Cherokee. Attended boarding schools. Worked as a cowboy, learned to twirl lariat. Joined Wild West Show, 1905. Added jokes to his act, became a New York vaudeville entertainer, appearing at Hammerstein's Roof Garden. Played in Broadway musicals, beginning in 1912 with *The Wall Street Girl*. Played in Ziegfeld Follies. Began making silent films, 1918. Moved to California, 1919, but returned to New York to play in 1922 version of the Follies. Began writing a syndicated column for the *New York Times* in 1922, eventually appearing in five hundred newspapers. Also wrote several humorous books. Easily made transition to sound films in 1929. An unpretentious man, he was beloved of his fellow Americans, and his death in a plane crash in Alaska shocked the nation.

Roosevelt, Franklin Delano, 1882–1945. Born into a life of privilege, graduated from Harvard and Columbia Law School, admitted to bar in 1907. Assistant secretary of navy in Wilson administration, ran as vice presidential candidate on defeated Democratic ticket, 1920. Stricken with polio, 1921. Resumed political career, elected governor of New York, 1928. Became opponent of power trust. Re-elected 1930. In 1932 defeated Herbert Hoover for presidency, re-elected three times. Failed to end Depression but served as inspiring national leader, using radio to great advantage through economic hard times and World War II.

Rosenwald, Julius, 1862–1932. Educated in Springfield, Illinois, public schools. Worked in New York City until 1885, when he established a clothing firm in Chicago with relatives. Purchased interest in Sears, Roebuck & Company in 1895 and rose to become president and chairman of the board. Contributed liberally to numerous endeavors, including five million dollars to the University of Chicago. Critical of the dead hand in philanthropy, he stipulated in 1928, when Rosenwald Fund was reorganized, that all its money be expended within a quarter-century after his death. The fund, in accordance with this requirement, completed its work in 1948.

Sarnoff, David, 1891–1971. Born in Byelorussia, reached New York in 1900. In 1912, while on duty as wireless operator in Manhattan, became sole contact with S.S. Titanic, struck by iceberg. For three days and three nights without rest he kept world informed of disaster. Protégé of Owen Young, rose to presidency of RCA in 1930. Foresaw development of broadcast radio. Took deep interest in development of television, responsible for NBC television exhibition at 1939 World's Fair in New York and founding of a TV station in New York, 1941. Also pioneered in development of color TV.

Schacht, Hjalmar Horace Greeley, 1877–1970. Born in Tingleff, Germany, and named for American editor; his parents had lived in New York. Graduate, University of Kiel. During World War I, financial advisor to German occupying authorities in Belgium. German Commissioner of Currency, 1923. President of Reichsbank, resigned 1930. Hitler reappointed him to the post, 1933. Left Reichsbank presidency again, 1939. Imprisoned for communicating with group plotting Hitler's murder. Tried as war criminal at Nuremberg, acquitted. Reestablished himself in West Germany as banker and economic advisor—thus achieving success under Kaiser, Weimar Republic, Hitler, and West Germany.

Schwab, Charles Michael, 1862–1939. From a grocery store clerk, Schwab rose rapidly as protégé of Andrew Carnegie. Chief engineer at main plant by nineteen, superintendent by twenty-five. By 1897 president of Carnegie Steel Company. Persuaded Carnegie to sell out to J.P. Morgan and became president of United States Steel, but left to build Bethlehem Steel as great armaments firm. Once the highest-salaried man in America, he lived high and died with few assets remaining.

Shearer, William Baldwin, 1874–1958. Sent to Geneva conference on naval limitations in 1927 as agent of three shipbuilding companies. In 1929 he testified about his role before Senate Naval Affairs Committee in self-dramatizing account. Died at Boca Raton, Florida. After his death his sister said that he had written a book of his experiences "so full of dynamite" that no publisher would touch it.

Smith, Frank Leslie, 1867–1950. Chairman, Illinois Commerce Commission, 1918–1920, 1922–1926. Elected to U.S. Senate (Republican, Illinois), 1926, but excluded because of Insull financing of campaign. Delegate to numerous Republican national conventions, the last in 1948.

Stewart, Colonel Robert Wright, 1866–1947. Law degree, Yale University; practiced law in South Dakota. Served in Spanish-American War, did not see action. General counsel for Standard Oil of Indiana, 1915. Chairman of the board for same, 1918–1929. After losing chairmanship in fight with Rockefeller, became director of Indiana Limestone Company, resigned in 1932. Lived last years in Chicago and Miami Beach, Florida.

Swope, Gerard, 1872–1957. Graduated from Massachusetts Institute of Technology, 1895. Joined staff of Hull House, 1897. Electrical engineer; became president of General Electric, 1922. Served on various councils during Depression. He and Young, who had taken GE's top positions together, retired together, 1939.

Wright, Orville, 1871–1948. With brother Wilbur, operated bicycle shop in Dayton, Ohio, and devoted spare time to study of flight. Experimented with gliders, flew them in 1899. Built wind tunnel in 1901, testing 200 wing surfaces, demonstrating fallacies of most previous work on flight. Orville first man to fly in heavier-than-air machine, at Kitty Hawk, 1903. Even after flight faced several years of skepticism. After Wilbur's death in 1912 Orville sold patent rights, got out of aviation business, and lost impetus for further research. Wright home and bicycle shop moved to Greenfield Village, 1938.

Young, Owen D., 1874–1962. A New York State native, graduate of St. Lawrence University, earned law degree at Boston University. Practiced law in Boston, joined General Electric in 1912, became general counsel in 1913 and chairman of the board of directors in 1922. Organized RCA, NBC, served on reparations commissions in 1924 and 1929. Never ran for elective office although often urged to by friends and editors. Embarrassed during Depression by revelation that he aided Insull with loan during latter's financial tailspin. Retired in 1939, taking up dairy farming at Van Hornesville, New York. Continued public service, was chairman of commission recommending establishment of State University of New York, 1949.

BIBLIOGRAPHY

Books

ALLEN, FREDERICK LEWIS. *The Lords of Creation*. New York: Harper & Brothers, 1935.

———. *Only Yesterday*. New York: Harper & Brothers, 1931.

BAKER, CARLOS. *Ernest Hemingway: A Life Story*. New York: Charles Scribner's Sons, 1969.

BERNAYS, EDWARD L. *Biography of an Idea*. New York: Simon & Schuster, 1965.

———. *Propaganda*. New York: Horace Liveright, Inc., 1928.

BORKIN, JOSEPH, AND WELSH, CHARLES A. *Germany's Master Plan*. New York: Duell, Sloan & Pearce, 1943.

BRAEMAN, JOHN; BREMNER, ROBERT H.; AND BRODY, DAVID, eds. *Change and Continuity in Twentieth-Century America: The 1920's*. Columbus, Ohio: Ohio State University Press, 1968.

BROOKS, JOHN. *Once in Golconda: A True Drama of Wall Street 1920–1938*. New York: Harper & Row, 1968.

BYRD, RICHARD E. *Little America*. New York: G. P. Putnam's, 1930.

CALLAGHAN, MORLEY. *That Summer in Paris*. New York: Coward McCann, 1963.

CHAPLIN, LITA GREY, WITH MORTON COOPER. *My Life With Chaplin: An Intimate Memoir*. New York: Bernard Geis Associates, 1966.

CHASE, STUART. *Men and Machines*. New York: Macmillan Co., 1929.

CLARK, ROBERT THOMSON. *The Fall of the German Republic*. New York: Russell & Russell, 1964.

DAVIS, ALLEN F. *American Heroine: The Life and Legend of Jane Addams*. New York: Oxford University Press, 1973.

DIGGINS, JOHN P. *Mussolini and Fascism: The View From America*. Princeton, N.J.: Princeton University Press, 1972.

DOUGLAS, PAUL H. *In the Fullness of Time*. New York: Harcourt Brace Jovanovich, 1972.

FOSDICK, RAYMOND B. *John D. Rockefeller Jr.: A Portrait*. New York: Harper & Row, 1956.

FREIDEL, FRANK. *Franklin D. Roosevelt: The Triumph*. Boston: Little, Brown, 1956.

GALBRAITH, JOHN KENNETH. *The Great Crash, 1929*. Boston: Houghton Mifflin, 1972.

GEDULD, HARRY M. *The Birth of the Talkies: From Edison to Jolson*. Bloomington, Indiana: Indiana University Press, 1975.

GOULD, JEAN. *A Good Fight: The Story of FDR's Conquest of Polio*. New York: Dodd, Mead & Co., 1960.

GRUENING, ERNEST. *The Public Pays*. New York: Vanguard Press, 1931.

HAYS, WILL H. *The Memoirs of Will H. Hays*. Garden City, N.Y.: Doubleday & Co., 1955.

HESSEN, ROBERT. *Steel Titan: The Life of Charles M. Schwab*. New York: Oxford University Press, 1975.

HOYT, EDWIN P., JR. *The House of Morgan*. New York: Dodd, Mead & Co., 1966.

INSULL, SAMUEL. *Public Utilities in Modern Life*. Chicago: Privately printed, 1924.

JOSEPHSON, MATTHEW. *Edison: A Biography*. New York: McGraw-Hill Book Co., 1959.

KAHN, OTTO H. *Of Many Things*. New York: Boni & Liveright, 1926.

KELLY, FRED C. *The Wright Brothers*. New York: Harcourt Brace & Co., 1943.

KETCHUM, RICHARD M. *Will Rogers: His Life and Times*. New York: American Heritage Publishing Co., 1973.

KOBLER, JOHN. *Capone*. New York: G.P. Putnam's, 1971.

KOCHNO, BORIS. *Diaghilev and the Ballets Russes*. New York: Harper & Row, 1970.

LARSON, CHARLES. *The Good Fight: The Life and Times of Ben B. Lindsey*. Chicago: Quadrangle Books, 1972.

LIEF, ALFRED. *The Firestone Story*. New York: McGraw-Hill Book Co., 1951.

LIFAR, SERGE. *Serge Diaghilev: His Life, His Work, His Legend*. New York: G. P. Putnam's Sons, 1940.

LINDBERGH, ANNE MORROW. *Hour of Gold, Hour of Lead*. New York: Harcourt Brace Jovanovich, 1973.

LINN, JAMES WEBER. *Jane Addams: A Biography*. New York: Appleton-Century Co., 1935.

LLOYD, CRAIG. *Aggressive Introvert: Herbert Hoover and Public Relations Management, 1912–1933*. Columbus, Ohio: Ohio State University Press, 1972.

LOTH, DAVID. *Swope of G.E.* New York: Simon & Schuster, 1958.

LYONS, EUGENE. *David Sarnoff*. New York: Harper & Row, 1966.

MATZ, MARY JANE. *The Many Lives of Otto Kahn*. New York: Macmillan Co., 1963.

MAYFIELD, SARA. *The Constant Circle: H.L. Mencken and His Friends*. New York: Delacorte Press, 1968.

MC DONALD, FORREST. *Insull*. Chicago: University of Chicago Press, 1962.

MILFORD, NANCY. *Zelda: A Biography*. New York: Harper & Row, 1970.

MORRIS, JOE ALEX. *What a Year!* New York: Harper & Brothers, 1956.

MORRIS, LLOYD. *Not So Long Ago*. New York: Random House, 1949.

MOSLEY, LEONARD. *Lindbergh: A Biography*. Garden City, N.Y.: Doubleday & Co., 1976.

NEVINS, ALLEN, AND HILL, FRANK ERNEST. *Ford: Expansion and Challenge 1915–1933*. New York: Charles Scribner's Sons, 1957.

PRINGLE, HENRY. *Big Frogs*. New York: Macy-Masius, 1928.

REID, ROBERT. *Marie Curie*. New York: Saturday Review Press/E.P. Dutton & Co., 1974.

SILVERBERG, ROBERT. *Light For the World: Edison and the Power Industry*. Princeton, N.J.: D. Van Nostrand, 1967.

SIMONSON, LEE. *The Stage Is Set*. New York: Harcourt, Brace, & Co., 1932.

SWARD, KEITH. *The Legend of Henry Ford.* New York: Rinehart & Co., 1948.

TARBELL, IDA. *Owen D. Young: A New Type of Industrial Leader.* New York: Macmillan Co., 1932.

THOMPSON, CARL D. *Confessions of the Power Trust.* New York: E.P. Dutton, 1932.

WALSH, JOHN EVANGELIST. *One Day at Kitty Hawk.* New York: Thomas Y. Crowell, 1975.

WERNER, M. R. *Julius Rosenwald: The Life of a Practical Humanitarian.* New York: Harper & Brothers, 1939.

YALLOP, DAVID. *The Day the Laughter Stopped.* New York: St. Martin's Press, 1976.

Periodicals

ABBOTT, PAUL. "Fever or Foresight?" *Outlook and Independent,* January 23, 1929.

ADAMS, MILDRED. "Here the President Finds Calm." *New York Times Magazine,* September 8, 1929.

ALLEN, ROBERT S. "Mr. Shearer Likes a Big Navy." *The Nation,* October 9, 1929.

American Mercury. "The Secretariat." December 1929.

ANDERSON, GEORGE E. "Ambassador Dawes." *Commonweal,* May 8, 1929.

ANDERSON, PAUL Y. "The Radio Corporation in the News." *The Nation,* January 1, 1930.

———. "The Radio Trust Gets the Air!" *The Nation,* June 26, 1929.

———. "The Sacred Radio Trust." *The Nation,* December 18, 1929.

BAILIE, HELEN TUFTS. "Dishonoring the D.A.R." *The Nation,* September 25, 1929.

BRADFORD, GAMALIEL. "The Great American Enigma: An Exploration of Henry Ford." *Harper's Magazine,* October 1930.

BROCK, H. I. "A Place de l'Opera for New York City." *New York Times Magazine,* February 10, 1929.

Business Week. "Blueprint of a Nation—in Red." October 5, 1929.

———. "Electricity Nearer Its Goal." October 12, 1929.

———. "The House of Morgan." September 28, 1929.

———. "Selling—With Sound Effects." October 26, 1929.

———. "Trade Association Is Keystone of Swope Stabilization Plan." September 23, 1931.

———. "World Battle Starts in Air and Under Sea." November 23, 1929.

CALLENDER, HAROLD. "As Dawes Moves in London's Spotlight." *New York Times Magazine,* September 1, 1929.

CLANCY, CARL STEARNS. "Aviation's Patron Saint." *Scientific American,* October 1929.

CONWAY, JILL. "Jane Addams: An American Heroine." *Daedalus,* Spring 1964.

CORTESI, ARNALDO. "Time Has Softened Mussolini's Frown." *New York Times Magazine,* July 21, 1929.

———. "Vatican and Italy Sign Pact Recreating a Papal State; 60 Years of Enmity Ended." *New York Times*, February 12, 1929.

DUFFUS, R. L. "Covering the News of Frozen Antarctica." *New York Times*, February 10, 1929.

———. "The Function of the Racketeer." *New Republic*, March 27, 1929.

———. "A Great Rocket For Exploring Outer Space." *New York Times*, December 15, 1929.

———. "The Most Traveled President." *New York Times Magazine*, January 6, 1929.

FLYNN, JOHN T. "Edward L. Bernays: The Science of Ballyhoo." *Atlantic Monthly*, June 1932.

———. "J.P. Morgan & Co.: A House Built on Favors." *New Republic*, June 28, 1933.

———. "What Happened To Insull." *New Republic*, May 4, 1932.

FORD, HENRY. "Light's Golden Jubilee." An Interview With Frank R. Innes in the July 20 *Electrical World. Review of Reviews*, August 1929.

———. "Machinery, the New Messiah." *Forum*, March 1928.

FRANK, WALDO. "Charles Chaplin: A Portrait." *Scribner's Magazine*, September 1929.

GAMMACK, THOMAS H. "May Radio Utilities Merge?" *Outlook and Independent*, June 19, 1929.

HARD, WILLIAM. "Superpower—Master or Servant?" *World's Work*, June 1931.

HODGINS, ERIC. "Heavier Than Air." *The New Yorker*, December 13, 1930.

HONAN, WILLIAM H. "Japan Strikes: 1941." *American Heritage*, December 1970.

JAMES, EDWIN L. "Owen D. Young Tackles His Hardest Task." *New York Times*, March 17, 1929.

———. "Restored Europe Soon To Face America." *New York Times*, March 31, 1929.

———. "Six Nations Give Views on Reparation Issue; Young in the Chair." *New York Times*, February 12, 1929.

———. "War Debts Dominate Reparation Question." *New York Times*, February 10, 1929.

———. "World Gold Control by War Bank Debt Visioned by Expert." *New York Times*, March 18, 1929.

———. "Young Regards Bank Chief Achievement." *New York Times*, June 8, 1929.

JOHNSTON, ALVA. "The Wizard." *The New Yorker*, December 28, 1929; January 4, and January 11, 1930.

JOSEPHSON, MATTHEW. "Chicago: A Modernistic Portrait." *Outlook and Independent*, January 30, 1929.

KAEMPFFERT, WALDEMAR. "The Age of Superpower Is Here." *New York Times Magazine*, September 22, 1929.

———. "Museum Will Depict Upward Climb of Man." *New York Times*, July 21, 1929.

———. "The Mussolini of Highland Park." *New York Times Magazine*, January 8, 1928.

KISCH, EGON ERWIN. "I Work With Charlie Chaplin." *Living Age*, October 15, 1929.

LENGYEL, EMIL. "Reich Calls on Schacht in Financial Tangles." *New York Times*, April 28, 1929.

LESCARBOURA, AUSTIN. "A Chat With Madame Curie." *Scientific American*, July 9, 1921.

Literary Digest. "After All, Einstein Is a Human Being." April 13, 1929.

———. "All Aboard the Lindbergh Limited!" March 2, 1929.

———. "Aviation's Twenty-Five Birthday Candles." January 5, 1929.

———. "The Battle of the Oil Giants." February 2, 1929.

———. "The Boulder Dam Deadlock Broken." July 13, 1929.

———. " 'Business Will Be Fine in Nineteen-Twenty-Nine.' " January 19, 1929.

———. "A Country Editor's 'Scoop' on the New Ford Car." December 3, 1927.

———. "A Cruiser Victory That May Aid Disarmament." February 16, 1929.

———. "Ford and Edison on the Inventions of the Future." December 7, 1929.

———. "The Ford 'Retractor.' " July 23, 1927.

———. "Henry Ford on His Plans and Philosophy." January 7, 1928.

———. "The 'Hoover Bull Market.' " November 24, 1928.

———. "How Japan Wants Naval Reduction." November 2, 1929.

———. "How Owen D. Young Ended the War After the War." July 6, 1929.

———. "An International Bombshell—'Germany Can Pay.' " January 19, 1929.

———. "Is Germany Really Paying Anybody Anything?" March 16, 1929.

———. "The Issue Behind the Cruiser Controversy." February 16, 1929.

———. " 'Johnny Strikes Up the Band.' " February 9, 1929.

———. "The Miracles of 2029." February 16, 1929.

———. "The Mystery of the Ambassador's Calves." July 20, 1929.

———. "O'Neill Wrestles With God." March 2, 1929.

———. "Philadelphia Justice For Chicago's Al Capone." June 15, 1929.

———. "Rockefeller Jr. Discovers Colorado." October 23, 1915.

———. "The Roosevelt Fight on Morgan Superpower." September 28, 1929.

———. "A Scientist's Blast at God and Sin." January 26, 1929.

———. "She Discovered Radium, But Hasn't a Gram Of It." April 2, 1921.

———. "A 'Sound' Merger: Radio-Victor." February 16, 1929.

———. " 'Strafing' New York From the Clouds." June 8, 1929.

———. "Success as Mere Luck." June 29, 1929.

———. "Ten Rules For Making Prosperity Stick." January 19, 1929.

———. "Wall Street's 'Prosperity Panic.' " November 9, 1929.

———. "Why America Likes the MacDonalds—And How!" November 2, 1929.

———. "Why Our Bankers Like Mussolini." February 13, 1926.

———. "A World Bank For Financial Peace." June 22, 1929.

———. "Zero Hour in the Rum War." November 2, 1929.

Living Age. "Reparations: A Setback and a Compromise." June 1929.

MARKEY, MORRIS. "Young Man Of Affairs." *The New Yorker*, September 20 and 27, 1930.

MARTIN, JOHN. "The Dance: A Changed 'Scheherazade.' " *New York Times*, October 20, 1929.

MC CORMICK, ANNE O'HARE. "Two Peacemakers: A Striking Contrast." *New York Times*, October 13, 1929.

MC COY, H.G. "How the 'Big Bass Drum' Sounded in Washington." *New York Times*, October 6, 1929.

MC GARRY, WILLIAM A. "Insull Lays a Specter." *World's Work*, April 1931.
MC HUGH, F.D. "Ford's Friend Edison." *Scientific American*, November 1929.
MC MULLEN, FRANCIS D. "The Army of Women Who Watch the Ticker." *New York Times*, March 31, 1929.
MENCKEN, H.L. "The Library: A City In Moronia." *American Mercury*, March 1929.
———. "The Library: Man and the Universe." *American Mercury*, July 1929.
———. "The Library: What Is It All About?" *American Mercury*, June 1929.
MERZ, CHARLES. "Our Second Billionaire." *World's Work*, April 1929.
MITCHELL, JONATHAN. "Trade With Russia Becomes Respectable." *Outlook and Independent*, July 10, 1929.
MOSHER, JOHN CHAPIN. "That Sad Young Man." *The New Yorker*, April 17, 1926.
The Nation. "The Disgrace at Geneva." August 10, 1927.
———. "Monopoly in the Air." December 25, 1929.
———. "The Scandal at Geneva." July 13, 1927.
———. "The Shipbuilders and Shearer." September 25, 1929.
NAYLOR, DOUGLAS O. "Now the Amazon Jungle Is Stirred By Henry Ford." *New York Times Magazine*, January 13, 1929.
New Republic. "The Purpose of the Cruisers." January 30, 1929.
New York Times. "American Tells of 'Borah Forgery.' " July 4, 1929.
———. "Anti-Semites Busy Again In Germany." April 21, 1929.
———. "Auto and Film Held Menaces of Home." February 25, 1929.
———. "Church Paper Sees 'Morals' in Oil War." March 2, 1929.
———. "Edison a Passenger in a New Ford Car." December 20, 1927.
———. "Ford, at 64, Faces Life's Biggest Job with His New Car." July 31, 1927.
———. "Ford Car's Debut Jams Showrooms." December 3, 1927.
———. "Ford Thinks Ancients Had Planes and Radios." December 18, 1928.
———. "Ford's Views on Europe's Needs." June 23, 1929.
———. "Fords Win Praise at Show in Waldorf." December 2, 1927.
———. "Forty-Five Dead, Twenty Hurt, Score Missing in Strike War." April 22, 1914.
———. "Inauguration Has World Broadcast." March 5, 1929.
———. "Japan Rehearses in War-Work Game." July 28, 1929.
———. "Laughter Lightens Curtis's Induction." March 5, 1929.
———. "Lindbergh 'Rescued' From Crowd on Landing; Complies with Demands To Make a Speech." October 21, 1929.
———. "New Morgan Yacht Costs $2,500,000." March 11, 1930.
———. "Orloff Is On Trial In Red Forgeries." July 2, 1929.
———. "Reparations Settlement Was Speeded Up To Get Young Home for His Son's Wedding." June 18, 1929.
———. "Rockefeller at 90 Cuts Birthday Cake." July 9, 1929.
———. "Russian Ballet Modified." January 26, 1916.
———. "Says Utilities Paid Woman Club Leader." October 5, 1928.
———. "To Call C.M. Schwab in Naval Inquiry." September 15, 1929.
———. "Trail of Insulls Leads Into Italy." October 8, 1932.
———. "Two Thousand Honor Brown as Charity Leader." May 24, 1929.

Newsweek. "Morgan: Wall Street's Thickset Banker a Squire in England." February 9, 1935.

NORRIS, GEORGE W. "The Power Trust in the Public Schools." *The Nation*, September 18, 1929.

The Outlook. "Mr. Rockefeller and the Colorado Miners." October 6, 1915.

Outlook and Independent. "Editorial: What of This Giant's Future?" January 2, 1929.

———"Hollywood's Italy." January 9, 1929.

OWEN, RUSSELL. "Byrd Fliers Survey Rockefeller Range." *New York Times*, March 10, 1929.

———. "Byrd Flies to Mountains, Finds Missing Men Safe; Gale Had Wrecked Plane." *New York Times*, March 20, 1929.

———. "Byrd To Fly To Aid of Mountain Party." *New York Times*, March 18, 1929.

PARKER, DOROTHY. "The Artist's Reward." *The New Yorker*, November 30, 1929.

PEARSON, DREW. "Ambassador Dawes." *Living Age*, July 1929.

PHILIP, P.J. "How Owen Young Made Peace In Paris." *New York Times*, June 9, 1929.

PINCHOT, GIFFORD. "The Gigantic Strides of Power Monopoly in the United States." *Current History*, April 1929.

POORE, C. G. "Ford on Lindbergh and Aviation Future." *New York Times*, May 20, 1928.

PRINGLE, HENRY F. "Mass Psychologist." *American Mercury*, February 1930.

———. "A Portrait Of Owen Young." *American Review of Reviews*, December 1927.

REIMANN, GUENTER. "How Farben Swindled Standard Oil." *New Republic*, April 13, 1942.

Review of Reviews. "A Noble Aim—To Make Everybody Rich." August 1929.

RIPLEY, C. M. "Our Amazing Electrical Genie." (Magazine unknown), September 1929.

ROOSEVELT, NICHOLAS. "If War Comes in the Pacific: An Imagined Conflict Between the Navies of Japan and the United States." *New York Times Book Review*, September 13, 1925.

ROTHBARD, MURRAY. "The Hoover Myth." *Studies On the Left*, July–August 1966.

SELDEN, CHARLES A. "Britain Gives Dawes a Rousing Welcome." *New York Times*, June 15, 1929.

SHEEHAN, ROBERT. "The Man From Pugwash." *Fortune*, March 1961.

SPEERS, L. G. "A Baron of the Petroleum World." *New York Times*, February 19, 1928.

———. "Edison Forecasts 'Hoover Prosperity.'" *New York Times*, February 12, 1929.

———. "Florida Flood Need Impresses Hoover." *New York Times*, February 17, 1929.

———. "The Way Hoover Will Meet His Big Task." *New York Times*, February 10, 1929.

STRAIGHT, MICHAEL. "The Scandal in Tungsten Carbide." *New Republic*, May 4, 1942.

————. "Standard Oil: Axis Ally." *New Republic*, April 6, 1942.

STRAWN, ARTHUR. "A Man Of Heart." *American Mercury*, October 1927.

WAGNER, PHILIP. "Cigarettes Vs. Candy: War Correspondence from a New Battle Front." *New Republic*, February 13, 1929.

WALKER, W. M. "J. P. The Younger." *American Mercury*, June 1927.

WALLACE, ROBERT. "A 'Lucky' or a Sweet—or Both!" *The Nation*, March 13, 1929.

WAMSLEY, W. F. "The Magnet of Dancing Stock Prices." *New York Times Magazine*, March 24, 1929.

WERTHEIM, ARTHUR FRANK. "Relieving Social Tensions: Radio Comedy and the Great Depression." *Journal of Popular Culture*, Winter 1976.

WILLIAMS, WYTHE. "Shearer's Methods at Naval Parleys." *New York Times*, September 16, 1929.

WILLIAMSON, S.T. "Dawes Uses His Own Diplomacy." *New York Times*, April 14, 1929.

WILSON, P.W. "John D. Rockefeller at Ninety." *New York Times Magazine*, July 7, 1929.

————. "The Man Who Talks For Britain." *New York Times Magazine*, September 29, 1929.

WILSTACH, FRANK J. "World Sway of Cinema." *New York Times*, October 14, 1928.

WINKLER, JOHN K. "A Mighty Dealer In Dollars." *The New Yorker*, February 2 and 9, 1929.

————. "Steel." *The New Yorker*, April 25 and May 2, 1931.

WOOD, RUTH KEDZIE. "Henry Ford's Great Gift." *The Mentor*, June 1929.

WOOLF, S. J. "The MacDonald of Lossiemouth." *New York Times Magazine*, July 21, 1929.

————. "Kahn Talks of Our Cultural Future." *New York Times Magazine*, November 24, 1929.

YBARRA, T.R. "Mussolini as Peacemaker." *Outlook and Independent*, March 6, 1929.

INDEX